THE MUTED
CONSCIENCE

THE MUTED
CONSCIENCE

*Moral Silence
and the
Practice of Ethics
in Business*

Frederick Bruce Bird

QUORUM BOOKS
Westport, Connecticut • London

Library of Congress Cataloging-in-Publication Data

Bird, Frederick B. (Frederick Bruce) [date]
   The muted conscience : moral silence and the practice of ethics in
business / Frederick Bruce Bird.
      p.   cm.
   Includes bibliographical references and index.
   ISBN 0–89930–652–7 (alk. paper)
   1. Business ethics.   2. Ethics.   I. Title.
   HF5387.B537   1996
   174′.4—dc20   96–591

British Library Cataloguing in Publication Data is available.

Library of Congress Catalog Card Number: 96–591
ISBN: 0–89930–652–7

First published in 1996

Quorum Books, 88 Post Road West, Westport, CT 06881
An imprint of Greenwood Publishing Group, Inc.

Printed in the United States of America

The paper used in this book complies with the
Permanent Paper Standard issued by the National
Information Standards Organization (Z39.48–1984).

10 9 8 7 6 5 4 3 2 1

Contents

Preface

The argument of this book can be briefly summarized: Although they possess moral concerns, many businesspeople do not actively and forthrightly voice these convictions in relation to their work. They do not confront colleagues who are engaged in questionable activities. They fail to speak up forcefully for their ideals. They mute their appraisals. They fail to bargain as hard as they might for their convictions. Their moral silence is the polar opposite of hypocrisy. Hypocrites voice moral convictions that they do not possess. People who are morally silent fail to voice and thereby often fail to act upon moral convictions that they in fact hold. These several forms of moral silence are in turn reinforced by diverse expressions of moral deafness and blindness. In various ways businesspeople turn morally deaf and inattentive ears to moral issues voiced by others. They often overlook moral concerns, fail to foresee the moral repercussions of specific policies, too readily fall back on stereotypes, and often simply do not recognize and acknowledge the numerous moral expectations that directly bear upon their work. Insofar as businesspeople are morally silent, deaf, or blind, a number of adverse consequences result. Problems go unattended, issues related to organizational accountability are aggravated, opportunities are missed, moral resources are not utilized, and extraneous transactional costs are multiplied. Although individuals are responsible for the degree to which they become morally silent, deaf, or blind, it is possible to identify a number of underlying factors that occasion these vices. At the individual level these include fear of being implicated as well as feelings of being ethically inarticulate. At the organizational level they include the various ways in which organizations block both bottom-up and horizontal communications.

The book concludes by examining ways by which businesspeople can and have overcome these vices. The key is to foster lively, honest, reciprocating conversations about moral concerns. By means of these kinds of communicative interactions, individuals can little-by-little and over time reduce their own moral silence, inattention, and blindness, helped in part by those with whom they are conversing. The book argues that ethics as a social practice consists of just these kinds of good conversations. The book surveys several different ways for cultivating these kinds of good conversations within corporate organizations.

This book is organized in keeping with this basic argument. Chapter 1 introduces the problem of moral silence and contrasts it with hypocrisy. Chapter 2 describes the typical expressions of moral silence. Chapter 3 analyzes different forms of moral deafness, which equates with moral inattentiveness. Chapter 4 explores the several dimensions of moral blindness. Chapter 5 examines the consequences of these vices for businesses and other complex organizations. Chapter 6 then analyzes the underlying causes for these vices by examining and weighing the significance of a number of cultural, individual, and organizational factors that occasion or reinforce moral silence, deafness, and blindness. Chapter 7 discusses what can be done to reduce or overcome moral silence and its accompanying vices, calling for the cultivation of good conversations, exploring ways these can be developed, and analyzing how these kinds of reciprocating, unfolding communications help over time to reduce moral silence, deafness, and blindness.

I am indebted to a number of people who helped me as I worked at developing this book. The initial interest and impetus came from Jim Waters, then at McGill University, who invited me to help him conduct a number of unstructured interviews with managers. Together Jim and I wrote an article titled "The Moral Muteness of Managers," which appeared in the *California Management Review* in 1989. Jim died suddenly in early 1989 before he was able to see our article in print. This article represents the skeleton around which this book has grown. Boston College, where Jim had been teaching, instituted a lecture series on business ethics in Jim's name in 1990. I presented the first lecture on the topic "The Role of Good Conversations in Business Ethics." In this address I initially presented material that I later developed as chapter 7 of this book. I am grateful to George Aragon, Richard Nielsen, and William Torbert—all of Boston College—who helped make arrangements for this colloquium and helped me as I prepared my talk and later as I wrote an extended version for published papers from the colloquium. I am grateful to the Social Science and Humanities Research Council of Canada, which funded two research projects in which I studied both how individual managers and then how corporate organizations managed moral issues. Throughout this book I cite examples based on this research. I have kept in confidence the identities of these individuals and corporate organizations at their request. I would like to thank Jeffrey Gandz of the University of Western Ontario and Manny Velasquez of Santa Clara University, who helped me with a number of these interviews. I am grateful to William Westley, Professor Emeritus at McGill University, Barry Hayward from OECD, and Travis Kroeker of McMaster University for discussing the ideas of this book with me and for their comments on a preliminary draft of chapters 1, 2, and 3. I would like to thank Louis Chauvin for his careful reading of these three chapters and for helping me prepare my bibliography. I am grateful to Diane Boulé for her work in preparing this manuscript for publication. Finally I want to express my gratitude to Eric Valentine, who first invited me to write this book and then patiently waited during the long gestation from conception to eventual delivery.

I would like to express special gratitude to my wife, Frances Westley, of McGill University, who initially suggested that I broaden my topic to include discussions of moral deafness and blindness. I have learned much from her about speaking up and listening attentively; she has been an engaging conversationalist and a dear friend.

I would like to dedicate this book to my father, Marion T. Bird, who tirelessly voiced his conscience for justice and for peace, and to my sister Carol, with whom I enjoyed many good conversations over the years.

CHAPTER 1

Introduction

MORAL SILENCE IN BUSINESS TODAY

Many people hold moral convictions yet fail to verbalize them. They remain silent out of deference to the judgments of others, out of fear that their comments will be ignored, or out of an uncertainty that what they might have to say is really not that important. They are morally mute. This moral self-silencing occurs in all domains. Politicians may fail to articulate certain ideas forcefully because they suspect that speaking out may cost them votes. Religious leaders may hold some of their convictions about unpopular topics in reserve knowing full well that many of their congregants will find such statements offensive. Even friends sometimes fail to raise questions about behavior they find objectionable for fear of alienating one another. Although moral silence is not peculiar to the domain of complex organizations and business especially, it finds many expressions there with extensive consequences.

People are morally mute when they fail to speak up about matters they know to be wrong. Many examples could be cited. In one company a number of workers took expensive office equipment home, purportedly to facilitate work off premises. Over time a considerable amount of equipment "walked off" in such a way that no one could account for it. For the company this represented a measurable loss, and it was resented by other workers who had not been party to the practice. In spite of this fact no one was willing to speak up and identify who was involved, even though many knew what was going on. When businesses engage in questionable practices, such as price-fixing, bribery, or evading environmental standards, it can be assumed that a number of people both know about these practices and personally object to them. However, many remain silent (Waters and Chant 1982).

People may be morally mute in other ways as well. They may fail to raise questions about activities that seem to call for further inquiry. For years certain industries such as textile manufacturing and asbestos production tolerated what seemed to be excessively high rates of sickness among employees before people began to seriously question the health consequences of specific production processes. In the maritime industry some ship crews treat fairly high rates for mishaps and incidents as normal without pausing to inquire what might be learned from these cases that could result in improved practices (Perrow 1984). Many people fail to dissent when they see colleagues engaged in activities they judge to be misguided. They may silently observe while they notice colleagues depleting the resources of a unit over the short term in order to advance their own careers within the organization (Jackall 1988). They may silently observe but not publicly object as their company appoints a few women to senior positions in what looks like a public relations ploy without dealing with the more systemic factors causing women to be underrepresented in senior management.

People are morally mute when they fail to defend their ideals and when they cave in too easily and do not bargain vigorously for positions they judge to be right. They are morally silent as well when they do not provide candid and comprehensible appraisals about the discourteous or offensive habits of colleagues and subordinates. Employees are not only out of line but also morally mute when they respond to what they judge to be unfair wages and working conditions by not voicing their objections but rather seeking their own justice by pilfering supplies or by absenting themselves at higher than normal rates.

Moral silence is correlated and reinforced by the related practices of moral deafness and moral blindness. The morally deaf fail to take notice of moral issues and concerns raised by others. They are morally deaf and not just incorrigible when their failures to listen arise not from ill will but from a kind of inattention or obscured attention that leaves them unable or unwilling to comprehend moral concerns and issues that call for their response. People can be morally deaf in several ways. They may dismiss the alarmed warnings of whistle-blowers as the self-serving cries of overwrought colleagues bent on getting others in trouble. They may respond to critical questions and voiced dissent as expressions of disloyalty or incomprehension by persons who do not have a really full view of what is going on. They may not appreciate and learn from the critical appraisals of supervisors because they view these primarily as exercises in humiliation and power.

Moral blindness complements, complicates, and often occasions moral silence and deafness. To be morally blind is to fail to recognize moral issues and concerns. Many people argue quite forcefully that ethical concerns are irrelevant to business practices. Some have even gone so far as to assert that attempts to raise moral concerns with respect to business are not only bad for good business practices but morally questionable because the persons raising these concerns often do so to trumpet their own special causes.

Although many firms and many businessmen and businesswomen attempt to conduct their businesses conscientiously, numerous moral problems face businesses today; many remain barely addressed and unresolved. Some would argue that a moral vacuum exists within the domain of business. Businesses have polluted the environment. They have made rivers unsafe for swimming and the air unhealthy to breathe. They have produced tons of toxic waste. Furthermore, businesses are depleting our natural resources. They are consuming scarce and limited supplies of fossil fuels. Even as businesses begin to address these environmental issues, other moral concerns seem to receive only scant attention. For example, thousands of deaths per year are attributed to occupationally related diseases. Avoidable on-the-job accidents befall numerous workers. Many firms either directly practice bribery or look the other way and hire agents who offer inducements to arrange deals for them. Employee theft remains an enormous problem. Whether they pilfer supplies, pad expense accounts, use company resources for their own private purposes without permission, or divert company funds into their own accounts, organizational members cost their firms billions of dollars every year. In 1973 the FBI estimated the loss from employee theft at $15 billion per year (Altheide, Adler, and Altheide 1978, 90).

As many firms are initiating programs in workplace diversity and employment equity, others might well argue that racism and sexism remain ongoing, barely-attended-to problems. Women and minorities are grossly underrepresented among senior management. A more serious problem, it could be argued, is the pervasive careerism that affects so many businesses. Losing sight of what might be good for their customers, investors, and employees generally, many businesspeople make their choices primarily in relation to calculations of what activities are likely to advance their own careers (Jackall 1988). A long list of other moral problems might be drawn, including the way many businesspeople neglect their families, the employment insecurity suffered by millions, cheapened products and services, and highly deceptive advertising. Any current list of moral problems in business would probably include as well the dubious practices in the thrift industry, including not only bad loans and risky investments but outright stealing (Mayer 1990).

Many of the moral problems in business are aggravated by the moral silence of businesspeople as well as by their correlative moral blindness and deafness. If people spoke up more readily about ethical issues that concern them, these concerns would more likely be addressed or attended to. However, it is not always that easy to get people to speak up. Moreover, giving vent to morally informed speech does not always help. Moral speech may assume one of several moralistic expressions that typically aggravate rather than help deal with moral issues in a responsible way.

Several forms of moral talk often exacerbate moral issues because they typically detract from organizational problem solving. In the process, they often serve to give moral talk itself a bad reputation. For example, many people use ethically weighted expressions largely to complain, voicing in the process their own vague sense that things are not going exactly the way they would like. Such moralistic carping is widespread. Envious of others' good luck, disappointed with their own lack of mobility, or disgruntled by contingent circumstances, people often reach for morally charged terms to voice their frustrations and sense of powerlessness. In the process, events that might best be described in morally neutral phrases receive a moral coloration that hints that things have turned out worse than they might have because of someone else's wrongdoing. Moral language used in this fashion frequently obfuscates the issues at hand. Language of personal blame and praise often has the same effect when it is used to address moral issues in business. Rather than asking about the factors that give rise to the undesired condition and inquiring what might be realistically done to alter these conditions, discussions become diverted by questions of who is to blame or who should be praised. Evaluations of the moral worth of individuals or organizations replace diagnoses of the problems at hand and hardheaded thinking and bargaining about what should be done.

These expressions of moralistic talk probably reinforce the existing tendencies toward moral silence. Because they are prevalent, they tend to give genuine moral talk a bad name. In order to avoid this kind of moralistic blathering, people often avoid moral expressions altogether except in relation to private concerns.

Here then is the thesis of this book: *Many people in business fail to speak up about their moral convictions.* They fail to do so in a number of different ways. As a result many of the ethical issues and concerns facing business are not addressed as fully, as clearly, and as well as they would be if people voiced their concerns. Moral silence is occasioned and reinforced by the correlative phenomena of moral blindness and moral deafness as well as the quite opposite and contrary practice of giving voice to moralistic concerns. In subsequent chapters, I examine typical instances of moral silence, deafness, and blindness drawn from my own field research and interviews as well as from public accounts. I examine the impact of this moral silence on business practice and the several cultural, individual, and organizational factors that give rise to and support moral silence. Finally, I examine ways of addressing this problem.

WHAT KIND OF A PROBLEM IS MORAL SILENCE?

Moral silence (like hypocrisy but for opposite reasons) represents a discrepancy between the moral—or in the case of hypocrisy, amoral or immoral—convictions people hold and their corresponding speech. One of the best ways to understand moral silence is to compare and contrast it with hypocrisy.

Moral Convictions and Moral Speech

To be morally mute is to be silent about one's moral convictions in settings where it would be fitting to give voice to them. Moral silence represents a condition exactly opposite of hypocrisy. Hypocrites speak as if they possess strong ethical convictions but then deliberately act to circumvent the very standards they name. They are two-faced: What they say does not correspond to the commitments they hold. We might say to their credit that hypocrites at least act in keeping with their convictions, adding, of course, that their convictions differ markedly from what they say they believe. For example, an executive of a large resource-extraction firm vociferously announced his company's commitment to government noninterference and free enterprise even while he was privately bragging about his successful efforts to lobby his country's government to raise tariff duties charged on a competitor's product coming from a different country. Another company proclaimed with great fanfare its commitment to green marketing even while it continued to sell a number of products that it knew failed to meet the standards it stated it was honoring. Hypocrisy occurs whenever people speak as if they both recognize and attempt to comply with ethical standards at the same time as they knowingly act to ignore or contravene the standards they overtly embrace (Hegel 1952).

Hypocrisy is widespread in business. A number of examples can be cited. Some companies vigorously defend legal compliance yet privately attempt to skirt tax laws that they consider to be unjust. One company defended selling materials with toxic levels above code because they privately felt that the existing legal standards were excessive and that their purchasers really didn't care. Another company passed off a cost-of-living adjustment as merit pay, even though the actual increments constituted a decrease in buying power. Subordinates act hypocritically when they pay lip-service deference to superiors, praising their efforts in public, and then seek to undermine them when out of the scrutiny of others. One manager systematically checked to see that his employees worked the hours and days that they claimed, yet he put his wife on the payroll for a regular salary for the occasional accounting services she provided at home. In all these examples, businesspeople give voice to ethical commitments that they knowingly do not seek to fulfill.

I cite these cases not in order to judge all such acts. Some of these examples are trivial, but others touch upon matters of great weight. There may well be situations, especially in negotiations, when we may temporarily make overt statements that are not fully in line with our private commitments. These examples serve as a point of contrast for indicating the particular character of moral silence. When people are morally mute, just as when they are being hypocritical, they make statements about ethical concerns that do not reflect their personal convictions. In both cases there is a discrepancy between what people actually believe and what they say they believe. In one case people speak as if they strongly hold convictions that they do not; in the other case people speak as if they do not hold convictions that they actually do. When they are being morally mute, people speak as if they are primarily motivated by nonmoral considerations of power, practicality, and personal advantage even while ethical commitments measurably affect their judgments.

Variations in Moral Convictions

In order to get a good sense of moral silence and why people with moral convictions sometimes remain silent, we need to consider briefly the relationship between moral convictions and moral action. We first need to recognize that people vary in the scope and strength of their moral convictions. Some people hold very strong beliefs about a very limited range of moral concerns. An individual may assume a militant stance opposed to using animals for laboratory tests but remain indifferent about most other concerns. Someone else may become quite fired up about a number of issues insofar as they affect the status and opportunity of women in business but not be much concerned about most other ethical dilemmas facing businesses. In contrast, other people may be mildly concerned about most issues but not feel particularly hot under the collar about any special concerns. Others may possess only a few moderate ethical convictions, for example, keeping promises and not telling lies to friends, and otherwise guide their choices by the pursuit of personal pleasure and advantage. Table 1.1 sketches these alternatives.

Table 1.1
Variations in Moral Convictions

Variations in the Scope	Variations in the Strength				
	immoral	non-existent	weak	moderate	strong
limited					single-issue cause fighter
moderate		the amor-alist			
wide	incorri-gible				
total					

We would expect morally concerned people to be moderately to strongly concerned about a moderate to wide range of moral issues. They would possess fairly strong convictions about a number of concerns. Their moral convictions would be bounded. They would see many concerns as being morally indifferent, as matters of personal preference or practicality. Those who see all decisions in a moral light are as problematic as those who are never able to see the ethical aspects of issues. The former moralistic positions treat ethics in an imperious manner that allows little or no room for the play of other considerations, from aesthetic taste to economic judgment, from political pursuits to personal affections.

Depending upon the scope and strength of a person's moral convictions, silence about moral concerns may be an honest expression of genuine moral indifference or an aggravated state of moral silence. Until we know a person's actual commitments, it is difficult to know. Theoretically, it is possible for people to hold very strong convictions and still be mute about them. However, it is difficult to imagine that someone would hold very strong commitments and not mention them at all. Still, this happens especially in highly regimented settings, such as under oppressive political regimes or in tightly run and strongly controlled organizations, where people are not invited or allowed to express their beliefs and feelings. People are likely to be mute about many of their moral concerns in what Etzioni (1961) described as coercive organizations controlled through hierarchical structures of command. As we will see, being mute often has the effect of dampening our moral convictions. When people speak up for their convictions, these commitments at the same time tend to become more articulate, clearer, and stronger. Hence we would expect that the range and strength of our moral convictions would become wider and stronger as we find ways of voicing them.

In the case of both hypocrisy and moral silence, a discrepancy exists between what people announce as their moral convictions and what convictions they actually hold. The fundamental problem in both cases is a lack of consistency between vocalized expressions of moral sentiment and the commitments that actually guide people's lives. Although a lack of correspondence between our convictions and how we act is a matter of concern, it is not the defining characteristic of either hypocrisy or moral silence. Both hypocrisy and moral silence may occasion, give rise to, reinforce, and/or seek to cover over morally discrepant conduct. In both cases actions fail to correspond to our overt statements because our convictions differ from our vocalized expressions, even though for the most part our actions largely reflect our convictions. Divergence between our convictions and actions typically occurs for reasons unrelated to hypocrisy or moral silence.

Discrepancies between Convictions and Actions

This point needs to be stressed because people typically understand hypocrisy as a discrepancy between conviction and action. This view is doubly wrong because (1) it fails to recognize the extent to which discrepancies between convictions and actions may occur for reasons that are for the most part morally neutral and (2) it fails to recognize that actions of hypocrites often quite closely reflect their real, but misrepresented, convictions. Even when our moral talk corresponds to our convictions, discrepancies between convictions and corresponding actions may arise for reasons that are largely morally neutral. Both behaviorists and idealists fail to appreciate this fact. Both naively assume that our actual behavior corresponds closely to the convictions we hold. Idealists assume that by applying ourselves, we can act in ways that fairly accurately reflect our commitments. Although we may not be able to accomplish all that we would like, given the uncooperative and often morally questionable resistance of others, we can nonetheless act conscientiously in keeping with our ideals. We may witness to our values, sometimes as men and women of conscience uncowed by the immoral and amoral forces surrounding us. The problem, idealists announce, is that not enough people possess strong enough convictions. What we need in business, politics, or law are more men and women of integrity. Behaviorists assume that our conduct reflects our actual commitments. In the final analysis, we act the way we do because we hold convictions that guide those kinds of behaviors. If we had different convictions, then we would act differently. Most behaviorists would go on to argue that it is fallacious to talk as if there were some kind of inner state referred to as our commitments different from our existing patterns of conduct. Rather our commitments simply refer to predominant patterns of behavior to which we have become accustomed over time. From a behaviorist perspective it makes no sense to refer to discrepancies between moral convictions and actions because the latter accurately reflect the only commitments worth mentioning. If we wish to improve moral behavior in business or politics, then we need to strengthen those forces that reward people for good behavior and punish them for bad behavior. All other strategies are likely to prove illusory (Scott 1971).

The arguments of both idealists and behaviorists make some sense. They separately recognize the strength of beliefs and ideals on the one hand and systems of rewards and punishments on the other. Both insist that in the end it is how people behave that really matters. Both seek greater consistency between how people talk and how they act with regard to ethical issues. However, both give rise to moralistic posturing because they underestimate the extent to which unwilled and not-easily-changed factors may cause us to act in ways that do not fully and accurately reflect our convictions (Nussbaum 1986).

A number of factors may cause us to act in ways that do not correspond to our convictions. For example, we may suffer from weak wills or weak convictions in some areas of our lives, even though we may possess iron wills and intense convictions about other concerns. People grow tired of doing good. They forget their moral lessons just as they forget names, formulas, and foreign languages. When rewards seem vague and objectives appear distant, when frustrations grow and opposition mounts, it is understandable that people become weary and that moral perseverance lapses. Because humans are fallible, they are prone from time to time to relax their moral guard. In the face of goods that tempt our desires and uncertainties that aggravate our sense of risk, we are often prone to become blurred in our moral vision and muffled in our moral hearing. Weak wills and weak convictions are just that. They lack strength and vigor. A weak will is not an ill will. Modest convictions are not the same thing as nonexistent convictions. When we act with weak wills, we set forth with limited supplies of moral energy. We are correspondingly more likely to get diverted, discouraged, or distracted. When our convictions are weak, we are more likely to get snared by plausible rationalizations that make our morally questionable actions seem excusable if not tolerable or even at times acceptable (Hare 1963, ch. 5). For these reasons, when we are only weakly committed to particular standards, we are prone to ignore, evade, or forget these convictions. Because the commitments are only modest, the divergence between our convictions and actions may be only slight. The divergence may appear more sizable if we talk as if our convictions were stronger and more vigorous than they are. However, such moral bravado represents something more akin to puffery than hypocrisy. Often such moral braggarts fool themselves more than others, and they do so without any intent to deceive.

Weak convictions are not just a matter of lazy volition. Nor does the existence of weak commitments in particular contexts predict equivalently weak convictions in other areas. By temperament people possess different strengths and weaknesses in different moral sentiments. Some men and women are by nature more risk aversive than others and hence more likely to demonstrate weaker wills when courage is called for. Some people, more than others, are gifted with greater capacity for stoic resoluteness in the face of tempting distractions. They are correspondingly able to show greater conviction in settings where others may become more easily distracted. Frequently, strengths with respect to certain virtues bring with them accompanying weaknesses in relation to other moral dispositions. For example, the capacity to empathize with the needs and requests of others may render some people less capable of steady determination in settings that call for hard bargaining. An ability for loyalty may render one less capable of dissenting. As any who have taken the standard Leggett-Meyers personality tests know, people differ in the way they orient themselves to others and to problems that arise in their interactions. These differences mean that by temperament people show greater and lesser aptitude for different types of moral convictions. I make these observations not to excuse all expressions of weak will but to recognize that it often requires greater perseverance and more energy for some to develop strong convictions in particular areas than for others. People are capable of cultivating their moral dispositions. But we are not all similarly gifted with respect to our basic moral dispositions (Aristotle, Bk i 1981; Kagan 1989).

Other factors also may lead us to act out of harmony with our convictions. Often, for example, our actions reflect compromises to which we feel we must consent in order to balance commitments to values that themselves are in conflict (Winch 1972). When we are forced by changing economic prospects to reduce our work force, our several commitments to job security, workplace equity, respect for long-time experienced workers, and regard for competent and skilled workmanship are likely to clash. To be sure, there are ways of balancing these several commitments. In the process, however, we are likely to assign a somewhat reduced value to one or more of these objectives. These kinds of clashes of commitments happen all the time. Labor negotiators must seek to achieve the best contract possible for the constituents they represent, knowing that these commitments compete for priority with other commitments to seek what is good for the organization as a whole, to speak the truth, and not to make compromises that are not matched and reciprocated by others. As a result negotiators often voice partial truths when they are asked to state their side's current and fallback positions. Though not overtly lying, they may hold back and not speak out about information that they regard as confidential and secret. To cite a further example, one plant manager found himself hard put to honor conflicting commitments to his employees' health and to legally imposed environmental standards. His own superiors had remained deaf to his concerns and asked him to resolve the problem on his own. The dilemma was this: The manufacturing process produced fumes and smoke that, when vented directly to the environment, exceeded the limits imposed by law. At the same time, retaining excessive amounts of this bad air within the plant was not good for the workers. Given the unwillingness of his superiors to address this problem, the plant manager opted for the compromise of venting the bad air at night when it would not be detected by neighbors likely to report to the environmental agencies of the government. This manager was neither weak willed nor hypocritical. He simply found himself in a place where he felt he had to find a viable compromise between several commitments, including the well-being of his own family and the advancement of his own career.

Those who interact regularly with several different constituent groups know that they must from time to time craft reasonable compromises between the clashing demands and expectations of these groups. To be sure, not all compromises seem comparably satisfactory. At times, we may feel like gifted statesmen who have mastered the art of the possible. At other times we may feel "compromised." However, whenever we are called upon to find ways of balancing opposing commitments, the ensuing courses of action are likely to be ones that do not allow us to fully honor the moral convictions we hold. We may in fact be doing the best we can under the circumstances. Nonetheless, our actions probably only partially reflect the convictions with which we set out to deal with problems at hand.

The moral lassitude that some people feel often results not directly from a lack of moral conviction but from an inability to assign priority among several competing convictions. An individual may not know quite how to balance his or her several objectives of being an attentive parent, an industrious and energetic executive, an active member of civic groups, a close friend to close friends, a committed professional, a likable and responsible colleague, a physically fit and regularly exercised adult, a well-read and thoughtful person, a culturally sophisticated appreciator of the arts, and an understanding and responsive spouse. This person's several engagements may appear both to himself and others as half-hearted, not because he doesn't care but because these several commitments compete for his attention and energy in ways that are personally exhausting. Comparable moral exhaustion occurs when people simultaneously feel strong impulses to pursue a good that appears attractive to them and feel that they ought not because it will distract them or yield morally questionable results. As a result people often undertake such pursuits but with divided wills. Their resulting actions mirror their convictions but only in a fragmentary way.

Three additional essentially nonmoral factors may cause us to act in ways that do not correspond strictly with our convictions. We may, for example, face resistance from others so that our own projects become difficult if not impossible. Our intentions are frequently frustrated in small and large ways by the opposition of others. In these cases failure to follow through on our convictions occurs not because of ill will or weak will but because of limitations in our capacities to influence others. To cite a case: The manager of an east coast plastics plant had been won over to an environmental perspective as a result of attending a workshop on environmental issues and listening over an even longer period of time to the arguments of his children. After several attempts, he was able to persuade the head officers of his company to invest in a plan whereby his plant could increase capacity and at the same time dramatically reduce the volume of pollution his plant had been venting to the atmosphere. This plan called for the construction of an incinerator that would burn the exhausts from the plant, filter a much higher percentage of potentially dangerous matter, and create steam that would be used to generate electricity. In order to go forward with this plan, the plant sought clearance from governmental environmental agencies, which it received, as well as from the municipal planning and zoning commission. The public hearings called to discuss this plan attracted a large number of people who voiced opposition because they felt that the plant was currently polluting too much, because they opposed incineration in principle, because they suspected that the overt environmental concerns of the company were just a public relations ploy, because they opposed the chemical industry generally, and because they wanted the plant to come forward with a plan that would reduce pollution even more. The outcome was that the plan was shelved. The pollution levels remained as high as they had been. Furthermore, the plant manager's own personal environmental convictions came to nought. He had to continue to manage a plant that was venting more pollution than he thought was either good or necessary.

Some people repeatedly fail to comply with their convictions because they consistently overestimate what they think they can accomplish. This frustration continuously plagues idealists, who frequently grumble about the amoral if not immoral stubbornness of others. Assuming that they can draw upon almost limitless energy as well as their ability to generate new ideas, their often quite impressive capacities to persuade others, their own perhaps somewhat overblown reputations, and/or the intensity of their own dedication, they too readily presume that they can realize their objectives because they are so determined. Many idealists never fully face up to the ways they miss the mark. Identifying so strongly with their own dreams and visions, they regard present frustrations as temporary obstacles that will be surpassed in time. Invoking their own resolutions, they characteristically assume that they will find ways to use their time more efficiently, to become more persuasive, and to handle ambiguous situations with greater pizzazz and command or whatever else is necessary. Idealists sometimes fail to recognize the extent to which their own lack of accomplishment may result from unacknowledged personal divisions of mind about the commitments they hold. We all know idealists who often set up for themselves very demanding agendas for what they hope to do. They do so because their objectives seem compelling and ignoring them seems irresponsible and unattractive.

It may be that idealists sometimes fool themselves with respect to what they are really committed to. They may believe too fervently in their own lines. The convictions upon which they act may be more modest and circumspect than those they voice in their own internal dialogues with themselves and announce to others. Such moral bravado, referred to previously, does not fully comprehend the penchant for genuinely and not self-deceptively overestimating personal capacity and external possibilities that is so characteristic of many idealists. These same traits also energize these people, enabling them to accomplish much more than they might otherwise be able to do. Idealists who make the pursuit of excellence seem easy often aggravate more skeptical realists who can cite innumerable cases where similar idealistic efforts turned sour or where highly lauded results were really made possible by the tireless work of others who scrambled to make these idealistic dreams come true (Niebuhr 1944).

Finally, people sometimes fail to act in keeping with their convictions because they do not choose well the means by which they seek to realize their objectives. Selecting means to accomplish ends is not always easy. Information available to us about alternatives and their likely consequences is usually limited, sometimes dated, and occasionally inaccurate. The intelligence that we bring to these choices is necessarily bounded. With the best of intentions we may set out on a course of action that yields unanticipated and unwelcome results. We can think of countless examples. A plant manager sought to cooperate more closely with environmental groups. He began collaborating with one well-known group. Others, both in the world of business and among the environmentalists, viewed this working arrangement as a form of collaborating with the enemy. As a result the overall relationship with environmentalists became more tense and acrimonious. In the 1930s the liberal if not radical-minded directors of the Tennessee Valley Authority in the name of democracy sought to develop working relationships with local conservative-minded farmers. They succeeded in establishing good working relationships, but as a result the aims and standards of their agency shifted markedly to the right. Although the agency successfully co-opted the local farming communities, it was in an unanticipated way also co-opted by them (Selznick 1949). In another example, a human resources manager staged a series of open forums with workers in hopes of generating closer, more harmonious working relationships. However, the meetings turned into rallies for the workers to stage even more hostile protests. In turn the manager had to assume a more heavy-handed approach with the workers than he believed was good or initially necessary. If they had been able to foretell their outcomes, each of these primary actors would have chosen alternative courses of action. They didn't know, and they picked infelicitous means to realize their objectives. As a result they were eventually forced by circumstances to act in ways that compromised their own convictions.

Table 1.2
Factors Causing Discrepancies between Moral Convictions and Actions

Weak and Irresolute Convictions
   Moral exhaustion, weak wills
   Lack of clear priorities; internal tensions between commitments

Other Factors
   Conflict between what different commitments call for
   Opposition and resistance by others
   Overestimation of what is possible
   Choices of infelicitous means

For a number of different reasons, explored in the preceding paragraphs and summarized in Table 1.2, people with genuine moral convictions may find themselves acting in ways that diverge from their commitments. The divergence in none of these cases resulted from either ill will or total lack of commitment. Although morally divergent behavior may vary markedly in its character and extent, it is a characteristic feature of all humans except some saints and some incorrigible sinners. As moral beings, humans typically experience tensions between how they say they ought to act and how they do in fact act. They variously experience this tension: as a pull of aspiration to do more; as the push of obligations not yet fully honored; as feelings of inadequacy, shame, or guilt; as the call to realize ideals or the recall to reciprocate gifts that have been graciously extended (Gouldner 1960, 1973; Nozick 1981; Etzioni 1988; Strawson 1974; Habermas 1990). Saints may experience no such tensions to the extent they feel that they fully comply with their own convictions. Forthright sinners and hypocrites may experience no such tensions to the extent that they possess no real moral convictions at all. All other humans are likely both to experience this tension and to act at times in morally discrepant ways. However, as we will explore further in subsequent chapters, although it may be human to err, it makes all the difference in what kind of errors these are and how extensive they are.

I have explored discrepant moral conduct at some length for several reasons relevant to our understanding of moral silence. This analysis provides a basis for criticizing the moralistic assumption that discrepant behavior necessarily represents either hypocrisy, lack of commitment, or malicious intent. It is important to criticize the moralistic stance because of the considerable appeal it has exercised on many who feel called to speak up about their moral concerns in relation to business practices. Additionally, as we review the causes of discrepant moral conduct, we can see that the essential feature of hypocrisy consists not in the divergence between conviction and action but in the discrepancy between verbal attestations and actual moral convictions or the lack thereof. Hypocrites typically comply with their own convictions, which happen to be amoral if not immoral. Furthermore, these several examples of morally divergent conduct also indicate that whereas such conduct occurs quite independently of whether men and women are morally mute or not, moral silence in turn tends to aggravate each of these several types of divergent behavior. We thus far have only touched on this problem, which we explore at greater length in chapter 6. The problem is that when people fail to speak up about their moral beliefs, their weak wills are more likely to falter and remain irresolute; their divided states of mind are more likely to remain confused. They are less likely to win support from allies or persuade those who oppose them; they will probably find less help as they seek to sort out conflicts between competing values; they are less prone to face up to their own overestimating zeal; and they are less likely to augment their own intelligence as they choose means to realize their moral objectives.

Reasons for Voicing Moral Concerns

People voice their moral convictions for diverse reasons. They may want to announce what they believe. They may be attempting to explain and justify their choices to others who have called their conduct into question. They may be bragging or attempting to testify to their own virtue. They may be invoking moral terms as a means of excusing otherwise morally dubious conduct. They may in fact be speaking ethically in order to cover up or distract attention away from self-serving conduct that is morally out of line. In contrast, people also use moral talk to persuade others, to negotiate bargains, to justify their judgments, to identify and criticize questionable beliefs and actions, and to address and solve problems. People also use moral discourse to articulate ideological defenses of particular arrangements of power and privilege and to criticize existing conditions from the perspective of valued alternatives. They voice moral convictions as well to police others, to promote reforms, and to vent their frustrations (Bird, Westley, and Waters 1990; Bird 1991).

People voice their moral convictions for quite varied reasons as Table 1.3 indicates. It is useful to recognize that they do so for reasons that are both laudatory and questionable. Giving voice to one's moral conviction is by no means necessarily a virtuous act. People are morally mute when they fail to voice their moral sentiments for whatever reasons in settings where such speaking up would seem expected and called for. As we review the list of reasons for voicing moral convictions, it is not difficult to see that situations may frequently arise when muting one's moral sentiments may well be virtuous if voicing is likely to result in rationalizing, carping, bragging, or demeaning. Moral silence is not a problem in these contexts. It is a problem, however, in many other settings where forms of moral voicing would be fitting.

Table 1.3
Reasons for Voicing Moral Concerns

Typical Forms	Typical Reasons
Interactive	To identify problems, to negotiate, to explore alternatives, to reach agreements
Formative	To inspire; to motivate, often using praise or blame; to cultivate moral character
Legislative	To determine rules and principles
Policing	To identify and punish violators
Ideological	To provide persuasive defense for particular arrangements of power and privilege; to criticize alternatives
Orienting	To provide personal guidance with regard to how one ought to lead one's life
Criticizing	To call into question the judgments and actions of others
Rationalizing	To provide moral-sounding rationales for morally ambiguous acts
Carping	To use moral terms to express personal frustrations
Bragging	To use moral expressions to call attention to one's own virtue often invidiously in relation to the failings of others
Demeaning	To shame and humiliate others; to attack and condemn oneself

Variations in Vocality

Given the opportunity to speak on specific topics, people respond in varying degrees: They say nothing, very little, a fair bit, or a lot. They may be comparatively close-lipped or effusive. We know that some people say more using a few well-chosen words than others who use many more words. Typically people say more when they are direct and less when their communications are filled with evasions, uncertain allusions, vague references, and not-well-formulated ideas. People say more when they are clear and articulate. They say more when they speak responsively to their audiences, attempting in the process to answer questions that have been raised and respond to concerns that have been voiced and doing so using terms and expressions that are familiar and comprehensible. Whereas some people may say little, others may on occasion say too much. People say too much whenever they overwhelm their audiences, giving them little chance to respond or reflect on what is being said. We use the term "lecture" in a derogatory manner to refer to this kind of forceful speaking at people. People also say too much when they nervously go on and on about a topic; their audiences are likely to become so irritated by their verbosity that they find it difficult to attend to their message. We can construct a scale running from mute to verbose to indicate how much people say when they have opportunities to speak about their concerns. Although this scale might be used to gauge any kind of speaking, it is particularly useful for identifying how people express themselves with regard to ethical concerns (see Table 1.4).

Table 1.4
Variations in Vocality

How Much Do People Say?	Characteristics of Their Communications
They are mute.	They fail to speak up or they say almost nothing. They speak using evasions, indirect statements, and vague statements.
They are articulate.	They speak directly using clear and fitting expressions. They speak intelligibly. They speak to their audiences. They do not muffle their communications.
They are verbose.	They overwhelm their audiences. They reiterate their points. They speak often at length but not to the issues at hand.

People are morally mute whenever they would be expected to speak up or out but they do not do so in any of the several ways previously mentioned; that is, to refer to their convictions as they negotiate or bargain, praise or blame, criticize or police, invoke principles or evoke visions, legitimate policies or criticize the policies of others. They are morally mute because on these occasions, but perhaps not on others, they either voice no moral sentiments or communicate in ways that obscure their moral beliefs and commitments. For example, even though working hard to create a fair and caring organization, they talk as if all that matters are greater efficiency, less conflict, and better margins. Though striving to create first-class quality for their customers, partially in hopes of cultivating customer loyalty, they talk as if all that they are concerned about are improved market share and satisfied investors.

VOICING AND NOT VOICING MORAL CONVICTIONS

In relation to any particular concern, people may in varying degrees possess relevant moral convictions or not, and in varying degrees they may voice these sentiments or not. As a result people can assume quite an array of different stances, some exhibiting a much higher degree of congruence than others. Table 1.5 charts these several different possibilities. Moral silence, like hypocrisy and rationalizing, represents one of several noncongruent alternatives.

Table 1.5
Congruent and Discrepant Relationships between
Moral Convictions and Moral Speech

How Vocal	Strength of Moral Convictions			
	None	Weak	Moderate	Strong
Silent or Mute	(a) Immoral (c) Amoral or morally indifferent		(b) Morally mute (d) Stonewalling	
Vocal or Articulate	(g) Hypocritical		(h) Rationalizing	(e) Pro-vocal voicing; responsible speaking (f) Problematic voicing (e.g., moralistic, ideological posturing)
Verbose		(i) Carping (j) Bragging		

Depending upon the state of their moral convictions, not voicing moral sentiments may or may not be problematic. The amoral or morally indifferent as well as the incorrigible stances are all consistent. It is appropriate not to voice moral sentiments in relation to concerns that we feel ought to be handled without reference to ethical considerations. Many decisions are best made strictly on economic terms, in relation to political goals, or as matters of personal taste.

Importing moral references into the discussion of these choices is likely to obscure the issues at hand and give the appearance either of special pleading or of attempting to discredit those with whom one disagrees. Importing ethical terms into such debates often renders them more intractable. It is likewise understandable for people not to dress up their confessedly immoral choices in moral language. Compared to the hypocrite, the avoidance of ethical talk in such cases constitutes a virtue of sorts.

People are morally mute when they fail to voice moral concern, in any of the several ways reviewed, in settings that normally evoke these sentiments. Here moral silence is just as inappropriate as moral voicing is with respect to amoral or immoral conduct.

In this book I am especially concerned about the failure to voice moral concerns. In subsequent chapters I explain both why this happens and what can be done to address this problem. However, even as I am interested in exploring ways to foster more speaking up about ethical concerns, I am equally interested in identifying and discouraging several ways of speaking up using forms of moral discourse that are either morally questionable or simply wrong.

For example, people are hypocritical when they voice moral concerns about matters about which they feel morally neutral or quite frequently possess consciously immoral intentions. When people speak hypocritically, they are using ethical language with immoral or amoral intent because such language variously serves to gain them favor and/or distract attention away from questionable practices. Rationalizing is a similar activity but differs in the degree to which people willfully seek to deceive and purposively seek to control the responses of others. Rationalizers use moral expressions, often invoking their own well-meaning intentions, in order to excuse actions they recognize as being questionable or dubious. Managers often use their heavy workloads to excuse their inattention to particular issues. In the process, they may refer to their many responsibilities, their recognized concern for other problems, and the justice with which they managed other conflicts. They offer what might technically be described as mitigating evidence in order to draw attention from their moral lapses and reduce their own sense of culpability. Rationalizers often refer to their conscientious attempts to fulfill as well as they can morally ambiguous assignments given them by superiors. One manager, caught offering kickbacks to customers in an East Asian country, rationalized that he had been mandated to do what was necessary to secure the contract as long as it seemed to be in keeping with local customs loosely interpreted. People often rationalize in relation to events when, because of weak convictions, they faltered in their attempts to realize their objectives.

Carping and bragging represent further examples of moral voicing that, even though valid to a degree, can easily become abusive and off-putting. When people carp, ordinarily they are complaining about real moral problems. Typically they name wrongs and slights intentionally committed by others. Moreover, in the process of complaining, they typically testify to heartfelt offenses to their own moral sensibilities. At the same time, they invoke these moral expressions to express their frustrations, to air their resentments, and to complain. As they complain, swear, and bitch, carpers typically seek to overcome their own sense of inadequacy, often occasioned by not mastering situations as well as they might, by making implicit if not explicit invidious comparisons of those they are disparaging. As a result carping often assumes the form of personal attacks on others. Even though these others may indeed be vulnerable, carping provides little or no basis for thinking about the sources of problems and how they might be rectified (Bird, Westley, and Waters 1990).

When we carp, we call attention to the wrongs of others, not infrequently wrongs that leave us worse off. In contrast, when we brag, we call attention to our own virtues and the ways we have benefited others. Although we might occasionally wish that moral braggarts would more modestly wait for others to sing their praise, we cannot fault them for speaking either with intentional deception like hypocrites or with the purpose of diverting attention like rationalizers. Rather, what we find objectionable is that they speak excessively. They continue at greater lengths than seems necessary to name and laud their own accomplishments.

Stonewalling represents a special case in which people deliberately avoid the use of moral terms—and insist upon this avoidance—because they do not want people to raise questions about actions they know to be debatable. Stonewallers may or may not possess moral convictions about the cases for which they keep ethically silent. They may remain silent because they see particular issues in morally indifferent terms best considered in relation to practical or political considerations and refuse to consider the explicit moral arguments raised by others. They remain essentially deaf to the moral concerns of others. I interviewed two accountants who angrily argued with each other about whether a particular transaction that one of them had negotiated involved ethically dubious arrangements. The one who had enacted the transactions failed to answer his colleague in terms of the questions that the latter had raised. The former insisted that moral considerations were irrelevant. He avoided rather than addressed the concerns that had been brought up. He did so—at least to my hearing—not because he wanted to hide something but because he really couldn't comprehend the moral issues to which his colleague pointed. His deafness in this case functioned to cut off the possibility of real debate about matters that his colleague felt should at least be discussed. Because this case involved deafness to the concerns of others, it differs in principle but not necessarily in practice from other cases in which the refusal to consider the moral aspects results from a closed-mouthedness intentionally adopted to close off debate. People typically stonewall when they recognize that particular practices or policies may legitimately be debated but do not wish to invite any such discussions. For example, a senior executive of a public utilities adamantly argued that his firm's decision to build a nuclear reactor near an active fault line had no morally debatable dimension. Although he may have been able to produce persuasive arguments about the safety features of the proposed reactor, he stonewalled when he denied what he also recognized: namely that questions of risk management and safety may be discussed in relation to relevant moral considerations (Douglas and Wildowsky 1982; Douglas 1992). Stonewalling is similar to hypocrisy. Both involve modes of communicating designed to lend the aura of legitimacy to practices that those making these communications recognize as being open to questioning. Stonewallers seek this moral acceptability by using morally neutral terms. Hypocrites do so by voicing moral convictions they do not hold.

Stonewalling provides an instructive example of people attempting to make real moral claims without using moral language. It has often been assumed that people must necessarily use moral language in order to communicate morally. Modern philosophers have analyzed moral expressions at length with this assumption in mind (Stevenson 1944; Hare 1952, 1963). I subsequently argue at length the opposite position: that people sometimes make their moral claims, arguments, and judgments more effectively when they do not use overtly ethical language. Stonewalling typically involves an implicit moral claim that the activity under consideration is legitimate in terms of accepted social practices and therefore does not need to be subjected to overt scrutiny and debate, which would have the effect of reducing this tacit validity.

Table 1.5 distinguishes between two different ways in which people voice their moral convictions. In both cases they neither silence their moral sentiments nor speak falsely about them. In both cases those speaking up about moral concerns are likely to have at least moderate if not strong convictions. The difference between the problematic and fitting voicing of moral concerns results from the way people speak up. I consider this distinction at length in subsequent chapters. At this point we can briefly refer to several salient factors that make some forms of legitimate moral talk problematic. In most cases moral talk becomes problematic if it is disproportionately put to certain kinds of uses. For example, moral talk becomes problematic whenever those using it become overly preoccupied with questions of praise and blame. Focusing excessively on the moral worthiness of individuals involved, either in the form of righteous or self-righteous praise or in the form of vilification and personal attacks, people voice intense moral sentiments but often in ways that do not allow for debate, negotiation, or problem solving. Instead of identifying conflicts or sorting out dilemmas in relation to alternatives, they narrowly express outrage and/or applause. Praising and blaming are acceptable moral activities, especially when we seek to motivate or deter. However too much attention to these kinds of questions at the expense of others becomes problematic. Moral talk is similarly problematic when it is used excessively for ideological purposes, either to justify or to condemn particular arrangements of power and privilege. Those who use every available occasion to sing the praises of their firms and their well-known philosophies or to rehearse the injustices visited upon the working class can quickly bore their audiences. Although they often augment the legitimacy of the views they uphold and rally support from those similarly minded (Gouldner 1976; Geertz 1973), these kinds of general testimonials and critiques do not help to negotiate resolutions of the issues at hand.

In a number of ways, which I explore in this book, moral silence, deafness, and blindness aggravate ethical issues faced by businesses. Therefore, we need to discover ways to encourage morally concerned people to become more vocal. When people who have been mute speak up, however, they may do so in ways that may be equivalently—if not more—problematic than their previous silence. No longer mute, they may voice moral sentiments in order to brag, rationalize, or carp, to advance and defend ideological convictions, or in a more moralistic manner to evaluate the personal or organizational moral worthiness of themselves and others. Even though these last uses for moral language are suitable in moderation for some settings, they can become excessive and offensive, especially when voiced in inappropriate settings. Furthermore, they do not really overcome moral silence with respect to the interactive, policing, legislative, formative, and problem-solving uses of moral discourse. This silence is a problem not only because it means that people are not voicing their beliefs and are not bringing ethical considerations to bear in relevant and constructive ways, but also because, by their silence, they are de facto allowing moral discourse to become disproportionately used by hypocrites, carpers, rationalizers, braggarts, moralizers, and ideologues. Their silence means that these questionable and problematic uses are not challenged as forcefully as they might be, in ethical terms, rather than just by the amoralists who seek to reduce the consideration of business issues in relation to ethical values.

I use the term *moral discourse* to identify any communications in which people voice moral sentiments or convictions, whether they do so using overtly moral language or not. Moral discourse is like a currency. People employ such discourse to initiate and maintain interactions, to render judgments, to establish rules, and to do a number of other activities previously discussed. Like any other currency, the value of moral discourse may become depressed or inflated. It is depressed when there is an insufficient flow of this discourse in circulation or when people attempt to interact and address their problems without it. This happens in pluralistic situations, when people are using different moral expressions and making unrelated moral claims such that it is difficult to reach agreement using common frames of reference. Moral discourse is depressed when few comprehend or are willing to respond to the claims made by those interacting with this verbal currency. Moral discourse is likewise depressed when few recognize or acknowledge the agreed-upon understandings and shared assumptions to which people allude when they address each other using this discourse.

In a way, moral discourse has become a depressed medium of communication in the world of business today. Some would add that this moral depression exists as well in government. Moral claims and arguments seem to fall on deaf ears when they are invoked, but more often issues fraught with moral complexity are discussed antiseptically (from an ethical perspective) as if they could be fully comprehended by economic analysis, opinion polling, and the well-turned phrases of conventionally wise media spokespersons and consultants. In a cyclical fashion, people avoid using this moral currency because others seem not to be using it. In this way being morally mute serves to perpetuate a milieu in which being mute seems natural because moral discourse seems to have become a devalued form of communicating.

If moral discourse were only just depressed, then it might suffice to get people to speak up more and to pepper their exchanges with greater reference to their moral beliefs. However, the contemporary situation is not that simple, because moral discourse appears inflated when viewed from some vantage points. Morally-weighted terms are continuously being imported into business discussions where it is not clear they always belong. Recall, for example, the moral expressions that have infused the discussion of Quality Management, the Pursuit of Excellence, and environmentally responsive business strategy, to name a few current views about good management. Recall as well the emphasis, invoked by many businesses, on corporate social responsibility, executive integrity, good citizenship, recycling, workplace diversity, level playing fields, organizational commitment, and just plain hard work. We could easily add to this list and then start another one that included all moral-sounding terms used by critics, prophets, and conscience-stricken businesspeople referring to the liars, sharks, and chizzlers in the world of business (Lewis 1989). Putting aside for the moment questions about the validity of the latter attacks or the veracity of well-meaning idealistic reformers, we may observe that the direct and indirect references and allusions to moral values are quite pervasive even if the overt voicing of ethics as such is more limited. A case can be made for arguing that moral discourse as a currency for social interactions has become inflated. If this condition were to exist, what would be the signs? Moral discourse would be inflated if there seemed to be too many moral expressions and arguments in circulation such that particular moral beliefs, assumptions, and arguments that once were viewed as being especially compelling lost their aura of authority. They could no longer readily be introduced as being self-evident. Rather, they would have to be explained and defended and compete with other moral arguments that seem to traditionalists to be more cavalier and superficial (MacIntyre 1981; Taylor 1989). It would be fitting to describe moral discourse as being inflated if people found that they often had to pile moral arguments on top of each other in order to get much attention because individual expressions had lost sanctity and value. When people too readily invoke moral sentiments, the value of this discourse is likely to decline. The extensive use of moral discourse to rationalize, to complain, to brag, to moralize, and to make politically persuasive and politically correct statements clearly aggravates this situation.

The contemporary situation appears a bit schizophrenic, especially in the milieux of business and large organizations. Moral discourse bears the marks at once of being both a depressed and an inflated medium of exchange and interaction. Moral silence adds to both problems. It perpetuates this depression by its silence. In addition, when people are morally mute, they add to the inflated state of moral discourse insofar as they might otherwise speak responsibly but de facto allow less intrinsically valued uses of moral discourse—to carp, rationalize, brag, moralize—to prevail.

MAKING A DIFFERENCE

This book is written in the hope of making a difference. After examining the several sources that give rise to moral silence, deafness, and blindness, I propose a number of steps that individuals and organizations can take to foster a lively, responsible, and effective speaking up and out about ethical concerns. Speaking up and out will make a difference in how well businesses and complex organizations address the many different ethical issues that they face. In the process, I set forth an alternative view of ethics as consisting characteristically not in rules and commands but in what I refer to as "good conversations," that is, especially, in interactive, formative, problem-solving, and self-orienting moral discourse (Bird 1991). This view of ethics is similar to that developed by the German philosopher/sociologist Jürgen Habermas; he refers to it as communicative ethics (Habermas 1984, 1987, 1990). The position developed here differs in being less utopian and more practical, more overtly influenced by the long history of casuistry, which viewed ethics in terms of good arguments put forward to resolve specific issues (Jonsen and Toulmin 1988) and more influenced by current versions of pragmatism (Bellah et al. 1991; Selznick 1992). Several fundamental assumptions inform this work. First, I assume that people in business and that contemporaries more generally hold multiple assumptions about the moral goods they think ought to be pursued, about the forms of reasoning most appropriate for justifying ethical positions, and about those standards to which they would assign highest priority. Although particular communities of commitment—whether they be religious, ideological, or ethnic—may share common beliefs regarding such goods, arguments, and standards, people in general do not (Stout 1988). Even though it is possible to identify a number of basic moral standards that human beings generally regard as authoritative and compelling (Bird 1996), naming these standards does not really eliminate the diversity already mentioned. People still will disagree, often quite fiercely, about the saliency of particular standards, about the priority of what they regard as good, about the relative weight to be assigned to moral and nonmoral values, and about the types of reasoning that might be used to sort out these questions (MacIntyre 1981). Various well-reasoned philosophical attempts to identify universally valid first principles (Gewirth 1978; Donagan 1977) or moral rules (Gert 1970) have not succeeded in overcoming this pluralism, in part because people still disagree about the kinds of reasoning they find most compelling and about the goods they value. However, this pluralism is no cause for despair or for assuming that we are left with a hopeless relativism. Although people may differ about their moral assumptions, they can still make themselves intelligible to each other. They can consider, counter, and concur with each other's arguments. Most importantly, they can reach agreements that facilitate their cooperative interactions. As Habermas (1984, 1990) has argued, these activities of considering, countering, concurring, and agreeing—along with correlative activities of evaluating and judging—are close to the heart of what people do when they engage in ethics.

While I do hope that, as a result of more speaking up, businesses and other complex organizations will be better able to limit unjust, narrowly self-serving, and injurious behavior and expand their ability to promote morally worthy objectives, I do not assume that it is either necessary or possible to bring about marked changes in the kind of people we are in order to pursue these objectives.

People vary in their moral predispositions as they do with respect to their temperaments generally. They vary in their inclinations for generosity and guardedness, in their capacities for entertaining new ideas and for fidelity to old ones, in their abilities to concentrate and to respond, in their propensities for collaboration or autonomy. They vary as well in their instincts for self-advancement and for team-building, for holding grudges, and for lightheartedness. Even though people display diversity in their natural moral dispositions, except for self-sacrificing saints and incorrigible sinners, most people possess viable mixtures of other-regarding and self-regarding dispositions (Niebuhr 1944). They are, as the Protestant reformer Luther once wrote, a bit of both sinners and saints. They are, as the eighteenth-century Scottish philosopher and economist Adam Smith declared, moved by both sympathy for others and self-interest. Smith's famous arguments in *The Wealth of Nations*, where he defends self-interest as a basis for economic cooperation, need to be balanced by the arguments he made and assumed in his earlier work, *The Theory of Moral Sentiments*, where he identifies the capacity for sympathy as a generic moral instinct (A. Smith 1970, 1976).

The relationship between organizational patterns and individual character is complex and not one that we need to resolve. We know that influences can go both ways. Particular individuals as they exert leadership can change the character of organizations for good and ill. When specific businesses decide to introduce programs to reduce informal discrimination against the advancement of women to senior management or when they make extensive efforts, far in advance of what is legally required, to reduce the venting of organic substances, these initiatives and ones like them are typically initially championed by specific individuals. A number of examples of individuals making a difference could be cited, such as the executive who made special efforts to have his company hire, train, and advance natives; or the steps taken by one internal auditor, at another company, to identify and correct loose reporting practices that were allowing a number of managers to take advantage of their company's free-spiritedness. Contemporary campaigns to foster executive integrity make sense (Nash 1990;

Srivastva and Associates 1988). It is impossible to create morally responsible organizations without in some way also attempting to foster or cultivate the moral character of the people who make up these organizations. Developing organizational policies and codes of ethics will probably not transform ethically dubious organizations into responsible ones unless at the same time actions are taken to welcome and reward the moral character of the individuals in these organizations.

However, there are limits with respect to what can be done to encourage moral development among adults. The most dramatic alterations in moral character take place within the context of groups of people marked by strong affectional ties, shared beliefs, and a common sense of identity—like families, religious groups, and ideological movements (Conn 1981). Such changes may occur in limited ways in therapeutic settings and encounter groups. Comparative studies by Kohlberg (1984a, 1984b), Perry (1968), and others show little evidence that measurable moral development takes place in the context of impersonal, complex organizations. Nonetheless, organizations can, in significant ways, either foster or stifle the moral dispositions of their members. I will subsequently show that the efforts organizations might make to encourage people to act on their moral convictions are not much different than those that also foster speaking up.

By creating and supporting arrangements that allow people to speak about their moral convictions, businesses and other complex organizations will augment the extent to which their members act on their moral convictions as well as restrain their own and others' antimoral inclinations. Speaking up can have a number of ethically beneficial effects. As people speak up, they are likely to receive support from others. A couple of well-known psychological experiments, discussed later at greater length, give evidence that people are measurably more likely to act on their convictions when they have opportunities to speak with others about the misgivings they feel regarding the instructions they receive from superiors (Asch 1951; Milgram 1974). By speaking up, people are more likely to encourage the moral dispositions of others as well. One of the characteristic experiences of many conscience-stricken managers is to feel that they are on their own, ethically speaking. Many businesspeople talk as if they were moral souls moving within an amoral if not immoral milieu. One manager confessed: "What is right in the corporation is not what is right in a man's home or in his church" (Jackall 1988, 6). Another manager complained: "I wonder if I am calling this an ethical decision as a way of letting out my unhappiness at the fact I cannot do what is right" (Toffler 1986, 201). After having interviewed several dozen managers several years ago, I was struck by the fact that so many managers expressed very similar sentiments of having moral convictions in the midst of countless others who appeared to have none. The commonality of this personal conviction belies its claim, however. It seemed that each of these morally convicted managers worked in regular interactions with others who felt similarly, but because none of them voiced their convictions, they remained unaware of the extent that others felt similarly. They held common moral convictions, but they did not hold them in common and hence they felt isolated (Waters and Bird 1987).

Finally, speaking up and out is likely to help restrain and curb actions motivated by our morally less desirable dispositions. Our impulses toward self-aggrandizement at the expense of others are likely to be modified and checked when others raise questions about them and appeal for collaboration. Some organizational members will inevitably seek their own ends to the injury of their own or other organizations. Some will seek to get away with criminal acts. However, the secrecy and silence that conspire to tolerate, collude with, or hide efforts to pursue these ends are more likely to be limited in organizational environments that encourage people to speak up in responsible ways (Waters and Chant 1982).

CHAPTER 2
Moral Silence

People are morally mute when they do not recognizably communicate their moral concerns in settings where such communicating would be fitting. Moral silence may assume a variety of forms. Businessmen and businesswomen are mute not only when they fail to speak up about flagrant abuses they become aware of and about which their superiors are ignorant but also when they fail to speak up for causes or projects that they judge to be morally valuable. They are mute not only when they fail forthrightly to dissent from policies they personally regard to be ethically questionable but also when they allow themselves to give less-than-candid evaluations of the workmanship of subordinates. I will introduce a number of examples, and I expect that some readers will respond initially by objecting that I have included cases that do not belong. Some may well ask why the act of not giving full, critical, and helpful feedback to subordinates constitutes an expression of moral silence. I will address this and other questions that will arise in the process and end by discussing instances when moral silence may be called for.

VOICING MORAL CONCERNS

We must begin with a theoretical issue that has considerable practical importance: In order to voice moral concerns, does one have to use overtly moral language? I argue that we can communicate moral concerns without having to use explicitly ethical terms and expressions and that we can fill our discourses with moral terms—words like "right" and "wrong" and "obligated" and "ought"—as part of communications in which no moral convictions are being expressed. I want to emphasize this point so that moral silence is not confused with the failure to use moral language or to cite or use acknowledged ethical theories and principles. Moral silence occurs whenever people fail to communicate moral concerns that they genuinely feel, regardless of how this failure takes place. People may fail to communicate moral concerns even when they are using moral language.

In order to clarify this issue, it is useful to consider what it means generally to voice or not to voice moral concerns. Whenever we invoke standards of how we ought to behave and we do so with assumptions that behaving this way will augment what is good and valuable, then we are voicing moral concerns. This simple statement incorporates a number of philosophical assumptions. I assume, for example, that the standards invoked possess the double features of being viewed as both compelling in the sense that we ought to comply with them and being attractive in the sense that action in keeping with them will promote conditions that are regarded as good, desired, and valued (Durkheim 1974). As an integral part of our lives as interacting beings, we humans invoke standards that are viewed both as being obligatory in the way that the followers of the eighteenth-century philosopher Kant have maintained and as promoting states that are regarded desirable as Utilitarians have argued. In their polar arguments, these opposing philosophical traditions have each seen with clarity only part of the intrinsic character of moral standards. Characteristically the standards we invoke are those that a number of us have already agreed to and regard as normative for how we ought to act. This agreed-upon character can assume varied forms. We may, for example, invoke shared standards that have been traditionally handed down from one generation to the next. We may more concretely invoke standards to which we knowingly and unknowingly consent or assent when we become part of organizations that have already adopted them. We may more informally simply refer to prior agreements entailed in promises we have made among ourselves. To be sure, we do not always just invoke already accepted standards. Sometimes we try to persuade people to adopt new standards. Even in this instance, we typically solicit agreements creating new standards by invoking, reinterpreting, and assigning lesser and greater importance to particular configurations of old standards.

When we act morally, we seek voluntarily to comply with agreed-upon standards because we feel that we ought to and because we think such actions will enhance what we judge to be good. Moral actions differ from nonmoral or amoral ways of acting in several ways. Moral actions are voluntary. They cannot be coerced. Actions are moral only if they are chosen and if there is an opportunity to act out of compliance with standards that have been invoked. Moral actions are not undertaken as a matter of personal whim or subjective taste. Often we act as we do because it suits our personal desires, tastes, or feelings. Such capricious action is amoral. Similar instrumental actions undertaken in order to realize certain objectives are morally indifferent insofar as our behaviors are not guided by normative standards of how we ought to act in these settings (Habermas 1984, 1990).

I offer this brief nontechnical account of morality as a background against which I can indicate ways in which people voice or fail to voice moral concerns without having to refer to their use or nonuse of moral language as a determining factor. This account also allows me to indicate several ways in which attempts to express moral concerns can become nonmoral.

Voicing moral concerns is a communicative activity involving others or at least one other person. Ideally when we voice moral concerns, we wish to do so in ways that both accurately reflect our own convictions and are intelligible and persuasive to our audience. It is not always easy to satisfy these two distinct objectives equally well. We may be so concerned to articulate our own views that our communications are either incomprehensible to others or off-putting, or both. Because of the strength of our convictions, we sometimes honor such voices of conscience. We have borne witness to our visions. In the face of threats, we have remained true to our commitments.

We hear stories of the families who through hunger strikes stopped wreckers from destroying old buildings to make way for condominiums; or of women who through years of perseverance finally persuaded senior managers to consider appointing women into their number. We admire the way in which Ralph Nader almost by himself convinced large automakers to introduce a number of safety features into automobiles, a move that they resisted for years. We can recall these and other examples because in each case those involved acted in ways that had the effect of communicating their concerns effectively to others. That is not always true for conscience-stricken prophets. Sometimes morally wrought individuals voice their concerns in highly charged language that is not easily understood by others. We may see that they are outraged by activities they think to be morally wrong but we cannot readily see exactly wherein the wrong lies or what the issue is in actionable terms. Even though they may offend or remain incomprehensible to others, however, these kinds of moral prophets at least strive to remain true to their own convictions.

At the other extreme it is possible to imagine people who strive to make their communications both intelligible and persuasive to others. Especially in settings where parties involved begin with different points of view and different background experiences, speakers may use terms of reference and invoke beliefs familiar and dear to the other. Subordinates often find themselves in this position when they want to identify what they judge to be flaws or faults in the actions and decisions of their more powerful superiors. In order to obtain a good hearing for their concerns, which do in fact challenge or call to into question previous policies or judgments of their superiors, they may attempt to phrase their arguments in comfortable terms. In the process, they may hold in check their most critical observations and focus on more incidental matters more likely to receive an agreeable and attentive response. The inclination to tell superiors what we think will please them is widespread. The same intent of attempting to state our concerns in images familiar and favored by others affects people in many other settings. Politicians are often accused of pandering to popular interests even when they may be convinced that unpopular policies, such as tax increases or restrictions on local government projects, are called for. Convinced that the baseline for all business activities is improved economic performance, many conscientious businesspeople purposely disguise their genuine moral concerns regarding particular personnel and marketing issues in the language of profits and losses. They use terms that they think others will find intelligible and persuasive. In the process, their own moral concerns often get lost to sight.

At both extremes people may fail to voice their moral convictions in ways that are understandable to their audience. At one extreme, people voice their concerns like solipsisms in terms comprehensible only to themselves or to those who already share their convictions. Some moral prophets appear to be speaking primarily to themselves. They seem more interested in gaining the applause of their like-minded followers than in seriously communicating with businesses they are ostensibly addressing. At the other extreme, people find themselves trying to fit their moral concerns into the agendas and vocabularies of those they are addressing so much so that they feel co-opted. Translated into the rhetoric and thought patterns of others, squeezed between lines in the others' program, they feel that their concerns have lost shape and force. They have been trivialized as they have been placed within frameworks borrowed from others. At both extremes people become morally mute as their particular moral concerns become inaudible to others.

Table 2.1
Variations in How We Voice Our Moral Concerns to Others

Solipsistic Discourse:	Ordinary Moral Discourse:	Overly Other-Directed Discourse:
We voice our convictions in our own terms with little effort to make them intelligible and comprehensible.	Mixtures of and tensions between both polar concerns.	We voice our convictions in relation to the agendas and terms of others.

For the most part, however, moral discourse takes place somewhere between these extremes (see Table 2.1). Insofar as we seek to communicate moral concerns to others who hold different beliefs than we do, who use different rhetoric and expressions, and who may disagree at least initially with some of our convictions, in any viable and engaged communication with them we will need to find ways of balancing our attempts to set forth our convictions clearly with attempts to translate these into expressions important to those with whom we are speaking. Temporarily we may end up nearer to one end of the pole or the other. We become morally unrecognizable whenever we stray so far to one extreme or the other that our audience never really hears the moral concerns we are attempting to raise.

When we voice moral concerns to others, we do so in order to persuade them to agree to positions or points of view we are defending. We seek to elicit a favorable response from them. We do so by giving reasons for our position. We try to make these reasons compelling. As a result of our speaking, we hope they will choose to act as we recommend. They can genuinely choose to do so only to the extent that it is possible for them to accept or not accept the reasons we give. These reasons must by their nature be ones that are understandable and debatable. Our discourse can embody moral terms but become amoral or nonmoral whenever we violate these basic conditions of seeking to persuade others by offering good reasons (Toulmin 1950; Habermas 1990).

When we voice opinions about ethical issues, we express moral views in essentially nonmoral ways. An opinion is a statement of personal feelings. Such statements cannot really be debated. They represent how we feel. They may do so with more or less accuracy, more or less veracity, or more or less authenticity. Opinions do not really make claims about the larger world or about the validity of particular arrangements. They only claim to disclose how we feel about these matters. They are testimonials to personal points of view. Depending upon who voices these opinions, we may assign them greater or lesser weight. We may choose to defer to the opinions of close friends or trusted authorities because we have found their views to be reliable guides. Rather than attempt to think through a choice on our own, weighing alternatives thoughtfully, we may at times simply defer to the opinion of someone we trust. Opinions provide no reasons for choosing other than referring to the tastes, feelings, or intuitions of the persons who voice them. Opinions are amoral because they provide no reasons for choosing. We may defer to opinions either because many people hold them—and siding with what many hold seems to be important—or because we hold in high regard those who hold a particular opinion. But such positions are essentially nonmoral because we provide no compelling, arguable reasons for our choices. The situation changes the moment we begin to provide reasons for our choices. Then we appeal to others to act on the basis of their thoughtful consideration of the circumstances. We also acknowledge their option of choosing not to act as we recommend because they disagree with the arguments we have marshalled. As long as we are only stating opinions, we seek their compliance on the basis of their deference to our feelings or our power, not because they have thought through the issues at hand and have become persuaded by our arguments or those of others to act as they choose.

This point needs to be stressed because people frequently merely state opinions when they think that they have stated their moral convictions or have articulated moral arguments. Sometimes people initiate an assertion of what they think ought to be done—hiring more minorities, marketing a product especially needed by elderly poor persons—by confessing that they feel this ought to be done or by naming someone of renown who also takes this position. As such, these are expressions of personal sentiment but not debatable arguments.

The polar opposite activity—commanding others to act without giving reasons why—is equally nonmoral. We may at times order others to act in ways we judge to be morally correct. However, we are acting nonmorally insofar as we simply compel others to act in this way without directly appealing to their considered judgments that this way of acting is in fact better. As parents we may justify such paternalism because we judge our children incapable as yet of fully considering alternatives and being able to live with the consequences of bad choices. We often provide moral arguments to justify commanding those we consider incapable of making genuine moral choices because of their age, mental or physical handicaps, or prior commitment to criminal or violent conduct that renders them unwilling or unable to listen openly to our arguments. The act of ordering others to act, however, is in itself basically a nonmoral activity. When we order, we force or compel people to act as commanded. Typically, we implicitly or explicitly threaten them with forcefully asserted sanctions if they refuse to comply. Those commanded are given no real choices as participants in whatever interactions or community is involved. They may, insofar as they are able, depart from this group or interaction. But this is not a really viable alternative for many people. Commands leave people with the mutually exclusive alternatives of either strict compliance or quitting, or, in the words of the economist Hirschman (1970), with the alternatives of loyalty or exit but without voice.

I stress this point because commands have often been invoked as a typical form of moral communication. The commands of parents are sometimes cited as one of the more elementary expressions of moral speech. Within certain types of organizations, such as armies, the police, tightly run ideological movements, and hierarchically structured religious groups, moral behavior is frequently commanded of subordinates by superiors. Even though commands are widely associated with efforts to gain moral compliance, they represent an exception to the basic character of moral communication. Commands are viewed as legitimate forms of moral communication only in settings where people have voluntarily consented to allow themselves to be ordered by their leaders as the prerequisite of their membership in particular groups or where they are regarded as incapable or unwilling of reaching considered moral judgments.

When I state opinions or when I make commands, I seek a favorable response from others based on their deference to either my feelings or my power. Others are not being invited to consider that recommended conduct is really better and more suitable than alternatives. Others are not invited to ask questions or make counterclaims or consider imaginative compromises. Deference is sought without invitation to think about whether this choice is really the one that ought to be made. The difference between these extremes is that the other is allowed to ignore opinions without fear of adverse consequences. But this is precisely not the case with commands. Except in those cases where statements of opinion are regarded as authoritative because of the position held by opinion staters, stating opinions does not really engage or make claims on others. When I state an opinion, I leave the other free to ignore my comments because those comments only represent my feelings. When I issue a command, in contrast, I allow the other no freedom not to respond as ordered.

In the one case I seek a favorable response not on the basis that this way of acting is good and fitting for diverse reasons but because I feel this is so. In the other case I likewise make no appeal to the appropriateness of the recommended action but rather use my power to seek compliance.

Both represent extremes where the voicing of moral concerns has become essentially nonmoral. Both exemplify states in which we become in practice morally mute even though we may be using moral words and expressions. In the one case, we whisper our moral concerns so that the other can easily not recognize or dismiss whatever moral claims we may hint at, except in those instances when we hope others will know to pick up the hints because of their existing deference to us. At the other extreme, we loudly shout our moral concerns so that others find themselves compelled to comply out of deference to the noise or the position from which it is coming. In both cases substantive moral claims are muted.

Table 2.2
Variations in the Connections Between Voicing Moral Concerns and Desired Responses Solicited from Others

Discourse in the Form of Stating Opinions:	Audible Moral Discourse:	Discourse in the Form of Commands:
I state my views as my personal opinions without giving reasons and leave others to respond as they choose.	I state my views or issue commands and give reasons for doing so.	I command others to act precisely as I have ordered without giving reasons and threaten sanctions if they fail to comply.

Recognizable moral discourse (see Table 2.2) takes place between these extremes. We recognizably voice moral concerns not only when we speak about them and acknowledge that we are making claims on how we hope others will act but also when we give intelligible justifications that are inherently discussable. They must be discussable insofar as we are seeking the voluntary, considered response of others. We recognizably voice moral concerns only when we leave others room to consider how they will choose to respond. To be sure, we may well attempt to make our position as persuasive as possible. Yet if our communication is to be moral and not just imperative, our voicing must allow and invite others to think about their alternatives, to explore the bases and objectives of their own actions, and correspondingly to inquire further, if they choose, about the reasons for our position. We might say that the activity of voicing moral concerns is by its very nature an engaged and dialectic activity. We cannot voice moral concerns without making some kind of claims on others. However, we cannot force or compel their response. We voice in order to elicit their conscious choices.

Typical Forms of Moral Silence

People are morally mute in businesses and complex organizations, as well as in other settings in several typical ways. I will introduce these several forms, which are outlined in Table 2.3, before describing individual types at greater length.

Table 2.3
Forms of Moral Silence

Negative Expressions
Not blowing the whistle on observed abuses, violations, or misconduct
Not audibly dissenting from policies and agreements thought to include morally questionable features
Not questioning or debating aspects of decisions thought to be morally debatable
Positive Expressions
Not speaking up for ideals
Not bargaining hard enough for positions that among other things advance morally valued objectives
Not Holding Others Sufficiently Accountable
Not providing adequate feedback either in supervisory or collegial relationships

The first or negative form is easiest to recognize. We are morally mute when we fail to raise questions about or call attention to what we regard as morally questionable activities. A manager is morally mute when she knows that a colleague regularly pads his expense accounts and she never raises the issue with him or others. One executive confessed how he had remained uncomfortably mute in labor negotiations as his confreres passed off what was essentially a small but not full cost-of-living adjustment as a pay raise. Although he was bothered by this sleight of hand, he said nothing and the negotiations proceeded on these terms. The example of moral silence that most readily comes to mind is the case of the person who knows of a serious wrong but fails to speak up. For example, we may know that members of our organization are providing money to bribe officials in other countries in contravention of local laws and of our own national conventions, but we say nothing, assuming that the practice is already known about. We may indeed find various ways of rationalizing what is going on but still feel troubled. Although it is easiest to recognize moral silence in cases of self-silencing by would-be whistle-blowers, this is only a more dramatic form of not dissenting or not raising questions about practices or policies that seem to violate moral standards we regard as important. We may be mute simply by not calling for further discussion of sales practices or marketing policies that strike us as clever and ingenious but also in some minor ways troubling. We may, for example, regard an advertising campaign that introduces invidious comparisons between the products of our company and a competitor as being especially creative in the way it called attention to strong features of our product but still feel bothered by the very selective and not-exactly-parallel way it displays these features. By raising questions early enough in the process, we might have been able to introduce modifications that deal with these troubling aspects. Thinking that we may be making a mountain out of a molehill, however, we remain silent. This represents an instance of moral silence, even if subsequently we are able to justify this silence as a temporary expedient that made it possible for us to gain a hearing for other issues we regarded as more vital.

People are morally mute as well when they fail to speak up strongly for moral positions they regard as important. Here they are not so much failing to call attention to abuses as they are failing to stand up for their ideals. This positive form of moral silence assumes two typical expressions. On the one hand, people fail audibly to champion moral programs and projects. For example, a bank manager spoke admiringly of how a competitor had developed a banking program in a low-income neighborhood that helped neighborhood organizations learn to keep their books and extended credit at somewhat higher risk to residents in connection with these organizations. He felt that his bank could and should develop a comparable program in other parts of town in ways that he believed would eventually expand the bank's customer base while offering a community service. He spoke briefly of his scheme with his superiors who dismissed it as impractical and too risky. Without trying further to develop on his own time a substantial portfolio for his idea, he spoke no more of it either to his superiors or other colleagues. Other examples of failing to speak up for ideals can easily be cited in relation to other kinds of community programs and environmental practices, as well as minority hiring and promotion. Many people do not even take as much initiative as this manager. Assuming ahead of time that they will receive unfavorable responses, they fail to make even the initial movements of inquiring about such proposed projects and discussing them with their colleagues. On the other hand, people assume a form of moral silence when they fail to bargain forcefully enough for positions they regard as morally valuable. This happens in many settings and around concerns that may not be especially targeted as ethical projects. A union representative may not assert his position vigorously enough and accept as a compromise an arrangement that seriously disadvantages his union. Growing impatient with lack of progress at the bargaining table and assuming that not much else could be gained, he softens his position. As a result, depending upon the clauses that were the objects of negotiations, workers may obtain smaller improvements than might be expected from comparable negotiations in other organizations with regard to educational benefits, grievance arbitrations, or other concerns. Equivalent occasions of soft bargaining may occur with respect to suppliers, customers, creditors, and government agencies with the result that particular organizations and their members receive less of certain desired goods (in the ethical sense) than they might have expected if bargaining had been more forcefully undertaken.

People are morally mute as well when they do not hold sufficiently accountable those with whom they interact. The problem here is that by not speaking up, we tacitly or overtly tolerate behavior that, though not being dramatically wrong or harmful, is inadequate. Eventually this tolerated inadequate behavior may cause difficulties in two ways. One, the effects of questionable practices over time may eventually result in serious problems. For example, carelessly undertaking credit checks for risky loans may in a cumulative way affect the credit-worthiness of a bank when bad loans mount up during economic reversals. Loose internal audit procedures may over time leave an organization without a clear sense of cost-effectiveness of its several operations. Two, tolerated inadequate behavior often becomes a problem for the persons whose conduct is not forthrightly held accountable. They become accustomed to working in ways that, though not gaining them accolades, do not gain them many candid appraisals. As a result they are not really challenged to learn from their mistakes. In time someone may get fed up and discipline them or let them go. Frequently, albeit not always accurately, these people complain that no one ever gave them a good clue as to their problems, especially earlier when they might have more easily benefited.

Finally, people are morally mute when in the course of ordinary discussions and debates they mask their moral beliefs and concerns. Several years ago I helped interview a number of managers about ethical issues that arose in the course of their work. Repeatedly as they mentioned particular events or issues, they expressed their concern for open disclosures, honest advertisements, just treatment, fair competition, and executive integrity (Waters, Bird, and Chant 1986; Bird and Waters 1986). They referred to these values not in answer to questions about their ideals but as terms they found useful at least privately to think about the specific events they were discussing. What was impressive to us as interviewers was the degree to which diverse sets of managers ended up invoking a common set of moral values. However, they all also confessed that they almost never made explicit reference to these values at work. Rather, when these events and issues had come up at work, they discussed them almost entirely using the language of finance, organizational politics, and business strategy. These interviewed managers felt that something was missing as a result. People camouflage their moral concerns in several ways. One manager, who went out of his way to arrange for corporate contributions to a number of environmental groups and institutes, described these activities in the language of smart business practices. Another riddled discussions of her human resources policies in the language of pop psychology and group work, even though she was concerned to overcome the unfair yet often unintended ways in which ordinary promotion policies discriminated against women who took pregnancy leaves.

I have set forth this initial survey of types of moral silence in order to indicate that people may be mute in several different ways, some seemingly much more innocuous than others. This survey is in part designed to tease out and expose some people who may never think that they succumb to occasional lapses of moral silence, precisely because they avoid particular nocuous forms. I argue later that it is difficult to avoid altogether any lapses because there may well arise occasions when temporary moral silence is morally justified. This initial survey also allows us to get a sense of how pervasive this problem really is, particularly when it occurs not only in blatant instances where individuals fail to report on fraud they have witnessed but also in more muted cases of inadequate feedback and masked moral commitments.

NOT WHISTLE BLOWING, NOT DISSENTING, AND NOT QUESTIONING

I introduce this discussion of occasions when people fail to call attention to moral wrongs by examining an often-reported case involving a faulty brake design prepared for an Air Force plane. The information on this case, which is included in several books and texts on business ethics, comes from Kermit Vandiver, who was one of the principal protagonists in the events that he describes (Vandiver 1972). In an article, "Why Should My Conscience Bother Me?," Vandiver gives an account of how the B. F. Goodrich Plant at Troy, Ohio, designed and built 202 brake assemblies for LTV Aerospace Corporation for the A7D light attack aircraft the latter corporation was assembling. The brake that was designed and later tested by the Air Force was seriously flawed, such that the test planes using them seriously overran the runway and the brake itself dangerously overheated. After official tests demonstrated these failures, B. F. Goodrich subsequently agreed at considerable additional expense to itself to build a new set of brake assemblies with five instead of the original four disks in each brake. Although no one was hurt in any of the tests, which were undertaken initially by B. F. Goodrich in March 1968 and subsequently by the Air Force in June 1968, someone might well have been. In going forward with official tests in June after they had experienced considerable difficulties if not outright failures in March, the company was knowingly exposing itself and others to potentially damaging and, in the case of the test pilots, mortal risks.

The question is: Why did the company proceed with tests by the Air Force when several people connected with the project had attempted to speak up about the faultiness of this brake design? When we ask the question this way, we are focusing on the moral deafness of managers and executives at B. F. Goodrich. I will in fact reexamine this case in the next chapter as an exemplary instance of moral deafness. Now, however, I would like to examine what we can learn about moral silence in this case.

During the initial phases while the brake was being designed for the company tests on actual airplanes, one young engineer, Searle Lawson, several times overtly questioned the safety and dependability of the brake design, which had been the work of another engineer, John Warren. Lawson was responsible for preparing the brake lining material. In the laboratory tests, no materials were able to perform as expected with the four-disk brake assembly. In his judgment the brake design was flawed. It should have included five disks instead. He argued his case both with Warren and his supervisor, Robert Sink, who also was responsible for keeping the people at LTV Aerospace informed. Sometime before the March tests, he raised these concerns in a meeting with Sink again and with Russell Van Horn, the manager of the design engineering section. The decision was made to go ahead with the project.

Retrospectively, we may ask why Lawson did not pursue his concerns further. He had data on simulated test results that were very convincing. To be sure, he addressed people who seemed to be deaf to his concern for various reasons. He probably had a sense that if the brake turned out to be faulty, as he had predicted, then the company as a whole would suffer both in financial terms and reputation. Moreover, he had a sense that the brake as designed was dangerous. Why didn't he go over the heads of his superiors with the data he had in hand? Why didn't he seek out the support of other junior engineers who might well have readily recognized the urgency of the problem? We don't have his account, so we cannot answer. We can, nonetheless, suspect in a sympathetic way that (1) he felt that he had little room to maneuver and (2) he expected that the test cases with actual planes would indeed confirm his arguments in ways that would move the company to recognize the flaw in its initial design.

During the next phase of this case, B. F. Goodrich prepared a report in which it recorded a fudged version of the results of its own tests. This report was forwarded to LTV Aerospace and the Air Force in preparation for the official Air Force tests. In March 1968 Vandiver was called to examine the initial March test results and to prepare graphs and other materials for this report. Eventually both he and Lawson were asked to write the report, for which they wrote the draft that with some minor but significant modifications was sent out by their company. Vandiver was alarmed by the test results. The tests were modified so that the planes were allowed to coast longer and fans were used to cool the brakes. Still the brakes overheated and in some cases melted down and the planes overran the distances in which they were supposed to stop. Vandiver raised his concerns with his supervisor, Ralph Gretzinger, and with Lawson. Gretzinger discussed this matter with his supervisor, Russell Line. Although Gretzinger was responsive enough to take this action, no one responded sympathetically. Vandiver went directly to Line, pointing to the risks to Goodrich's reputation if some action was not taken to alter the brake design. He urged Line to speak to the chief engineer, H. C. "Bud" Sunderman. Line refused. Eventually Vandiver and Lawson, failing to get any satisfactory response, consented not only to prepare technical material for the report but to write the report. They knowingly wrote a fudged report that included descriptions of tests not undertaken as well as altered data on tests that did occur. They included in this report a sentence in which they said that the brake assembly did not meet the requirements spelled out in the relevant documents. This sentence was subsequently made positive in the official report. Vandiver, Lawson, and Warren refused to sign the report that they had largely written.

Why didn't Vandiver attempt in some ways to speak up more forcefully? He knew that the brake design was flawed, and he made several initial attempts to bring this concern to coworkers and several supervisors. Initially he was not at all mute. But he seemed to have become so. He confesses to preparing fudged test results without fully explaining who ordered this and in what ways he might have been able to write a more accurate report. He doesn't explain why by himself or with Lawson he did not bring more accurate information on the test results to more senior executives who would, we would expect, quite readily see how their company was going to be not only embarrassed by the official Air Force tests but also put at risk of endangering the lives of the pilots involved. Vandiver did raise these concerns with Warren, who seems to have recognized the problem but argued that the fudged report did not technically amount to fraud even though it was wrong. Why didn't Warren join Vandiver and perhaps Lawson in telling the truth about this matter to more people in the corporation? To be sure, jointly they did enter a whisper of protest by not signing. Without a clear statement of their reasons, however, this whisper was hardly audible.

It is not my interest to blame or criticize anyone in this case. Threatened with dismissal, it is not easy to speak the truth, even in a case like this where the corporation was clearly bound to benefit from hearing the truth. My interest is to gain some understanding of the factors that lead people to soften or silence their criticisms not only in cases where criticisms are likely to be in the organization's interest but also in cases where this may not be so. In a not untypical way this case involves people who began by speaking up but then became mute and silent until after the events in question had come and gone. Even though we can sympathize with them given the deaf responses of those to whom they initially spoke, we can still ask what factors in themselves and their organizations led them not to speak up and out more forcefully in order to gain sympathetic ears from others.

This case illustrates well the characteristic dilemma experienced by people who feel that they ought to bring attention to bear on questionable proceedings but typically feel caught with polar alternatives, both of which feel extreme and uncomfortable. As they were writing the preliminary test results report, Vandiver and Lawson saw their alternatives as being either to knuckle under in a show of feigned loyalty and support for actions they judged to be fundamentally wrong or to expose these wrongs in ways that seemed to put their jobs on the line as well as those of the persons they would be accusing. They saw few alternatives, and though not being fully mute, they offered a faint protest, set forth as much, it seems, to disclaim responsibility as to issue a recognizable warning.

There are a number of ways of speaking up to bring attention to questionable activities and correspondingly a number of different ways of being mute if we do not voice our concerns when we learn of these activities. Richard Nielsen (1987) wrote an ingenious article in which he surveyed a number of different ways in which executives can blow the whistle on perceived wrongs. He found examples for each of twelve different ways of protesting against unethical behavior. His list includes the following different strategies:

(1) secretly blowing the whistle within the organization; (2) quietly blowing the whistle, informing a responsible higher-level manager; (3) secretly threatening the offender with blowing the whistle; (4) secretly threatening a responsible manager with blowing the whistle outside the organization; (5) publicly threatening a responsible manager with blowing the whistle; (6) sabotaging the implementation of the unethical behaviour; (7) quietly refraining from implementing an unethical order or policy; (8) publicly blowing the whistle within the organization; (9) conscientiously objecting to an unethical policy or refusing to implement the policy; (10) indicating uncertainty about or refusing to support a cover-up in the event that the individual and/or organization gets caught; (11) secretly blowing the whistle outside the organization; or (12) publicly blowing the whistle outside the organization.

Nielsen describes a variety of tactics for bringing attention to real or potential wrongs. His list might be transposed negatively into a series of ways of being mute insofar as people fail to pursue these kinds of options and instead remain silent in the face of observed wrongdoings. One might well ask what can be gained by such a negative list. Why review all the ways people silence their moral concern or outrage? There are several answers to this question. One answer is that this list, like Nielsen's, provides suggestions of ways of speaking up that avoid the two extremes of either complete silence or voicing only with alarm and outrage. The second answer is more complex but is related to the first. Consider the following list of variations in moral silence with respect to questionable activities:

1. Feigning loyalty—One acts in vocal support of questionable activities but may privately carp. One may whisper objections but not in ways that others clearly comprehend.
2. Not questioning—One may whisper objections but not voice them either publicly (in meetings) or discreetly with colleagues, superiors, or officers in reasoned statements.
3. Not dissenting—One may voice questions but not be willing in the end to dissent from policies or practices judged to be wrong. Dissent is a form of loyal opposition.
4. Not threatening—One may dissent quietly but firmly but not threaten any further objection either in the form of not cooperating with the questionable practices or blowing the whistle on them.
5. Not refusing to cooperate—One may make threats in hopes of persuading others to act but be unwilling to carry through in the form of refusing to cooperate.
6. Not blowing the whistle discreetly—One may be willing to refuse cooperation but unwilling to inform others in superior positions or in the public about questionable practices.

7. Not blowing the whistle publicly—One may be willing to blow the whistle quietly
    within an organization but unwilling to inform those outside the organization about
    wrongs or questionable conduct.

If we look at the series of positions outlined here, we can observe that people
are often not absolutely mute but only relatively so. They may whisper an
objection that practically no one understands. They are not fully mute, to be
sure. But they have not voiced their concerns in ways that correspond to either
their convictions or what they might do, given more imagination. Or, in another
situation, an executive may question but not overtly dissent, as one manager did
from a marketing policy that assigned sales quotas for rewards to the sales
representatives of a public utilities. Where a manager both was able to exert
greater voice and felt in good conscience that a wrong was being perpetrated,
he would be relatively mute if he only hinted at his concerns and did not utilize
more fully his real opportunities for voicing. In the case just cited, the manager
loyally dissented yet helped to administer a policy he thought was wrong
because, he argued, utilities ought not attempt to force unwanted or unneeded
products and services on their clients as did the marketing policy in question.
This executive did not go so far as refusing to cooperate. His position on this
policy was subsequently confirmed by a court decision.

The list just presented surveys a series of positions moving from silence to
loudly vocal. Typically people are mute not because they fail to blow the whistle
publicly on serious wrongs but because they fail to attempt in some less noisy
ways to voice their concerns and bring attention to other less blatant instances
of questionable conduct. Clearly, how vocal we ought to be and how mute we
in fact allow ourselves to be depends on several factors, including the
seriousness and urgency of the observed wrong. There is no need for public
exposés about minor infractions that can be taken care of over a period of time.
Not only do such public cries of wolf discredit those who voice them, but they
underestimate the extent to which those accountable for questionable activities
may be willing and able to respond to direct questioning. However, to stop with
whispered objections to serious problems rather than venture to dissent or
threaten noncooperation or in fact refuse to cooperate is to stop far short of what
might be possible. How vocal one ought to be and correspondingly how mute
one is depends as well on our real opportunities. We may possess significant
power either because we hold positions of influence or because we control
scarce resources in the form of technical know-how or contacts or access to
credit. In the Air Force brake case both Lawson and Vandiver may have
possessed more potential power in the form of firsthand knowledge of the tests
than they realized. With greater power or more opportunities come greater
possibilities of voicing more vocally and with greater impact. Finally, whether
and to what degree our particular responses to unethical conduct are mute
depend as well on what ways of speaking out are likely to occasion desired
responses. There is no need for overkill. If speaking discreetly is likely to yield

better responses than public protests, then this form of speaking may well be preferable. In practice, we ought in a serial manner to attempt to voice our concerns first in quieter and more discreet ways and then in louder and more public ways when the former fail to elicit sympathetic responses.

The conscience-stricken employee who learns of serious wrongs and fails effectively to alert others in a timely fashion represents moral silence most starkly. The failure to blow the whistle in a dramatic way characterizes the way the morally mute often muzzle themselves or speak only with a whisper at the time while occasionally saving louder outcries for later. We will subsequently examine several of the factors that render would-be whistle-blowers mute. In the meantime we can acknowledge that speaking out in these settings is often very difficult. Would-be whistle-blowers often feel as if they would be putting their jobs or positions at risk at the same time as they are accusing others of outrageous moral lapses. Even when they are convinced of the correctness of their private judgments—and often they feel besieged with doubts—they feel as if they would be speaking as prosecutor, judge, and jury because the offensive acts seem so clearly wrong. Until they speak, they really hear of no other moderating views on the matter except for the tacit but, in their minds, unknowing acceptance of the legitimacy of existing relationships. Speaking up seems to occasion so much trouble in highly moralistic tones. So, many would-be whistle-blowers remain just that. Although the plight of the mute but would-be whistle-blower is exemplary, however, it is probably not typical. Whistle-blowing is often an heroic act often best undertaken when other less dramatic forms of calling attention have failed. Frequently, people are morally mute not because they fail to expose illegal acts, major flaws, or fraud but because they fail to voice dissent or raise questions in more ordinary circumstances. Consider this list of typical instances in which mute managers held their tongues about conduct they found questionable:

1. A manager with an alcoholic boss did not know whether to report him or to speak to him. She did nothing.
2. A manager felt that his company was charging excessive prices for a product widely used by those suffering from AIDS. He did not know whether or how to raise his concern.
3. A manager was upset when a superior raised prices for a particular product, with disastrous results, and then used a marketing manager as the scapegoat. Wondering whether he should expose this action as a sham, he did nothing.
4. A purchasing agent learned that the manager of a work group had arranged to purchase a product needed for production at a much higher price than might be paid from another supplier. He feared that the product also produced more noxious side effects during the manufacturing process. He did not fully trust the manager's disclaimers about the side effects but recognized that the latter had legitimate prerogatives regarding these kinds of purchasing arrangements. He recognized that the manager often used this same supplier, which the latter defended as a good working arrangement. Not knowing with whom he might raise his concerns, the

purchasing agent remained silent.

5. A number of nurses felt that several doctors were taking heroic efforts to prolong the lives of tiny, premature babies even though the survival rates for very, very young babies was extremely low. Although they admired the doctors' successes, they felt that in too many cases these efforts meant only putting these tiny infants through prolonged suffering. Not knowing how to raise their concerns, they remained silent, and many of them became disenchanted.

6. A number of women managers silently accepted a situation in which no women were promoted to senior executive positions. They rationalized that really only engineers were appointed to these positions (not true) and that individually many of them were doing better than they had expected.

7. A number of managers privately groused about the ways many senior executives seemed to take great liberties with company perks. However, these managers never raised their concerns openly within the organization.

8. A manager did not know what to do when government agents showed him low bids submitted by others.

What is noticeable in most of these cases, drawn from my research and similar studies undertaken by others, is that managers are mute in the first place because they fail openly to raise questions about practices that do not seem at the outset to be self-evidently wrong.

FAILURE TO SPEAK UP FOR IDEALS AND TO BARGAIN HARD

I now consider a quite different form of moral silence that occurs when people fail to stand up forthrightly on behalf of their own commitments. This, too, is a sin of omission but committed not by failing to call attention to questionable activities but by failing to promote worthwhile activities. This form of moral silence is especially difficult to document because people feel less conscience-stricken by this kind of moral silence and silence here results in few exposés by outraged investigators. People may feel less fully challenged and fulfilled because they neglect to speak up for and promote their dreams and ideals, but they rarely feel guilty. At the same time it is hard to generate prophetic protests about missed opportunities. Nonetheless, moral loss is occasioned by failures of people to advocate their ideals, to champion their valued projects, and to bargain aggressively for their commitments.

Often silence in relation to valued projects represents opportunities foregone or delayed. Much later, people will recount stories of their youthful dreams of creating safer, less risky products, or of somehow combining accounting careers with their interest in the arts, or their visions for hiring and retraining long-term unemployed young adults. They then recount how the exigencies of work made these visions seem unrealistic and as a result they relinquished them. For the isolated examples of managers who find ways of combining their interest in altruism with their business careers, either by donating spare time to civic projects or by taking short leaves to work on these endeavors, there are hundreds more who confess that no such arrangements seem possible to them. Silence in these cases usually occurs in unasked questions, in unpursued inquiries, and in the unadvanced entreaties for support from others. All too frequently most of us accept without further debate the conventional wisdom about what is possible, and we abandon our dreams and visions little by little—sometimes without really noticing that we are doing so.

We become morally mute as well, not absolutely but relatively so, whenever in the very process of speaking up for our ideals and commitments, we speak too softly or obscurely. When we speak out for our projects too quietly or too indirectly, our concerns are too easily overlooked or dismissed. We may make peace with our consciences by saying something. Nonetheless, our dreams, visions, and commitments remain effectively unrecognizable to others. As I interviewed managers, I heard tales of numerous proposed projects that received little or no support. In many cases these projects were never forthrightly championed. In some cases this weak advocacy was probably fitting for schemes that were at best unrealistic, too costly, or of uncertain benefit. But in other instances proposed schemes for improved community relations, training programs for handicapped workers, and environmental projects remained dead letters for lack of any vocal champions.

Mute advocacy is best illustrated in relation to difficult negotiations. I will look at labor negotiations, but we could consider as well negotiations with customers, creditors, suppliers, government agencies, or competitors. There is a moral dimension to these processes not only in relation to specific clauses dealing with rights and wrongs but also in the fact that the parties to these deliberations seek the good of their own constituents. Negotiating is a process that takes place over time as parties move from initial bargaining positions through one or many intermediary stages until they reach agreements. Negotiation may take place speedily or become protracted. The parties may be open or guarded. Often the process involves give and take. A good negotiator will bargain hard and will make concessions only to the degree that they are equivalently matched. In difficult negotiations one or both parties may be tempted to yield concessions to more speedily reach agreements and thereby avoid the extra costs of strikes or lockouts. A negotiator becomes mute by compromising prematurely before she has fully and aggressively stated her position. She becomes mute by accepting early closure prior to attempts, using both persuasion and pressure, to gain more favorable outcomes. From time to time both management and labor negotiators retrospectively may feel that they yielded too easily to the other side and as a result reached agreements that seriously disadvantage their constituents. They are relatively mute not because they yield but because they decide on their own to hold in check some of the arguments, threats, and bargaining chips they might voice if negotiations went on longer.

FAILURE TO HOLD OTHERS ACCOUNTABLE

We are morally mute as well when we fail to hold accountable others with whom we have entered into ongoing agreements and contractual relationships. This form of silence requires an introductory explanation. In any voluntarily agreed-upon relationship—in organizations and at work especially, but in any other areas as well—we are expected not only to honor our agreements but also to hold others accountable to do so as well. Most simply understood, accountability is a form of control whereby we check to see if others have complied with explicit and implicit terms of governing agreements and then reward or punish them accordingly. Correspondingly we are mute to the degree that we fail to communicate clearly to others our judgments about the ways they honor, exceed, and fail to honor these explicit and implicit expectations. Holding others accountable involves more than calling attention to blatant violations of organizational rules and values. It involves letting others know where they stand and how well they are doing. We are mute to the extent that we fail to keep others informed about our considered judgments of how they are performing in relation to the agreements that establish and guide our interactions.

Complaints about the mute ways in which people fail overtly to hold others accountable often arise in relation to poorly conducted performance appraisals. As a part of my research, I listened while a number of managers told stories of the inadequate appraisals of their colleagues. One executive said: "I inherited a manager who had sloppy dress, bad teeth, and poor personal hygiene; previous managers couldn't bring themselves to give him feedback. I went through a period of trying to gentle him into improving but eventually got around to telling him directly how appearance was putting people off and hurting his career." Another manager complained: "We have a lot of people in my company who don't know where they stand. Half-truths or incomplete pictures are drawn. The truth is bent and the employee is not dealt with in a forthright and honest fashion with respect to his performance and his prospects." If what these managers say is true, large numbers of employees are not being candidly informed about the quality and character of their work.

Silence in these settings is a moral concern for a number of reasons. Because they have not been kept forthrightly informed, employees may justifiably feel mistreated if they are suspended or threatened with suspension for conduct about which they have not been warned. One manager commented: "I had a 30-year-old woman who was not performing, and I told her we wanted her to go. She said, 'Look, I've been here for 12 years; this is the first time anybody has spoken to me about my performance; so you have a responsibility to not only tell me but to do something about it.' We struck a deal—we hired a placement agency, and she didn't have to leave until she found a job she liked." The failure to voice criticisms of the performance of subordinates also means that the latter are not extended opportunities to learn and grow from their own mistakes and shortcomings. Silence here also has the added consequence of unfairly loading added burdens onto subsequent supervisors who eventually have to confront the poorly performing subordinates who have never received true performance appraisals. Additionally, insofar as managers mute their performance evaluations, organizations as a whole may well receive less good work from these employees than they could appropriately expect and from which they could potentially benefit.

More is involved in holding others accountable than simply informing them when their performances fall below expected levels. Correspondingly, silence entails more than simply the failure to adequately communicate these evaluations. We become accountable whenever we enter into agreements with others. As participants in agreements, we are expected to hold each other accountable and to keep each other informed about how well from our perspectives the others are performing in terms of these agreements. This is a two-way, interactive activity. In face-to-face relationships characteristic of friendships, some partnerships, and some collegial relations, we often hold each other accountable by means of informal, day-to-day conversations. Incidents arise in which one person acts in unexpected and unanticipated ways and the other communicates his/her disappointment, surprise, or pleasure. On an ongoing, unfolding basis, partners, friends, and colleagues may adjust and modify their basic agreements by means of casual face-to-face discussions. Face-to-face communication, as I will indicate shortly, can misfire or be distorted in many ways. I am introducing it here as a clear, rather idyllic example. We can use this example to see more clearly what is involved in holding others accountable.

As we can see from this example, all those involved in agreements—not only those in supervisory positions—hold each other accountable. As partners hold each other accountable, so can subordinates and superiors. Subordinates can be expected to inform their superiors about the degree to which the supervisors are holding up their ends of the bargains governing the subordinates' work. They may complain if superiors fail to provide promised conditions necessary for them to fulfill their expected assignments or if their compensations are less than agreed upon. They may object as well if superiors fail to provide the leadership and direction expected of them. Additionally, we can see from this example that holding others accountable involves several different kinds of communications. Initially we need to communicate our expectations as well as our understandings of the expectations of the others with whom we are involved. This is as necessary and as useful for superiors and subordinates as for friends or partners. We cannot presume that others view agreements exactly as we do unless we have openly discussed this matter with them. These initial expectation-setting exchanges also provide occasions when participants in agreements can attempt to elicit from each other promises to provide the conditions they think they need to achieve what others expect of them (Culbert and McDonough 1980). Holding others accountable necessarily involves communicating our evaluations of their performances as well as our responses to their evaluations. In face-to-face as well as in more impersonal and complex relationships, all participants to agreements may communicate evaluations and responses.

I have just described the basic skeleton of an interactive model of accountability. This model contrasts with the simple compliance model, which people frequently have in mind when they talk of accountability, especially in organizations. According to the simple compliance model, superiors communicate expectations to subordinates and then judge the degree to which the latter comply. This model is one-sided. It doesn't work well for a number of less strictly hierarchical relationships between partners, friends, collaborators, colleagues, and coworkers. It fails to recognize the extent to which holding others accountable is a continuous and often responsive activity. The complex, interactive model in contrast views accountability as a two-way, interactive, and ongoing activity involving sets of different exchanges initiated to establish expectations, to gauge performances, and to reinforce or adjust expectations accordingly.

People are morally mute in relationships of accountability whenever they fail to communicate clearly and understandably both their own expectations and evaluations of others and their responses in turn to the expectations and evaluations of others. Silence here takes several typical forms. One is the superficial performance appraisal. Often performance appraisals become so routine that they lack any real substance. They often become one-way communications with few opportunities for subordinates to voice their expectations and interpretations and assessments with respect to the conditions of their assignments. Silence occurs as well when people fail in the first place to spell out clearly what they expect of others. What happens is that certain expectations are usually very clearly spelled out but many others are left vague or implicit. Universities expect their faculty members to teach and to contribute to learning and/or the arts. Sometimes universities are not very clear about the kind of balance they expect particular professors to strike with regard to these expectations. However, they are typically even less clear about the collegial and professional responsibilities of faculty. Professors are expected to spend some of their time engaging in an assortment of collegial and professional tasks—from serving on departmental, divisional, and university committees to reviewing manuscripts and research applications; from assuming occasional administrative tasks to being available and accessible to offer assistance to colleagues. Even though informal assessments of real and potential collegiality probably play a large role in decisions to hire and promote, the criteria used to make these assessments are almost never clearly spelled out and communicated. Lacking clear criteria to gauge collegial and professional activities, too often universities substitute overt criticisms of measurable activities such as publications (or the paucity thereof) for the mute yet critical assessment of poor collegial and professional performances (Cowan 1994).

The recent interest in organizational codes of conduct in part represents a response to a previous condition in which organizations failed to communicate clearly and explicitly how they expected their members to behave in relation to a set of overt moral concerns. Typically these codes spell out standards for handling conflicts of interest, using organizational resources, interacting with minority group members, and participating in community and political activities. A number of companies have enacted these kinds of codes and are further augmenting and revising them because they recognize that they had not been very clear and overt in communicating what they had expected. In more recent years, codes originally drafted in the 1960s and 1970s are being expanded to include paragraphs on sexual harassment and workplace equity as organizations recognize a need to identify these kinds of expectations more clearly.

People mutely hold each other accountable whenever the interactive process of communicating and responding to expectations and communicating and responding to evaluations becomes blocked or distorted. In face-to-face relationships this often happens when people silence their criticism because they do not wish to offend. Their loyalty, based on mutual affection and long periods of cooperation, may make them reticent to call attention to incidents that seem small, even though they may readily voice complaints regarding other matters that have been ongoing occasions for disputes. In hierarchical relations, subordinates frequently fail to voice their assessments of how well their superiors have worked to establish conditions conducive for them to meet the task assigned to them. Too frequently they let superiors set the agendas and the tone for their interactions, and superiors in turn fail to recognize the ways they are accountable to their subordinates. Superiors often provide imbalanced evaluations of subordinates that overly focus on immediate and measurable outcomes rather than on the quality of performance. Many supervisors fail to provide genuine and concerned feedback. One interviewed manager commented: "Our managers are chicken to confront in the performance appraisal interview. All our employees have satisfactory or better ratings, and everybody has potential. It's just not true." While preparing a dossier that marshalled evidence in support of promoting more women into senior management, several women discovered that women at the same supervisory and managerial levels as men usually received higher performance ratings. They used this information to support their campaign, but they suspected in private that higher appraisals for women occurred in many cases because male supervisors were often reluctant to be really candid in their criticisms of their female subordinates.

CONCLUSION: WHEN IS IT RIGHT AND WRONG TO BE MORALLY SILENT?

In a number of different ways people mute their moral sentiments and convictions. A surgeon who accidentally operates on a patient's left eye rather than the right says nothing to the patient because he knows that he was scheduled to perform the same operation later on the other eye. A manager remains silent although troubled when she discovers that her company has been spying on fellow employees. A subordinate privately complains but says nothing about the inconsistent and careless direction of a supervisor given to occasional bouts of excessive drinking. A manager suppresses from an employee's personnel file all references to a previous history of irregular work performances associated with a period of mental instability.

Generally, it is wrong to be morally mute whether moral silence assumes the form of not raising questions, not voicing criticisms, not speaking up for ideals, not bargaining strongly enough in support of one's position, not holding others accountable, or camouflaging one's genuine moral commitments. Thus far I have primarily described several expressions of moral silence. It is now time to more fully indicate why moral silence in these settings is morally wrong.

One, it is wrong to silence our moral convictions because harm will occur that would otherwise not occur. This is a straightforward utilitarian argument. For the most part I alluded to utilitarian arguments as I have surveyed the several forms of moral silence in the preceding paragraphs. I described the ways that problems have not been addressed, opportunities have been missed, and rights have been ignored because people have failed to speak up. I further examined the ways questionable behavior has been tolerated and dilemmas have remained intractable because people have failed to voice their privately held moral concerns. In most of these cases moral silence resulted in consequences most people would judge to be less favorable not only to specific individuals but to their organizations more generally. Additionally, it is wrong to remain silent about mistakes, near accidents, and careless practices even when no apparent harm results, because the failure to report results in lost opportunities to learn from these incidents in order to avoid future ones in which harm might well result. Harmful consequences in these cases consist of the missed opportunities for early intelligence. Utilitarian arguments like these possess a pragmatic persuasiveness. The adverse consequences of moral silence are many-sided and extensive in ways that matter to the overall well-being of businesses and complex organizations. As the example of the faulty airplane brake case well illustrates, the company as a whole suffered when those who knew found it difficult to alert more senior officials about the design errors that rendered the brake unreliable.

Two, people should not mute their moral convictions because silence in practice often represents a form of deceit. Although I make reference here to practical activity, the second argument is essentially principled. The basic assumption here is that it is wrong to lie, to deceive knowingly and intentionally, either by what one says directly or by what one refuses to say. Most characteristically, lying assumes the form of deliberately distorting what one says with the intention of misleading others. Several basic arguments have been used against lying. It is wrong to lie, for example, because it is impossible to extend universally the permission to lie. It cannot be regarded as a principle valid for everyone in all settings. It is wrong to lie, furthermore, because lying itself is a parasitic activity. It can be beneficial to lie only so long as we can assume that most of the people most of the time will tell the truth. If we all assumed that others were likely to lie a good part of the time, then we would act differently, seeking greater guarantees, using more surveillance, and acting with greater suspicion and less trust. Social cooperation would greatly suffer. It is worthwhile lying only when others are likely to assume that we are telling the truth and when others are themselves likely to tell the truth. Lying is therefore wrong (Bok 1978). Not disclosing what one knows when asked is not exactly the same thing as lying. There are a number of occasions when being silent is not only an acceptable but a morally preferred course of action. In many settings, however, not disclosing amounts to the same thing as lying. When one holds in silence information that others would consider vital if they knew about it, then not disclosing can be as intentionally misleading as if one uttered a direct lie. Not speaking up results in presenting a distorted and deceptive representation of what is actually going on. The principal actors in the Air Force brake case were deceiving equivalently as much by not revealing the faults they found as they were by fudging their reports on subsequent tests. The arguments used against lying work equally well against failures to disclose information others are likely to consider vital. It is impossible to will that all persons would remain silent, if they held onto information we considered vital to our lives. We do not wish to be intentionally misled whether by what others say or by what they do not say.

When people fail to blow the whistle, raise questions, champion ideals, or hold others accountable, they often do so with little or no conscious intention of deceiving or misleading others. There are exceptions, to be sure, when supervisors deliberately lead along underperforming subordinates, when informants wait for misfortunes to happen rather than blow the whistle, or when constituents bargain mildly in hopes of showing others up as overpowering bullies. Moreover, those hoping to succeed in tacitly violating prior agreements clearly have a vested interest in not reporting on their own questionable activities if they feel at all troubled by them. Insider traders typically use evasion and silence as much or more than direct deception to draw off the inquiries of others whose trust they are violating. However, these are exceptions. Characteristically, those who are morally mute do not directly aim to mislead. Sometimes when people are morally silent, they recognize at that time that their failures to speak up will result in distorted representations of what is really going on. Vandiver knew this in the Air Force brake case. Many times, however, people recognize the distorting and misleading effect of their silence only later when questioned by others. Some both before and afterward fail to acknowledge the way their silence miscues and misinforms others. Nonetheless, their willful silence has that effect. As a result others proceed with their activities without fully knowing problems that have not been brought to light.

Three, people ought to voice their moral convictions when appropriate because the failure to speak up and speak out is self-compromising. When people fail to speak up about wrongs they know are undetected, when they fail to champion projects that they value, and when they fail to hold others accountable, they are likely to feel that they are being untrue to themselves.

They may well experience a loss in the sense of personal integrity and self-worth. They have allowed their convictions to be ignored. They have allowed wrongs to be tolerated. They have in some measure not been faithful to their own ideals and commitments. Often in addition to these feelings of self-compromise, they may additionally experience feelings of resentment. People often feel angry and jealous when others seem to benefit from conniving they knew about but failed to report. They often feel particularly slighted, especially when it seems that a timely word on their part, if really heard by others, might have turned things around in ways that would have benefited them. When people are morally mute, they are likely to experience some diminution in their sense of self. Rather than asserting themselves at an opportune moment, they remained silent and thus more at the mercy of forces beyond their capacity to influence than would be the case if they had spoken up. Rather than being participants in unfolding events by speaking up, they have become observers with the unspoken feeling that they might well have had something important to contribute (Nietzsche 1927).

The problem with moral silence is that, similar to lying, it is often self-reinforcing. When people intentionally lie, they often find it necessary to lie further in order to cover their initial lie. Additionally, having succeeded with their initial deception, they are often tempted to try again, particularly if no one seems to complain or seems to be especially injured in the process. Processes of self-rationalizing kick in. If they seem to benefit personally from this deception and no one else seems to be measurably harmed, then those engaged in the original deception are tempted to neutralize moral standards they otherwise honor, rationalizing that special circumstances warrant their particular evasions (Cohen 1955; Matza 1964). Equivalent psychological impulses affect the morally mute. If they have been mute and nothing really untoward seems to have occurred, they can be easily persuaded that it was okay to remain morally silent, especially if they feared that speaking up might have put them at risk. They can similarly feel that it is necessary to cover their silence with further silence lest it be discovered that they knowingly failed to speak up (Klitgaard 1988; Bok 1983, 177).

It is wrong to be morally mute. Nonetheless, we need to acknowledge exceptions when moral silence is justified. At least three exceptional situations come to mind. One, during protracted bargaining, negotiators can justifiably not disclose what they regard as their final positions. Neither partner in these negotiations is expected to disclose appreciably more than the other. Negotiating in good faith simply requires that each side in a reciprocating fashion attempt to match the disclosures of the other. Although the final agreements can take place only when both sides finally disclose where they stand, the process of negotiating itself requires that bargainers retain some information as well as their own private views of the extent to which they are willing to compromise. Timing matters here. Though it is wrong to enter into agreements intentionally withholding vital information from the other, it is not only not wrong but actually fitting to withhold some of this information during the process of negotiating to the extent that the other likewise withholds.

Two, it is wrong intentionally to defame. People can speak moral truths but do so in ways that inappropriately expose others to shame, public ridicule, or malicious gossip against which the latter cannot readily defend themselves. This kind of exposing is not justified when other, more private settings are available for raising the same concerns. The contemporary German Protestant theologian, Dietrich Bonhoeffer (1955) gives the example of a school boy being asked in class by his teacher whether his father was still drinking too much. The teacher in this case was defaming the boy and his father. The same question could have been asked privately under circumstances that allowed the boy to explain his father's condition more fully and defend his own honor as well as acknowledge the difficulties he faced. Bonhoeffer argues that it was probably truthful for the boy in class to evade the teacher's direct question and to dissimulate. The issue here is one of setting. If people are being accused of some wrongdoing, it is only fair that they be allowed to defend themselves appropriately. Sometimes it is very difficult to mount credible defenses in public, especially when one is accused of personal wrongdoing. People remember the accusations long after they have forgotten about how these cases eventually were resolved. Therein lies the wrong of much gossip. To be sure, gossip often amounts to no more than frivolous chatter. It sometimes assumes the form of malicious degradation of others, however, in which those accused have no opportunity either to know or defend themselves against accusations voiced by others.

Three, it is wrong to divulge confidences to which others possess no legitimate claims. Friends rightly keep personal secrets. Organizations appropriately guard their trade secrets. Members of private societies protect the confidences known only to sworn members. Family members guard their own internal intimacies from the unwelcome scrutiny of others. Whenever we openly or tacitly promise to keep secrets, we are obliged to do so unless there are overriding reasons not to. The question is: When do such reasons count enough to make a difference? There is no simple answer to this question. Two different considerations each possess considerable weight. One may, for example, judge that it is in the best interest of the other with whom one shares a confidence to divulge a shared secret. As a physician you may attempt to persuade your patient to inform his spouse that he is a carrier of the HIV virus. In rare cases, but especially with children, you may choose to exercise this paternalistic initiative on your own. The other reason for revealing confidences reflects judgments about how vital the secret information is or might be to others from whom it is being withheld. Today most neighbors of industrial plants consider any information about toxicity of fluid, solid, and air emissions to be vital to them. Attempts to retain this information on the grounds that the levels are insignificant are treated with suspicion. Nearby residents counter any such claims with arguments that they should be allowed to judge for themselves when emission levels are significant and when they are not. Although there are good reasons for keeping confidence when appropriate, it is easy to suspect that sharers of secrets are prone like thieves to honor and protect each other to the disadvantage of the uninformed whose ignorance of this information they are likely to exploit. Still the obligation to keep confidence is weighty and should be overridden only when we can make a persuasive case that divulged secrets will be either in the best interest of those sharing the confidence or truly vital to interests of those who have been kept uninformed.

Although we can identify several exceptions, the basic principle is clear. It is wrong to be morally mute not only because harmful consequences are likely to occur but also because silence often in practice consists in a passive if not active form of deception and because the act of being mute is frequently self-compromising. Nonetheless, there are times and settings when it may not only be possible but morally justified to be morally silent. These exceptions are instructive. In each case the exceptions are temporary or relative and not absolute. Timing matters in several ways. For example, we ought not accuse others publicly until we have attempted to raise our criticisms privately in ways that allow others to explain and/or defend themselves. Otherwise, we might wrongly affect another's reputation because we lacked sufficient information or comprehension of the issues involved. The issue is not about whether we speak up but rather about when and how we speak up. Timing matters in other ways as well. It is best to speak up when the chances are best that we will be heard. Often we find others unable or unwilling to understand and respond to our morally wrought messages. It may thus be in our interests to prepare our intended audiences: to begin with information whose importance others are likely to acknowledge and then later add information about which they will probably be resistant. The model of partial and then increasing disclosures over time can be applicable not only for hard bargaining negotiations but also whistle-blowing and the championing of ideals. Additionally, as I have already discussed, careful judgment needs to be exercised with respect to keeping in confidence information that may be vital to the interest of others. The moral imperative to keep promises is not absolute when the retention of shared secrets allows for unjustified harm either to the parties involved or others. Because of the importance attached to keeping promises, it is clearly better to persuade those sharing a confidence vital to the interest of others to speak up on their own before we divulge their secrets as outsiders. Although it is wrong to be morally mute, moral blabbing is not the answer to this problem. We ought to speak up with care and responsibility.

CHAPTER 3
Moral Deafness

People are morally deaf to the degree that they do not hear and do not respond to moral issues that have been raised by others. For example, engineers identified and informed their superiors about defects in the engines built for the rockets that were to take a number of astronauts into orbit around the earth. Knowing that the O-rings in the rockets did not perform well in cold weather, some engineers warned against launches on very cold days. The Vice President of Engineering of the firm involved initially hesitated to sign the order for launch for the scheduled launch date as a result. His superior in turn counseled him to assume fitting managerial responsibility and sign, which he did. These superiors remained effectively deaf to the dangers entailed in the warnings that they received. Subsequently, the O-rings' engines failed in the way the engineers had warned, the booster rockets exploded, and the astronauts died (Werhane 1991). Although hindsight is clearly sharper than foresight, we can and should still inquire why the warnings were not clearly heard, fully comprehended, and adequately responded to. In the Air Force brake case previously considered, Vandiver and Lawson informed their superiors of faults in brake design. Their supervisors failed to respond to these warnings and instead instructed them to prepare reports that hid these faults or actually covered them up. Why did these supervisors not hear more fully and clearly and respond more appropriately to these warnings, especially when the weakness of the brakes would certainly become apparent in subsequent Air Force test flights? Were the superiors in both of these examples willfully malevolent? Did they clearly comprehend the dangers that they were warned about and then recommend actions that deliberately and callously put others in grave danger? I doubt it. Although the courts might decide otherwise on technical legal grounds, I doubt in either case if the senior executives were maliciously liable. It was not in their interest to mandate activities that would likely endanger people and bring discredit to their firms. Rather, I think in both cases, for a number of reasons they were effectively deaf. They were guilty of selective inattention or of so hearing the particular information they received that it seemed less important and critical than it later proved in fact to be.

In these cases, executives were morally deaf because they failed to listen carefully and respond adequately to warnings by others. They were deaf to a particular kind of moral message. We can think of other examples that would illustrate the way people have been deaf to a wide variety of other moral messages as well. For example, during the 1960s and early 1970s environmental groups produced studies about the extent of air pollution, about the dangers of toxic poisoning to water tables, and about the probabilities of exhausting within the near future a range of limited natural resources. Few local or national governments responded. Few businesses modified their practices as a result. Although many governmental and business groups subsequently heard this message and responded with varying degrees of commitment and resistance in the 1980s and 1990s, fewer did so earlier. People are morally deaf to the degree that they fail to comprehend and respond fittingly to any kinds of moral messages, whether these messages assume the forms of warnings, protests, idealistic calls for reform, persuasive arguments, considered judgments, or attempts to solicit agreements.

MORAL DEAFNESS AS INATTENTIVENESS

To be morally deaf is to be unresponsive and inattentive to genuine moral issues raised by others in spite of personally possessing genuine moral convictions. To be morally deaf is not to lack moral sensitivities. It is to be in a state where we fail to hear, recognize, and pay attention to the moral concerns addressed to us by particular others. People are typically morally deaf only part of the time or with respect to some, rather than all, concerns. In contrast, what especially characterizes those persons with acute and sensitive moral ears are their attentiveness and responsiveness. A number of contemporary philosophers have argued that the heart of morality is the capacity and disposition of humans to respond and be attentive to others. They have made this argument in different ways but affirm similarly that to be genuinely moral is to be responsive to others. For example, H. Richard Niebuhr, the Protestant theologian, argued that the morality of humans is characterized not so much by their capacity to follow rules and principles or by their capacity to bring about beneficial results—both of which are noteworthy—but by their capacity to respond willfully to the needs and wants of others. This capacity to respond renders humans responsible. The morality of humans is correspondingly to be gauged by how responsive they are. Viewed from this perspective, Niebuhr argued that it is possible to become too preoccupied with adherence to rules and principles as well as too preoccupied with particular objectives so that we become unresponsive to the unfolding events and persons around us (Niebuhr 1963). In his influential philosophical meditation, *I and Thou*, the Jewish philosopher Martin Buber (1958) contrasted a responsive I-Thou orientation to the world and others with a more mechanical and unresponsive I-it orientation. Buber argued that both orientations are necessary. By means of the latter, we gain objective knowledge of the world. The latter orientation, however, often leaves us incapable of recognizing and responding to new developments and, more importantly from Buber's perspective, leads us to see the world and our relationship with others in too impersonal terms. A similar line of argument was developed more fully by another modern Jewish philosopher, Emmanuel Levinas, who maintained that the true beginning of ethical reflection is to take seriously the existence and claims of the other. Philosophers, such as seventeenth-century thinker René Descartes, who begin their reflections by thinking about the self, its capacity for knowledge, its will, and its rights, wrongly construe the actual experience of humans, who first become aware of themselves as selves in response to the actions of others who address them and care for them (Levinas 1969).

To hear and respond to moral concerns is to be attentive and turned on. We do not have a word that neatly describes the opposite of deafness the way that "vocal" describes the opposite of silence. Still, the word "attentive" evokes the corresponding sets of concerns. It signals that we are alert, ready to respond, and able to distinguish communications that make sense from noise. This latter ability makes the difference between simply being aware that something is being broadcast or sounded out and the ability to recognize sensible sounds that correspond to language, music, or other comprehensible sounds. Our ears may be able to recognize that strangers are speaking a foreign language that we cannot hear and comprehend unless we have learned it ourselves. As a result we are not really able to hear with comprehension what these others are saying. We cannot be attentive to their discourse. Our capacity to be attentive is based on our capacity both to recognize forms and patterns and to stay tuned in without letting our attention drift away. Even our capacity to hear others speaking languages with which we have little familiarity is relative to our ability to attend to what is being said and not to other matters.

Attentiveness involves at least four distinguishable activities. First, to be attentive means that we are ready to listen and to receive whatever information is being communicated. We are oriented toward those who are speaking or sending and not elsewhere. People often don't hear particular messages because their attention is directed elsewhere. A woman executive in charge of quality control for a pharmaceutical company described how she complained regularly to her superiors for fifteen years about their failure to promote women into senior management. Suddenly a Glass Ceiling Task Force was organized and women were promoted. Although she applauded this response when it finally came, she knew that for years no one had really been paying any attention to her messages. Senior management's attention was directed elsewhere.

Second, to be attentive implies being ready to recognize patterns and meanings. To be attentive is to be prepared to make sense out of what others communicate. Otherwise, communications sound like noise, like random senseless sounds. To be sure, moral complaints, requests, and arguments of others often become noisy cacophonies of competing voices variously pushing their own projects and making demands upon our resources and goodwill. To make sense of what otherwise would sound brutish and senseless often requires that we undertake one or more of the following useful operations. We may need to listen to competing messages one by one. We may need to secure someone's help to translate what is being said into terms we comprehend. Prophets of particular moral causes often become so engrossed with their subject that they overlook the fact that they frequently and casually resort to their own particular vocabularies and diction, which are not fully comprehended by those not so involved. Sometimes we cannot really comprehend the messages of others unless we slow down our listening. At high speed, unfamiliar messages sound blurred. In practice, to hear unfamiliar messages means that we probably need to give others enough time to make their case fully. The real message becomes trivia.

Third, to be attentive means being ready to focus and to distinguish what is really important from what is not. Often we can comprehend and translate into familiar terms what others say but remain unprepared and unable to identify the significance of their messages. We get distracted by supporting arguments or illustrative anecdotes. We understand literal communications but do not know or are not ready to connect them with concerns that matter to us. To be ready to focus entails being prepared to assign weight and significance and being disposed to relate messages that are being received to ongoing commitments. If we are going to focus on what others say, we cannot remain passive receivers just listening and comprehending. We must be ready to make sense in such a way that we acknowledge that messages are addressed to us and require from us some kind of relevant response. When we focus on the messages, especially moral ones, that others address to us, implicitly we acknowledge ourselves as being connected to these messages, which not only communicate information but also call for our responses. To focus then entails a readiness to assign importance.

We may, of course, assign importance in ways that strike those communicating to us as being radically different. For example, we may respond either with sympathy or antipathy. In the first case we would indicate that we identify with their message and wish to count ourselves as fellow supporters of the views being communicated to us. To be sympathetic is to feel with others: to join with them or share with them the feelings and values that they communicate. Antipathy is the opposite: to be repelled by particular feelings and values; to find them abhorrent, off-putting, or without any attraction at all. Clearly, two alternative and contrasting responses to the moral concerns voiced by others are to feel either so moved positively that we can see these concerns as our own or so moved negatively that we seek to oppose or counter them. A third possibility is to experience no feeling at all in response to concerns raised by others. Our response may be one of apathy. We may feel neither attracted nor repelled, without sympathy or antipathy. People are apathetic if they listen to the moral concerns of others with complete indifference, without being moved at all either positively or negatively. In many ways apathy is a greater barrier to those raising moral concerns than antipathy. At least the latter exhibits a recognition that moral concerns are being voiced, even if those concerns are being opposed. A neutral, apathetic response is no response at all.

These thoughts on sympathy, antipathy, and apathy lead us to comment on the fourth characteristic of attentiveness: being ready not only to listen, to comprehend, and to focus but also to take interest in the messages addressed to us. Taking interest is the opposite both of apathy and antipathy. To take interest implies an openness to consider and be moved by what the other says. We cannot take interest and at the same time be indifferent and blasé about the concerns raised by others. Minimally, when we take interest in what others say, we are prepared to spend at least some time thinking about and considering the importance of their messages. To take interest in what another says means at least listening with the open possibility of being attracted or affected by their concerns. Taking interest does not require our sympathy. We can be interested in the issues raised by others without having to see them as our own. Interest may lead to sympathy, but it need not. To see a message as interesting is simply to recognize it as worthy of thought and possible action. We may decide that a particular project is interesting but, having considered it in relation to our own commitments, we decide to respond in ways quite different from those who initially informed us. To be ready to take interest in what others say does require that we partially empathize with their concerns. If we are interested in what they say, then we must at least to some degree be ready and willing to comprehend their particular points of view. We must be prepared to attempt to understand why they raise the concerns they do. We must be ready to appreciate the realities of the issues in question as they see them. Nonetheless, taking interest does not require that we be fully empathetic in the sense that without any puzzlement or question on our part we can genuinely understand the particular perspectives of those others addressing us. To be sure, empathy is not sympathy. It does not entail any sense of shared feelings or compassion. Still, full empathy does imply full comprehension of the others' point of view. The latter is not always easy to achieve. Less is involved in simply taking an interest. It means both a readiness to consider what others say and a readiness at least initially to consider those concerns in the ways they are raised by those addressing us.

Being attentive then means that we are ready to listen, comprehend, focus, and take an interest in the messages addressed to us and to do so without either apathy or antipathy, with some minimal empathy, but where full empathy or sympathy are not required. Correspondingly we are morally deaf to the degree that we are not attentive and thus not ready to listen, comprehend, focus, and take interest in the moral messages addressed to us.

Three characteristics are associated with the muffled attention of the morally deaf, one of which I have already briefly mentioned. The morally deaf become apathetic, complacent, and negligent with the moral concerns raised by others in their surroundings. From the perspective of those voicing moral issues, the morally deaf appear apathetic, acting as if they just do not care about these matters. For example, environmental activists protesting against clear cutting forestry practices again and again ask how forestry companies could create what seems to them utter devastation. "Don't they care?" they wonder. It seems incomprehensible to them that these companies would proceed this way, even when they replant, because of the impact of lack of plant diversity on animal life. Although I recognize both that this situation is complex and that some genuine compromises have been initiated between particular firms and environmental groups, my immediate concern now is to observe that many forestry companies seem from the perspective of environmental groups not to care about consequences of their practices on animal life. Similarly, it could be argued that many industrial firms for years, until forced to do so by legislation, seemed not to care very much about accidents to their employees. Although protests were launched from time to time by employee groups, accident rates among industrial workers remained high for years, especially during the beginning of this century. Protesters wondered: Didn't these companies care that their employees were injured and occasionally maimed? Textile manufacturers for years allowed, and in fact forced, employees to work under conditions that occasioned for many lung diseases and hearing losses. From the perspective of those ill-affected, these companies seemed not to care. They seemed not only apathetic but also complacent.

Complacency is a dominant feature of muffled attention. To be sure, businesses often have weighty reasons for not responding positively to the moral cries of every prophet and protester. They must exercise discretion and respond with judgment. However, a reasoned reply addressing the concerns of others is quite a different response than an indifferent one that complacently tolerates questionable conditions that have been overtly criticized. For example, for years the executives in one firm largely ignored periodic complaints from women managers who wondered why, with one or two notable and noticeable exceptions, they were never considered for senior management positions. In a turbulent market, senior executives had many other concerns to worry about. Many of the women managers in higher middle management became complacent as well. They found ways of rationalizing: They did not really feel comfortable hobnobbing casually at sporting events or golf; they did not cultivate the informal alliances that seemed to play such a key role in promotion decisions. Although the issue was raised from time to time, nothing was done. Both senior management and many potentially affected women remained complacent. However, this situation changed almost overnight when a new CEO announced that he thought something should be done. Complacency among both senior management and women managers disappeared. Women managers more overtly complained, and senior management more readily listened.

In some cases muffled attention gives rise to actual negligence, which in turn can be either slight, serious, or legally liable. Later in this chapter I examine several cases in which muffled attention resulted in situations where businesses became legally liable for harm they could have averted if they had paid attention sooner. Earlier in this century before the adoption of workmen's compensation programs, firms often ignored safety precautions for their workers in ways to which I have already referred. They argued that workers knew the risks they faced when they agreed to work. Workers were therefore responsible for their own workplace injuries not only because they knew about the chances of accidents but also because injuries often seemed to occur because operators made careless mistakes. Warning of the possibility of operator errors, many firms didn't listen to the complaints of injured workers. As compensation laws were passed and as the courts gradually began to take another view of these accidents, increasingly firms that failed to heed the warnings of workers with respect to dangerous conditions were judged to be legally negligent (Nonet 1969). A similar evolution occurred in relation to the industrial uses of asbestos. Those construction firms and other businesses that failed to respond to widespread warnings were judged to be negligently liable for harm suffered by workers excessively exposed to these fibers.

Often those raising moral issues complain that others neither hear nor comprehend them if the latter fail to support their proposals and concur with their arguments. It is, however, naive and infantile to expect that hearing will necessarily lead to sympathy and assent. Others who oppose our projects may hear and understand our positions quite well but choose for their own reasons to take alternative views. Attending to the communications of others does not require that we share the commitments of those who address us. It does, nonetheless, require that we be willing to enter into debate with them and explain both our distinct concerns and why we give less weight to the arguments and evidence they have put forward. Attending to others means that our responses to them should not assume forms of address that would be practically the same whether we spoke to one group or another. If our discussions with others, especially those with whom we disagree, assume the form of alternating monologues, then neither we nor they are really attending to what each other says (Piaget 1951). Attending to others calls for us to take what others say seriously enough so that in our responses we attempt to reply to the particular concerns and issues they raise, even if in the process we reach quite different conclusions.

It is not necessarily a sign of integrity when public figures say practically the same thing to the diverse audiences they may be called upon to address. To be sure, such consistency means that they are probably not pandering to these groups, saying whatever they think may please them. But this same consistency may also reveal that they are not really listening attentively to the particular constellations of concerns voiced differently by these diverse groups. If they were, then they might well seek to rephrase their messages in ways that addressed the specific issues raised by these varied audiences.

Moral deafness is often invoked by the morally mute as the primary cause for their own silence. To be sure, there is considerable merit in this claim. When Vandiver and Lawson received no positive responses from their immediate superiors, they judged that their efforts to speak up were futile. Many others have reached similar conclusions although perhaps too hastily before they imaginatively explored other alternatives. A corresponding argument might be made to read the other way: Many people are effectively morally deaf because others do not voice their moral claims loudly and clearly. They only whisper their concerns. Subsequently I explore the ways moral blindness, deafness, and silence reinforce each other. At this point I am briefly introducing this interrelationship in order to observe that the reticence to voice moral concerns and the disinclination to hear and respond to these concerns are fairly widespread. If we think that only others ever mute their concerns or muffle their attention, we are probably especially saintly, overly zealous, and/or not being entirely candid about our own episodes of moral silence and inattention. Hence, as I write about these problems, I try to present a broad range of examples so that we all may recognize occasions when we have acted mute or deaf, either for good or not so good reasons.

In the remainder of this chapter, I discuss four major types of moral deafness. First, I examine cases in which people did not really hear what was being said because they did not want to have to hear and respond to bad news. In these instances people usually listen and comprehend but fail to focus and take an interest in the messages addressed to them. I then pursue this line of analysis further and review cases in which people might have but did not seek out relevant information. I argue that active listening sometimes requires seeking information and not just waiting until it comes to us. Of course, in some cases I review, people did not hear because they did not really listen in the first place. Third, I look at cases in which people did not really hear what was being said because they failed to comprehend. Finally, I examine cases in which not hearing occurred because of the failure to consider issues and concerns more fully from the perspective of others.

MORAL DEAFNESS AS NOT BEING READY TO HEAR BAD NEWS

Most of us would rather hear good news, indifferent news, or no news than bad news. Inherently a goodly part of the news is bad. For several reasons we would prefer not to hear such news, especially if it is likely to affect our lives. Such news may inform us of a downturn in our fortunes or distress suffered by friends or loved ones or colleagues. It may reveal serious shortcomings in the behavior of someone we had highly esteemed. It may make us aware of failures on our own part: perhaps carelessness or lack of diligence on our part that allowed certain unfortunate practices to go on unchecked; perhaps intentional shortcuts we had taken assuming that they were not important and no one would notice. Whatever the causes, we do not like to hear bad news, because often such news, insofar as it bears upon our lives, also implicates us. I use the word "implicate" not in order to raise questions of guilt and blame but in order to indicate that bad news usually calls for some new and added actions that we must take time now to arrange. In addition to whatever we had already been doing, bad news calls for us to take on something more, either diverting our energies now to this concern or adding these activities on top of our current undertakings. Moreover, these additional activities not only typically require added time and resources but also require us to do things that are unpleasant: We may have to engage in nasty confrontations; we may have to recall products; we may have to acknowledge our previous careless inattention; or we may have to expend resources that are already limited.

Typically people do not blatantly refuse to listen to bad news. Rather they find ways of neutralizing it. They listen to reports carrying bad news and then treat this information as being of little importance. They discover ways of reinterpreting messages so that the bad news, placed in a different context, appears to be not so bad after all. They find ways so that others and not they are held accountable and expected to undertake whatever needs to be done to rectify the bothersome or aggravating conditions. As I have already noted, plant managers found ways for years to view accidents that happened to industrial workers as the product of operator errors.

This reluctance to hear bad news can be illustrated by a number of cases. For example, in a number of developing countries Nestlé had been marketing a powdered formula to be mixed with water for bottle-feeding babies. Nestlé began receiving complaints from a number people who asserted that this product was causing babies to become sick with diarrhea. Initially Nestlé protested their innocence. They countered by arguing that if children became sick, it was because users of their product were not taking proper precautions. Nestlé recognized that their product was not itself the cause of the problem; rather the problem stemmed from mixing the powdered formula with water that was contaminated. Nestlé argued that if users failed to boil the water as instructed or failed to use purified water, then the error lay with the users. Critics argued that the real error lay with Nestlé for vigorously marketing their product in areas where purified or boiled water was difficult to obtain and where women instead ought to be encouraged to breast-feed because breast milk is the best protection against this problem. Nestlé was convinced that their marketing practices were acceptable because consumers bought their product of their own free will. Nestlé did recognize that a problem existed but did not see it as theirs to do something about. Eventually, Nestlé much more fully heard and comprehended the complaints addressed to them. This required them to be prepared to assume responsibility for changing the situation. It required, in fact, the willingness to consider an altered marketing strategy. The critics had been asking Nestlé to assume a much greater responsibility for how their product was used. They argued that Nestlé's marketing strategy contributed to uses that in themselves brought about the problem. Nestlé had heard and responded to complaints about their product. They had been reluctant to hear and respond to complaints about their marketing strategy. However, after a number of protests, they got the message. They did not cease marketing their product as many critics had proposed. But they did market it in developing areas as a supplement and not as an alternative to breast-feeding and attempted to provide clearer, more-urgent instructions on the proper preparation of water for use with it.

Another often-cited example of not wanting to hear bad news involved the Ford Pinto. In 1968 Ford began designing a subcompact car that eventually became the Pinto. Ford's objective was to produce a very affordable automobile, and they endeavored to save on expenses in many ways. They decided to place the fuel tank behind and not above the rear axle and left only nine or ten inches of crush space between the tank and a very thin bumper. The crush space was less than in most other American vehicles or foreign subcompacts, and the bumper was less substantial than in most other American-designed cars. In addition, the differential housing had exposed bolt heads that were in position to puncture the fuel tank on serious impact. The Pinto was then tested in a rear-end crash—the Pinto was stationary, and another vehicle hit it traveling at increasingly higher speeds. When the second car was moving at only twenty-one miles per hour, the tests showed the fuel tank rupturing and causing dangerous spillage of gas. In April 1971 a production review meeting took place at Ford and considered whether to install protective devices in Pintos that would have reduced the danger of fuel tanks being ruptured by rear-end crashes. These would have cost $4 to $8 per automobile. In spite of tests that showed their vehicle to be very vulnerable to fuel tank ruptures from rear-end collisions and in spite of the knowledge that significant protection could have been added at a small cost, Ford decided to proceed with production and marketing. People within Ford had alerted Ford to some real dangers that their vehicles posed for those who drove them. Ford decided to discount this information. In 1971 and 1972 the cost to respond would have been minimal: Production schedules would have been stopped temporarily in order to make minor changes; cars already sold would have been recalled. At the time, the results of the crash test represented bad news. To respond seriously to this information would have cost Ford in time and money, although not much in either case. Ford assumed a deaf ear. Later they were forced to respond at much greater costs. In May 1972 a Ford Pinto was hit from behind while stalled in the middle lane of a highway. The fuel tank ruptured, and the car went up in flames. The driver was killed, and one passenger suffered serious burns. Ford lost a subsequent court case and eventually had to recall and fix the Pintos it had sold (Bear and Maldonado-Bear 1994).

In both of these cases it is possible to argue that Nestlé and Ford initially acted as they did simply because they were motivated by crass financial considerations. Clearly these kinds of factors did play a part. I argue, however, that they played a larger role than they might otherwise because in both cases these firms did not fully attend to complaints and warnings addressed to them. They listened, but they were not ready to comprehend fully or to focus clearly. They remained complacent about the dangers of which they were informed.

The reluctance to attend to bad news is particularly well illustrated by events that preceded by months and years the disastrous sinking of the ferry boat *Herald of Free Enterprise* near the port of Zeebrugge, Belgium, in 1987. The ship had been launched in 1980 as part of a fleet of twenty-two ships ferrying passengers and cars across the English Channel and in other parts of Europe. The ships were part of European Ferries, which was owned by Townsend Thoresen, which in turn had been purchased in early 1986 by the Peninsular and Oriental Steam Navigation Company (P & O). The *Herald of Free Enterprise* capsized within ninety seconds of leaving the port. The bow doors to the car deck had been left open, and because the ballast water had not been completely pumped out, the ship was sailing three feet lower. As the ship surged forward, water entered the deck through the open doors at the rate of 200 tons per minute. These waters flowed to one side and unbalanced the ship, which went over on its side. One hundred and eighty-eight passengers and crew members out of a total of 539 lost their lives. Many others were injured. It was the worst peacetime shipping disaster for the British since the sinking of the *Titanic*.

Shipmasters who captained the ferries had warned the management of Townsend Thoresen regarding most of the immediate factors that played a major role in this disaster. There were several immediate causes. The bow doors had been left open because the assistant boatswain, who was supposed to close them, had been excused by the boatswain to return to his quarters while the ship was in port. He fell asleep there and did not return. Those sailing the ship presumed that the doors were closed when they left port, but they had no direct means to verify this. In the meantime water had been pumped into ballast tanks to lower the ship to make it easier for cars to drive onto its car deck. This was not pumped out before departure, leaving the bow deck three feet closer to the water level. The forward surge of the ship made the bow drop even more. There was no draft gauge on the bridge to indicate how high or low the ship was riding in the water. European Ferries had put pressure on their shipmasters to keep their schedules. Extra time was not spent correspondingly to check on whether these tasks were in fact performed as expected (Boyd 1988).

The management of European Ferries had been duly warned about these dangers. In 1983 a shipmaster had alerted management of the need to more accurately monitor the draft of the ships. Captain Martin complained that the ship's draft was not regularly read before departure and that the figures entered into the logbooks were often erroneous. He also complained of the failure to inform the master of the number of passengers and the tonnage the ship was carrying. This information would help the shipmasters ascertain how low their ships were sailing in the water. It might well be argued that the captains themselves could on their own assume responsibility for these matters. In this case, however, one captain alerted senior management of practices he considered to be dangerous. He also made reference to sailing at too high speeds in fog. Captain Martin wrote additional memoranda highlighting these matters. Senior management basically ignored them. They later explained their response by saying that if the captains were really concerned about these matters, they should have come into management offices and banged on their desks. In any case, if the captains felt very strongly, senior managers later rationalized, they could have refused to sail.

In early 1984 a chief engineer wrote senior management to express his concern that the ballast pumps on ships docking at Zeebrugge took too long to do their job. He warned that ships were as a result in danger of leaving port too quickly (before all the ballast water had been pumped out) in order to keep to schedule. He noted how the amounts of ballast were only loosely and inaccurately gauged. In order to get the attention of his superiors, the chief engineer also observed how ships that sailed with excessive ballast used extra and excessive amounts of fuel. Senior management felt that the chief engineer was grossly exaggerating the problem and regarded the expense for high-speed ballast pumps (approximately $45,000) to be prohibitive. They listened but neither focused nor took any real interest in this problem.

In 1985 the captain of the *Pride* wrote senior management to argue that a warning light ought to be installed on the bridge that would indicate whether the watertight doors on the bow and stern were closed or open. The shipmaster raised this concern because two years earlier an assistant boatswain had fallen asleep on his ship and had forgotten to close the doors. In this case the ship sailed safely with the doors open. Senior management circulated the memorandum. Other managers scoffed at the request. One wrote: "Do they need an indicator to tell them whether the deck storekeeper is awake and sober? My goodness!" Another wrote: "Nice but don't we already pay someone!" Another wrote simply: "Nice!"

In 1986 a shipmaster complained that the ferries were sailing with excessive numbers of passengers, exceeding posted limits and the supply of life-saving jackets and boats. In hopes of pleasing customers and making profits, these limits were being ignored. The captain observed that no accurate count was kept of numbers of passengers. Senior management considered the issue briefly but made no serious effort to deal with the problem. Many memos sent by the captain never received a response.

In late 1986 and early 1987 Captain Kirby, who sometimes captained the *Herald of Free Enterprise*, wrote to senior management to express concern regarding dangers to the safe navigation of the ships because of the way the ships were manned. He pointed out that many crew members were not used to working closely together due to the excessive rotations of officers and crews. He observed that the long hours of work left crew members less than always alert. In January 1987 he wrote:

I wish to stress again that the *Herald* badly needs a permanent complement of good deck officers. Our problem was outlined in my memo of the 22nd of November. Since then the throughput of officers has increased even further. . . . To make matters worse the vessel has had an unprecedented seven changes in sailing schedule. The result has been a serious loss in continuity. Shipboard maintenance, safety gear checks, crew training and the overall smooth running of the vessel have all suffered. (Boyd 1988, 366)

It has been argued that marine transport proceeds according to customs and practices that, taken as a whole, are error inducing. Although accidents that do occur usually happen as a result of the errors of particular operators, the system of marine transport as a whole is far more error provoking than air transport. This occurs, the sociologist Charles Perrow (1984) has argued, because national and international regulations for marine navigation are far more varied, the economic pressures are more immediate, the shipboard management excessively centralized in captains, and certain navigation risks too lightly taken as customary aspects of the business. For example, ferry boat passengers are rarely alerted to safety precautions the way airline passengers routinely are. Although these factors help to explain the higher rates of navigation accidents in marine transport, they explain only in part why the management of Townsend Thoresen was so inattentive to safety concerns raised by their own shipmasters and chief engineers.

With hindsight we can conjecture that this catastrophe might not have happened if steps had been taken to respond to the warnings reviewed. For example, if senior management had attempted to address the ballast problem either by installing quicker pumps or by insisting on closer monitoring, the *Herald* might have sailed higher in the water and been less vulnerable to the bow waves entering the open bow doors. If senior management had installed a warning light on the bridge, the ship would not have sailed with its door still open. If senior management had taken steps to organize their officers and crews so that they were used to working with each other, the officers might have exercised better surveillance over the work of subordinates and the bow doors would probably not have been left unattended. Hindsight is clearer than foresight, however. What we can observe now is that in each case these warnings addressed to senior management assumed the form of bad news.

Senior management might have responded to the concerns raised in several ways. They might have taken these warnings quite seriously without necessarily having to comply exactly with the recommendations proffered by the captains and engineers. With respect to the draft issue, in consultation with the shipmasters they might have developed some internal regulations and monitoring measures to make sure that no ship sailed too low in the water. Because of the need to raise and lower the deck level at Zeebrugge, they might then have had to alter their schedules. Or they might have decided to maintain their schedules but installed quicker ballast pumps as a resolution to the problem that was overall more economical, especially when added fuel charges for heavier ships were taken into account. Similarly, they might have explored alternative ways for double-checking safety precautions, including the closure of the bow and stern doors. Additionally, they might have attempted to address the problem of overworked crews and the excessive throughput of officers by introducing new schedules of work or at least by alerting crews of their ships to risks of poor communication attendant on these staffing arrangements. These are not entirely idle speculations. I introduce these possibilities in order to indicate that senior management might have both focused on and taken serious interest in the warnings addressed to them in these and other ways that would have still allowed them discretion, judgment, and their own efforts to balance conflicting demands.

Instead they treated all these warnings as if they were unimportant. To respond as requested—they explicitly said and implicitly suggested—would be too expensive and would drop into their laps problems that the captains themselves might deal with better. Although they read and circulated a number of the memos addressed to them, senior management acted as if they did not fully hear what was being said. Although they listened and comprehended to a degree, they did not focus on and take a genuine interest in these warnings.

People often muffle their ears to bad news because it challenges them to think about matters in new ways, because it forces them to recognize that customary practices and habits fell short in protecting against the unfortunate events that occasioned the bad news, and because taking this information seriously requires that they expend extra resources. Sometimes we screen out bad news that seems trivial. We do this by treating it as news for someone else or as temporary alarms that will pass. Often these kinds of responses make sense. If we were to attempt to respond to every bit of bad news, we might not only become overburdened and distracted but more importantly we would lose sight of our own particular purposes and responsibilities. Still, we need to remain attentive to significant bad news. If not, bad news is likely to become even worse news. We need to find ways to take these messages seriously without being overwhelmed by them. In these cases, senior managers were not able to do this.

MORAL DEAFNESS AS NOT SEEKING OUT BAD NEWS

People sometimes fail to attend to moral messages because they do not listen for them in the first place. Not listening can be a product either of not seeking out relevant and interesting information or of actively putting ourselves in positions where we are not likely to hear. The first approach is more passive, the latter more active. Both produce comparable results. We fail to hear and understand moral communications because we listen at most only to bits and pieces of what has been voiced. We do not receive full messages. The causes may be multiple: Others have only hinted at their concerns and wait for us to indicate our interest; organizational structures block communications or force them into patterns of official rhetoric, where they become distorted; not wishing to implicate ourselves by listening too sympathetically, we delegate others to receive and deal with particular classes of issues; or, not wanting to have to deal directly with bad news, we ask for summaries only and hope that others will use their discretion to sort out these matters. Whatever the causes may be, on the basis of partial information, we might have assumed more active responsibility to seek out fuller pictures of the moral messages addressed to us. We are morally deaf to the degree that we let matters stay where they are while we wait either for fuller and clearer communications or, more characteristically, for none.

Occasionally senior executives intentionally do not want to know fully the arrangements of agents they hire for fear that this information, if known by them, might implicate them as being ultimately responsible for questionable practices. If it could later be shown that the executives were in fact fully briefed regarding dubious actions of company agents, then they could as a consequence become legally liable (Stone 1975). It becomes more complicated when agents can engage in activities that are legal in their own countries but illegal in the executives' home countries. After the United States government's enactment of the Foreign Corrupt Practices Act in 1978, a number of companies chose to use agents to negotiate their contracts in foreign countries. Companies drew up guidelines and codes that stated that company employees as well as hired agents must obey local laws. Many companies then hired agents either on fairly generous fixed commissions or percentage commissions and instructed them to negotiate local contracts, but never audited their actual expenses. One interviewed executive confessed: "We use agents overseas, and probably all sorts of things go on between them and the ultimate buyers, including bribery. But I don't think it's any of my business. We offer a product at a competitive price; it's up to them whether they buy it or not."

The disinclination to seek out bad news has assumed many forms. For example, many entrepreneurial and professional firms have been disinclined to look too closely at the entrepreneurial practices of their executives. University professors, for instance, often engage in consulting practices and sometimes establish their own firms through which they may receive contracts and research grants that in turn may place them in conflict of interest with their academic responsibilities. Professors may receive both regular full-time academic salaries as well as generous stipends from their outside activities to which they may occasionally devote excessive amounts of time. Many universities allow their professional staff to exercise greater discretion over the use of their time than most businesses would accord to the professionals who work for them. The issue, however, is not the amount of discretionary time, which has a long well-defended tradition within universities, but the degree to which universities as complex organizations attempt to keep track over how this time is used and to what degree these uses promote the larger interests of their organizations.

One free-spirited entrepreneurial firm exhibited a comparable disinterest in auditing the activities of its executives and professionals. The firm had grown quickly in part because of the initiative exhibited by its executives and professionals. Many of the latter also greatly benefited by the expansion of the firm. A number incorporated their own small firms and contracted to supply the parent organization with diverse parts and services. A marketing manager created a small firm that then contracted to box and ship products for the senior business. No one kept close account of these arrangements by tracking how particular individuals used company time and resources to develop subsidiary firms that then received fees for which they had formally contracted. Although these arrangements added to the costs of the parent organization and they personally benefited selected, entrepreneurial individuals, no one attempted to track these deals during the period when the firm was rapidly expanding. Confronting these individuals would have resulted in conflicts with some of those whose initiatives had contributed most to the firm's early successes.

A comparable disinclination to seek out bad news is exhibited by many pharmaceutical companies that only passively look for adverse reactions to their products. They wait for their sales representatives to inform them of accounts related to the latter by local physicians and pharmacists. Because most of their products have been fairly rigorously tested before the companies begin market sales, this disposition to wait for bad news rather than deliberately to seek it out often makes sense, especially because more active auditing can add expense. Nonetheless, failures to seek out adverse drug reports more actively from medical practitioners can from time to time leave these companies vulnerable when scattered individuals do in fact experience adverse side effects. In a tragic way the A. H. Robins company failed to attend to early adverse reports regarding the intrauterine contraceptive device it began marketing in 1971.

Between 1971 and 1974 A. H. Robins sold several million Dalkon Shield IUDs. This particular IUD had an adverse effect on many women who had them inserted in their uteruses. Although the company advertised a contraceptive rate of nearly 99 percent, more than 5 percent of the users became pregnant and 60 percent of these subsequently miscarried. Many women experienced extraordinarily heavy bleeding during menstruation; many suffered from pelvic infections; by 1985 eighteen women had died from septic abortions or pelvic infections while using the Dalkon Shield. By June 1985 A. H. Robins had paid out $578.3 million in compensation payments to affected women and $107 million in legal fees (Parry and Dawson 1981; Mintz 1985).

Why didn't A. H. Robins respond more quickly when concerns were initially raised about the Dalkon Shield? I will focus on this question rather than attempt to evaluate the extent to which this company was guilty of either criminal or moral wrongdoing. The courts have judged them liable. The company certainly tolerated or quite consciously allowed morally questionable practices such as circulating advertising that misrepresented the pregnancy rates of women using the IUD. With hindsight we can conclude that A. H. Robins acted irresponsibly not to test this product more rigorously before they marketed it. As a medical device it did not at that time fall under the stringent testing guidelines required by the Food and Drug Administration in the United States for pharmaceutical products. Still A. H. Robins might have ordered equivalent tests in order to make sure that its product did not pose undue risks to the people using it. Viewed retrospectively, it was clearly in the company's interest, as well as the interest of all the women who were ill-affected, for A. H. Robins to be more responsive to early adverse reports. Why was the company not more attentive?

Beginning in 1970 a number of people both within and outside the company began to raise questions about possible dangers of the Dalkon Shield to the health and safety of the women who used them. Several people within the company voiced concern about the multifilament construction of the string attached to the IUD, which allowed it to be retracted if desired after it was inserted. They raised concern that the string might act as a wick, allowing harmful bacteria to enter into the uteruses of the women with the IUD. William Crowder, who was responsible for quality control at the plant manufacturing the IUDs, raised this concern in June 1971. He rejected one shipment of 10,000 IUDs on this basis and proposed heating the ends of the string to prevent wicking from occurring. His concern was shared by the plant director but not by their superiors. At the time this was more a theoretical issue than a report of real harm. Nothing was done. At about the same time, A. H. Robins' salespeople began to report on complaints from doctors who told of higher-than-expected pregnancy rates and difficulties and trauma when trying to insert the IUD. Salespeople also passed along rumors that competitors were telling women not to buy the Dalkon Shield IUD because of the danger that its string might "wick" bacteria into their uteruses. During the first year of sales, A. H. Robins had not yet received much evidence that might have prompted recall of the product or initiation of extra tests with respect to its health and safety. Still, the company might have more actively sought out information with respect to the use of the product. At this stage they seem to have discounted whatever bad news they received by seeing these accounts as the product of operator errors—poorly inserted IUDs.

In 1972, however, more alarming concerns were raised. A doctor from Utah wrote the company complaining of pelvic infections in five of the ten IUD-using women whom he had assisted. Another M.D. from a medical school in South Carolina voiced the same concern. In April an article appeared in a journal, *Advances in Planned Parenthood*, announcing pregnancy rates as high as 24 percent after fourteen months for women using the Dalkon Shield. In June, Planned Parenthood announced that half of the cases of perforated uteruses that they heard of involved the Dalkon Shield. In June a medical consultant to A. H. Robins, who also happened to be an original investor in the Dalkon Shield, reported high rates of pelvic infections for women who became pregnant while using the IUD. He recommended that the company directly propose the removal of the IUD in cases where women missed their periods. The company responded overtly to none of these messages. They chose not to explore whether these warnings were portents of something more alarming. Given the number of IUDs they were selling and given that many viewed this contraceptive as possessing less-adverse side effects than contraceptive pills, A. H. Robins' response may seem comprehensible. Nonetheless, the warnings they received were very serious and would have seemed even more worthy of consideration if they had been investigated at all. The company seemed to be neither listening to nor comprehending these warnings, much less focusing on them and taking an interest in them.

During 1973 the company received more messages of concern. During congressional hearings on intrauterine devices held in May, the company admitted that it had received 400 complaints out of sales of 1.8 million. They probably had heard many additional informal complaints as well. The complaints included references to higher-than-expected pregnancy rates, excessive bleeding, difficult insertion, and pelvic infections. In May a woman in Arizona had died of pelvic infection while using a Dalkon Shield, and the company probably learned of this death by December. In September the company learned that the Centers for Disease Control had begun to keep statistics on problems related to the use of IUDs. How was A. H. Robins responding to this information? We don't fully know. Overtly they made no gestures to investigate the complaints and warnings they received. Perhaps they feared that if they knowingly began any investigations, their sales would markedly suffer. Perhaps they feared implicating themselves in future lawsuits if they now undertook tests they might have taken but did not take earlier. Perhaps they believed that the stories of infections, higher pregnancy rates, and excessive bleeding were exaggerated. They made no concerted efforts to apprise themselves of the seriousness of these complaints and warnings. Later in June 1974 the FDA ordered the sales of Dalkon Shields to be stopped.

This is an extreme example of the disinclination to investigate messages that seem to bring bad news. At its core the choice not to investigate warnings like these represents a tacit choice not to perform audits. I have just reviewed several cases in which people elected not to undertake audits of the performance of agents, colleagues, employees, and products. In the root meaning of the term "audit," these are choices not to hear. In the past few decades there has been a growing interest in performing social audits. That is, a number of observers have argued that the formal practice of internal auditing ought to be expanded to include auditing as well the social performance of corporations (AICPA 1977). I would agree with them that the practice of auditing—of consciously attempting to hear what is going on in and around organizations—should be expanded. I would extend the auditing practice even further, however, although not necessarily as formal processes. Rather, I argue for the need to remain attentive and correspondingly for the need to be ready to investigate warnings that may portent further difficulties. The failure to audit or investigate in these circumstances leaves organizations vulnerable for even worse difficulties. To be sure, organizations and individuals can easily become distracted by attempting to respond to all issues and messages addressed toward them. We must be selective. We become most skilled, however, at not responding to trivial concerns not by ignoring at the outset most warnings and claims that seem muted and without urgency but rather by ongoing attentiveness combined with occasional concerted audits so we gain an educated sense of what matters.

MORAL DEAFNESS AS NOT COMPREHENDING

Occasionally we suffer from moral deafness not because we do not listen and not because we fail to take an interest but because we have failed to comprehend the information we have received. In these instances we become morally hard of hearing because we misunderstand, confuse matters, or respond to concerns in keeping with presumptions that are inappropriate. We may well be responsive but act in ways that reveal our incapacity to clearly comprehend the shape and significance of the messages addressed to us. Typically we mistake shadows for substance, symptoms for underlying causes. Correspondingly our responses are often ill-suited, poorly timed, and off-putting.

This form of moral deafness is well illustrated by the response of a large, multidivisional, and multinational corporation to the problem of product shrinkage in its hardware manufacturing plant. The plant suffered from excessive losses of tools and equipment. Plant executives correctly saw that employees were borrowing without explicit permission or that they were stealing. Initially they defined the problem as one of employee misconduct. They decided that the appropriate response was to pay particular employees extra to serve as informants to discover who was taking tools and equipment and to report this information to senior management. Senior management learned of the shrinkage problem and chose to respond in ways they judged to be quick and effective. However, they misjudged the issue at the outset. The extensive theft by employees was in large part a symptom that the employees felt underpaid and unfairly treated (Altheide, Adler, and Altheide 1978). The overt shrinkage problem was the surface manifestation of a deeper, more troubling morale problem. This problem was correspondingly aggravated by the initial response of management. Employees cynically referred to their bosses' secret CIA operation and privately determined how they could get away with even more. The overall effectiveness of their work suffered further. The cost to the plant in terms of poor and half-hearted performance, absences, and thefts, as well as the added cost for secret surveillance far exceeded what it would have cost for improved working conditions and modestly higher wages and/or benefits.

Many organizations suffer from attendance problems. Typically this problem manifests itself by high rates of sick leave and other excused and unexcused absences by employees. The problem also assumes the form of excessive rates of late arrivals both at the beginning of work periods and after lunches or breaks. Low attendance rates are costly to businesses, which correspondingly perform less work as a result. A number of consultants and businesses have tried their hand at developing attendance-enhancement programs. Some of these programs have met with notable as well as modest successes. For example, attendance rates among employees at Canada Post improved significantly as a result of a concerted effort that included giving rewards to people with the highest attendance records, keeping track of attendance, and personally talking to employees about these matters. In spite of these successes, attendance-enhancement programs are prone to focus on a symptom, namely attendance, rather than on possible or real underlying causes, such as the degree to which employees and managers feel organizationally committed. By means of low attendance rates, employees may well be indirectly voicing criticisms about the terms and conditions of their work.

For example, there were high absence rates among the nonphysician medical staff of an urban hospital, especially among nurses, technicians, and service employees. The hospital administration attempted to determine the meaning of this problem, which added measurably to the costs of running the hospital. They responded in several ways at once with mixed success. They treated it partly as an issue of organizational control. They established a formal attendance-enhancement program. In keeping with this, they kept tabs on absences and late arrivals. They instituted pep talks to encourage workers to pull together. In order to save money and put pressure on absent workers, they did not find replacements for absent workers after the first day. In this way they added to the workloads of the remaining workers, who, they hoped, would bring peer pressure to bear on absent and tardy coworkers. Although generally well-intentioned, these programs did not work well. They had little impact on attendance rates. Some already committed workers became more conscientious. Others cynically thought that the hospital used these programs primarily to save money and treat them like children. Many nurses felt that their higher-than-average absence rates reflected the fact that they were exposed to more diseases by the nature of their work and cautioned likewise to stay away from work if they showed the slightest cold symptoms. Although the hospital appropriately regarded the attendance problems as an indirect message from their employees, and although they regarded it with appropriate interest, it is not clear that they fully appreciated what the message was.

Other responses were more fitting and indicated a greater comprehension of concerns of their staff. After discussing matters with members of the nursing staff, a new director of nursing instituted significant changes in staffing arrangement and work schedules. The nurses had indicated that many wanted to work part-time and most preferred to work longer hours rather than more shifts. The hospital allowed for these changes. The turnover rate among the nursing staff dropped dramatically, although the absence rate itself improved only modestly. On the basis of further discussions with nurses, technicians, and others, the hospital administration began to see that the absence rate, insofar as it was higher than could be expected, was mostly a symptom of another, larger problem: namely, the sense shared by a number of different groups that their performance and their skills were taken for granted and not really valued for their true worth. It is to the credit of the hospital that it began to comprehend this message, which was voiced mostly indirectly—although occasionally quite directly—by several different groups of people working at the hospital. Indirectly, nurses and other staff took advantage of liberal sick leave policies not because they did not care about their work but because they were upset by the way the hospital treated them. What they wanted was greater involvement in determining the conditions of their own work. Over time the hospital more fully comprehended the significance of high absence rates and through several different kinds of responses have attempted to address underlying concerns.

In neither of the two cases just cited had issues been directly raised by workers themselves. Privately, amongst themselves and with their immediate supervisors, workers had voiced their concerns. They did so sometimes hesitantly, often defensively, and frequently as carping complaints because they typically presumed that their organizations were not really interested in their concerns. The organizations did stop to listen and did take an interest. With the exceptions already noted, however, they attended primarily to the surface manifestations, which were costly to the organizations, rather than seeking to audit these situations more thoroughly.

Organizations can overcome their initial uncomprehending deafness to particular problems. The hospital administration began to comprehend the attendance problem with greater clarity. Sometimes, comprehending occurs more quickly or abruptly. The New York and New Jersey Port Authority experienced such a dramatic change in awareness several years ago with respect to a problem they had with homeless men using their terminals for places to hang out and sleep (Dutton and Dukerich 1991). This case is interesting because it shows that organizations are often more likely to listen with understanding to some people rather than others. The Port Authority had worked hard to establish itself, in the eyes of its employees especially, as a caring organization. It operated the air and bus terminals around New York City. It had attempted to create and maintain good working conditions, and it sought to treat its employees with fairness and justice. The problems arose with respect to their refurbished bus terminal near Times Square in Manhattan. A number of homeless men began to use the waiting room as a place to find warmth and shelter when it was cold and wet outside. They began to sleep on the chairs and benches. Many regular customers buying tickets and waiting for buses found the presence of these homeless men off-putting. The regular customers were made to feel uncomfortable. The terminal seemed more crowded and slovenly and a less agreeable place both for passengers and workers. The Port Authority had remodeled the building with the exact opposite aim of making it a place that well served the needs and interests of its customers and employees. These objectives now seemed to be undermined. Responding to the vocal complaints of these constituent groups, the Port Authority moved to contain if not eliminate the perceived problem. Initially they seemed to listen, comprehend, focus, and take an interest in the concerns raised by these groups. They hired private police officers to act as bouncers, to ask people using the terminal as a dormitory or refuge to go elsewhere. This response appeared to address the concerns raised by employees and customers. However, it was not as simple to implement as it was to initiate. At least two further complications were involved. For example, it was not always easy to distinguish customers who were sleeping in the terminal while waiting for their next bus from the homeless men. Overly zealous guards mistakenly affronted genuine customers, many of whom wore older clothes for bus travel. Furthermore, guards became abrupt and pushy when they attempted to cajole or force noncustomers out of buildings. Their activities became disruptive to customers and employees. Hearing well is not the same thing as exercising good judgment. In this case the response to the problem was not working as well as hoped.

The problem had not disappeared. Disruptions and protests occurred as a result of the attempts by the Port Authority to police the problem. The media responded, and eventually in the late 1980s an article about the problem appeared in *Newsweek*. The article posed a major threat to the Port Authority's image of itself as a caring organization. In their own terms, the Port Authority began to see the homeless men less as a policing problem and more as a moral issue. They viewed this problem as both an obligation and an opportunity for them to assume a measure of social responsibility to help unemployed and homeless neighborhood men who had looked to them for assistance. They began to view them as stakeholders who could legitimately seek some kind of assistance, which the Port Authority and others might be able to offer. Eventually the Port Authority, together with other community groups, helped to construct several hostels where these men could find temporary shelter and sustenance. The Port Authority altered their stance to the homeless men because media coverage had threatened the Port Authority's self-image.

Initially the Port Authority had both listened and taken an interest in this problem largely as it was voiced by employees and customers. They had not fully comprehended the issues involved and how difficult it would be to police the problem away because they had not really paused to listen to the homeless men or to the professionals seeking to deal with the problems of these men. Eventually the needs and wishes of these men were voiced by the media, who spoke out on their behalf. As a result the Port Authority began to recognize that the Port Authority and the homeless men coexisted in the same neighborhood in ways that impacted on each other. The semipublic spaces of this neighborhood, including those owned by the Port Authority, had been treated as meeting, sitting, resting, and eating places by passersby, shoppers, and passengers, as well as by these homeless men. The homeless men had not made their case directly and clearly. The media played a key role in giving voice to their plight (Fisse and Braithwaithe 1983). Although in the end the Port Authority acted in response to concerns voiced on their behalf, they did so only after they attempted to balance claims voiced by several different groups including local customers, employees, senior management, and directors, as well as these men. Although they had originally only partly understood this problem, their comprehension became fuller and clearer as they listened to the views of those they had not previously considered. Ultimately, this was not only or primarily an issue concerning the best way of dealing with vagrants. It was an issue concerning the allowed uses of the semipublic space in the terminal in which several different stakeholder groups, including employees, customers, passersby, and residents, as well as these homeless men, had an interest. This issue was fully compre-hended only when the company paused to hear several different accounts and sought for a solution that would satisfactorily balance them in keeping with their self-image as a caring organization.

Failure to comprehend the moral messages of others occurs for diverse reasons. We may not be able to make sense of their rhetoric, or we hear only fragments. In the examples just considered, organizations initially failed to understand fully particular concerns because they attended too exclusively to accounts of only some of the interested parties. In many ways these cases present typical conditions in which several different groups are involved in an issue and they voice their corresponding concerns quite differently. We can become partially deaf respecting these concerns if we listen only to some witnesses and if we focus too exclusively to surface manifestations without also listening for signs of underlying causes.

MORAL DEAFNESS AS NOT TAKING INTO CONSIDERATION THE ACCOUNTS OF OTHERS

In order to be attentive to moral concerns addressed to us by others, we need neither to sympathize nor even to fully empathize with them. If we seek genuinely to hear them, however, we must take into consideration their accounts of their concerns. We sometimes become morally deaf not by not listening and not by not focusing but by trying to weigh and evaluate their messages almost exclusively using our own frames of analysis. In the end, we will almost certainly render our judgments of what we hear by calling upon our own experiences, beliefs, commitments, and interpretive schemes. Even when we listen intently to others, as we make judgments, we will for the most part translate the concerns and claims of others into terms and points of reference we already understand, accept, and utilize to test and establish the validity of what we perceive by our senses and intuitions. Often we retranslate the concerns of others into our words and syntax almost without consciously being aware we are doing so. After hearing someone's account, we reply, "I know what you mean," and then restate their concern in our terms. Frequently others recognize their concern restated in our terms and correspondingly confirm our understanding. Sometimes, however, others fail to recognize their concerns in our accounts. We become morally deaf when during this process of listening, restating, and judging, we fail to give due weight to the accounts of others.

The issue is not whether as subjective selves we can ever really objectively know others (Schutz 1967), but more simply whether our interpretations and understandings of their concerns fittingly respect their own attempts to state, explain, and justify their concerns. Our accounts become reductionistic and inattentive to the degree that we forthrightly dismiss others' attempts to articulate, interpret, and defend their positions. This kind of reductionistic inattention has been exhibited by a long history of secular interpretations of religious practices and beliefs, as well as by particular religious interpretations of other religions (Bellah 1970, 1974; Robbins, Anthony, and Curtis 1973; Anthony, Robbins, and Curtis 1974). The religious practices of others are often regarded as being based on illusions (Freud 1957), false consciousness (Marx 1977), idolatry, or superstition. It is not necessary to become committed believers in order to respect the accounts others give of their beliefs and practices, whether in the fields of religion, ethics, or business. We need not concur with their judgments and commitments in order to give fitting credit to the importance with which they hold their points of view.

Whenever we attempt to size up and understand circumstances involving others, we cannot treat their own accounts of these circumstances as if they were peripheral or discountable. Their accounts are integral to the reality of the circumstances in question. Their accounts may seem farfetched or self-serving, intentional smoke screens or naive wishes. Nonetheless, they are part of the reality and must be given due weight for the role they play, especially to the extent that those involved seem genuinely to believe in them. We cannot hope to understand the actions of others apart from attempts on our part to comprehend the meanings they subjectively attach to these actions (Weber 1978). We must take their accounts seriously for a second reason. If as a result of our own judgments we wish to solicit the cooperation of others, we will need to communicate with them in terms they are likely to recognize and understand. We may then seek to show how our judgments can be understood in relation to their accounts. Rather than baldly discrediting their interpretations, even when we disagree with them, we are likely to want to point to their misunderstandings as much as possible by using the frames and terms of reference with which they are already familiar (Nussbaum 1986). In this sense as well, we must seriously consider their accounts if we are to attend to the concerns of others.

To consider the accounts of others means to listen intently enough in order to be able to reliably recount and relate to them and others their views as articulated from their perspective. We can do this without having to be able emotionally or sympathetically to understand their feelings and without having to agree with their views. Nonetheless, unless we consciously work at listening well for their accounts, most of us are prone to selective hearing, during which we tune out accounts of experiences and ideas that seem strange, contrary, foolish, naive, or threatening. At times we are too ready to file the accounts of others into our familiar mental sets without listening carefully enough to see that we may need to augment or modify our frames or at least recognize that the other's account cannot be as readily and simply accommodated to our frames as we had initially thought.

A few concrete examples will make this theoretical discussion more intelligible. For many years, especially during the early years of industrialization, managers and trade unionists remained deaf to each others' accounts. To be sure, each became familiar enough with the rhetoric and arguments of the other so that they could pillory and mock them. It is not clear that each really understood the others' accounts as they were articulated from the perspective of the others. Quick to defend themselves against the exaggerated caricatures by which the others depicted them and determined to rally their own supporters behind their own programs of action, each tended to discount the accounts of their antagonists. Each saw the accounts of others as self-serving excuses for what they regarded as questionable tactics like lockouts and strikes. Each felt that the others were actively promoting what they most feared: either regulations and contractual commitments that would suffocate enterprise or increased economic insecurity that would leave them destitute. It is not necessary here to review the controversy-filled history of industrial relations in order to argue that the protagonists in these conflicts frequently failed to comprehend these issues from the perspective of the others' accounts. To accomplish this task, neither side needed to sympathize or agree with their counterparts. What was required was that each listen intently and thoughtfully to what the others were saying, asking occasional questions in the process to clarify both the meaning and importance others assigned to the bits and pieces of their accounts. As they heard each other more fully and clearly, the character of their debates changed over time. Instead of reacting to reactions, each side gained in appreciation of what others regarded as their primary interests (Selznick 1969).

For a long time a comparable partial deafness muffled the concerns raised by women who judged that they had been sexually harassed by business or work associates. A number of women felt that no one was prepared to listen when they complained of superiors or colleagues who were overly familiar, aggressive in making personal advances, and/or disposed to use their power to solicit sexual favors. To be sure, many women who had been harassed did not directly speak up. Tacitly or overtly they had been warned or threatened not to say anything. Those who did voice their concerns often did so quietly and indirectly, talking these matters over in guarded tones with friends. It has often been structurally difficult for victims of these attacks to talk about them within their businesses or organizations because either their immediate supervisors or their close associates have been the source of their problem. Frequently, when women who have suffered from harassment were brave or angry enough to complain, the others who listened seemed to discredit their accounts. After listening to their stories, the others then pointed to ways that the women who raised these complaints had seemed in a friendly fashion to welcome or at least not overtly to resist the initial advances of the men who they claimed harassed them. Women making these complaints claim that their listeners repeatedly sought to implicate them, to indicate that they were somehow involved—if not in inviting these unwelcome advances, then at least in not more directly stopping them.

Harassed women's accounts were not taken seriously. The listeners of these accounts recognized that incidents did occur in which women felt they had been abused, compromised, used, or embarrassed. Typically, however, the organization members who officially listened seemed to credit only parts of their accounts. Listeners seemed to suggest that women making complaints were not so wholly victimized as the latter's accounts implied.

Women's accounts of alleged harassment can be regarded seriously without thereby having always to treat them as completely valid, objective assessments. They should never be dismissed. They articulate facts, recognitions, and assessments that are an integral part of the larger picture, which must also include the accounts of any others involved. Any person placed in a compromised position may resist the unwelcome advances of another less forcefully than they otherwise could. They may well admire or like the other person but not appreciate these particular verbal or physical gestures. They may later feel a genuine reluctance to admit that they were exploited, seduced, or harassed not only because of the professional or personal regard they may still hold for the other but also because they do not want to acknowledge an otherwise covered-over weakness on their own part. For several reasons they may remain silent after initial unwelcome advances. None of these sorts of admissions discredits subsequent accounts when they later talk of being used and victimized. Realities here are often complex.

A step in the right direction has been taken by the policy adopted by many organizations of saying that if people genuinely feel they are harassed, they have a right to make complaints that will be dispassionately investigated. This policy does not require that listeners wholly agree or sympathize with the stories of those who claim to be harassed. It does, however, require that their accounts be taken seriously enough to be listened to, recorded, and investigated and that attempts be made often informally but also formally to resolve the conflicts that the formal complaints have now become part of.

CONCLUSION: WHEN IS IT RIGHT AND WRONG TO BE MORALLY DEAF

It is not always easy to remain attentive to the moral concerns raised by others. Our attention fades. We listen to what interests us or to surface stories. We become distracted by other interests. Sometimes others whisper or camouflage their concerns. Or their accounts become so convoluted that we cannot easily distinguish core plots from irrelevant subplots. In particular most of us do not readily welcome bad news and may muffle our ears unaware so as not to hear. We may either hope to put off hearing until later or hope that someone else will listen and respond. Because in situations of conflict it requires much effort to listen to each party's accounts and additionally to weigh and balance them, we sometimes listen very selectively.

There are thus a number of reasons why we may become inattentive. Even though we listen to what others say, we may become inattentive because we do not fully comprehend their meanings, because we fail to focus our attention, or because we do not take real interest in their concerns. Given the several factors that may occasion inattention, full, alert attentiveness represents a genuine state of moral excellence.

Even though it may be difficult to achieve and maintain this attentiveness, we ought to be morally attentive for three major reasons: (1) We ought to be morally attentive because the consequences of inattention are frequently harmful if not devastating. This a utilitarian argument. (2) This is complemented by a principled argument that states that we ought to be morally attentive because it is unjust to others to be inattentive to their concerns and claims. (3) Finally, I consider a purposive argument that maintains that we ought to be morally attentive because to be inattentive is by its nature to be immoral.

One, I have already considered a number of cases where the results of not listening or not seeking out moral concerns had dire consequences for the organizations and people involved. We ought to be attentive because otherwise we are likely to overlook information vital to our organizations, to the lives of people affected, to the larger society, or to the environment. This argument is both credible and persuasive. The difficulty with this argument arises in its application. It is simply easier with hindsight to point to instances where people became inattentive than to prepare ourselves to be readily attentive so that occasions of muffled hearing occur less frequently. Inattention especially arises from several causes: namely, turning our attention away from bad news; regarding information that turns out to be important as trivial; and not actively auditing situations critical to us.

The crisis in the American thrift industry during the 1980s was aggravated by the inattention of auditors, executives, and managers for all these reasons. As early as 1981, articles appeared warning of impending problems (Mayer 1990). Executives and auditors failed to follow up leads of suspicious activities, treated concerns raised about overextended credit as trivial, and did not heed warnings about the precarious character of many investments funded by thrifts (Galbraith 1990). Industry executives seemed to be looking the other way, inattentive to widespread instances of excessive risk taking and gross negligence, in addition to the more notorious cases of outright fraud (Bear and Maldonado-Bear 1994). In the end a large number of savings and loan associations went bankrupt as a result of these practices, costing the federal government over $100 billion. As the scenes were being set for one of the worst financial disasters in American history, most of the industry's executives and auditors, who might have been more attentive, exhibited little concern or alarm. To be sure, many people took advantage of suddenly more lenient banking regulations combined together with generous government guarantees on savings accounts (up to $100,000) to engage in criminal activities. I doubt, however, if we will fully learn the lesson of this debacle if we focus primarily on instances of felonious activity and do not also examine the numerous ways law-abiding and otherwise responsible bankers, managers, and accountants paid less-than-full attention to concerns raised about careless thrift practices in the 1980s more generally.

Two, it is unjust to be inattentive to concerns raised by others whether harmful consequences ensue or not. The basic principle involved here can be stated as follows: When we become inattentive to the claims, demands, and issues voiced by others, we become at the same time less aware of how they represent themselves. We are as a result more likely to misrepresent them and correspondingly to depict them primarily from our frames of reference. I have argued that inattention tends to aggravate the extent to which we miscomprehend situations and fail to consider the accounts offered by others. In these several ways, inattention leads us not only to belittle the claims and concerns of others but also to treat them with less than the respect as others they are due. Fundamentally the principle of justice calls for us to give to each person his/her due (Aristotle 1953). Although people may merit markedly different rewards depending on their efforts and contributions, each person is due at least our respectful attention to his/her own self-representations unless or until these are proven to be deliberately fraudulent. When we are inattentive when others address us, we fail to acknowledge their claims even to our minimal attention. In a lesser or greater way, not according attention when others address us denies a fundamental claim to minimal attention that each person can expect of others. Even though others do not inherently possess rights to our sympathy, consent, or even empathy, they do possess a right to receive from us a minimal hearing if and when they address us with legitimate moral concerns.

Three, to be inattentive when addressed by others undercuts our fundamental morality as human beings. A number of moral philosophers have made a stronger case than this. They have argued for sympathy rather than just attentiveness to others. The eighteenth-century philosophers David Hume, Jonathan Edwards, and Adam Smith, the twentieth-century sociologist Emile Durkheim, and the twentieth-century philosopher Max Scheler have argued that sympathy for others or benevolence towards others is the fundamental moral sentiment. In answer to the question about what kind of will is intrinsically good, Edwards (1969), for example, did not reply like the philosopher Kant, to describe duties undertaken for the sake of duty. Rather, looking more at the substance rather than the form of goodwilling, he argued such a willing is characterized by general benevolence. In *The Theory of Moral Sentiments*, which he wrote twenty years before *The Wealth of Nations*, Smith argued that moral sentiments are rooted in our sympathetic feelings for others and our concerns about their feelings of approbation for us. Without some kind of sympathetic attachments to others, Durkheim (1961) argued, moral concerns are reduced too much to regimentation by external regulations. The German sociologist Ferdinand Tönnies (1957) argued that sympathy and benevolence lead us to act on behalf of others and to join with them in communities of attachment. It is in these associations characterized by strong affections and fellow feelings that people are nourished and morally strengthened. Although sympathy clearly motivates generous and sometimes altruistic moral actions, I argue that we do not need to feel sympathy for others to be minimally morally responsive to them. All that is required is that we remain attentive whenever they voice genuine moral concerns.

I have already argued that not to be attentive when addressed by others is not to recognize their humanity and that inattentiveness is unjust. I now move this argument one step further to maintain that we need to be attentive to others in order to maintain our own sense of humanity. To be human is to recognize that we live with others and that from time to time both we and others address each other to coordinate our activities, to cooperate, to seek help, to request distance and less interference, and to demand respect. To maintain our own sense of humanity as selves who inherently interact with others, we do not need always to ascend to the heights of compassion. We do, however, need to be responsive enough at least to hear and attend when they raise legitimate concerns regarding their being and well-being.

The case I have just made both for attentiveness and against moral deafness does not require us to respond to every query or demand addressed to us. To be attentive does not entail being readily available and accessible to all who might choose to voice their concerns to us. There are occasions when it is morally fitting to ignore or evade concerns addressed to us. For example, people may illegitimately or fraudulently seek our attention. We may be solicited by someone posing as a beggar who is not. Antagonists may urge us to take their respective sides in a conflict for which we legitimately choose to remain neutral. A child seeks our assistance for a problem that both we and she know she ought to address herself. A colleague seeks our reticence about his questionable pursuits. In all these instances, others are seeking to implicate us in activities from which we legitimately seek to be free. In the end, we must exercise our own good judgments. We are responsible for setting the agendas of what concerns we will in fact respond to. We relinquish this responsibility if we passively let our attention be ordered by whatever concern others address to us. We may choose for good reasons not to attend to particular calls upon our attention. In part these choices are made de facto. We can after all attend to only so many queries, requests, and invitations. As we respond to some, we inherently put ourselves in position of not responding to others. Our attention becomes directed in several ways that leave us directed away from other potential concerns. Yet in no case is this a static matter, because our attention continually shifts. Finally, we are responsible for what we choose to attend to.

In none of the instances I have just reviewed does the choice not to attend to another's concerns indicate inattentiveness on my part. In all of these cases, I have remained attentive enough to get a good sense of what the other sought to say to me. The choice to evade or ignore was a decision not to identify with, not to become a partner with, or not to intervene on behalf of. In order to decide to ignore or evade these demands and inquiries, I had to be attentive enough, open always to further clarification, to get a good sense of what was being said. To be attentive is to hear enough to be aware of what is going on. Being attentive does not commit us to giving active and full attention to all others. It does, however, commit us to being ready to give full attention whenever this seems called for.

CHAPTER 4
Moral Blindness

People are morally blind when they fail to see or recognize moral concerns and expectations that bear upon their activities and involvements. Moral blindness can be as innocent and trivial as failing to recognize the appropriate etiquette for greeting strangers or confirming agreements or as serious as not foreseeing the harmful consequences likely to ensue when making overly risky investments with someone else's funds. We are morally blind both when we don't recognize the moral dimensions of organizational life and when we overlook pressing moral issues. Our moral vision can become dulled, distorted, and dimmed in many ways just as our ordinary vision does. For example, we can become morally blind when we fail to acknowledge our own moral sensitivities, when we misperceive overt moral issues, and when we become so preoccupied with a part of a problem that we ignore the larger reality of which it is a part. We become morally blind as well to the extent that we lack perspective or foresight on moral concerns. Typically people who become morally blind hold moral convictions with respect to certain issues and readily perceive related moral problems though simply not seeing other moral concerns. Except for a few incorrigible souls, rarely are people totally morally blind. For most people moral blindness is only partial. People who otherwise see clearly, fully, and with perspective from time to time become dim-sighted morally, seeing only as through glasses darkly.

Often moral deafness is triggered and sustained by some form of moral blindness. The directors of European Ferries did not hear moral concerns raised by their shipmasters and engineers in part because they were morally blind in several ways: They failed to recognize often enough the importance of safety concerns in their business; they failed to perceive the risks involved; they failed to acknowledge the extent to which they complicated matters by the competitive pressures they put on the ships; and, most importantly, they failed to foresee the impact of their manning and management policies on the ways responsibilities were actually exercised on shipboard. Similarly, A. H. Robins was not attentive to early concerns raised about the Dalkon Shield because it was afflicted with particular forms of moral blindness. A. H. Robins failed to recognize early the risks that its product entailed. It also failed to acknowledge its own responsibilities for monitoring problems of women using the product. By its own account, the Port Authority did not initially respond correctly to the homeless men problem, because it was misperceived as a policing rather than a moral issue.

WHAT IS GOOD MORAL SIGHT?

People become morally blind to the extent that their capacity for moral sight becomes impaired. Before exploring the characteristic features of moral blindness, we must therefore have a look at what we mean by moral sight. Considering the long history of debates about the epistemological and phenomenological grounds for moral judgments, the discussion here will be brief. It is introduced to serve as a necessary point of reference for our examination of moral blindness. Beginning with the ancient Greek philosopher Plato, philosophers have indicated that the ways we view the world in turn influence our evaluation, objectives, and judgments. Plato in particular argued that people are often misled in making moral decisions because they allow themselves to be deceived by appearances and misled by conventional wisdom (Plato 1960a, 1960b). His arguments have been echoed by many others including Galbraith's exposés of the folly of conventional wisdom (Galbraith 1990, 1992).

Simply stated, moral sight refers to the capacity to see moral realities. These realities in turn encompass a wide variety of phenomena, some of which are more empirically obvious than others. These include particular ethical problems, social obligations, moral objectives, promises, normative expectations, valued principles, benevolent sentiments, critical judgments, and cooperative agreements. Moral realities are of several kinds. There are, first, the concrete problems, issues, demands, and conflicts that claim our attention. We may correspondingly be considering how to raise children, how to allocate scarce resources, how to punish an employee who has been confiscating company supplies, and many other matters. At the same time, our considerations of these kinds of concerns are in turn influenced by a different set of moral realities: namely, the beliefs, normative expectations, exemplary stories, well-respected arguments, honored precedents, and/or senses of duty that shape and affect how we regard the initial issues and problems that attracted our attention. Specific issues and normative expectations are two quite different types of realities. When we make moral judgments, we connect these realities together. In practice we relate them to each other by means of a third set of moral realities: namely, our own sense of ourselves as moral agents. Our moral vision may become more focused on one or more of these several types of moral realities. For example, we may become acutely troubled by conflicts and dilemmas in our business life but have little idea of how to sort them out. Or, in contrast, we may possess strong beliefs and commitments that we don't know quite where and how to apply. Or, further, we may become preoccupied by our own sense of virtue or guilt and worry more about whether we are really doing the right thing than whether actions taken address current problems. Ideally our visions of these several kinds of moral realities overlie each other. Because they vary in kind and in the ways they attract our attention, we are not always successful in lining up our moral visions.

Seeing these realities involves perception as well as other forms of sight. To fully see moral realities means all of the following: perceiving or being aware of these realities, recognizing or appreciating their significance, conceiving or understanding their importance, foreseeing what is likely to develop in relation to them, envisioning what we might do to realize our ideals, and acknowledging our own responsibilities in relation to these concerns. Moral sight includes more than just physical seeing. It involves our minds, hearts, and wills. Moral seeing is primarily a kind of knowing that includes perceiving, recognizing, understanding, and foreseeing. But it is also a way of appreciating as well as a way of orienting ourselves willfully with reference to moral concerns.

When we say to others with regard to a moral concern, "I see what you mean," we typically have in mind several of these aspects of moral sight. We mean to tell them that we are aware of their concern, we recognize what is involved, and we have some understanding of its significance. We may additionally be indicating that we can foresee how these concerns will develop or unfold, and we may also wish to acknowledge our own sense of its importance to us.

Moral sight is multidimensional, just as is physical sight. When we see well with our eyes, we engage in several different kinds of seeing although usually not in exactly the same moment. We observe details, shifting our focus from those near to those farther away. We recognize patterns and configurations. We see how things are moving or changing and often gain a sense of where and how they will further develop and unfold. In varying degrees we may be able to see and appreciate contrasts, shades, and perspective. Likewise in varying degrees we may be able to imagine or infer what we do not directly see. What we think we see is as a result a composite of our several closely, and usually spontaneously, interwoven acts of seeing. Similarly what we think we see morally is typically a composite of several, interrelated acts of moral sight. These include observing moral concerns, recognizing their features, conceiving their significance, foreseeing their likely developments, sensing overall patterns, imagining what we hope might happen, and acknowledging our own involvements and concerns about these matters.

Moral sight is not as much a constitutive aspect of our interactions with others as is moral speech or moral hearing. How we speak and attend to others directly establishes and affects our social interactions. How we see does so less directly. To be sure, how we look at others or how we view problems does affect our interactions. For example, whether and how frequently and in what settings we look directly at another's eyes make a difference. To gaze too intently, especially when the gaze is not reciprocated or invited, is invasive (Goffman 1967). However, this "looking at" is only one dimension of moral sight. For the most part, how we perceive, recognize, conceive, foresee, acknowledge, and envision do not so much directly shape our interactions as they affect the latter indirectly by influencing in turn how we listen and how we speak. Our moral sight affects the understandings, dispositions, presuppositions, beliefs, and convictions that we bring to our interactions.

I can illustrate how differences in moral sight affect how people respond to moral issues by looking at a specific moral concern: namely, the fair treatment of minority group members within business organizations. When this issue arose several decades ago, it was viewed in markedly different and antagonistic terms by different groups. Some saw in this issue evidence of blatant prejudice, some saw no issue at all, and others saw evidence of people unable to work as hard, as effectively, and in as timely a manner as majority group members. Some people perceived a moral problem here, and others did not. Even when they recognized the problem, groups differed in how they conceived of it and what they foresaw would likely happen. They held different visions of what they thought ought to be done. People have seen this problem in many different lights over time. The focus has shifted partly as a result of changing laws, changing circumstances, and increased concern to reduce outright forms of discrimination. In more recent years the problem has been viewed differently. From a concern with eliminating barriers to entry, the focus has broadened to include efforts to reduce overt as well as more subtle forms of internal discrimination. In recent years these concerns have been pursued under rubrics calling for affirmative action, employment equity, and workplace diversity. Each of these labels identifies a slightly different way of viewing issues related to the fair treatment of minority group members. More generally, they each reflect and qualify the moral seeing by which we view these related concerns. In turn our views of these issues affect both how attentive we are to the voiced concerns of others regarding these issues and the ways and degrees to which we feel called to voice our related concerns.

Because humans have been influenced by multiple traditions of ethical thought, some especially identified with particular religious, political, national, and ethnic communities, we readily recognize that people hold different moral views. This is a fact shaped by cultural diversity. It is also probably valid to argue that some traditions of ethical thought enable people to see moral issues with greater clarity, more perspective, and more lively attention than do others. Even though I do wish to identify criteria for evaluating variations in the goodness of moral sight, however, I do not wish to judge moral traditions as a whole. This is too large and complex a matter to take on. Rather, I wish to take

an approach that is more personal and practical. Whereas we may debate forever
the relative excellence of different moral and ethical traditions as spectacles
through which we view moral concerns, we can in the meantime attempt to
establish generic criteria for judging the marks of good moral seeing by
individuals. Furthermore, we can in turn use these criteria as benchmarks, if we
wish to, to gauge the relative strengths and weaknesses of particular traditions
of moral thought judged in terms of their capacity to promote good moral sight.

Table 4.1
The Marks of Good Moral Sight and the Dimensions
of Moral Blindness Characteristics of Absence

Marks	Characteristics	Parallels with Ordinary Vision
Not perceiving well	- Not observing fully: losing sight of issues, problems, standards. - Not foreseeing: failing to envision the consequences of current activities. - Not recognizing the moral dimensions of organizational life.	Shortsighted; farsighted; tunnel-visioned
Not seeing clearly and reliably	- Misinterpreting or misconstruing issues and problems: The problems of ideological bias and self-deception. - Stereotyping.	Astigmatism or blurred vision
Not seeing with a lively eye	- Lacking vision: Not seeing opportunities; not being able to read the signs of the time. - Lacking engagement: Seeing ourselves as observers and not actors and participants.	Unable to see contrast, color, perspective; viewing with fixed focus

I propose three general criteria for gauging the goodness of our moral sight.
Good moral sight ought to be perceptive, clear and reliable, and lively (see
Table 4.1). Why do I select these marks? There are several reasons for selecting
these as the criteria for good moral vision. One, our moral sight ought to keep
us informed. It should provide us with as much relevant information as we need
or want. It is less good to the extent that it leads us to overlook or not see

relevant moral considerations. Our moral seeing is perceptive to the degree that it provides us with relevant information. Two, our moral seeing ought to be clear and reliable. It does not help us to receive distorted or blurred visions of what is going on. Good moral vision represents realities faithfully and with clarity. Additionally, good moral vision also helps us keep track of our own relationship to moral concerns. In this way moral sight differs at least in degree from ordinary physical sight. As viewing subjects, we are inherently part of any moral concerns we picture. We are not just subjects receiving visual sense data. When we view moral realities, we are looking at concerns, issues, or obligations that matter to us. Our moral seeing is reliable and clear to the degree that it also gives us a clear picture of our own moral involvements. Three, our moral sight ought to be lively. It ought to spark our interest. It ought to waken our attention. It ought to move us and touch the springs of our motivations. Our moral seeing ought not to leave us indifferent and detached. Good moral sight ought to elicit and enliven our several senses of obligation, commitment, compassion, and outrage, depending upon the particular objects of our concern. Good moral sight ought to keep us fully, reliably, and lively informed.

Good Moral Sight Is Perceptive

Good moral sight ought to be perceptive so that we actually see moral issues and concerns and do not overlook them. We may gauge perceptiveness both in depth and breadth. We may miss moral issues and concerns by regarding only surface appearances and failing to investigate problems that do not directly announce themselves. We may fail to see moral realities because we do not look around broadly enough. We may readily respond to traditional, well-defined moral concerns and fail to take account of new issues and concerns more hazily understood. For example, many people remain confused and undecided how to judge a wide range of previously not encountered copyright issues related to the development and uses of information systems.

Three related forms of moral seeing together determine how morally perceptive we are. How well we perceive reflects in turn how broadly we observe moral concerns, how well we recognize and understand their patterns, and how good we are at foreseeing how current concerns will unfold over time. These three different acts of moral seeing affect the range and depth of our moral perception. By our observations we become aware of broader or narrower ranges of moral concerns. By our recognitions we become familiar with them. By our foresight we are able to get a sense of their growth and development over time. Our moral seeing is less perceptive to the degree that our observations are narrow and restricted, our capacity for recognition is only slight, and our ability to foresee remains atrophied. When this happens, our moral seeing becomes constricted in ways equivalent to being nearsighted, farsighted, or tunnel-visioned in our ordinary seeing.

Our ability to perceive moral realities is inevitably limited. The extent of our observations, recognitions, and foresight is bounded. We can receive and attend to only so much information at one time. The limits vary. Because of their intelligence or the conceptual spectacles with which they look at moral concerns, some people may be able to receive and process more information than others. Some people are more perceptive because they are ready to receive more information. Others may simply be more eager to learn. Nevertheless, in all cases perception is necessarily selective. When we are viewing some concerns, we almost inevitably must turn away or not notice others. As we focus on patterns, we typically pay less attention to detail. Several factors may influence what we select to perceive. Many people wait and respond to whatever concern gets their attention. This passive approach leaves people vulnerable to whoever or whatever distracts them the most. Others establish rigid criteria of moral priorities but then remain insensitive and unresponsive to concerns filtered out by their predetermined moral agendas. Because perception is inevitably selective, we cannot judge excellence here just by gauging the extent of information that people are able to receive. Rather, the most perceptive are those able to observe, recognize, and foresee the greatest amount of truly vital information. Because people differ in their moral beliefs and commitments, we cannot force any genuine consensus about what constitutes really vital information. Which approaches to moral sight are truly most perceptive is a matter that is inherently open to ongoing discussions.

Good Moral Sight Is Clear and Reliable

Good moral sight ought to be clear and reliable. It ought to represent faithfully and without distortion the moral realities that we are observing. Good moral vision enables us to see problems clearly uncontaminated by self-serving points of view or excuses. It enables us as well to recognize with clarity our corresponding obligations and commitments. Moral vision is less good to the extent that it occasions confused interpretations and deceptive accounts. Clarity and reliability of vision are promoted in several ways. Our seeing is clearer to the degree that we are not distracted by other matters. We see with greater clarity to the degree that we are able to establish a fitting focus that enables us to see issues in their settings in ways that neither abstract from relevant particularities nor become immersed in irrelevant detail. Knowing how to focus appropriately on moral issues is a noteworthy accomplishment, one for which we can gain greater skill over time. It is the art of being able to distinguish what genuinely matters from less relevant information and of being able to identify what factors are most decisive. Finally, our moral vision is more reliable to the degree that it is not distorted by accounts of external problems, normative expectations, or self-perceptions that are themselves deceptive. We may be deceived by others who give us one-sided accounts of issues and concerns. We also deceive ourselves in several ways: by voicing greater commitments than we are in fact ready to act on and by hiding from ourselves our own feelings and self-judgments.

Our moral sight is good, much as our ordinary physical sight is good, insofar as it clearly and reliably represents objects of sight to us. In our moral seeing, we seek to avoid the factors that produce the equivalents of blurred vision and astigmatism. Each of these leaves us with vision that distorts and misrepresents the objects of our sight. If our eyes suffer from blurred vision or astigmatism, we seek to correct for the causes of these problems through operations and/or special glasses that will enable us to see with clarity and without distortion. People who suffer from blurred vision or astigmatism end up with inherently idiosyncratic views of things in the sense that their views do not correspond to those held by others who do not experience this problem. Correspondingly, their sight becomes more objective, in the sense of being equivalent to that held by others, to the degree they correct for their astigmatism or blurred vision.

A number of strategies exist for attempting to reduce blurred vision and astigmatism in our moral sight. It is often assumed by the proponents of particular ethical views that their moral systems provide clear and reliable views to those who adopt them. I examine this claim later. In the meantime, it is useful to look at two other strategies. One, we can reduce blurred and astigmatic moral seeing by efforts to enhance self-knowledge and self-candor. In whatever way honest self-knowledge may be promoted—whether through personal reflection, feedback from close friends, confession, or therapy—it helps to correct for the tendencies both for excessive self-idealization and self-criticism regarding our own moral involvements. Two, we can enhance the clarity and reliability of our moral sight by attempts to adjust our own accounts with those held by reliable others. We can consult others to gauge the extent to which they see problems, normative expectations, and our own roles in ways similar to us.

Good Moral Sight Is Lively

Good moral sight ought to be lively. Our moral seeing is lively both to the degree that it engages us and to the degree that the objects of our sight remain living realities. Our moral vision becomes dull and deadly to the degree that we are moved neither by our sight of concrete concerns nor by our vision of normative expectations. Moral visions that are simply catalogues of problems and tables of rules usually don't engage us. Informed by moral visions of this sort, we can in a detached manner cite endless issues and invoke endless rules but without much sense that these concerns matter to us or anyone else. Our vision of moral realities lacks vividness, color, contrast, and perspective. Dull moral sight corresponds to impairments of physical sight that leave people unable to distinguish colors, tones, contrasts, and perspective.

Two factors especially foster dull moral sight: (1) an overly fixed focus by which we view moral concerns and (2) a detached viewing in which we fail to look at our own involvements.

How does fixed focus affect our moral sight? We can gain a sense of what is at stake here by examining the problems occasioned by fixed focus with our physical sight. As we look at objects, ordinarily our focus rapidly shifts from detail to detail, from overall patterns to light and color and shade, from foregrounds to perspective, from an analytical scrutinizing to synthetic attempts at appreciation. As I mentioned previously, our overall vision results from the composite putting together of these several types of seeing. People who make movies recognize this fact. They know that they can evoke a fairly vivid sense of a place or events by rapidly combining together a variety of quite different shots.

Fixed focus brings with it certain benefits. By looking closely with a steady gaze, we are often able to describe what we see in much greater detail and with greater accuracy than when we let our vision wander and move. Modern science has produced significant findings by detailed observations.

In his historical study on the origins of modern medical science, the twentieth-century philosopher and social critic Michel Foucault criticizes the extent to which these practices became preoccupied with the static observing of the signs and symptoms of illness. Rather than interacting with persons and seeking to help individuals become healthy, science became concerned with examining particular malignancies and illnesses which it tried to heal or remove. Like the subsequent fictional character, Sherlock Holmes, medical doctors tried to become skilled at looking carefully for telltale signs that would help them diagnose and solve medical mysteries. Using magnifying glasses, thermometers, and other diagnostic instruments, doctors attempted to make careful and exhaustive descriptions using ever more finely tuned classificatory schemes. Foucault argues that what particularly characterized this practice was the fixed gaze of the doctors and clinicians. Foucault criticizes this stance (1) because of its preoccupation with looking only at observable surfaces rather than looking as well at less clearly expressible depths and (2) because of its silent perceiving, sometimes even in depth, but not interacting. Foucault acknowledges that the modern clinical approach has yielded enormous benefits. Under the diagnostic gaze of clinicians, however, people as living human beings have often been lost to sight. What we see are signs and symptoms. A fixed focus also has the consequence of obscuring other matters or other ways of looking. The clinician's fixed focus did not allow for the reflective eye of the philosopher or the interactive viewing of the friend or lover (Foucault 1973).

Our moral sight becomes lively to the degree to which we see concerns with different foci. In making this point, I am not arguing that it is desirable to see moral issues neutrally as impartial observers (A. Smith 1976). To gain a lively vision, it is not necessary to see moral issues from both or multiple sides. I use the phrase "different foci" to identify the presence of different kinds of seeing in relation to the same object of concern. Thus, our seeing is more lively if we regard details as well as overall concerns, if we pay attention to foregrounds as well as backgrounds, if we attempt to assess likely outcomes as well as probable causes, and if we envision the good we would like to emerge and acknowledge our own interests and involvements. Our vision remains fixed to the degree that it becomes dominated by only one kind of moral seeing. Focusing too intently in one way, we fail to regard matters in other ways. Viewed from a single focus, objects of concern appear static and isolated: We fail to look enough at contexts, prior developments, and likely outcomes, as well as the views of others involved.

Our moral sight becomes dull as well when our viewing becomes too detached. When we become detached in our ordinary vision, we see things and we take in information, and we may do so with greater clarity than when we become overly involved. In the process, we also treat what we see as if it does not matter to us. Unengaged vision has served as a model for good scientific observation. It is not a fitting model, however, for an artistic viewing of the world nor for how lovers gaze at each other. As lovers certainly and often as artists, we are part of the world we are viewing. We are not just looking at a world that is independent of us.

We are in part the objects of our own moral sight. Whatever issues or problems attract our attention, whatever standards and objectives, obligations, and ideals we use to see them, we must also necessarily picture our own accountability and responsibility in relation to these concerns. Many questions might be asked: Is this an issue we ought to act on? Can we make a difference? Given our position and our previous promises, are we expected to act? Is this an opportunity? Are we needed? Where do we fit in relation to this particular set of moral concerns? As long as we are viewing the world with moral sight, these questions should not be evaded or avoided. To be sure, as with ordinary sight, people may address these questions with myopic vision, such that they hardly ever make out the contours of these concerns from the perspective of others but primarily see these concerns in terms of dealing with their own guilt, self-righteous pride, opportunity for glory, or reputation. Such nearsighted moral sight lacks clarity and reliability. Too much detachment is also a problem. If we distance ourselves too much from moral concerns, we take ourselves out of the picture and we lose interest.

Our moral sight is also lively to the degree that we are able to see connections between the diverse things we see—multiple issues, normative expectations, and our own roles—in relation to images and symbols that help make sense of them. To the degree that moral realities remain disconnected from each other, to the degree, for example, that we cannot connect our own feeling of obligations or integrity to concrete problems or see the interrelationship between different aspects of these issues, we also feel less engaged. Our vision is more lively to the extent that we can envision relationships. We often use the word "visionary" with just this significance because visionaries are able to envision connections, usually in relation to future possibilities, that allow and challenge us to act in ways that seem to make a difference.

Ethical systems serve like spectacles to facilitate our moral sight. Ethical systems assume many forms. They are embodied in political ideologies, in religions, in ethnic traditions, in organizational cultures, and in philosophical systems. They point to what kinds of issues ought to deserve our attention and in relation to what kinds of normative expectations we ought to view them. They provide images, stories, arguments, and precepts to help us recognize moral concern. They may set forth typical scenarios in relation to which we may envision how concerns will develop. They establish priorities and frames of reference so that we can make distinctions and see patterns. Typically they challenge people to be honest about their own accountabilities and involvements. With their stories, codes, legends, and precedents, they often offer reservoirs of potential imagination that we may bring to bear on particular issues.

Ethical systems not only instruct us what to look at. They also help shape the way we look. In particular they help in the development and formation of conscience. Humans probably possess some innate moral senses related to respect for others, compassion for those in distress, care for those we love, and the desire to realize our own self-images. These vague sentiments are coupled with other feelings, such as the desire to gain the approbations of those we trust (A. Smith 1976) and the sense that we ought to keep promises and reciprocate gifts (Gouldner 1960), to produce basic elements of conscience. But given the capacity of humans for self-deception and the strength of other self-interested desires, these moral senses do not amount to much unless they are cultivated and developed. Ethical systems seek to do just that. They cultivate and form consciences through informal and formal educational systems and through family and communal rituals. They seek in varying ways to cultivate a wide awake sense of conscience that in turn enables us to see moral concerns with lively, clear, and reliable perceptions (Conn 1981).

WHAT IS MORAL BLINDNESS?

Having looked briefly at the characteristics of good moral sight, we are now in a position to examine the general character of moral blindness. I sketch the general problem here before reviewing several prevailing forms of this phenomenon in the remainder of the chapter.

We can analyze moral blindness in relation to the three qualities or excellences of moral sight discussed above. Correspondingly, I examine moral blindness as a deficiency in moral perceptiveness, as an impairment in the clarity and reliability of our moral seeing, and as an incapacity that deadens the otherwise liveliness of our moral vision. To be morally blind is to see less well in these several ways. Often, as I indicate subsequently in this chapter, the problem is not that we do not see moral realities; rather, the problem is that we do not see them very well—that is, perceptively, clearly and reliably, and lively.

I have adopted this approach to moral blindness for several reasons. One, the handicap that many people face is not one of not being able to picture these several kinds of moral realities. They can bring them to mind. The perplexing problem they face is knowing how to line them up in some way that gives them a sense of perspective and agency. Too often these several kinds of moral realities seem unrelated or at least very difficult to bring together to enhance their own sense of vision. Though the discussion that follows here does not directly address this problem, it offers ways to reduce the problems of moral blindness that emerge from this perplexity.

Two, to be morally blind is not to be incorrigible without any moral sight at all. As in the case of both moral silence and moral deafness, those who are morally blind do not lack all moral convictions and sentiments. The problem in all these cases is that people do not bring into play capacities for moral speech, hearing, and sight that they possess but do not utilize as fully as they could. For several reasons, they have allowed these abilities to atrophy. Typically they perceive and recognize some moral realities though overlook others.

Three, because people hold many, different, and at times antagonistic ethical views, I have adopted an approach that is ecumenical or public. I am not setting forth a new synthesis that claims to overcome this problem. Nor am I defending a particular ethical philosophy as more adequate than others. I am not therefore arguing for a particular moral vision. Given the plurality of views, I am proposing ways of helping people to reduce their moral blindness no matter what philosophies, ideologies, or moralities they and others already hold. Rather than propose how people should rank their normative expectations, I discuss ways of making people see these realities with a more lively, perceptive, and clear vision, and I leave to them the task of assigning priorities.

MORAL BLINDNESS AS NOT PERCEIVING MORAL CONCERNS

Perhaps most if not all people possess moral blind spots. They simply overlook moral concerns that seem to be staring them in the face. They can give quite accurate accounts of their worlds but leave out issues or concerns that are in front of them but which they succeed in looking past and moving around without being aware that they are doing so. These blind spots assume several forms. Often they occur in relation to issues and concerns we simply overlook and do not observe. For example, moving to a foreign country as a sales representative, we may fail to observe differences in social etiquette in ways that initially offend our hosts. Or we fail to see a particular problem like harassment as a moral issue that concerns us. Often blind spots occur with respect to the future consequences of present acts. We fail to take a hard-nosed look at the likely consequences of present projects. In the short run many activities look much better than they do when viewed from a long-range perspective. A decision to fudge a quality control report, on the basis of a probably accurate judgment that the error lay in the way the testing was performed rather than in the product, may make considerable short-run sense when retesting would involve costly delays in production and distribution, but it can cause long-run problems if the error in testing is not really examined and corrected so that the same kinds of probably erroneous results do not appear again. Blind spots assume still another form: They occur in the form of the failure in the first place to recognize the moral dimensions of business activities. Many businesspeople are morally blind about specific concerns because they simply fail to see the extensive degree to which moral expectations affect managerial tasks.

Moral Blind Spots: Overlooked Moral Issues

Viewing the history of business activities from the present, it would be possible to identify an extensive list of issues that are now treated as being of pressing moral concern but that received little overt attention in the past. For example, for centuries people tolerated slavery. Now and then particularly troubled souls would protest, but many otherwise morally concerned humans simply assumed its existence. Neither Christians nor Stoics directly protested against slavery in any major way until early modern times. For years business-people paid little attention to the problems associated with high noise levels in factories. Although they recognized that the smoke stacks of factories emitted smelly and foul substances, they ignored for long periods the recognition that these exhausted substances might be dangerous to other persons and environmental resources.

It is not unusual for people to ignore issues when the latter are especially aggravated and then begin to pay attention to them as they become improved. During the 1950s there was little public attention to the problems of poverty in the United States. Compared to the depression and the war years, circumstances seemed much better. These were the years of suburban expansion. More Americans lived in their own family dwellings. During a great building boom, new schools, shopping markets, churches, factories, and homes were constructed, especially in the areas surrounding the big cities. This seemed to be the age of affluence (Galbraith 1958). It was not until the early 1960s that people began to voice concerns about poverty after Michael Harrington published his book, *The Other American*. A number of people became especially vocal about this issue. Thousands of antipoverty programs were initiated at the local, state, and federal levels. Beginning in the middle of the decade the national government even waged a "War on Poverty." What is interesting about this example is that by all the usual indices of poverty, the extent of poverty was much worse in the 1950s than in the 1960s. The number of families living below the government-designated poverty line was much greater. Preoccupied by other matters, otherwise comfortable Americans overlooked poverty and the attendant deprivations it caused until the mid-1960s, at which time, ironically, the extent of poverty had become measurably less (Bird 1973).

For periods of time, businesspeople have been at least momentarily blind about a number of concerns that have now become integral to their ordinarily ethical agendas. Businesspeople have variously overlooked issues of harassment, workplace equity, fiduciary responsibilities, the emission of toxic matters, and unsafe products, as well as many other concerns that in time they have attempted to address more directly. Often moral blindness is temporary.

Not Foreseeing the Consequences of Current Activities

Many people perceive moral issues in the present fairly well but fail to foresee the ways by which their present activities are likely to give rise to unanticipated and unwelcome developments. Many practices seem perfectly acceptable in the present because we fail to recognize the way they give rise to injuries and problems that we do not immediately expect.

At times the failure to foresee serves as a device that allows people to get away with questionable practices. For example, even otherwise excellent managers often become preoccupied with advancing their own careers. The instinct to do so is natural, and they are often handsomely rewarded by their organizations by working at projects that in the short run improve their chances for promotion. A typical strategy is to attract and expand resources within units that one is managing in order to promote programs or projects that at least temporarily seem successful. If these innovations look good to senior management, the executives who engineered them often succeed in attracting appointments to more senior positions. On the surface this kind of activity seems to be pretty standard if not beneficial to their organizations. Companies are often encouraged to foster entrepreneurial initiative among their managers (Peters and Waterman 1982). Such initiatives do foster innovations and organizational learning and overcome the lethargy associated with more bureaucratic attitudes. This same preoccupation, however, with personal career advancement often leads to two other less defensible consequences. On the one hand, managers can become so wrapped up in advancing the interests of their own units—and their own careers in the process—that they lose sight of what is good for the corporate organization as a whole. Competing against other units and other executives for organizational resources, they begin taking part in turf wars that are organizationally costly. On the other hand, these career-advancing executives are prone to draw too extensively upon the resources of their units in order to produce attention-getting developments. They are thereby in danger of depleting the resources of these units at least temporarily. In many instances the costly by-products of their projects do not show up immediately. Many such wonder-working executives have been able to outrun the costly consequences of their policies, which in turn have been charged to the unfortunate executives assigned to manage their now resource-thinned units (Jackall 1988).

Atrophied moral foresight can be a product of success. In a book titled *The Icarus Paradox*, Danny Miller (1990) analyzes how a number of very successful companies fell into reversals as a result of pursuing too single-mindedly policies that had initially led to their successes. He describes how corporations are led to emphasize too greatly their strengths in ways that lead to not keeping track of issues and concerns. They fail to foresee how their virtues in sales, engineering, research, and/or organizational development need to be balanced by other concerns. Blinded as it were by their own especially strong abilities, they lose awareness of other critical factors in their environment, they fail to recognize serious problems as they begin to arise, and they become less self-aware. The lack of foresight raises moral concerns in these cases because of the impact of these policies upon how these organizations steward the resources entrusted to them by investors, creditors, and employees—all of whom suffer losses as a result of corporate failings.

Occasionally the lack of foresight simply takes the form of shortsightedness. Not only the petrochemical industry in particular but the public more generally can be accused of shortsightedness in their current uses of oil and natural gas, for example, since the known supply of these resources is certainly limited. There is not an endless available supply. For example, many industry spokespersons estimate supplies of natural gas available until sometime after the middle of the next century. However, from a larger historical perspective, that is a very short period of time. What will happen then? What alternative sources will we tap for energy or for the compounds with which we make many of our plastics and synthetics? When a petrochemical company describes its future as being very promising due to sixty years of reserves of natural gas, innocent observers can easily begin to wonder. To be sure, sixty years constitutes a long time in the history of an organization that in its present form is two decades old and stretches back in earlier forms another few decades. It is also a long time in the history of the current board and executives. It is also a long time in relation to the life expectancies of all the current customers of their products and services. It is, therefore, not surprising to perceive a sense of optimistic buoyancy in these announcements of sixty-year reserves. Nonetheless, it is also possible to argue that at organizational, industrial, and national policy levels, it is time to begin thinking about how to address the problems that will arise as this nonrenewable, natural resource first becomes more scarce and then is exhausted.

Moral shortsightedness can accompany well-intended, morally defended projects. Many forestry companies for long periods of time have felt justified in lumbering so long as they made a serious effort to plant trees in the areas they lumbered. In part this represented smart business over the long run because by replanting regularly, they were establishing a crop of trees that they could harvest forty or fifty years in the future. Regularly replanting was both a conscientious act and good business. Forestry companies took some pride in these efforts and posted signs along highways in order to let the public know how many years ago they had planted or replanted trees. In some areas the signs indicate that several crops of trees have been harvested from the same lands. The implications are clear: Lands that now look bare will shortly be covered with thousands of trees that will grow from small saplings to large trees. Moreover, this is not a new policy invented to capture some green market. As the signs along the highway indicate, some of these companies have been doing this for most of this century. Still this policy is open to criticism. The forestry companies clearly recognized certain moral issues, such as the need for reforestation, but they remained blind and shortsighted about others: namely, the way in which this method of harvesting and planting trees affected all the other plants and animals that inhabit forests.

With respect to this issue, the forestry companies were morally blind rather than being either naive or corrupt. They were not without some conservation concerns, even though these were connected by self-interest to ensuring the possibility for further future harvests. Their environmental commitment, however, was clearly limited. They give little attention for long periods to the effect of their policies on the animal life of the forests. They were not innocent, because others have throughout the twentieth century raised these issues and campaigned to set aside parks and forests in order to protect and preserve both plant and animal life in the wild. These concerns have been raised much more vocally in a number of countries including the United States, especially since 1970 when Congress enacted legislation to protect endangered species. This legislation has been invoked to stop logging in certain redwood forest areas of the Pacific Northwest in order to protect a rare species of owl that had been listed as an endangered species. Consequently, as these concerns have been raised about the way certain logging and replanting policies threaten wildlife, forestry companies that do not seriously attempt to revise their policies in some ways to take account of these concerns can be credited with being morally blind, at least with respect to this issue.

It is better to be motivated by goodwill than by self-aggrandizement. However, goodwill is not a guaranteed antidote to moral shortsightedness. Men and women of goodwill sometimes allow themselves to be duped by people who are less scrupulous. By means of another example, we can gain a clearer idea of the ways moral shortsightedness can subtly affect our otherwise seemingly farsighted goodwill. Beginning in the first part of the century a number of people in South Florida invested considerable effort to make what they thought was better use of vast semitropic areas. They wanted to reduce the dangers from flooding. They wanted to make good agricultural use of swampy areas by draining them. Even though this was not an initial objective, they also sought to set aside reserve areas for parks, such as the Everglades National Park. Over the years from 1900 through the 1970s and especially in the two decades after the Second World War, huge investments were made by the state and federal governments in one of the world's largest public works projects. Ostensibly their aim was to promote land reclamation and flood control. At the outset these goals seemed worthy and comparable to the famous efforts by the Dutch both to build dikes to protect their lands from periodic flooding caused by storms off the North Sea as well as flooding in the Rhine River delta and to create new and reclaimed lands in areas of the Zuider Zee. A vast array of public projects came into being in South Florida. The meandering Kissimmee River was straightened and channelized. Extensive dikes and levees were constructed. An extensive system of canals was built. A number of pumping stations were erected, and large quantities of water were pumped from lower to higher levels with the purpose of making as much use as possible of fresh water before it entered the ocean. As a result of these efforts, much more land was developed for agricultural purposes. Between 1960—the year when the United States started its boycott of Cuban products, including sugar cane—and 1975, there was a sixfold increase in land set aside for growing sugar cane. The people who developed these projects sought to make what they regarded as the highest and best possible uses of these lands. During these years only a few critics raised their voices. In 1949 Marjory Douglas wrote *River of Grass*. She protested that these public projects had turned South Florida from what it was by nature, a river of grass, into something artificial, a highly managed and widely used area dedicated to agriculture, outdoor sports, flood control, and tourism.

These public projects did not solve all the flood problems, and they gave rise to a number of unforseen and unsought-after consequences. Some of these were comparatively innocuous, such as the silting up of the newly dredged riverways. Others were more serious, such as the impact of these changes on the flight patterns of birds and encroachment of salt water into lands and waters that had been fresh-water territories in the past. As a result, beginning in the late 1970s new efforts had to be invested to undo what had been earlier done. The channelization of the Kissimmee River turned into an ecological catastrophe, sluicing sewage from Orlando to Lake Okeechobee. New efforts began to return the river back to its old, meandering course. The South Florida Water Management District now faced the prospect of undoing what it had previously undertaken for the most part with the best of intentions. Why had those initiating these projects not foreseen the consequence entailed by their designs? Is this just one of those unexpected pieces of bad luck? Although questions about this project will undoubtedly remain contentious, it seems possible that some of these adverse effects might have been anticipated, especially if the conservation aims had been as weighty for the designing engineers as the land reclamation objectives. The interest in making the economically highest and best uses, however, meant that conservation concerns were given lesser priority, especially in the late 1950s and 1960s during the great boom in sugar cane production (Light, Gunderson, and Holling 1995).

Aside from continually being aware of the possibilities, there are no guaranteed formulas that, if strictly followed, will ensure that we do not from time to time see with moral blind spots and/or shortsightedness. Factors that lead us to overlook or not foresee moral issues are multiple. It is too easy to cite blatant examples and think that only others because of their narrow-mindedness are ever prone to these forms of faulty perception. Probably the most serious error is to think ourselves immune to these problems.

Not Recognizing the Moral Dimensions of Organizational Life

Many people fail to acknowledge the way in which normative expectations shape and color many of the characteristic features of organizational and interorganizational encounters. This failure to recognize these moral features takes several typical forms. Many businesspeople seem to exploit their own self-serving partial moral blindness to find excuses to serve their own interests. The overt case they make is that they are allowed to do anything that is not explicitly prohibited by law. Furthermore, they are often willing to hire extra lawyers in hopes of winning adjudications that allow them the greatest freedom from external interference. This stance treats as matters of personal preference or self-interested calculations questions of whether to honor professional standards, gentlemen's agreements, and the normative status of virtues like probity, integrity, honesty, reliability, and civic responsibility. The shared cultural status of these moral expectations is denied. People can instead choose to adhere to these standards if that is their personal choice or if it seems to be good for their businesses. The moral dimensions of organizational life are accordingly reduced to several contrasting extremes: the charitable discretion of individuals who choose to be large-minded, the tactical moral acts undertaken to advance business interests, and legal standards imposed by government decrees and court judgments.

This self-interested nonrecognition differs slightly in character and in practice from the moral amnesia of those who often act in keeping with moral standards whose existence they fail to perceive. Those affected by moral amnesia recognize moral features of business life insofar as they in practice defer to them or even sometimes invoke them, while overtly arguing that these standards either do not exist or are not moral. In spite of the fact that those affected by moral amnesia seem to be doing two different things at once—both recognizing and not recognizing moral features of business activities—this position is not atypical. This mind-set is well-illustrated by the essay of the Nobel laureate Milton Friedman (1971) in which he argued that "The Social Responsibility of Business Is to Increase Its Profits." From this title, and from a quick reading of the essay, it would seem that Friedman is arguing that the moral responsibilities of business extend no further than making profits as long as this is done legally. The essay in fact makes a strong case against executives attempting to use their corporate positions to deal with problems like unemployment and pollution. Executives ought not meddle with such concerns, Friedman argued, because they lack the relevant expertise to manage these issues well and because they have been given no mandate by the boards to whom they are responsible to expend limited company resources on these concerns. Friedman notes that these kinds of social involvement might be defensible if it could be demonstrated that corresponding actions in turn were in fact good for business in some way. If they were, then they should be defended in the latter terms rather than invoking essentially misleading talk about corporate social responsibility.

Friedman's position seems to be pretty clear, especially given the increasing agitation for businesses to assume a more proactive stance with respect to environmental issues and the continuing pressures for employment practices that enhance employment security and reduce the frequent short-terms layoffs and hirings due to temporary market fluctuations. Friedman seems to be arguing that executives have no moral responsibilities other than to run their businesses in keeping with the law in ways that increase profits for their investors and owners. Friedman's argument is less clear, however, and much more moral when we begin to examine the arguments he mounts in defense of his position. For example, he mentions that businesses should be run without committing fraud, without intentional deception, and in keeping with standards of fair competition. Although only briefly mentioned, these words allude to an extensive range of normative standards that variously assume the form of expected virtues, professional rules, and organizational codes. Friedman additionally acknowledges in passing that businesses should act in keeping with societal values. This acknowledgment would seem to mandate quite a wide range of moral concerns for executives if the larger society seemed to be concerned, as it increasingly has become with environmental issues and as it has from time to time demonstrated with the problems of unemployment. Probably in making these observations, I am extending Friedman's references far beyond where he intended them to be taken. Nonetheless, he does seem to recognize other moral considerations as relevant for business. These recognitions are taken even further when in the middle of his essay he argues that one of the reasons executives ought not expend company resources on various social causes is because in doing so they would be taking away economic values to which others—including investors, employees, and customers—have greater claims. Although he gives prominence to the investors as the employers of the executives, he makes a case as well for the way such social projects may have the effect of taking money away from workers, which might be diverted to higher wages, or away from customers, which might assume the form of lower prices. In the process in rudimentary form, Friedman has sketched a stakeholder view of the firm, a view that presumes that well-run businesses in different degrees owe something to each set of stakeholders who help to make it possible for them to do business well. Friedman's argument well exemplifies the moral amnesia that affects many businesspeople who vocally deny that ethics has much relevance for business although they indirectly acknowledge or defer to moral realities in their practices and communications.

To a degree moral amnesia seems fairly innocuous. In practice, however, it functions by default to support the ideology that reduces the mandate of business to profit maximization. Because successful businesses find ways to cultivate and develop most of their relationships with their major stakeholders, this slogan presents a distorted image of the complex set of considerations that good executives seek to balance. This formula and the moral amnesia that it excuses in practice is cited in order to defend the autonomy of managers over any groups, including investors, who might seek to reduce their discretionary power. The motto is used especially to argue against conceding any power to trade union groups or to government regulations and regulators.

Whatever particular expressions it has assumed, this failure to recognize and acknowledge the moral dimensions of organizational life has the effect of turning ethical concerns in business over to a number of specialists and regarding other businesspeople as the bearers only of their own private moralities. Ethics becomes at best associated with a number of very special concerns at the edges of business activities, like philanthropic projects, legal wranglings, or proper accounting procedures. This view is not inaccurate. It is just not complete. More than others, people in public affairs, internal auditing, legal counsel, and human resources directly deal with issues that are overtly discussed in moral and ethical terms. However, ethical concerns do not stop there. To delegate moral concerns to these staff people is to ignore the much wider moral responsibilities facing all businesspeople.

MORAL BLINDNESS AS NOT SEEING MORAL CONCERNS CLEARLY AND RELIABLY

Often people fail to acknowledge moral concerns not because they have overlooked problems but because they have not seen relevant issues clearly and reliably. Their vision has become distorted. As a result they oversimplify or overcomplicate—they emphasize certain features excessively or fail to give enough attention to others. Often in the process they see things in ways that seem to serve their own purposes more than might be expected. Their vision has become blurred or distorted not because they lack sufficient information, but because of flaws or errors in the way they are arranging this information. They are bringing to their viewing particular points of view that engender these consequences. In part their distorted viewing can be explained as the product of the particular ideas and frameworks they use to process information. And in part it can be explained by their own disposition to see things as they do.

Misinterpreting or Misconstruing Issues: Problems of Ideological Bias and Self-Deception

Before exploring this topic further, it will be useful to discuss a relevant example. During much of the past thirty years, liberals and conservatives have debated the relative merits of public spending for welfare. Liberals have defended welfare programs as they are and championed additional programs and projects they believed worthy of support. They have invoked the neediness of the poor, homeless, uneducated, unemployed, and sick. The conservatives in contrast have expressed concern about excessive public spending, about the high interest rates on public debts, about specific programs that have involved waste, and about other programs that have proven futile in even making a gesture to address the problems at which they have been aimed. Whether they favored more or less generous programs, more or less financial restraint, both liberals and conservatives have largely thought of poor people as the primary beneficiaries of these programs. In a fundamental sense both groups have been wrong in this assumption. The primary beneficiaries of public welfare programs have been the middle and higher classes. This statement remains true even if we do not consider old-age pensions and public-subsidized educational programs—both of which provide most of their support for the middle and upper classes. If we think of income transfer programs aimed at meeting publicly defined needs, then we would include not only public assistance but also unemployment benefits and family assistance, as well as a wide range of exemptions and provisions that allow people to reduce their taxes depending upon a number of factors including dependents, tuition payments, mortgage payments, and contributions to retirement savings plans. Both sides of this debate failed to clearly see the way income transfer programs aided not only and not especially the poor but many others who were far from poor (Plotnick and Skidmore, 1975; Tussing, 1975).

In many instances contemporary executive defenses of very high executive salaries represent another example of seemingly distorted vision. During the past decade and a half, chief executive salaries generally have risen faster than inflation and faster than the profit margins of the firms they manage. How do these people justify to their organizations the salaries they have requested and been awarded? I have in mind here not just their salaries but all the additional benefits they receive, including stock options, housing allowances, and other perks. Clearly they cannot really defend their increases by citing their contributions to their firms' productivity and/or increases in the cost of living, although these arguments have been invoked among others. The vocal defenses for executive salary increases have not been made exclusively or even primarily by chief executives themselves. In many cases, these are the rationales cited by boards for the salary awards they have decided upon. They have additionally defended their huge salary packages on market forces. The argument assumes this form: Without really competent executives, their firms would languish. Really competent executives are, however, a scarce commodity. In order to attract skilled executives and retain them so that they are not attracted to other firms, firms need to award them handsome salaries. Market forces do have to be taken into account, and the market in chief executives is quite different from that for other personnel in less demand. Although this argument has some merit, it does not explain fully the considerable differences among executive salaries. It is possible, of course, to adopt a cynical view that rationales offered in defense of increasingly high executive salaries amount to nothing much more than smoke screens to obscure people from looking too closely at what amounts to a combination of greed for wealth and possessions and conspicuous consumption. This argument, however, cannot stand by itself because the boards must eventually approve these awards. Even if we allow that a significant proportion of board members are either chief executives of other firms or anticipate such appointments, that would not explain why other board members have been willing to divert corporate funds in this direction. None of these several rationales or arguments fully accounts for this phenomenon. However, if we assume that each of the several actors involved has allowed himself/herself the benefits of partially distorted and obscured sight, then we can believe that many of the chief actors have been fairly sincere as they put forward these arguments. It is almost as if the main actors have been caught up by a contemporary fad—this one concerning the significance and privileges of chief executives—and have not examined too thoroughly the credibility of the rationales they have offered.

Historically, two different but complementary explanations have been offered to explain why people often look at their own involvements with distorted vision. The first examines the way people adopt ideological biases, and the second analyzes factors that give rise to self-deception.

A controversial history surrounds the analysis of ideologies. Controversies have been ignited by accusations from one or more groups who have discovered distorted, often self-serving accounts in the economic, political, and religious beliefs of others. Groups have often traded critiques. While engaging in these critiques, these parties have mutually assumed that in their public philosophies groups often present distorted or skewed views of the world that function to justify arrangements of power and privilege that serve their interests. Typically, those making these accusations assume that they are freer of this tendency than those they are accusing. Beginning with the nineteenth-century philosopher and economist Karl Marx, Marxists became masters of ideological critiques. They demonstrated ways in which the economic theories and political philosophies of nineteenth and twentieth-century classical and neoclassical economists and liberal political analysts closely reflected the interests of the commercial and higher classes (Marx 1977; Mannheim 1936; Lukacs 1968; Habermas 1971). In a clever exposition of this approach entitled *The Eighteenth Brumaire of Louis Bonaparte*, Marx wrote about the civil and political conflicts in France between 1848 and 1851. He demonstrated how many of the eventual positions of groups and individuals can be accounted for by analyzing what the economic interests of these groups were likely to be (Marx 1963). It is, of course, possible in response to demonstrate ways in which Marxists' accounts in turn serve the political and economic interests either of the working classes or more narrowly of the trade union movement or the political left (Mannheim 1936). As they traded critiques, these analysts assumed that it is possible to develop a form of scientifically grounded political discourse that does not suffer from the distorting character of the popular ideologies being submitted to scrutiny (Sutton et al. 1956).

In the last several decades an alternative, less contentious view of ideologies has been proposed largely by social scientists. According to this view the public philosophies of any group are likely to reflect the economic and political interests of these groups. Groups articulate public philosophies, moreover, not just to describe the world the way it is but also to call attention to aspects of that world that may be problematic and to indicate ways in which following their philosophy is likely to address these problems. Public philosophies incorporate both judgment about what is real together with judgments about what ought to be actual. They are set forth, additionally, in rhetorically appealing ways both in order to rally popular support for their views and to indicate why alternative views are less adequate. Any group that communicates its public philosophy is likely to do so in ways that reflect the inherent ideological character of this discourse (Geertz 1973; Gouldner 1976). Utilizing this social scientific approach, Bendix (1956) analyzed the history of management ideologies from the scientific management Frederick Taylor set forth at the beginning of this century to more recent human relations theories. He demonstrated how these ideologies function, among other things, to legitimate the authority and privileges of senior management and to justify various means to control their work forces.

We may summarize this social scientific perspective as follows: As they publicly defend their policies and positions, people are likely to exaggerate, to call greater attention to some wrongs than others, and to emphasize some virtues more than others in ways that seem likely to arouse public support for their positions and discredit alternative views. These kinds of distortion seem to be an inherent characteristic of this kind of communication. It need not lead to distorted accounts of the world as long as people consider alternative views as complements and recognize the rhetorical character of these communications. Correspondingly, we can expect that various management and trade union philosophies will not only identify particular problems and how they can be solved but do so in ways that seem to foster the interests of some groups more than others. From this perspective no group is immune from the possibility of making ideologically biased statements. These become problematic, however, only if they are taken too literally and too exclusively.

For example, trade unions have developed philosophies that expose difficulties and injustices suffered by employees and propose ways that these problems can be overcome. While calling attention to unsafe and unhealthy working conditions and unfair wages and the problems of economic insecurity, these philosophies also defend the right of workers to form collective bargaining units and to have their interests represented by specific trade unions. During recent, generally successful efforts to organize custodial workers into collective bargaining units, trade union spokespeople have especially called attention to the fact that many of these employees, who worked for small custodial firms, lacked good health care programs. Not always, however, have successful unionization drives resulted in clearly better health care plans. Nonetheless, officials may still feel justified in making this kind of plea because they judge that in the end it is in the best interests of workers to be represented by trade unions than not to be. Rarely are union spokespeople strictly Machiavellian. For the most part they genuinely believe what they say, giving less attention to the way unionization augments and supports their power and more to the believed benefits to the workers they represent.

Recent defenses of charismatic executive leadership have an equivalent ideological character. Charismatic leaders are celebrated for their vision, their capacity to win loyalty, and their ability to accomplish more than expected. Compared to other kinds of leaders, they seem to be admired more than autocratic leaders and to be more inspiring than bureaucratic leaders. Furthermore, it seems that there are ways to cultivate charismatic appeal (Conger and Kanungo 1988; Conger 1989). While allowing that charisma can be abused, affirmations of this kind of highly personal leadership call little attention to the way such leaders are also less accountable and answerable to their organizations and to their tendency to overextend both those who work closely with them and their organizations more generally (Weber 1978, Part II; Bird 1992).

Analyses regarding self-deception complement those regarding ideological bias. In this case, however, the focus of analysis has typically been on individuals rather than groups. The basic assumption is that people sometimes like to think of themselves in more complimentary forms than just the ways they are actually behaving. In the process, they hide from recognizing or acknowledging certain unsavory and uncomplimentary but real aspects of their own involvements. This line of analysis, initiated both by the founder of psychoanalysis Sigmund Freud (1958) and the nineteenth-century philosopher Friedrich Nietzsche (1927), argues that people often are inclined to kid themselves about what kind of people they really are. They often fail to admit the extent to which they are motivated by feelings of aggression, vengeance, resentment, greed, and self-aggrandizement. The core problem is not strictly cognitive but rather volitional. They deceive themselves about their motives because they are unwilling to acknowledge and avow some of the motivations that in fact move them. The problem of self-deception is, moreover, particularly tricky. It is difficult to catch yourself doing it. When you are aware that you are deceiving yourself, you may be accused of entertaining an illusory but willful fantasy. You are not suffering from genuine self-deception (Fingarette 1969). To the degree that they are deceiving themselves in some way, people are likely to give well-meaning accounts that leave out how supposedly neutral actions in fact serve their own ends in especially self-serving ways.

Expressions of distorted vision accompany many accounts of current empowerment programs. These programs aim to give workers, usually as part of teams, greater discretion over the timing, pace, conditions, and character of their work. Rather than simply working to fulfill directives imposed through a chain of command by their supervisors, workers themselves are asked to participate more fully in allocating tasks among themselves and holding each other accountable. Immediate supervisors are asked to change their roles so that they act less like foremen and directors and more as coaches and facilitators. Workers genuinely experience themselves as having greater discretion. They often feel more involved in trying to make sure that they achieve their team-chosen objectives. Are they exercising greater power and influence? To the extent that these programs work as intended, they do so at least with respect to the conditions of their own involvement. However, senior management has not really reduced its power and controls. These empowerment programs do not bring into being workers' councils or large numbers of worker representatives on boards. Workers are not given greater say in organizational strategies, although their suggestions on minor tactics may indeed be welcomed. These programs often load supervisors with greater responsibilities but less direct authority with consequences it is too early to determine. On the whole I suspect that these programs have much to offer in helping to foster greater participation and organizational commitment among workers. It is not clear how much real power they create for workers. They do, however, in less announced and less acknowledged ways serve to reinforce and legitimate the authority of senior management. They continue to establish the parameters within which particular units operate. Under many empowerment programs, however, they bear less of the onus for the difficult decisions about who gets laid off and which particular projects are downplayed or promoted. It may indeed be difficult for senior management to see the ways empowerment programs reinforce their own authority. Some external critics, however, have been especially aware of this aspect and have criticized these programs both on this basis and on the failures of these programs that promise more than they actually deliver (Rinehart 1978; Gandz and Bird 1996).

Stereotyping

We see moral concerns unclearly as well when we use stereotypical images to respond to and think about complex moral problems. Galbraith has argued that we are too ready to accept conventional wisdom as a reliable guide (Galbraith 1967, 1973). People often think of many of the features of business activities in relation to stereotypes. Stereotypes are preformed ideas, which may fairly accurately apply to some situations at the same time as they present distorted images when applied to other situations. The tendency to stereotype is pervasive and grows out of the efforts both to offer brief, easily recognizable but essentially neutral caricatures and to offer equivalently brief summary judgments about others. As a result stereotypes are rarely wholly wrong. But they often present overly simple and misleading accounts.

Stereotypes have been formed about people and about situations. For many years businesses operated with the assumption that fresh, clean air was essentially a free and limitless resource. Because wind currents often take away polluted air and bring in fresh air and because bodies of water absorb the pollutants that are washed out of the air, it seemed that this caricature remained valid. During the past two generations especially, people in urban areas around the world have discovered that fresh air is neither limitless nor free. To make or keep the air clean and fresh has required ever more expensive filters on cars and smokestacks. Before industrialization, this caricature often seemed trustworthy. Even with industrialization, it seemed valid in areas especially blessed by favorable winds and the good fortune of placing their major smokestack industries downwind from their residential areas. In this case, the relevant stereotype was not a prejudicial account of another group but a simplifying caricature that became increasingly false with industrial development but was still held onto by those who resisted efforts aimed at reducing willful air pollution.

It is far easier to see stereotypes in the eyes of others than to recognize our own. Where others may accuse us of stereotyping, we may often see sympathetic defenses. Where others see in our images misleading characterization, we often see insightful assessment. The following example well illustrates some of the ambiguities associated with the use of possibly stereotypical images. A fairly large business in the transportation industry in the Southwest made considerable efforts to hire native people. They hoped to hire enough natives so that the composition of their work force equalled or exceeded that of the larger population in their regions of the country. They developed a number of related tactics with this goal in mind. They offered training apprenticeships to young natives. They actively recruited among native groups. They deliberately sought to subcontract some work to native-developed firms. Recognizing that the cultural backgrounds of native and others employees might be different, they developed educational programs so that non-native employees would be more appreciative of the cultural characteristics of natives. As a result of these initial efforts, the company appreciably increased the native proportion of its work force. These efforts were exemplary, and the company received fitting public commendation for its efforts. They had addressed and overcome the popular stereotype that native people were unwilling and incapable of working alongside non-natives as part of regular industrial work forces.

Over time the program was not as successful as at its inception. Two problems in particular seemed difficult to solve: Few natives were promoted to positions much above entry level and a number of natives began to drop out of the work force. After several years the proportion of natives in the work force was appreciably lower. The firm began to investigate why this was happening. The causes seemed to be multiple. Some natives withdrew for better positions or to assume political roles in their local communities. Some suddenly took off in response to crises in their families or neighbors back home. The company attempted to become more understanding. They made apologies both to other employees and for the natives. They argued that natives were often late, for example, because many of the latter possessed a different sense of time and that they worked at a more casual pace because they were culturally less ambitious than non-natives. A number of the natives, though remaining very grateful to the company for its initiatives and interests, felt that their immediate supervisors or colleagues used these kinds of caricatures in order to not consider their own achievements and potentials more seriously. Their accusations assumed several forms. In a number of cases, natives felt that they had not been treated fairly because their supervisors or colleagues assumed that they were too casual in their work habits. In other cases, they criticized the firm itself for tolerating many natives who acted in keeping with these caricatures when many natives were able and already prepared to work in as timely and industrious manner as any other employees.

This case presents an interesting example in which it is often easier to criticize the caricatures used by others than to look closely at one's own. Who was really right? Were some of the natives who complained about being stereotyped using arguments to excuse their own lack of achievements? In the hopes of avoiding censure of its well-intended policies was the company at times too willing to excuse absences and casual work habits among some natives? Was the irritation expressed by coworkers often really a manifestation of their continuing inability to appreciate legitimate cultural differences? Was the company stereotyping when it made too much of these cultural differences? There is no simple answer to these questions. As we attempt to acknowledge and work with cultural differences among our work forces, we are likely to use existing and invent new caricatures to capture the decisive aspects of these differences. At the same time, we must somehow find ways of exploring how caricatures can be associated with legitimately different ways of working but not in ways that disfavor or privilege any group. This is what workplace diversity means. It is no small task. It is one that leaves open the possibility that our best efforts to overcome old prejudicial stereotypes may give rise to new, less obvious ones that still tend to exaggerate or characterize in distorting ways.

MORAL BLINDNESS AS NOT SEEING WITH A LIVELY EYE

We can be morally blind as well not because we fail to perceive issues and not because our vision becomes blurred or distorted but because our viewing remains flat, static, fixed, and lacking in imagination and engagement. One way of putting this problem is to say that we become morally blind when our viewing lacks vision—that is, when our seeing lacks scope, a sense of opportunity, and passion. What visionaries do is look at problems in such a way that people begin to see genuine openings to act to address and overcome current difficulties. To be morally blind is to look at problems without a sense of possibilities generally as well as for oneself in relation to them.

Lack of Vision

Morally concerned people sometimes become overwhelmed by the problems they see. More than others, they may courageously look at the difficulties and hard choices these dilemmas entail (Toffler 1986). They can in the process, however, view these concerns with too fixed a focus. For example, the eighteenth-century philosopher Kant posed a famous case involving issues of lying and truth telling. In this case a man who belongs to the enemy's army is looking for a soldier from your country who is hiding in a house. The enemy soldier wants to seize the soldier and probably kill him. If the homeowner answers truthfully, the enemy knows that the house is unguarded and that the soldier is hiding within. He will recognize that he can proceed with his aims without much opposition. Kant asks whether it is okay for the homeowner to lie in this instance in order to protect the loyal soldier from being seized and probably executed. Kant rejects such utilitarian calculations as being essentially amoral. He insists that we possess a categorical imperative always to tell the truth. When we begin to introduce exceptions and excuses, we open the door for people to invoke all manner of seemingly important considerations that undermine the ethical status of the principle against lying. People will then tell just as much of the truth that seems to be in their interest or in the public good. These judgments then become merely relative, and as a result it becomes difficult to know whether others are in fact speaking the whole truth or not. Kant argues that we ought to be able to universalize the maxims that guide our actions. Some followers of Kant have adopted a softer version of Kant's position. They have argued that all that we are required to do ethically is to act in keeping with maxims that we could will that all those similarly situated would likewise invoke. In this situation, we could then find an ethical justification for telling white lies by assuming that others placed in the same setting as the homeowner might find it acceptable to deceive in order to protect the loyal soldier. I think this modification goes too far from Kant's position. It allows for the introduction of various relative cost/benefit considerations. The contemporary moral philosopher Sissela Bok (1978) defends a stance very close to Kant's when she argues that it is morally wrong to lie except in cases where life or survival is clearly at stake.

I think a case can be made that both Kant and his utilitarian critics see dilemmas like this with too fixed a focus. They assume that the homeowner is allowed to give only one answer. But is this assumption valid? While the homeowner is considering how to answer, would it not only be possible but also desirable for him to ask a series of questions of his own? Could he not only inquire about the enemy soldier's objectives, his name, and his background but also about other topics, about whether he has been looking for a long time and how far he is from home? The homeowner might begin by not answering and then answering by talking about extraneous matters such as the weather or difficult conditions of the roads at this time of year. He might refer in general terms to his very strong cousin whom he is expecting at some point of time that is as yet unclear. Even in Kantian terms, strictures against lying do not require that we reveal secret information to others unless that information is of legitimate and vital concern to others (Bok 1983). In broader Kantian terms, the homeowner might respond to his interlocutor by silence, by extraneous talk, by evasion, and/or by asking questions of his own without having to lie directly. To be sure, these verbal tactics may not work any better than straight lying in getting the enemy off the track. However, they give fuller appreciation of the fact that these interactions occur over time and that those involved often have opportunities to raise as well as to answer questions.

If we approach this dilemma with too fixed a focus, we seem to be presented with either/or solutions, neither of which appears morally acceptable: We either defend lying to protect against the potential wrong of seizing someone we wish to protect or we insist on truth telling but then seem to make the homeowner into an unwilling accomplice of an immoral act. Alternatively, looking at this dilemma from several different perspectives, we can propose several alternative responses—silence, extraneous chatter, and questions of his own—that are consciously evasive. These constitute a number of ways of acting that can legitimately take place between the initial question and a full and complete answer. This time provides an opportunity for the homeowner to initiate actions of his own, which might include calling upon neighbors, rattling the enemy soldier, and stalling until someone else happens along the street. These evasive tactics may well work so that the homeowner in the end can remain a not-lying truth-teller as well as a clever defender. But, we can still ask, whether evasive responses are really excusable if not legitimate. Clearly, if our responses to others are always evasive, then we undermine our relations with others. We fail to take them seriously. Moreover, not to provide answers to legitimate questions is equivalent to lying, especially if we hold information that is vital to their legitimate interests. Temporarily, however, evasion may be a justifiable tactic. It can be challenged by others if, as in protracted negotiations, it means that we are not bargaining in good faith. But it also buys time during which we can explore alternative responses to difficult choices. One of the primary problems with the way this question about truth telling was originally posed was that it focused so fixedly on choosing between particular alternative answers that it failed to envision alternative ways of answering as part of timely but time-consuming ongoing conversations.

At times we indeed face dilemmas that require either/or decisions—but not always or as often as we frequently are led to believe. With a lively imagination, we can frequently turn either/or questions into both/and answers. Often we can do this by finding a new alternative that represents a creative synthesis of the posed opposites. Both the philosophers Hegel (1956) and Kierkegaard (1941) explored ways to discover solutions to deeply engrained oppositions by viewing alternatives as critical moments in developing processes that led at other critical moments in time to creative new syntheses. Finding apt answers was not, from their perspective, just a matter of reasoning well and creatively. It was also a timely exercise in exploring the possibilities of the moment, which typically differ from those of previous and subsequent times.

Among other traits, visionaries are people who can sense possibilities where others see mutually unappealing alternatives. They are people who can read the "signs of the time" (Vatican II 1965). Reading the signs of the time means sensing both what can now be done, even though we previously thought it could not, as well as sensing what cannot now be done, even though we feel it should be. We appropriately celebrate real innovators: people who sense new opportunities. In response to the suggestions of the Rev. Leon Sullivan, one of their board members, General Motors developed a new strategy for their businesses in South Africa in the mid-1970s. They found an alternative between simply abiding by the apartheid laws, which they considered unjust, and selling off these plants and investments. They decided to continue their businesses but to ignore a number of the apartheid regulations regarding interracial work forces, interracial promotions, and interracial housing. Technically this was a corporate act of civil disobedience for which they could be prosecuted by the South African government. To protect themselves against such actions and to further the cause that they had now embarked upon, General Motors solicited the support of other North American firms with businesses in South Africa. After a few years several hundred firms had adopted the Sullivan principles. This was an innovative response to a difficult dilemma.

It is not always possible to be quite so innovative. By the late 1980s a number of people felt this compromise was too compromised. The political climate in South Africa was changing. In order to help bring about a true end to apartheid, increased political and economic pressure from outsiders seemed desirable. At this point in time even Rev. Sullivan urged the divestment of South African holdings as a way of forcing political change in South Africa. To see with a lively moral eye is to be able to recognize when certain kinds of action are timely and when they are not. To be morally blind is to view issues like these out of time.

When organizations lack vision, it often seems more difficult to accomplish assigned tasks and impossible to take on anything new. Organization members look at their resources and assignments with fixed gazes. Other departments, divisions, and individuals appear as antagonists ready to gobble up scarce resources and opportunities. Accordingly, units often divert a goodly portion of their energies to protect themselves against this threat and to advance their own interests (Ackerman 1975, ch. 4; Jackall 1988). What happens when vision is absent is well illustrated by events at a medium-size university. The president felt comfortable with a collegial style of leadership. Rather than dominating meetings, he allotted much time for deans and other administrators to state their views. He wanted to be a low-keyed consensus-builder. As funds became scarcer, departments became more defensive and wary. Cuts would have to be made somewhere. Where? The executive council called into existence two high-level committees: one to consider ways of containing costs and enhancing revenues and another to establish university priorities. The first committee invoked lofty rhetoric but came across no models to help them sort out their assignment. The second committee considered various criteria for gauging priorities but in the end ranked departments by assigning them grades from A through D. Needless to say, in a university setting, the departments with below-average grades were outraged. These committees attempted as best they could to manage the difficult issues the university faced. Their failures did not result from lack of goodwill and intelligence. The problem in large part was that they were just sorting and re-sorting existing information in a setting where most of the alternatives seemed unappealing to most and too self-aggrandizing for a few. What they all lacked was an imaginative vision of their shared sense of what it was that they were all about.

Some organizations possess this kind of vision about themselves. Essentially they are able to articulate a clear sense of the particular good(s) that they as organizations have the special competence to realize and enhance (Selznick 1957). Good visionary leaders help organizations to understand this about themselves. They are able in engaging ways to identify the organization's common good. Organizations can sometimes do this for themselves, often with the assistance of consultants who can help top administrators and others see more clearly what they value in common. Articulating a common vision is not always possible, but when it does happen, a number of corollary experiences often occur. To the extent that this vision is real and not just idealistic dreaming, units within the organization often feel that much less defensive and competitive. They see themselves through the vision as being integral to realizing objectives they and other organizational members both value and feel skilled to accomplish as they draw upon their different but complementary talents and resources. Correspondingly, they feel that they can spend less time trying to defend and expand their turfs and more time realizing their part in the organization's overall objectives. With a clear and appealing vision, they sometimes can do even more. Energy that had been diverted into organizational politics and careerism is freed for other purposes that may well bring with them the added sense of esteem connected with being part of what seem to be genuinely worthy projects (Westley 1992; Weisbrod 1992).

Imagination is the critical ingredient for any vision. Without imagination issues become polarized. Organization members caucus to defend their own interests and expose the weaknesses of competitors. Issues increasingly seem posed in exclusive either/or categories. Often this lack of imagination is rooted in the fixed ways people look at the concerns that confront them. Marshall McLuhan (1962, 1964) argued that the problem is that people look at issues in too linear a fashion. This hypothesis, however, seems too simplistic. It is more accurate to argue that people lack vision because they cannot imagine alternative possibilities. But this formulation just restates the problem. It is more helpful, I think, to assume that we fail to see the "signs of our time," to see opportunities in our difficulties, because we fail to look at our circumstances from enough different angles. Harvard Medical School professor Harold Gardner argues that humans possess and can cultivate at least seven different, distinct forms of intelligence. He identifies these as numerical, linguistic, artistic, physical, spatial, personal, and social (Gardner 1983). By bringing an additional form of intelligence to bear upon particular problems, we may well be able to see possibilities and not just problems. Looking with other forms of intelligence may not provide answers; however, it may enable us to see possibilities we overlooked and it may put familiar problems in new light in ways that occasion new observations and ways of seeing. From this perspective we can become partially morally blind not by not perceiving issues and not because our vision is distorted but because our seeing lacks vision and imagination. Because we see things too exclusively from particular points of view, too fixedly in terms of given habits of mind, and too statically in relation to future possibilities, issues become protracted and alternatives become polarized.

Lack of Engagement

Often our viewing of moral concerns becomes dim and dull because we are looking at matters only as detached observers or as affected sufferers rather than as agents and participants. Either we do not see ourselves as part of the picture or we see ourselves passively, almost as if we were puppets pushed and pulled by others. If we see ourselves as only acting in our organizations in keeping with scripts developed by others rather than as actors as well as script editors and revisers, then we are likely to misperceive problems and overlook opportunities.

When it concerns human problems that affect our own lives, mathematical and linguistic problem-solving abilities are not sufficient. After reviewing a wide number of experiments and studies, the neurologist Antonio Damasio (1994) demonstrated that people with otherwise good to excellent cognitive abilities are unable to deal with perplexities in their own lives if the parts of their brains controlling emotions have been damaged. The rational abilities of these persons, which tested high in ordinary paper-and-pencil tests, were unable to help them address personal and social problems. Damasio writes:

There is a particular region in the human brain where the systems concerned with emotion/feeling, attention, and working memory interact so intimately that they constitute the source for the energy of both external action (movement) and internal action (thought animation, reasoning).

Without a sense of active personal involvement, it is often very difficult to think about problems in ways that make them seem solvable.

Karl Marx and several of his followers understood this problem particularly well. They referred to it as the problem of false consciousness. Their insights were occasioned by the frustrations they experienced in their not-always-successful attempts to organize workers to take active roles to change for the better the circumstances of their own laboring. Marx argued that many industrial workers were alienated because they failed to recognize the ways in which the economic value of the organizations for which they labored was in large part produced by their own efforts. In a mind set Marx referred to as the fetish of commodities, they saw economic value in money or in things they made rather than in the laboring that transformed otherwise only potentially useful matter into usable and valued commodities. Marx also complained that workers failed to see themselves as collectively producing historical developments through their overall interactions (Marx 1906, 1963; Marx and Engels 1947). Lenin (1963) elaborated on these themes in an early essay called "What Is to Be Done," where he argued that industrial workers too often develop what he described as a "trade union mentality" because they have such small ambitions: They seek only to increase their wages and/or to improve their working conditions rather than combine together actively to democratize the workplace and to democratize society. Having made this observation, Lenin then proceeded in an autocratic and undemocratic fashion to justify forming a hierarchically controlled party that would inform and persuade workers of their real interests, which the latter seemed unable to grasp on their own. Marx and Lenin were correct to observe that many organizational members regard themselves passively as observers or sufferers affected by the decisive actions of others. Marx and Lenin were also perceptive enough to recognize that organizational members, by their collective dissents or strikes, could temporarily bring pressure to bear to produce changes that seemed fairer. Marx and Lenin were wrong insofar as they felt it was appropriate for them to inform industrial workers of their real interests and insofar as in the name of workplace democracy they justified oppressive forms of control by state or party bureaucrats.

Although there may be good reasons for adopting a passive attitude, this resignation prevents us from seeing the real but perhaps less dramatic ways in which we both contribute to the current circumstances by choosing to play our parts the way we do and could alter these circumstances by changing the ways we play them. Many of us feel like the protagonist of Albert Camus' novel *The Fall*, who felt conscience-stricken because he witnessed and did not act to prevent a suicide attempt. We experience ourselves similarly witnessing disasters and unfortunate turns of events but do nothing except perhaps to confess, if we are morally sensitive, our own sense of moral impotence (Camus 1956). Camus' protagonist reflects the author's own anguished sense of impotence with respect to the social changes affecting Algeria, where Camus was born. In the 1950s Algeria was moving toward national independence from France. Although Camus sympathized with the social aspirations of the Algerian people, he found repugnant the terrorist tactics used by the independence movement. The increasingly militant stance taken by both sides of the nationalist issue left little room for reasonable, liberal discussions and negotiations. As he had been active in the resistance movement during the Second World War, Camus would have preferred to take an active, engaged part in the social and political transformations of Algeria. However, he seemed to be reduced to the role of a helpless, inactive, and correspondingly guilty observer. Sometimes, and with respect to particular issues, we may have no other options. But that rarely happens, as Camus himself testified in other works. In the novel *The Plague* especially, he argued that we can find ways to fight against the social, cultural, and physical pestilences that threaten our communities (Camus 1947). Even as he was writing *The Fall*, Camus was not just a passive observer of the events unfolding in Algeria. He had become an articulate protestor of the self-destructive ways in which his fellow Algerians were destroying each other because of the uncompromising positions they took.

Camus was an impassioned and engaged observer. Unlike the protagonist of his novel *The Stranger*, who seemed to possess no affect or care for his mother, the man he accidentally killed, or his own death, Camus (1942) felt deeply moved by what he saw. He saw also that there were many different ways to resist forces of destruction and human denial. One could attempt to heal the wounded, educate the ignorant, and undermine aggressors. One could collaborate with reformers or protest wrong. In his major philosophic work *The Rebel* especially he explored the different responses taken by Europeans in modern times to overcome injustice and expand freedom. People did not need to detach themselves. If they did, they would end up strangers to themselves, like the central subject of *The Stranger*. If nothing else, they could at least protest and confess their own limitations and thereby establish some bonds of compassion and understanding with others similarly situated (Camus 1951).

CONCLUSION: WHEN IS IT RIGHT AND WHEN IS IT WRONG TO BE MORALLY BLIND?

Moral blindness assumes a number of characteristic forms. We are morally blind to the degree that we fail to perceive moral concerns, to the extent we see these concerns with a distorted vision, and to the degree that our viewing remains fixed, dull, and unengaged.

Even though the case against moral blindness seems as self-evident as the cases against moral silence and moral deafness, still it is instructive to examine both the reasons why it is wrong to be morally blind and the exceptions. As with the previous discussions of moral silence and deafness, I think we misperceive these phenomena if we regard them as merely exceptional forms of behavior of which only a few others are guilty. From time to time most people will occasionally fall into these moral failings. My concern from the outset is to help us find ways of recognizing and limiting the extent to which we perpetuate these deficiencies.

At least four different arguments can be made against moral blindness. One, from a utilitarian perspective, moral blindness is wrong because of the harm to which it gives rise. Morally blind people overlook important issues, fail to foresee the untoward consequences of otherwise benign actions, and squander organizational resources on internal squabbles because they lack a vision of the organization's good. Because I consider other consequences in the next chapter, I do not elaborate on these consequential arguments here except to observe that moral blindness occasions consequences that are both harmful and organizationally costly.

Two, from a pragmatic perspective, moral blindness is wrong because it is simply unrealistic. It is unrealistic not to acknowledge our own involvements, not to foresee the consequences of our acts, not to be on the lookout for stereotypes, and not to look at problems from several different points of view. It is unrealistic as well not to recognize the moral expectations that shape organizational interactions. To be genuinely realistic, we must not only recognize the limits but also the extent to what is possible. Earlier this century a number of moral realists attempted to puncture the naive presumptions of moral idealists, who thought that science, reason, democracy, and goodwill would together lead humans toward a morally superior future. Repeatedly the moral realists argued that it is irresponsible to aim for objectives that cannot be fulfilled easily. People instead ought to embrace realizable ideals. The realists argued that people invoke lofty, impractical ideals more often because they want thereby to witness to their own virtuous sentiments than because they want in a realistic manner to work toward constructive change. The realists called for sober and practical social assessments. From the perspective of their critics, moral realists appeared too often in the role of apologists for the current social and political arrangements. The issue is: What is really possible? It can be just as unrealistic to seek to undertake social or organizational reforms with insufficient resources as it is to refrain from any reforms without imaginatively exploring all possibilities. It is just as unrealistic to underestimate obstacles and difficulties as it is to underestimate the benefits to be gained from heightened motivations, greater cooperation, and less conflict.

Three, from a purposive perspective, moral blindness is wrong because it obstructs the possibilities for moral learning. By means of our seeing, recognizing, acknowledging, perceiving, and viewing, we learn in several different ways. Potentially, we not only acquire knowledge but we also gain in understanding, insight, and wisdom. Because the world around us is continuously changing and because we continuously encounter organizations, people, and problems we have not met before, if we are not learning, we will become more helpless, less tuned to the world around us, and less aware of our own limitations and potentials.

Four, moral blindness is wrong because it fosters and perpetuates self-deception. If we misperceive what others are doing, if we fail to foresee the direction of current practices, if we accept distorted accounts from others as real, and if we fail to recognize the moral expectations of our organizational environment, we are correspondingly going to run amiss in our self-perceptions. It is impossible to retain a fully lucid and accurate account of our own moral character at the same time that our moral vision is impaired with respect to others.

Although the case against moral blindness is very strong, I can think of at least two settings in which a measure of moral blindness seems excusable, if not acceptable. In both of these settings permissible expressions of moral blindness are temporary and tactical. Thus, in the first instance it is justifiable at least temporarily not to look too closely at certain phenomena in order to focus more sharply and closely at others. We cannot look everywhere at once. We cannot pay attention to anything unless we focus our sight. Putting something in focus, however, involves taking other things out of focus. If we are going to look closely at future probabilities, we may temporarily have to examine less closely other matters such as our own involvements or other ancillary issues. If we hope to achieve a really good sense of one concern, we may need to stay with it for a while and let other issues bide their time. Nevertheless, because we cannot clearly and fully see anything unless we focus, we are always vulnerable to overlooking something as our focus shifts. Therefore, we need to build in ways of regularly reviewing not only to keep track of familiar concerns but also to be alert to emergent ones. In this case the excuse for temporary blindness becomes at the same time a reminder for the need to recognize and re-vision because of the high probability that the very process of focusing will lead us to be blind-sided with respect to moral issues, concerns, possibilities, and limits that make a difference. There are no conceptual spectacles and no visual exercises that can eliminate this possibility. We cannot be ever-vigilant, even though this sounds high-minded and virtuous, because we all need breaks and retreats and because we must from time to time focus more sharply and for longer periods on particular concerns. The continuously networking manager may keep herself fairly well informed (Kotter 1988). Still, if she is going to exercise vision and perspective and understand matters in depth, she must focus.

The second case for justifiable moral blindness is more a matter of appearance than reality. Frequently for tactical reasons it is useful temporarily to overlook moral failings in oneself and in others. Focusing too hard and too long on particular problems often causes us to lose perspective. It might be argued that overlooking wrongs and mistakes is a way of guarding against another manifestation of excessively fixed focus. After all, most of us are tempted at times to dwell on fallings and failings, especially when they are unexpected, or they give us opportunities to crow at others, we feel especially caught out, or we are soliciting sympathy. Depending on our own personal dispositions, we may dwell excessively either on the speck in the other's eye or the speck in our own. We can indeed become overly preoccupied with particular failings in ways that make too much of these matters and divert us from other concerns. In such instances, we might then argue that it is useful to overlook some of these issues. What is really critical in these cases can be seen by examining the difference between forgiving and forgetting. To forget is to act as if something never happened. To forget is to develop amnesia or retrospective blindness. We do this all the time with respect to small, insignificant errors and mistakes because they don't matter. We may attempt to do this as well with larger, more troubling accidents and wrongs. We may rationalize that no good purpose is served by putting someone into a lot of trouble over an incident that is now past. Why rehash and expose all the old hurts? When we forgive, we assume a different strategy because we do not forget or act retrospectively blind. We don't act as if nothing happened, as if no mistakes have occurred. We acknowledge errors and reflectively attempt to learn from them. For tactical reasons, however, we do not call attention to them. We acknowledge instead the value of the ongoing collaborative efforts and institutional commitments. In this sense forgiving is like an act of mutual face-saving in which those involved tacitly or explicitly acknowledge the errors or mistakes but temporarily focus on dealing with the problems and opportunities at hand and restoring the working relationships and institutional connections. We can, of course, forgive our own errors as well as those of others. However, forgiving well is an art. We do not forgive by forgetting nor do we forgive when we dwell too much on particular failings. It is necessary that we recognize and acknowledge and signal this even while we focus attention on getting on with the tasks and prospects of the moment. In a way this kind of overlooking is the exception that proves the rule. In this case what appears as momentary or tactical blindness is not really an example of moral sightlessness at all.

There are a number of settings where this moral overlooking can be called for in business and organizational interactions. Organizations sometimes publicly adopt this tactic with partners and collaborators in order to work at maintaining their working relationships even while they may privately acknowledge errors and mistakes in their past dealings. Occasionally, when organizational members have been caught violating in minor ways organizational guidelines respecting uses of office supplies, business expenses, conflicts of interest, and unprofessional conduct in relation to other employees, it is wise to deal candidly with these matters at a private and confidential level while publicly diverting attention away. Making too great a scene about these concerns typically does not act to deter others. Rather the usual response is to encourage people to become even more zealous in their efforts to cover up. However, these are clearly exceptional cases. Moreover, those involved in these tactical maneuvers are not really morally blind. They see but without a fixed focus.

CHAPTER 5

Consequences of Moral Silence, Deafness, and Blindness

In the three preceding chapters, we have looked at different expressions of moral silence, moral deafness, and moral blindness. These represent three different but interrelated deficiencies with respect to the corresponding moral virtues of speaking up for moral concerns; attentively being ready to respond to moral issues; and being able to perceive, recognize, and acknowledge moral realities. Moral silence, deafness, and blindness are vices. Like any other vices, these identify shortcomings gauged in relation to their corresponding virtues. They differ from other vices, such as intemperance, timidity, foolhardiness, greediness, imprudence, and spitefulness, because they describe ways people recognize and communicate about moral concerns rather than any particular concerns as such. The corresponding virtues of moral sight, hearing, and discourse are basic to moral life, no matter what other particular virtues—such as justice, compassion, industry, or honesty—people honor. As a consequence, these vices in a correspondingly destabilizing way undermine moral responsiveness and communication. These vices are morally desensitizing. They render individuals insensitive, unattuned, apathetic, and silent with respect to moral concerns of whatever kind.

This chapter examines the consequences of these vices. It looks first at the impact of these vices both generally and on organizational life in particular. Chapter 6 then analyzes the causes that give rise to these vices. With an eye to what might be done to reduce and overcome these vices and their attendant consequences, Chapter 6 indicates the ways particular cultural, individual, and organizational characteristics give rise to them.

The major problem with these vices is that they reproduce themselves, creating, extending, and reinforcing moral apathy and insensitivity. Each of these vices is both the primary cause and the consequence of the correlative vices. As people become blind to moral concerns, they correspondingly become inattentive and silent. Their deafness leaves them unable to correct for or recognize their blind spots and distorted seeing. Their inarticulateness and silence means that others are never called upon to attend to or see moral issues in the first place.

We can see how these vices re-create and support each other by reviewing a simple example. In this case an organization faced a problem because employees had reached a point where they were appropriating excessive amounts of company resources for their personal uses. The problem began innocently enough with liberal policies that allowed employees a measure of discretion in using company supplies, vehicles, phone lines, computers, secretarial services, and labs. Many of the employees were well-educated professionals or semiprofessionals and shared a common sense of commitment to the mission of the company. Many worked very long hours and took their work home with them. The liberal policies made sense. However, individuals gradually took advantage of the situation. Company vehicles were employed for personal use. Managers arranged for company technicians to help them with household problems. Expense accounts were padded and submitted even when no company business was involved. While ostensibly working for their company, some individuals used their offices and company time to manage private businesses of their own. In several cases the amount of time involved with their private businesses exceeded or almost equalled what they devoted to the company's business. These changes occurred incrementally. Exceptional uses of company resources by individuals, justified by particular circumstances, were cited to rationalize regular or at least occasional uses. Given the team-spiritedness of the company, what were originally excused as executive privileges were claimed as well in a discretionary way by many lower executives and middle managers. Several people were overextending their privileges and fudging on the rules. Privately, they found ways either for rationalizing their own actions as excusable or for regarding them as so trivial that they could easily be overlooked. Nobody is perfect after all. A number of managers involved in these practices took a more open position and declared that these kinds of opportunities and privileges were among the entitlements they deserved as professionals and as hard-working, long-time employees who had contributed to the company's develop-ment and expansion. Overall the situation was a bit soft and mushy. Many people were aware that the uses of discretion had been overextended. In individual cases, however, they either chose not to say anything because a friend was involved or they felt implicated, or they were not sure just where to draw the line. In many cases they simply did not see what was going on or chose not to investigate surface indications further.

In this case moral silence gave rise to and received support from moral deafness and moral blindness. People who were concerned chose not to speak up, partly because they felt that they too had been involved and partly because they were not clear about the issues. The questions raised by those who were concerned were typically not heard or not answered. They received replies that spoke of company traditions and professional discretion. Many did not recognize that the company as such endorsed any moral standards bearing on these practices, did not wish to look at the consequences of these practices on the long-term well-being of the corporation, or did not wish to acknowledge their own involvement. Because many people did not see any moral issues, they neither spoke up nor comprehended the queries of those who expressed concern. Because many people failed to hear their concerns, others either failed to speak up or gave up in their attempts to raise questions or to point to what they considered abusive. Because managers who were morally concerned about these practices failed to voice their views and questions recognizably, others never heard or were not able to comprehend the extent to which acceptable practices had become abused.

Potentially, a number of moral issues were at stake in this situation. Even though it was clear that some employees were using company resources excessively for personal use, it could also be argued that the company itself had not explored adequately enough the fitting ways of allocating rewards, opportunities, tasks, and burdens among and between its professional and nonprofessional employees. Rather than looking closely at the proper way of managing its explicit and implicit contractual relations with its highly skilled professionals, it had attempted to avoid having to do so through team spirit and generally liberal attitudes. Did some abuses arise because individuals were not being properly rewarded, compared to others, for their extensive efforts? Or, was the issue really one of being too permissive and not taking supervisory responsibilities seriously enough? The point is that these and other moral questions might have been raised but were not. For a long time a number of people felt increasingly uneasy about the way these practices were evolving but hardly any concern was recognizably and clearly voiced or heard when it was. Moral silence, deafness, and blindness occasion and succeed each other in such a way that in many organizational settings people become accustomed to acting as if moral issues just didn't arise.

Aside from observing that these vices reproduce each other in ways that foster moral insensitivity, we can indicate six other direct consequences of moral silence, deafness, and blindness for organizational life. These consequences are outlined in Table 5.1 and are addressed over the rest of this chapter.

MORAL WRONGS AND MORAL ISSUES ARE NOT ADDRESSED

As a result of moral silence and its associated vices businesses and organizations fail to attend to wrongs and moral issues, often with costly results. Because they are morally mute, organizational members fail to alert organizations with respect to problems and concerns, and they fail to dissent audibly from policies they consider morally questionable. Because they are morally deaf, they are not prepared to respond to bad news or to seek out further information with respect to potentially bad news. Because they are morally blind, they fail to perceive issues and concerns, they fail to recognize fully and clearly the moral dimensions of organizational life, and they fail to foresee the morally questionable consequences of current practices. Moral silence, deafness, and blindness are costly. I have already cited a number of examples where some combination of these vices meant that actions were not taken in a timely fashion to identify and stop practices that eventually proved costly to the organization and/or dangerous or damaging to others. As consequences of the moral silence, deafness, and/or blindness of organizational members, businesses have failed to detect and cease the production and marketing of faulty or dangerous products, to recognize and correct excessively risky practices, to identify and apprehend individuals making abusive use of organizational information and resources, and to alert themselves in due time to the untoward consequences of current practices they have not fully and thoughtfully examined. These failures have been costly. Customers have been hurt and in some cases died. Environments have been damaged. Businesses have had to pay enormous costs after the fact to reimburse those harmed and to seek favorable court judgments. Although we cannot be certain how things would have turned out if people with consciences had spoken up more audibly and articulately, listened more attentively, and/or seen with greater clarity, vision, and lively sight, we can reasonably conjecture that matters would have turned out much better. Accordingly, a strong case can be made that smart business sense would lead business organizations to want to confront these problems and to find ways to overcome them.

It is as if businesspeople attempted to discuss the intricacies of their work with the vocabularies of first graders. They could talk about many of the issues that concerned them but would be hard pressed to explain—much less understand or recognize—many of the problems they must address regarding finance, human resource management, subcontracting, and purchasing. Concerns would be overly simplified. Many issues would become invisible. As in negotiations between people using different languages, many concerns would become inexpressible. When people act morally mute, deaf, and blind, they effectively reduce the vocabularies in relation to which they can identify, interpret, and address problems arising in business. With reduced vocabularies they become less responsive on a day-to-day basis to what are at the moment ordinary everyday moral concerns. To be sure, most of the time they remain responsive to crises. In spite of the degree to which businesspeople may suffer from moral silence, blindness, and deafness regarding day to day activities, they often retain an ability to see and know how to respond to fundamental crises. Many problems, however, would not become crises if they had been addressed sooner. Many crises are not handled well and many lesser issues are not addressed at all because people are attempting to communicate about them with decisively reduced vocabularies.

Table 5.1
Consequences of Moral Silence, Deafness, and Blindness

Consequences	Associated Forms of Moral Silence, Deafness, and Blindness
Wrongs and moral issues are not addressed.	Not blowing the whistle (2)* Not dissenting Not being ready to hear bad news (3) Not seeking out bad news (3) Not perceiving issues (4) Not foreseeing issues (4)
Accountability problems are aggravated.	Not blowing the whistle (2) Not bargaining hard (2) Not providing adequate feedback (2) Not comprehending issues (3) Not taking into account the account of others (3) Stereotyping (4)
Moral stress is increased.	Camouflaging moral concerns (2) Increased self-deception (2,3,4)
Moral resources are ignored and neglected.	Not speaking up for ideals (2) Lack of attentiveness (3) Lack of vision, imagination, and engagement (4)
Extraneous transactional costs are increased.	All of the above
The role of ethics is marginalized and confused.	All of the above

*Refers to number of the chapter where this topic is discussed.

With reduced vocabularies people become reluctant to raise questions and enter into discussions with others. As a result they are much less likely to dissent or counter current practices about which they may have serious doubts. In the absence of discursive communication with others, people are much more likely to imitate the conduct of others around them and follow the directions of superiors even though they doubt the fittingness and rightness of what they are doing. A research experiment conducted in the early 1970s illustrates this tendency. The researcher placed want ads in the paper and then arranged appointments with unsuspecting subjects who came to a waiting room at a designated time to find two other people waiting. The other two were assistants of the researcher but appeared also to be waiting. After the subject had been waiting for a period of time, the two others began to take off their clothes without talking. In many cases the subject, without saying anything, did so as well even though there was no instruction from the researcher to do so (Frank 1988).

ACCOUNTABILITY IS AGGRAVATED

Moral silence and its associated vices additionally aggravate problems of accountability. We can best see how these vices affect patterns of accountability by first examining what is involved when people hold each other accountable. Organizations seek to hold their members, constituents, and stakeholders accountable in several different ways, depending upon the character of their relationships. When we hold people accountable, we seek to make sure that they act in keeping with promises and agreements they have made. However elaborate the auditing practices, we hold people accountable by using some means to determine how well they are performing, gauged in relation to expectations established by prior understandings, contracts, or arrangements. We hold others accountable through performance appraisals, internal and external audits, departmental reviews, and contract renegotiations as well as through informal inquiries.

Although we often think of the activity of holding others accountable as a one-way process by which supervisors check on the performance of subordi-nates, in principle this is a two-way, reciprocating activity in which both parties to any agreement or understanding check on how well the others are living up to their expectations. For example, if a supervisor gives a subordinate a special assignment, such as organizing a special training session for part of the sales force, the supervisor then holds the subordinate accountable by periodically checking on the latter's plans and progress. The latter can also check on how well the supervisor has acted to provide the conditions and resources that the subordinate requested in order to perform the task as expected (Culbert and McDonough 1980). We hold others accountable in relation to prior agreements and promises. The latter are inherently reciprocal. Just as others are consenting to perform certain tasks or to act in particular ways, so we also are promising, whether explicitly or implicitly, to do our part. The latter may involve rewarding others when they complete their tasks, providing suitable settings where they can undertake their work, not interfering with their activities, and making designated resources accessible for them.

Although at its core holding others accountable is a simple, albeit reciprocal, activity, it is possible to identify five distinct elements involved in this process. Often we focus on a few of these and fail to give sufficient attention to the others. I will discuss each briefly in order to show how moral silence and its associated vices aggravate problems of accountability. One, we establish criteria by which we audit others. A number of issues arise in relation to these criteria. The criteria may become too detailed or too broad. They may focus excessively on output or on process. They may not fully be comprehended or they may be interpreted differently by the parties involved. They may be one-sided: They may be spelled out for one party but not for the other. Two, we provide methods for auditing how well others perform. An extensive range of options is possible. We can use unannounced spot checks, formal appraisals, anonymous surveys, informants, interviews, secondhand accounts from other relevant observers, the reports of confidential whistle-blowers, and financial and organizational audits, as well as informal and formal accounts by the other. One concern regarding auditing procedures is whether we are attempting to utilize one or several different types of probe. Any one auditing probe comes with its own focus and perspective. Often it is useful to supplement these with others to obtain a fuller, more lively accounting. Three, we need to arrange for means both to verify these audits as well as to challenge them. No audit is perfect and fail-safe. It may overemphasize particular criteria. It may look too much at overt results and not enough at less observable conduct. It may rely too heavily on particular sources of information. Those being audited need to be able to review the audits and to challenge both their descriptive assessments and their interpretations of these. We need to provide arenas to resolve disputes that may arise in the process. Four, we need to identify and find ways of implementing reasonable and fair sanctions and rewards. The procedures for identifying and hearing the cases of people who violate agreements must be fair. The rewards and punishments should be fitting. Finally, we need to establish means for reviewing and changing accountability procedures and criteria. In order to be kept up-to-date, systems of accountability need to be reviewed and adjusted. Are they performing as well as expected? If not, they need to be modified and changed.

Every accountability system is a web of interacting communications. The parties involved communicate to establish criteria, to audit each other, to verify and challenge their audits, to reward and sanction, and to adjust and change the overall process. Any particular system of accountability works only as well as the communications that are integral to it. A system of accountability that is overtly one-way will be less effective than one that is two-way. One that provides only one means of auditing and little opportunity for discussion will be less reliable and less well-regarded than one that utilizes several auditing procedures and welcomes discussion.

Probably the most effective accountability systems are the ones that mix formal and informal procedures in ways that allow for occasional probes as well as regular, more formal audits. This might be illustrated by the ways good partners or colleagues keep track of each other's work. Initially, they attempt to be clear about what they expect of each other, often communicating this as much through verbal cues as through more formal written agreements. Furthermore, they continuously interpret and adjust these understandings as they become familiar with each other's particular competencies and weaknesses in relation to their collaborative objectives. They audit each other regularly by reviewing verbally what each has done, by considering objective financial or production measures, by attending to what those involved say about the work that is being done, and by asking questions and making inquiries. They also periodically stop what they are doing, step back from the ongoing flow of work, and take stock of how things are going. They may order some formal auditing probes for these sessions and seek out the counsel of reliable third parties in order to avoid mis-seeing or mis-hearing something important because they are too close to matters at hand. They will consider their results as part of give-and-take assessments in which they will be especially interested in gauging the quality of the partnership itself. Much of the auditing occurs as part of regular, everyday communications as the partners express concerns about activities that fall below expectations, offer suggestions on how to deal with factors that give rise to these shortcomings, propose new demands, and respond to criticisms. Formal auditing probes of several kinds are consulted regularly as well as more formal appraisals. Taking account of the others as a result is rarely regarded as a one-way policing activity. It is simply seen as a dimension of ongoing interactions whereby the partners seek to keep track of what is going on, to offer critical yet instructive assessments, and to do so reciprocally, checking their own accounts and interpretations against those of their partners. To the degree that partners remain open to each other and have been able to generate an atmosphere of trust, these accounting procedures serve as means of keeping in touch rather than ways of trying to uncover untold secrets.

This is an ideal picture. Still, each partner must regularly take account of what the other is doing. In these kinds of face-to-face relationships, however, much of the auditing, verifying, challenging, sanctioning, and adjusting takes place on an ongoing basis rather than through formal probes. The latter are in fact often regarded more as resources to be consulted rather than the accountability system itself. Accountability systems become integrated with regular interactions in large part because the communications between partners assume so many forms at so many different levels. When communications are not so regular and reciprocal, not at once both formal and informal, and not characterized by as much openness and trust, accountability systems typically become more formal and distinct. Greater emphasis is placed upon regularly commissioned audits and appraisals. More attention is devoted to securing objective accounts and to searching for hidden information and more energy channelled into protecting potentially embarrassing information that people do not wish to be disclosed.

Accountability systems become aggravated when they do not do what they are expected to do in a timely and reliable manner. Dysfunctional accountability systems manifest the following symptoms. One, they do not allow us to know what the others are really doing. Instead of clear, accurate, and relevant information, we possess only a rough sense of what others are in fact doing. Two, they do not encourage and allow us to inform the others about what we expect and need from them. The others lack a clear sense of our assessments of how our relationships are working and what we expect them to do. Three, audits and probes provide, at best, restricted accounts and serve largely to police. They do not provide occasions for mutual learning and adjustments. Four, accountability systems possess little respect and regard. As a result, people often cooperate with them only begrudgingly as onerous obligations. Because they trust them only minimally, they are also likely to withhold information they think may be misconstrued.

An aggravated accountability system is one in which the flow of information between parties is stilted, restricted, often obstructed, and distorted. Although they are rarely fully dysfunctional, the accountability systems of many organizations exhibit a number of the signs of aggravation just listed. Most fall below the model of the ideal partners. Formal audits and appraisals often provide at best static, limited accounts of what others are doing with few explanations for why these are happening as they are. Many people regard these periodic probes with a mixture of trepidation, hostility, and fantasy, hoping that well-kept secrets won't be betrayed and that information obtained won't be used against them and may somehow enhance their opportunities. Outside of formal collective bargaining settings, subordinates rarely communicate clearly about what they need and would like in order to realize what is expected of them. Too often auditing probes provide after-the-fact information rather than lively, reliable accounts of actual processes and activities. It is as if they keep people informed about the score of a football match but give no indication of how well the play was proceeding.

In several ways moral silence, deafness, and blindness aggravate these problems. One, to the extent that they are morally deaf, people become inattentive to concerns raised by others. They fail to pursue clues, follow tips, and investigate what lies behind surface disturbances. In this way they let matters slide. We have already reviewed a number of examples where pharmaceutical companies failed to investigate incident reports, where shipping companies failed to respond to concerns raised by their captains, and where supervisors failed to take seriously alarms raised by subordinates. Additionally, to the degree that auditing probes do not consider the accounts of those being audited, the latter will begin to distrust them. Subordinate employees and working units often treat with disdain the probes sent by senior administrators for them to fill out and complete. They seem to be intrusive instruments that require their time and energy to complete but offer them no real opportunities for learning or for communicating their own concerns in their own terms. Organizational members joke about the enormous piles of paper wasted for these ventures, which seem to them to possess little real benefit.

Two, to the extent that they are morally blind, people are likely to rely on static, stereotypical accounts of what others are doing. They treat audits as a means either of confirming what they already expect or as a means of uncovering people who are taking privileges with their discretionary opportunities. This view, although widely held, differs dramatically from the working arrangement of our ideal partners who regarded their ongoing audits of each other, which were largely informal, as a way of fostering collaboration and mutual adjustment.

Three, to the degree that people are morally mute, they are likely to aggravate accountability systems in several ways. They are not inclined to bargain assertively for their own points of view when the initiating agreements are being negotiated or renegotiated. Nor are they as likely to assert their own interpretations of these or to criticize directly or counter the feedback they receive. Consequently, accountability systems are prone to becoming one-way policing arrangements rather than opportunities for mutual tracking of each other. To the degree that they are morally mute, supervisors, partners, and contracting parties are less likely to provide full and candid feedback. As a result they leave the others with an unclear picture of where they really stand and how well they are doing. Insofar as they are affected by moral silence, individuals will be less likely to voice concern and raise questions about activities that seem questionable. Essentially, by remaining silent about these matters, they cut off many of the informal forms of communicating that augment and round any lively, reciprocating accountability system. Informal probes often consist of nothing more than queries and comments that invite clarifying responses and discussions. By not voicing these concerns, people de facto reduce accountability systems until they become not much more than formal auditing measures. By variously curtailing and channelling communications, moral silence and its associated vices aggravate accountability systems, which work best to the degree that communications are open, lively, multileveled, and reciprocal.

MORAL STRESS IS INCREASED

Moral silence and its correlative vices exacerbate the problems of moral stress. Managers experience moral stress when they feel that they ought to act in ways that conflict with each other and they do not know quite how to resolve these dilemmas. They experience moral stress when their superiors order them to lay off a long-time employee and their conscience tells them that the person has not been given sufficient warning and the company has not provided adequate termination benefits. They experience it when they ship out faulty goods because it is in the best interest of the company, which knows that only a small proportion of customers will ask for the replacements for which they qualify. They experience it when they pass on technological information from a first vendor to a second vendor because the company now wants to do business with the second. In these and countless other examples, businesspeople find themselves placed in the very difficult position of making moral choices, which they may subsequently rationalize as the lesser of two evils, in which they are violating at least some moral standards while pursuing actions they feel in part obliged to perform. They feel uncomfortable both about the processes of choosing and about the decisions they feel they ought to make. The issues are complicated. Advancing the company's interest is not an indifferent matter. They have promised to do this as part of their job, and it is wrong to break promises. Furthermore, not pursuing these interests may put people out of work or endanger the good name of the organization.

A measure of moral stress is an inherent feature of all serious deliberations about difficult moral dilemmas. It is a sign that the judgments matter, that there are genuine alternatives, and that choices require thought and consideration and cannot be resolved by simply invoking this or that ethical formula. Managers who experience no moral stress probably either lack sensitivity to the plight of others, are content in an unfeeling way to invoke moral formulae rigidly, or lack a sense of conscience altogether. A degree of moral stress is a sign of moral life. Stress levels become intensified and exacerbated, however, whenever people don't know quite how to sort things out, when they feel constrained by superiors to render decisions that leave them personally troubled, and when they do not know where and how to draw the line between what they judge to be legitimate practice and questionable ones. They experience both uncertainty and the pressure to reach a judgment. Greatly increased moral stress levels in these settings are rarely productive. Blindly people grasp for moral straws. They cite random precedents. They blame it all on their bosses. They invent facile excuses. They attack others who question them. They self-deceptively deny that they were ever considering moral claims for problems like these that can and should be judged in strict business terms.

Businesspeople who experience moral stress do not necessarily make bad choices. Their eventual decisions may be ones that, with greater room to reflect, they would subsequently justify as being morally responsible. In the meantime, however, they do not feel that way. They feel uncertain and troubled. They feel constrained to act in ways they think are not right. They feel that they do not have much room to consider alternatives and they frequently arrive at choices by considering what they think their superiors feel ought to be done. They often feel caught between subservience and a heroism for which they feel ill-prepared.

In *Tough Choices: Managers Talk Ethics*, Barbara Toffler sets forth the accounts of approximately thirty managers she interviewed, almost all of whom experienced high levels of unrelieved moral stress. One manager felt conflicted about his bank's financing of arms shipments to Third World countries. He was troubled as well by the bank's failure to do something about the sloppy bookkeeping of Third World borrowers because this would lead the latter into increasing financial difficulties. In both cases he wondered whether he ought to act more directly to do what he thought was right. Several managers continually felt uneasy by compromises they felt they had to make on quality control decisions in order to allow the company to meet production deadlines. Several managers expressed their discomfort when having to let go long-time employees with outdated skills who were otherwise excellent workers and colleagues. Another manager felt torn by how to handle the case of a woman who complained of sexual harassment but had lied in another instance about jury duty. This same manager also confessed to his own uncertainty about how to handle his own personal involvement with a consultant hired by the company. As the title of the book indicates, interviewed managers felt that they faced tough choices, that they were not clear about how they ought best resolve the dilemmas they faced, and they felt uncomfortable about the decisions they had made or were about to make (Toffler 1986).

Almost all these managers experienced the degree of moral stress they did because they also felt isolated from others as they were considering what to do. They felt that morally they were on their own. An interviewed manager put it this way. He was told by his superior that if he was not able to settle the case at hand, his superior would put someone else in the position who would. It was if he was being told that he was in the kitchen by himself doing what had to be done. If he couldn't stand the heat of this situation, then he shouldn't be there. It seemed to be assumed that making these kinds of tough choices on one's own builds character. Whether it does or not, it certainly increases and intensifies moral stress. Faced with an interviewer asking about moral issues in business, manager after manager related examples of settings where they faced comparable tough choices but felt there was no one at work with whom they could talk over their tough choices.

Moral silence and associated vices help to create and sustain these high levels of stress by the ways they foster and reinforce the moral isolation of managers from each other. Most of the managers interviewed by Toffler and by Waters and others had not talked about their particular moral dilemmas with other managers (Waters, Bird, and Chant 1986). They had been morally mute at their place of work even if they were subsequently quite vocal with their interviewers. At work they tended to camouflage their moral concerns, voicing them indirectly as if they were raising practical, organizational, or financial considerations. Additionally, those who did speak up, usually very quietly, found little response from other managers who seemed to be tone deaf to the concerns that were being raised. The moral stress these managers experienced was intensified by their isolation, which meant that those involved often viewed these issues statically with little imagination. With greater imagination, a number of these cases would seem less perplexing and less tough. It is hard to be imaginative, however, when we feel stressed and when we are not able to seek out suggestions from others. Moral silence and deafness in these cases often occasion a fixed focus on these issues that thwarts imaginative consideration of unexamined alternatives. Issues tend to remain posed in either/or rather than both/and categories and remain that way both because of and as a result of the moral isolation of those deciding and the stress they are experiencing.

MORAL RESOURCES ARE IGNORED AND NEGLECTED

Business organizations are enhanced and energized to the degree that they can call upon and count on their members and constituents to be moved by a range of moral sentiments, such as basic honesty and the sense of fair play. To the extent that these sentiments seem to be absent or in short supply, organizations must exert extra efforts to accomplish their tasks. Correspondingly, to the degree that organizational members are affected by moral silence and its associated dispositions, they are likely to dampen their expression of these desired sentiments.

For example, most business organizations hope that they can count on their employees to be honest, to act with probity, to respect the property and resources of the organization, to be attentive to work-related needs and interests of their colleagues, to keep their promises, and to cooperate with others on team projects. They hope that their employees will be able to accept responsibilities and to perform their work well without needing too much supervision. Additionally, they hope that employees will utilize the resources entrusted to them, including their own time, effectively and efficiently without undue waste. Often they also hope that members and constituents will demonstrate a willingness to learn and be instructed. Concisely, business organizations hope that their employees will express and act on the basis of a number of dispositions, all of which exhibit a measure of moral character, some with greater strength and overtness than others. Business organizations hope that their members and constituents will possess and act on these sentiments because the work of the organization is easier and more productive when they do. From the "human relations" approach to management to the contemporary interest in "quality management," businesses have been attracted to management styles that promise to help cultivate these sentiments among their work forces. For example, many businesses have sought to "empower" their workers not simply because they hope that as members of teams the latter will exercise greater discretion but also because they hope that individually their workers will demonstrate team spiritedness, a willingness to learn and adapt, an interest in making more effective use of limited resources, and a disposition to seek out and serve the interests of the recipients of their work (Hammer and Champy 1993).

Clearly, many workers fail to exhibit these sentiments openly and vigorously. Consequently, business organizations may variously seek to cultivate these sentiments among their members through their recruitment and promotion practices, training programs, and human resources policies. These endeavors, however, often fail. They fail to the degree that organizations are affected by moral silence, deafness, and blindness, because efforts to cultivate these sentiments typically proceed indirectly under other guises and names. The fact that business organizations are seeking to foster particular constellations of moral sentiments is not directly acknowledged. Rather, the focus shifts to current shibboleths, recruiters look for workers with congruent values, executives talk of quality management, and organizations become deeply involved in restructuring and reengineering. Although the latter may well identify worthwhile objectives, they suggest but do not really identify candidly the degree to which these organizations hope to cultivate a number of explicit moral sentiments among their members.

The irony here is that a number of these workers already exhibit a number of these sentiments, at least privately. They care about friends and family and even their work and are willing to take risks on their behalf, especially if they are likely to be recognized for their efforts. They believe in keeping promises, avoiding deceit, conserving resources, being loyal, treating others fairly, and accepting their responsibilities. When asked how they deal with difficulties and issues at work, they consistently invoke or allude to these and other virtues to explain their own private thoughts about these matters (Bird and Waters 1986). They also confess, however, that neither they nor their organizations overtly talk about these virtues and their importance. Consequently, individuals less forthrightly act on the basis of these sentiments, which are neither openly named nor honored.

By stifling moral communication, moral silence, deafness, and blindness also reduce the possibilities for more advantageous cooperation with stakeholders, competitors, and adversaries with whom relations may be strained. In settings where two parties repeatedly interact and where each can gain extra benefits by cheating on their arrangements so long as the other plays fair, it is actually in their mutual best interests to cooperate but to retaliate in a tit-for-tat manner if the other cheats. Several researchers have used both live subjects and computer models to investigate which strategies best serve the interests of parties in these situations. Where there are no expected repeat interactions, it is in the best interests of parties to cheat so long as they can reasonably expect the other to play fair, because if both cheat, they will be worse off than if they cooperated. Still, if one party thinks that the other will cheat, it is in his interest to cheat as well, because he will be less worse off than if he is taken advantage of. Where repeated interactions are likely, then each party will gain the most by cooperating so long as the other can be counted on to cooperate as well or respond in a tit-for-tat fashion to violations. What matters in these settings is to find ways of distinguishing potential cooperators from those who seek to appear this way only to take advantage of others (Frank 1988; Axelrod 1984).

Moral discourse functions as one means among others by which people may signal to each other their willingness to cooperate to their mutual advantage. Even though this means can be abused by hypocrites, it still provides opportunities for signalling willingness to cooperate that are absent when this discourse is stifled or shunned. In settings where people suspect that others may take advantage of their goodwill and reliability, people are likely to become protective of their own interests and opportunistic about chances to advance these at the expense of others who naively keep agreements in good faith. Excessive self-serving behavior can be costly to organizations. Individuals can seek their own ends at the organization's expense (Jackall 1988). The organization itself can become mired in struggles with the suspicious, self-seeking moves of its stakeholders and competitors. In all these settings it is mutually advantageous to develop arrangements that are more cooperative and less ridden by the suspicion of self-seeking duplicity. It is in the mutual interest of would-be cooperators to find ways to signal their dispositions to each other (Frank 1988). Open communication where parties overtly disclose these moral sentiments constitutes one way of accomplishing this end. Moral silence, deafness, and blindness undercut this possibility. Consequently, the potential for greater cooperation is often dissipated in the process.

One resource especially affected by moral silence and its correlative vices is the potential for idealistic ventures among organizational members. Clearly, organizations can benefit from encouraging members who mobilize followers and energies to pursue worthwhile objectives that aid workers, neighbors, customers, or others. Organizations can learn from these initiatives and can gain both in repute and in morale. Countless examples of these ventures can be cited. For example, one interviewed manager assumed the initiative to develop a corporate foundation that supported the arts; another bank manager worked to develop credit unions to help community groups in low-income neighborhoods; another worker persuaded his company to send him for several weeks every year to help with school programs in Central America; and one manager developed a cooperative recycling program between his firm and a local grocery store chain—he later recruited a "green team" of company volunteers to help man these recycling centers on weekends. Other examples can be named, such as the woman who campaigned for years for women employee rights until she finally found a champion in a newly appointed senior vice-president, or the workers who lobbied for more smoke-free work areas. These initiatives, arising from the middle and bottom of organizations, were all undertaken because of the idealistic vision of particular organizational members.

Moral silence and its correlative vices tend to stifle and dampen this idealism. The vices make this idealism seem out of place, gauche, and awkward unless sanitized by presenting every such venture in terms of its cost/benefit contribution to organizational ledgers. When this idealism is translated in the argot of good business sense, however, it loses its vision, much of its originating impetus, and its special capacity to elicit extra energies and commitments from other organizational members likely to be excited by its high-minded and moral qualities. These idealistic ventures work best when they are unabashedly just that—idealistic in large part because it is in these terms particularly that they are able to call for and gain extra efforts. Moral silence and deafness muzzle exactly these sentiments. Initiators instead speak up for their ideas in whispers. Others remain largely inattentive unless these ideas can be restated in strictly business terms. The springs of idealism are reduced to a trickle.

EXTRANEOUS TRANSACTIONAL COSTS BECOME GREATER

Organizations necessarily invest a measure of time and energy attempting to make sure that people do what they are expected to do. Broadly stated, this is a control function, which organizations exercise through supervision, surveillance, and sanctions. They also invest efforts in making preparations so that they are ready to accomplish what they hope to accomplish. Broadly stated, these are preparation functions. Leaving aside training programs, they exercise these functions by negotiating arrangements with the several constituent groups with whom they interact and by recruiting manpower as needed. These efforts in control and preparation are necessary to put organizations in position to perform well. They amount to transactional costs because they are not integral to the organizations' primary activities as such and do not result in any direct payoffs. They help to engender benefits only by helping to shape organizations so that they are fit to act effectively to realize their goals. Ideally these transactional costs should be kept to a minimum.

In well-run organizations, these costs remain limited and small. Organization members work industriously and cooperatively with little need for direct surveillance. They perform their tasks as expected with little need for extrinsic pushes and pulls to move them to do what they are supposed to do. They feel satisfied that the assignments and rewards they receive are both fitting and fairly allocated. They possess a lively sense of working together in ways that promote their collective as well as their individual ends. Correspondingly, organizations realize their ends with minimal investments in control and preparation functions.

Many organizations fall far below this ideal. In order to achieve their objectives, they divert considerable resources into several control and preparation functions. I refer to these as "extraneous" transactional costs because in well-run organizations these kinds of extra investments are kept to a minimum. One, in settings where it is not possible to count on workers performing as expected, organizations create more supervisory positions to guide employees and to track that they are performing as expected. To be sure, in a self-fulfilling pattern, augmented supervisory ranks often seem to signal a stubborn disposition among workers to do the minimum they can get away with. Two, similarly in these organizational settings, auditing functions often assume a policing character. Extra efforts are invested in formal attempts both to make certain that employees perform correctly and to uncover those who have secretly either violated these rules or diverted organizational resources to their own ends. Three, when the relationship between organizations and their primary constituent groups become strained, the negotiations surrounding these relationships become protracted and often hostile. This situation can occur with suppliers, customers, community groups, or regulators, but it especially happens in relation to employee associations. In some companies these negotiations regularly become aggravated and long-lasting and correspondingly consume considerable amounts of organizational time, goodwill, ingenuity, and staff. Four, in organizations with high turnover and absence rates, additional time and energy must be invested in filling positions permanently or temporarily left vacant. Moreover, additional efforts usually need to be invested to prepare these replacements so that they can perform as expected with others. In all four of these instances, extra organizational resources are diverted to activities that would not need to be undertaken in a smoothly running organization. These are extraneous transactional costs.

Several factors can add to these costs. An aggressive union can make labor negotiations tough. A volatile labor market can increase turnover rates. Overly aggressive supervision can leave workers wary. When employees feel that they are being treated unfairly, they are more likely to fudge the rules. Still, although only one factor among others, organizations characterized by moral silence, deafness, and blindness are especially likely to require these extraneous transactional costs. This probability occurs largely for reasons we have already examined: These organizations are often characterized by aggravated accountability systems, intensified moral stress among employees, stifled moral sentiments, and diffused moral idealism. These several factors together combine to deflate goodwill and dissipate trust. Correspondingly, rather than gaining cooperation through moral persuasion, organizations find themselves forced to use more explicit control devices that amount to extraneous transactional costs.

THE ROLE OF ETHICS IS MARGINALIZED AND CONFUSED

One of the major consequences of moral silence and its correlative dispositions is that ethics ends up playing greatly reduced, marginalized, and confusing roles. If people rarely voice their moral concerns, seldom respond to those voiced by others, and frequently fail to recognize the moral aspects of issues at hand, it is no wonder that ethics as purposive discursive talk about moral concerns plays little or no role. We might find it surprising that there is any room at all for ethics in relation to business practices. Still, businesspeople do express concern about ethics in spite of the general moral amnesia. Many companies have developed codes of conduct. Moreover, when the issue of ethics comes up, businesspeople often bring out stories of blatant abuses and violations, usually committed by notorious figures (Lewis 1989), accounts of particularly wonderful acts of altruism and justice, and confessions of occasions when they were put into compromising positions. These sinner and saint stories are as much a part of the milieu of business as codes of conduct for large businesses and the pervasive denial that ethics has much relevance for the really difficult organizational and business decisions that have to be made.

On a day-to-day basis ethics tends to be restricted to the role of identifying and limiting noncompliant behavior that threatens to harm the interests of business organizations. Ethics is associated with formal codes and efforts to identify those who violate these standards. Little attention is accorded to ethics in relation to other potential roles, such as addressing and resolving problems, enhancing morale, identifying and mobilizing consensus to realize the common good of organizations, and facilitating conflict resolutions. It has been argued that ethics is primarily concerned with the question of how to live really good lives (Nussbaum 1986; Williams 1985). In milieux affected by moral silence, deafness, and blindness, this simple but encompassing focus is reduced to questions about disciplining rule violators. The larger, more constructive roles for ethics are lost to sight. In these milieux ethics is typically regarded as a particular vocational specialty, like accounting or offering legal advice, exercised by those who deal with these kinds of behavior problems.

It is interesting and ironic, however, to observe that at the same time that businesspeople deny the general relevance of ethics and formally marginalize its role, they continue to utilize morally loaded phrases and images to talk about how business ought to be managed. They use words that invoke normative standards of how to act and that bring with them connotative moral associations. They talk of "quality" management, the pursuit of "excellence," "responsible care," "efficiency," "credibility," "accountability," and "walking the talk." They have borrowed the term "value," first used in moral philosophy and later by eighteenth and nineteenth-century economists like Adam Smith, John Stuart Mill, and Karl Marx, all of whom doubled as moral philosophers. Even as businesspeople call upon their lawyers to adjudicate disputes, they talk of honoring explicit and implied promises, as well as fair and unfair contractual obligations. They invoke notions of fiduciary responsibilities, customer service, and the need to respect good long-term working relations. These terms are probably coined and used because they function indirectly both to arouse the corresponding moral sentiments and to set forth normative standards of how people ought to behave. Still the use of these words and images hardly relates to ethics, if for no other reason than that ethics is a conscious reflective activity. Nonetheless, the use of these terms bears witness to the degree that business-people indirectly recognize the need for ethics under some guise, even if, as a correlate of their moral silence, deafness, and blindness, they have marginalized its more overt roles.

CONCLUSION

In this chapter, I have been arguing that it costs organizations when they foster circumstances in which their members and constituents are morally mute, deaf, and blind. These costs assume several different forms as organizations correspondingly expose themselves to increased risks, aggravate feelings of stress, and deplete the goodwill of their workers and stakeholders as the correlates and consequences of moral silence, deafness, and blindness. Insofar as these vices become pervasive, accountability problems intensify, extraneous transaction costs grow, and many ordinary issues and conflicts become more difficult to resolve. For several reasons, it is in the best interest of businesses to address these vices and to seek ways to overcome them.

With the exception of the passing reference to moral stress, thus far I have examined the impact of these vices primarily in relation to organizations and their activities. However, the impact of these vices on individuals, their consciences, and their interactions also needs to be considered. Becoming morally mute, deaf, and/or blind costs individuals as well. Our moral silence, deafness, and blindness prevent us from acting in heroic, self-sacrificing, and saintly ways. They impede us from acts that require great risks or expose us to sharp criticism and vicious counterattacks. These vices affect us in more immediate and less dramatic ways. In ways that I examine at greater length in the next chapter, moral silence, deafness, and blindness directly filter and muffle how we experience and express our consciences. Moral speaking, hearing, and seeing are the sensuous expressions of our consciences. When these become muted, deafened, and blurred, our consciences are correspondingly affected. Although most of us retain our sense of conscience in relation to crises, on an everyday basis our sense of conscience becomes weakened and blunted. Because our conscience represents the call for integrity, when we muffle and mute this call, we also thereby lose the corresponding integrated sense of ourselves. We may remain quite aware of our roles and the several faces and personae we carry into our diverse relationships, but we become flatter and more hollow to the degree that we allow the sensuous dimensions of conscience to atrophy. Not attending to the moral concerns voiced by others, not acknowledging as such the normative expectations that bear upon our work, and not voicing moral sentiments we feel—all have the affect of cutting off the springs of our consciences. We may do this in little or big ways. The effects are cumulative. Weakening our sense of conscience is personally costly. As a result we become less morally active. To be sure, our consciences do lead us to act in responsible, caring, honest, and accountable ways. But they do more. They also represent the instinct within each of us to be true to ourselves, to be faithful to ourselves, and thereby to be integrated as selves. As the twentieth-century Protestant theologian and philosopher Paul Tillich (1963) argued: The real voice of conscience is not an alien voice imposed upon us—rather, it is the call to act in such ways that the various parts of our selves fit without self-deception or dissimulation.

Becoming morally mute, deaf, and/or blind also affects our interactions with others. To the extent that we mute, muffle, and blur our moral voicing, hearing, and seeing, our relations with others are likely to become more mechanical and more superficial. These consequences follow from the ways moral silence and deafness in particular cause us to leave out of our interactions a fairly extensive range of concerns that we do not voice or do not respond to when expressed by others. Depending upon the forms of moral silence and deafness that affect us, we may not voice or hear expressions of ideals, direct and candid feedback about performances, suspicions of difficulties, and feelings of disappointment, as well as conflict-engendering complaints. Our conversations may as a result be less aggravated, less full of debate and argumentation, and less emotionally vociferous. They are likely to be more placid. But they are also likely to touch on a much smaller and safer range of topics, be more evasive, and less engaging.

CHAPTER 6

Underlying Causes of Moral Silence, Deafness, and Blindness

People affected by moral silence, deafness, and blindness are like people who possess weak consciences. By nature such people are neither amoral nor immoral. They possess moral convictions, which they may discuss privately, about many matters. But the voice of conscience within them seems timid, not easily aroused, and slumbering. Consciences are not unwavering realities. They may be weak or strong, lifeless or vigorous, unformed or well formed. Individuals who are morally mute, deaf, and blind are moved by consciences rendered weak by being largely voiceless, inattentive, unresponsive, and partially blind. These people may still affirm moral beliefs and often act on them. For the most part they are likely to comply with expected moral rules. Occasionally they will probably be moved to extend themselves on behalf of others, now and then object at least privately to injustices, faithfully adhere to most of their commitments, and regularly seek the well-being of the associations of which they are a part. Although their consciences—like gyroscopes—may help them maintain a measure of balance, they do not energize, enliven, convict, and inspire them. Moral silence and its associated vices are the expression of people with tepid consciences (Aristotle, Bk vii, 1953; Lukes 1971; Matthews 1971).

Why are people morally mute, deaf, and blind? Why do these people possess consciences that seem so weak, voiceless, inattentive, and without vision and recognition? We now turn to this question. We ask this question not just academically but in order to discover ways to address and reduce the problems we have just reviewed. We ask this question in order to prepare ourselves to consider more fully—as we do in the next chapter—what can be done to cultivate milieux in which people act with lively and vigorous consciences.

The phenomena that we wish to explain, namely moral silence, deafness, and blindness, especially as these occur within business organizations, exist simultaneously at both an individual and a collective level. This is necessarily the case because of the interactive character of these vices. To be sure, in the end specific individuals are either morally vocal or mute, morally attentive or unresponsive, morally perceptive and farsighted or partially blind and unimaginative. Their display of these vices and their correlative virtues, however, affects others because these directly deaden or enliven the character of the communication between the parties. Collectivities shape and define these patterns of communicative interactions as much as the individuals who engage or fail to engage in them. Although organizations do not possess consciences the way individuals do, it is appropriate to describe and analyze how well organizations voice or mute moral concerns, respond to or turn a deaf ear toward these voiced concerns, and recognize and acknowledge their reality and importance with a lively vision—or fail to. Still, it is well to remember that organizations do not do this as abstract realities but by means of the actions and inactions of individuals who are part of them. Organizations and associations frequently channel, limit, and shape these actions and inactions in ways that are both influential and identifiable.

Because these vices directly affect our interactions, they cannot be fully mastered and overcome by individuals on their own. Individual actions to voice, attend to, and see moral concerns in their work and in their organizations are encouraged and supported by the comparable actions of others. We must therefore examine these phenomena and their causes at both the individual and collective levels.

Each person is responsible for the strength or weakness of his/her own conscience and for the corresponding degree to which his/her conscience is vocal or silent, attentive or unresponsive, seeing or not seeing. Several factors, however, may act to help cultivate and strengthen or to weaken and frustrate the springs of conscience. In the remainder of this chapter, I examine a number of factors that influence people and organizations so that they are more disposed to be morally mute, deaf, and blind.

CULTURAL FACTORS

People identify what they mean by culture in different ways. Following Geertz (1973), and Weber (1978), I think of culture as the webs of meaning by which people communicate, interpret, and guide their conduct. More specifically I regard culture as the sets of symbolic forms and expressions that people use to communicate and make sense out of their lives. We may variously group and label these sets as learning, law, the arts, language, religion, folklore, science, rituals, philosophy, and prevailing beliefs. These symbolic forms and expressions provide the vocabularies and syntax by which we think, order our experiences, bargain, solicit assistance, play games, entertain ourselves, and engage in any activities in which we are either communicating with others or with ourselves. Cultural symbols are contingent upon historical constructions. They change over time and vary from locale to locale. Even the symbols by which we express what we regard to be "common sense" vary from one historical period to the next and from one setting to the next (Geertz 1983).

When we examine cultural influences, we analyze the way particular sets of symbolic forms and expressions—because they are so pervasive in specific historical settings—in turn affect the way people think and communicate about their experiences. We may, like Galbraith (1992), look at how conventional wisdom shapes people's expectations and judgments. By focusing on organizational cultures, we may examine the way particular myths and rituals affect how people communicate and cooperate in specific businesses and corporations. By grouping these symbols more broadly, we can, like Hampden-Turner and Trompenaars (1993), examine variations in the ways people in seven different nations think about and organize their business activities. In all these cases cultural forms influence us by shaping and limiting the vocabularies we use; by providing the legends, philosophies, and beliefs that are regarded as worthy of knowing and citing; and by determining what is assumed to be common sense. Cultural influences accordingly are broad and pervasive. They affect all those within particular cultural settings to the degree that the latter use the same sets of symbols to communicate and make sense.

Broadly considered, cultural factors influence the incidence of moral silence, deafness, and blindness by restricting and channelling the vocabularies by which people express their moral sentiments and by providing conceptual and symbolic images as spectacles that limit and distort what they see.

In the following paragraphs, I consider four cultural influences (see Table 6.1). Each constitutes a particular set of beliefs and assumptions, which are widely but not universally held today. Each affects how people identify, think about, and respond to moral issues. As I examine these sets of cultural symbols, I also attempt to gauge the degree to which they can be held individually and collectively responsible for the expressions of weak consciences exemplified by moral silence, deafness, and blindness.

The Prevailing Economic Philosophy

A number of observers have criticized the prevailing economic philosophy because of the moral stance that it seems to take and/or fails to take. The basic argument runs as follows. This philosophy has established what amounts to an orthodoxy, and alternative beliefs and assumptions are roundly discounted and treated as unrealistic, silly, and nonsensical. This philosophy assumes that economic actors can be counted on to seek what are their rational self-interests. To do otherwise is to act in irrational ways that do not make economic sense. These critics argue that these sets of assumptions operate like any reigning orthodoxy as conversation stoppers. They claim that people who wish to express alternative ideas are not really listened to. In particular, critics argue that the prevailing economic philosophy assumes that moral considerations play no significant role in the decision making of economic actors that cannot be explained better by the latter's attempts to maximize their self-interests. In actual business decision making, these critics argue, individuals are correspondingly forced to either translate their moral concerns into the language of economic self-interest or not raise them (Jackall 1988).

Table 6.1
The Impact of Cultural Factors on Moral Silence, Deafness, and Blindness

Cultural Beliefs and Symbols	Historical and Cultural Setting	Impact on Moral Silence, Deafness, and Blindness
Current economic philosophy (Focus on rational, self-interest)	Nineteenth and twentieth centuries	Constricts moral perceptions; limits moral vocabulary
Beliefs about the inevitability of particular circumstances	Universal and recurrent phenomena	Fosters self-deception, respecting the justice and legitimacy of difficult and degrading conditions
Beliefs regarding the role of legal action	Twentieth century, especially North American	Restricts and rigidifies moral perceptions; tends to disqualify non-legal people as moral speakers on specific topics
The cultural ethos of tolerant and expressive individualism	Contemporary ethos	Affects moral perceptions, recognitions, and vocabularies

A constellation of economic beliefs about rational self-interest clearly is influential. This can be demonstrated in several ways, including examining the hold that these ideas have on business school students. Even after studies have been read and analyzed that demonstrate that managers actually are motivated by diverse considerations—which include the enhancement of their own status and maintaining ongoing relations with suppliers out of loyalty even if these are less economic—many students insist on claiming that all this behavior can be explained by efforts to maximize profits and pursue self-interest. After having taught at Harvard Business School, the sociologist Amitai Etzioni, whose work is discussed below, expressed his frustration with students who steadfastly embraced the self-interest arguments despite considerable evidence he had marshalled to the contrary. Etzioni attempted to demonstrate in business school classes what most sociologists and anthropologists would take for granted:

namely, that people, even as economic actors, are usually motivated by a range of considerations including irrational habits of heart and mind as well as value commitments in addition to the pursuit of their self-interests (Weber 1978). The influence of this philosophy, however, is eloquently demonstrated by the form of arguments that critics like Etzioni and the economist Robert Frank make: namely, they seek not to supplant but only to supplement this philosophy.

Both Etzioni and Frank argue that the assumptions about individuals rationally pursuing their self-interest provide distorted and constricted views of how businesspeople actually act. Etzioni cites large numbers of psychological and economic studies to demonstrate that people act as much on the basis of values and emotions as rational self-interest. He proposes a codetermination model that better explains why so many people act charitably, forego free rides, protest injustices even at their own expense, and engage in equivalently non-self-interested behavior (Etzioni 1988). Frank acknowledges that in the long run what people seek is to protect and enhance their self-interest. It is not in their best interest, however, to seek this objective in every setting. In many different arenas of life long-term relationships foster our best interest. This can be true for friendships, marriages, partnerships, communities, and so forth. As a result humans have to be persuaded into making commitments, which are likely at any given moment to be less materially and psychologically rewarding than opting instead for interactions with alternative others. Frank argues that several emotions, from the desire to seek revenge and anxiety about harm and rejection by others, through empathy and fatigue, coax individuals into making commitments, which in turn ironically serve our long-run interests. He thereby observes: "We may thus concede that material forces ultimately govern behaviour, yet at the same time reject the notion that people are always and everywhere motivated by self-interest" (Frank 1988, 145). He argues that material incentives often prompt people to act in ways that undermine their ultimate material interests.

Etzioni and Frank have written large-scale scholarly treatises attacking basic assumptions in the prevailing economic philosophy because they regard these assumptions to be overly simplistic and thereby seriously misleading and because these assumptions blind people from recognizing, acknowledging, and acting on moral considerations. In part they are accusing economists and businesspeople of a form of self-deception whereby they fail to identify and avow the moral values that already influence them both unknowingly and privately. In part they are also arguing that people are likely to make less wise decisions to the degree they allow themselves to be misled by the economic rhetoric of rational self-interest. Frank adds: "Largely as a result of the self-interest model's influence, our bonds of trust have taken a heavy beating in recent years" (Frank 1988, xi).

Does this economic philosophy render people more likely to be morally mute, deaf, and blind? Although these sets of cultural beliefs greatly influence the rhetoric and arguments by which businesspeople discuss the issues they face, their influence is still limited. These beliefs largely affect the moral sight of businesspeople. The arguments by critics such as Galbraith, Etzioni, and Frank seem reasonable: This philosophy leads many people to misperceive a number of issues and concerns, not to foresee the long-run consequences of what seem to be smart short-run moves, and to deceive themselves with regard to many of their own motivations. By this means, indirectly these cultural beliefs may affect how people hear and voice moral concerns. I think, however, that it is easy to overstate this argument. Many businesspeople still respond to moral concerns and speak out about them in spite of the influence of this reigning orthodoxy. In any case, this philosophy has aroused a diverse body of critics and dissenters among both professional economists and businesspeople. Its influence is therefore moderate and not dogmatic or exclusive. Furthermore, morally aroused businesspeople find that they can effectively voice their positions both by using alternative rhetoric borrowed from philosophy, religion, or politics and by utilizing the maxims and symbols of economic philosophy to express moral concerns not now usually entertained by this philosophy.

Assumptions about the Possibilities for Effective Change

Many people accept distressing, dangerous, and degrading circumstances because they presume that these cannot be easily and effectively changed. In a book focusing on the working classes in Germany between 1848 and the 1930s, Barrington Moore, Jr., inquired why people acquiesce and do not protest against conditions that threaten, harm, or undermine them. In *Injustice: The Social Bases of Obedience and Revolt*, Moore (1978) examines this history and also considers generally the factors that seem to persuade people suffering from injustices not to rise up more forcefully to object. Moore argues that many people acquiesce in distressing circumstances because they judge them to be inevitable. He points to the examples of untouchables who tolerate unbelievably difficult conditions because they believe it to be their fate. Many laborers put up with dangerous, insecure, and filthy working conditions for comparable reasons. They see no way to bring about positive changes. Moreover, unsuccessful exhibitions of anger are likely only to make matters worse.

Assumptions about the possibilities for effective change vary from culture to culture, from one historical period to the next (Douglas and Wildowsky 1982). What people are willing to endure without protest is greatly affected by what they think they can change. The French social analyst, Alexis de Tocqueville (1955), commented in the middle of the nineteenth century that revolutions are most likely to occur when social conditions are improving, because only under these conditions is the aura of inevitability overcome sufficiently so that it seems possible to protest and revolt. Contemporary protests by women about injustices in the workplace fit this pattern as well. As women have entered the labor force in greater numbers and received more opportunities for advancement, continuing injustices seem less tolerable. The recognition that effective change is possible makes existing slights and discrimination seem less acceptable even though conditions in general have been improving. As a consequence the extent of protest increases.

Many people have become inured to unjust, excessively risky, and demeaning business practices because they assumed that these conditions were inevitable and could not be easily and effectively altered. Many businesses live with high rates of workplace accidents and with unhealthy and excessively noisy working conditions because these seem to be inherent in the kind of work being done. Textile factories long assumed that there were no alternative ways of operating except those that included high noise levels and high lint contents in the air. Many board members passively have gone along with the current inflation in executive salaries because this seems to be part of a powerful trend, even though these raises are not correlated with higher productivity, larger marginal returns, or greater executive leadership.

In what ways does this aura of inevitability affect the degree to which people in business are morally mute, deaf, and blind? These cultural assumptions do not constrict their vocabularies but they do limit what they see to be possible. Beliefs about opportunities for effective change are often quite realistic. Possibilities for reform expand once some reforms have already been introduced, but they remain limited to the degree that even small changes are obstructed and opposed. It is easier to protest against environmentally damaging practices today when more numerous business-environment schemes have been introduced than a generation ago when environmental issues excited much less interest. Often it is not primarily beliefs about inevitability that discourage protest and advocacy but the fact that powerful interests oppose proposed changes. To the degree that judgments that effective change seems doubtful reflect realistic assessments, people holding these views are not morally blind. They may, nonetheless, deceive themselves into thinking that many morally questionable conditions in their businesses and industries are morally indifferent or even acceptable not because they genuinely judge them to be so but because they presume incorrectly that these circumstances cannot be significantly altered in the foreseeable future. Such self-deception is a form of moral blindness, which indirectly can render people both more reluctant or hesitant about speaking up and less responsive to the related moral concerns of others.

Beliefs Regarding the Role of Legal Action

A number of businesspeople treat many of the moral issues that organizations face as the special provenance for legal actions and legal judgments. Legal counsels have been asked to prepare organizational codes of conduct. They are typically consulted when stakeholders and constituents complain either about unfair contractual stipulations or failures to honor contractual obligations. For example, when a community group protests that a factory's air emission exceeds healthy limits, legal counsels are typically consulted to determine exactly the extent to which corporations are culpable, accountable, and responsible for remedial action. A large number of moral standards related to business practices have been codified by legislation. Particular laws concern diverse activities—from the proper disclosures of corporation information to investors to truthful labeling of products, from the protection of minorities to allowable discretion in calculating the replacement costs for capital expenditures. Accordingly, legal counsels are consulted about practically all the moral issues that arise within businesses that concern some form of conflict or some violation of standards. Although this tendency is found in most modern businesses in some measure, it is much more pronounced in North America. North Americans are more prone to turn moral conflicts into legal disputes than are people in other industrialized societies.

As a consequence of these tendencies, organizations often delegate the handling of many moral issues to legal experts. The latter become the designated experts in interpreting what is really at stake and in officially voicing the position of the organization on these matters. Other organizational members who wish to raise moral concerns about issues that are legally construed are often treated as lacking appropriate legal knowledge and experience. Their formulations of issues are often treated as being naive and misinformed by legal experts. Essentially they are counseled that they are likely to misinterpret moral issues unless they take into account and defer to legal protocols about what matters and how these matters should be handled. Often protestors have been informed that no real issues exist regarding matters as diverse as pollution, dismissals, and harassment so long as there have been no violations of the letter of legal codes and collective agreements as these have been interpreted by relevant court judgments and grievance proceedings. Correspondingly, many moral issues have come to be defined and understood largely, if not primarily, in terms established by legal codes and arguments rather than by broader moral standards and objectives.

To what degree do these views about the role of legal action in business affect the extent to which people voice, hear, and see moral concerns? These beliefs and corresponding practices influence individual and corporate expressions of conscience in two ways. One, they affect the vocabularies in relation to which moral issues are identified and discussed. In this way they shape how issues are perceived and how they are mentioned. A case can be made for arguing that deference to the legal model tends to influence people in a reductionistic way to view concerns excessively and statically in legal terms. Two, deference to the legal approach serves to create and legitimate a division of organizational labor in which experts in law play a preponderate role in addressing and resolving moral issues involving conflicts over contractual relations and compliance with legal, organizational, and regulatory codes. These practices in turn greatly influence organizational norms about who is expected to speak up about these kinds of moral concerns as well as when and how they should do so. In practice they foster milieux in which moral silence may be expected among most organizational members about these kinds of issues.

Still, it is easy to exaggerate the extent to which beliefs and practices about legal action actually cultivate or reinforce morally weak consciences. They affect how a number of issues are seen and the language in which they are typically discussed. They legitimate the principal role of legal experts in handling many of these issues and thus tend to disqualify others as primary players. However, other organizational members can still respond and speak up about these concerns even if they must at times channel their efforts through legal experts and legal language. These beliefs and practices constitute a constraint rather than an obstacle to moral voicing and responding.

Cultural Mores That Support Beliefs in a Tolerant and Expressive Individualism

Many observers have argued that the tolerant, highly subjective, and individualistic moral attitudes of many contemporaries leave them without much moral vigor and stamina. This argument, which has been rendered in several different versions, makes two basic points. The first is that during the post—Second World War years a recognizable shift in moral beliefs and values has occurred that places greater value on individuals expressing themselves and seeking their own personal well-being and allowing others to do so as well in their own ways. The second point is that this popular moral philosophy encourages individuals to be more self-preoccupied (Yankelovich 1981). A number of eminent social analysts have attempted to characterize and diagnose the causes of this shift in popular moral attitudes. The sociologist Ralph Turner (1975) analyzed this shift as a change from an instrumental to an expressive view of the self. Rather than thinking of ourselves in terms of roles, responsibilities, and our real and expected accomplishments, we regard ourselves in relation to our feelings and the ways we express these. Fellow sociologist Daniel Bell (1976) made an analogous argument, noting the extent to which people set their priorities and form their identities much more in terms of their roles as consumers of goods and services rather than as producers and workers. Bellah and associates (1984) analyzed the emergence of a therapeutic individualism that both encouraged and legitimated the individual preoccupation with personal well-being. Sennett (1974) examined an equivalent shift in terms of the decreasing interest in public affairs combined with an increasing investment in private activities.

These beliefs constitute a diffuse popular moral philosophy expressed and communicated by the media of popular culture. These beliefs have helped to occasion, and received support from, several correlative moral assumptions. One of these is the belief in tolerating and not openly criticizing the moral beliefs of others (Wolff, Moore, and Marcuse 1965). Some people hold ultraconservative views; others are flaming radicals. Some people believe in honoring ethnic traditions and preserving ethnic languages; others think of themselves simply as individuals without ethnic backgrounds. So long as no one seeks to impose his or her views on others, then all moral views should, it is argued, be treated equivalently. In fact, some have gone so far as to argue that it is ethnocentric to attempt to criticize the moral views of others, especially if these are associated with other cultures. A second correlative view is that moral positions essentially amount to personal opinions about moral concerns. We refer to these as value preferences, assuming in the process that they amount to nothing but personally arranged and ranked feelings about moral matters (Rokeach 1968, 1979; Bloom 1987). The value clarification approach to ethics illustrates both of these characteristics. According to this school of thought, people are expected to be able to identify and clarify their ethical positions by subjectively ranking value preferences. Moral positions as such make few claims upon us. They possess no real self-transcending authority because they merely reflect our personal and subjective beliefs and priorities.

Without attempting to gauge the actual influence of this popular, even though vaguely expressed, moral philosophy, I think most observers would agree that many people in contemporary industrialized societies justify their activities by invoking these and comparable beliefs and images. This vague moral philosophy is probably more popular in certain areas, such as urban areas, and among identifiable populations, such as young adults and the middle-aged. Does this philosophy of expressive and tolerant individualism render people morally mute, deaf, and blind? Does it function to dampen the growth of conscience? Again, it is easy to credit this moral philosophy with more real influence than it in fact possesses. It might in contrast be argued that these moral attitudes largely consist in after-the-fact expressions of changing and already-altered patterns of conduct. This moral philosophy has had an ambiguous influence on the articulate and lively expressions of conscience. Although on the one hand, in the name of tolerance, it seems to encourage people to silence their moral criticisms, on the other hand it still legitimates the expression of individual points of view. Nevertheless, it does tend to blunt the expression of moral convictions, whether these are set forth by ourselves or others, insofar as these are regarded as opinions and value preferences rather than as articulately reasoned and defended judgments.

Conclusion: The Role of Cultural Factors on Moral Silence, Deafness, and Blindness

We have examined four constellations of cultural symbols that have had some impact on how people regard and communicate about moral issues in business. Although these belief syndromes at times limit the vocabularies by which moral issues are discussed, they have primarily influenced moral seeing rather than moral hearing and voicing. Even when all four of these cultural factors are taken together, they cannot really be blamed or credited as major causal explanations for the fact that so many people seem to be guided by weak consciences. They do affect how people perceive, talk about, and listen to accounts of moral concerns. But they do not really obstruct such conversations. Rather they shape where and how these communications can take place.

None of these factors can be easily changed with the exception of the sense of inevitability associated in the past with a number of abusive conditions from high accident rates to tacit discrimination against minorities. That these cultural beliefs regarding rational interest, the role of legal action, and expressive individualism are widely accepted as valid need not provoke despair. Some moral philosophers have adopted this stance in part because ethical pluralism makes it difficult if not impossible to achieve rational resolutions of moral disputes (MacIntyre 1981). Rather I think the pervasiveness of these cultural beliefs should be regarded as an historical fact of the same sort as the facts that we inherently learn specific mother tongues or that we signal friendship by utilizing specific culturally determined gestures and signs. These cultural beliefs are part of the historical circumstances in which we live. We must take account of them. To the extent we judge them to be misleading and distorting, as I do, we are challenged both to critique them like a number of authors I have cited and to find ways of articulating our concerns both using and ignoring these belief systems. Although these cultural syndromes may restrict and distort our field of vision, they do not prevent us from seeing and learning to compensate for their blurring and constricting influences.

A number of moral philosophers have thought that it might be possible, as well as desirable, to discover and utilize modes of moral expression that are free of culturally specific trimmings and substance. Such moral expressions would be in keeping with reason as such or would at least be free of any historically contingent trappings. We can see the attraction of this vision in contemporary philosophers like Habermas (1984, 1987, 1990) and Rawls (1971), each of whom attempts to determine good judgments by imagining what people would decide if they were in culturally free circumstances where people communicate without reference to current ideological and religious beliefs, differing status, or their own material interest and actual loyalties. These remain ideal and utopian fantasies. As morally responsible men and women we can and must find ways of cultivating the growth and expression of our consciences, utilizing and expanding upon the cultural expressions available to us in our own particular, historically contingent circumstances.

INDIVIDUAL FACTORS

Whether individuals exhibit weak consciences is largely the responsibility of individuals themselves. Whether organizations exhibit the equivalent of weak consciences is the responsibility of both individuals singly and groups of individuals in their organizational settings. It is not enough simply to observe that individuals are accountable for the vibrancy of their own moral voicing, hearing, and seeing. If we genuinely hope to understand and hope to reduce the extent of moral blindness, deafness, and seeing, we must also inquire about those factors that most decisively affect their moral dispositions and competencies. In the following paragraphs, I consider several factors that manifestly affect the degrees to which people voice, hear, and recognize moral issues. These factors in different ways impede the cultivation and growth of the active expression of conscience. Both individuals and organizations can take initiatives to reduce the impact of these factors.

Before considering these factors, we need to review two other influences that affect the degree to which individuals are morally vocal, attentive, and seeing in relation to particular concerns but that are not actually evidence of either weak consciences or accompanying expressions of moral silence, deafness, or blindness.

One, individuals vary in their moral temperaments. Some people are capable much more easily than others of acting with courage, demonstrating magnanimity, exercising self-restraint, feeling empathy, and expressing sympathy. People are not equally gifted in their capacity for exhibiting these virtues. Some people are more uninhibited; others are more inhibited and correspondingly likely at times to be more irritable, fearful, and timid (Aristotle Bk i, 1981; Kagan 1989). Still each person can develop his/her particular constellation of gifts so that no adult is excused for failing to act with these dispositions insofar as he/she can. It is just that people's capacities differ. As a consequence some people find it easier to listen comprehendingly to the moral concerns of others. Some people more readily can assume the risks of voicing concerns. The fact that people vary in their gifts for different forms of moral virtues must be taken into account both to avoid being overly judgmental about the conscientious efforts by others as well as ourselves to raise and respond to moral concerns and to acknowledge realistically our own strengths and limitations. This fact also reminds us that what matters are the efforts people make to strengthen their own consciences and their corresponding capacities for moral voicing, hearing, and seeing. Nonetheless, we can accomplish this objective only by acting on particular concerns in relation to some of which we may be more capable of exhibiting strong virtues than others. Consequently, individuals may remain comparatively inattentive around a concern that calls for much empathy, a virtue for which they feel ill-suited, though being able to demonstrate quite a lively conscience on behalf of another concern that requires them to courageously protest, an activity that comes much more naturally for them.

Two, individuals occasionally exhibit moral silence, deafness, and blindness in relation to specific issues because they have already committed themselves to respond to other issues. Clearly we do not possess the time, energy, or dispositions to respond to all issues that may concern us. For example, we may involve ourselves with neighborhood improvement while attempting at work to bring about more forthright and less misleading sales strategies with the result that we feel we have little time to join in the campaigns for minority hiring. Although we must often make decisions about where to invest our moral energies, we can also fool ourselves into essentially rationalizing cover-ups. We can invent well-meaning excuses to explain lack of voicing and attentiveness rooted more in laziness, timidity, or hard-heartedness than in competing commitments. Still, people often attempt to excuse their reluctance to voice and respond by invoking their support of friends who may be implicated, prior promises they have made to act in specific ways, and their loyalty to the organizations they feel they may be betraying if they were more overtly vocal and responsive. These may provide the bases for justifiable but tactical decisions to remain at least temporarily and overtly silent and unresponsive. It is easy to mislead ourselves, however. What matters is the extent to which we have really thought these matters through and that we remain genuinely attentive even though we may appear publicly to be unresponsive. I will make an observation here that I build upon in the next chapter: It is often difficult to know whether or not we are deceiving ourselves when we do not consult with others who in an empathetic but objective manner can help us sort out these decisions. Even though this rationale can be invoked self-deceptively, in principle our lack of involvement with particular moral issues may spring from genuine prior commitments.

In the following paragraphs, I discuss five distinct but at times interrelated and overlapping factors that decisively impact on individual expressions of moral silence, deafness, and blindness (see Table 6.2). These factors represent fears, competing preoccupations, and deficiencies that obstruct and frustrate the expected growth and vigorous expressions of personal conscience. I have not included lack of moral concern or ill will among these factors because throughout this work I have been examining the lack of involvement by people who possess moral sentiments and convictions. I have correspondingly described these people as being guided by weak consciences rather than no consciences.

Fears of Further, Uncertain Engagements

People express reluctance to get involved because they fear that such engagements will expand and expose them to even further, less clearly understood and less clearly bounded involvements. They fear the open-ended character of most involvement. People draw back from speaking up or responding to others out of fear that they might otherwise be biting off more than they can chew. They may feel willing to make a few steps over territory with which they are already familiar but fear that these movements will involve them in much more extensive journeying over less well-charted areas. They fear being exposed to the influence of events and forces that appear likely to affect them in unknown ways that are not easily controlled or limited.

These fears assume several typical and interrelated forms. For example, people worry about overextending themselves. What they fear is that they will lose free or discretionary time so that what and how they act will be determined to a greater extent by events and forces not at their command. It is like signing up for jury duty on the assumption that one week will be spent, only to find out that the corresponding tour of duty is expected to last a minimum of two months. As events unfold connected with the topic about which they have been considering speaking, people fear that they will find themselves called upon again and again to meet, speak, protest, and organize. They feel apprehensive about the possible claims that might be made of them should they speak up or respond. People also experience this fear as anxiety about becoming more vulnerable to the criticism, evaluations, hearsay, caucusing, and pressuring by others. Once they have spoken out or responded, they fear that others will then feel free to comment on their actions, to tell them how they should act now and in the future, as well as how they should have acted in the past. By speaking out and responding, they fear that they may expose themselves to ridicule, comments, and oppositions against which they in turn will have to oppose and defend themselves. Many people confess that they withhold comments and criticism about particular practices they privately regard as questionable because they are not sure that they have enough of the picture to make good judgments. Privately, they say, they may be wrong. They worry about making mistakes that not only may discredit themselves but also make themselves appear to be harboring suspicions. The black leader Malcolm X once said, invoking both usual meanings of the term, that the only dumb questions were the ones not voiced (Malcolm X 1973). Many people, however, hold back their questions and comments because they fear that others will view them as being simplistic, naive, stupid, or silly.

One typical but not readily acknowledged form this fear of uncertain engagement assumes is the fear of disillusionment. Having committed ourselves to others as friends, mentors, or leaders or having committed time, energy, and talents to our organizations, we are often very reluctant to acknowledge the ways these others may have betrayed our trust, commitments, and confidence by specific acts we regard as wrong or questionable. Often in these circumstances, people are overcome by strong but opposing feelings. They feel outraged by the questionable actions, which it seems likely were willfully committed at the same time as they hope that their suspicions are groundless. They don't want to be confronted directly with the trust and admiration betrayed by others. They don't want to have to admit that their trust was in some measure misplaced or at least too naively and carelessly placed. Caught by fears of being disillusioned, individuals sometimes will actively reinterpret information so they do not perceive and recognize openly its significance regarding possible wrongdoing by trusted others.

This fear of further, uncertain engagements is an aggravated form of the anxieties that all humans experience about the personal consequences of any open-ended engagements. Once we get involved, we cannot be certain how things will turn out, how much we will be asked to do, and whether we will meet disappointment and criticism or success and approval. Most of the time, as we are falling in love, joining associations, starting new ventures, or even responding to colleagues, the initial moves seem so attractive and challenging, or so unquestionably necessary, that we do not really consider all the negative possibilities. When they are about to take moral stands forthrightly, however, some people become overwhelmed by anxieties about these kinds of uncertain possibilities that they think may subsequently lead to unwelcome further involvements, vulnerabilities, disillusionments, and/or disappointments. In these cases, apprehensiveness often occasions moral paralysis.

Table 6.2
Individual Causes of Moral Silence, Deafness, and Blindness

Causal Factors	Characteristics	Impact on Moral Silence, Deafness, and Blindness
Fear of further, uncertain engagements	Fears of being vulnerable and not in control	Need not but often does aggravate moral deafness and blindness; occasions moral silence
The sense of resignation and futility	Anxiety that efforts will be trivial; assume that one must act like a saint or be a sinner	Aggravates and provides excuses for moral deafness and blindness; occasions moral silence
Fears of being implicated	Fears that speaking up will either involve one in questionable acts or occasion the discovery of implicating facts	Need not but does aggravate moral deafness and blindness; occasions moral silence
The claims of other preoccupations	Causes people to become distracted	Need not but often aggravates moral deafness and blindness; causes some people to be hesitant about speaking up
Ethical inarticulacy	Inability to voice moral concerns clearly so that others can comprehend	Reinforces moral blindness and deafness in others; occasions miscomprehension of issues; renders people reluctant to speak up

The Sense of Resignation and Futility

Morally conscientious people sometimes fail to voice and respond because they feel overwhelmed by feelings of resignation and futility. Issues seem too large. Possibilities for meaningful change appear too remote. Interrelations and means of approaching matters seem too complex and inaccessible. Morally sensitive people ask themselves: How can I have any measurable affect on the me-first careerism rampant in my organization? How can I change the sexist and discriminatory practices of senior management? What hope can I have of ending the practice of payoffs and bribes in our foreign markets when these seem so pervasive? What chance do I have of halting the extensive ways fellow managers and employees appropriate company resources for their private uses? Feeling powerless, these people sometimes begin inventing their own excuses or repeating other often-cited ones about the greedy, amoral character of business practices.

Beneath these excuses and beneath the feelings of resignation that they reflect, we often find assumptions that link moral action generally to heroic moral action. People begin to feel resigned because they feel incapable or unprepared for heroic actions and think of less grand moral actions as being either amoral, fundamentally compromised, or insignificant. Idealistically they associate all moral action with absolutes or standards of excellence and regard other moral gestures as expressions of self-interested or conventional behavior. Moral action, they assume, ought to be self-sacrificing and in keeping with universalistic standards. They fail to clearly recognize the difference between ideals and ordinary moral expectations (Fuller 1964).

The tendencies to confuse and conflate these different types of moral standards are very pervasive. People regularly fail to distinguish heroic standards of excellence, which all people may aspire to realize but usually only few achieve, from minimal obligations, which all are expected to comply with or be counted as apprehensible moral sliders. Often we discuss particular moral principles, such as ones about honesty, without clearly distinguishing between the minimal obligation of not intentionally deceiving others by what we say or do not say and the standard of excellence that calls for us to speak the truth. The latter represents an ideal in which our communication in a lively manner seeks to foster comprehension and insight and appreciation while still doing justice to the complexities and depths of what is being considered. Storytellers, poets, and scientists in different ways are often better equipped than most of us to communicate various faces of truth. The same confusing and conflating of different levels of moral expectations occur with respect to notions of benevolence. Regularly people conflate the ordinary, minimal moral obligation of reciprocity, of caring for those who care for us, with the standard of excellence that calls for people to be altruistic or charitable to others with no expectation of corresponding reciprocation. The history of Christian ethics is filled with examples where this confusion has been made. The apostle Paul, for example, several times intermixed counsels of mutual benevolence, "love your neighbor as yourself," with counsels to be willing to make sacrifices for the other to the point of giving up one's life for the other. Although these are two quite different kinds of standards—one is minimal and in a sense obligatory, and the other is ideal and in a sense optional—Christian ethicists often have used them interchangeably (Troeltsch 1960; Bird 1981b).

Some individuals seem to resign themselves to inaction because, assuming that the only worthy moral action is heroic, they feel incapable or unprepared for heroic moral action. Associating moral voicing with prophetic protests or visionary revelations, for both of which they genuinely lack gifts and calling, they resign themselves to whispers, private grousing, and silence. Associating moral hearing with visible displays of sympathy that they can neither feel nor simulate, they become inattentive, not wishing to be bothered by information they can neither readily assimilate nor identify with. Associating moral seeing with a profound and lively intellectual mastery, they hang on to their current, often unexamined moral assumptions. Not wishing to look too closely at these because they seem comfortable and important, they resign themselves to seeing selected moral concerns but without much sense of perspective or purpose.

Fears of Being Implicated

People sometimes fail to speak up or respond to others because they fear that by these actions they will be implicated. They fear that their speaking or responding will lead to revelations about their connections with the wrongdoings to which they are pointing. As well, they fear that by speaking or responding they will be engaging in morally questionable practices themselves. These are quite different fears, which I discuss separately, even though both represent anxieties that, by acts of conscience in the present, people will be implicated as both fallible and faulty individuals.

First, morally sensitive people remain silent at times because they fear that they will be implicated in the wrongs that they are thinking of speaking about. These fears may have one or more of several bases. For example, though I may feel impelled to raise questions about what I regard as serious violations of safety precautions, I fear that the supervisors and engineers guilty of this carelessness are likely to be angered by the subsequent inquiries and that the latter in turn are likely to uncover my own extra efforts in arranging a contract with a supplier who happens to be a long-time friend. Even though I think that the latter is defensible both in terms of the procedures used in contracting for these services and in terms of the benefits to the corporation, still I feel vulnerable to criticisms that I may have violated conflict-of-interest guidelines. Because I know that the supervisors and engineers I am thinking about openly criticizing also happen to know of my relationship with this supplier, I fear that they may retaliate and that I may in turn be roasted on technical grounds. In this example the grounds of feeling implicated are distant and accidental. Usually they are closer and more direct. Thus, using the example just cited, suppose that I am fully aware of the careless neglect of safety precautions, which in this case involved the hurried loading of not-carefully-cleaned boxcars with toxic chemicals. I know of this problem because of my responsibility for arranging for train transportation schedules for completed products going to diverse locations as well as the arrival of varied supplies. I am not directly responsible for arranging the loading of wastes, but I have put pressure on those involved because of my overall concern for scheduling. I knew that some shortcuts were being taken, but I said nothing because everything seemed to be working just fine. However, if an accident occurred—and a serious one occurred in the original events on which this account is based—then it is likely that I too would be implicated because I both tolerated and seemed to foster the careless loading practices. Thus, no matter what alibis I may voice, fundamentally I fail to speak up in a timely manner because I fear that the subsequent investigations will find me acting in ways that promoted the abuses about which I am about to blow the whistle.

Sometimes we feel implicated because we have not reported on wrongs, even though we neither caused nor encouraged them, or have acted to cover them up (Miceli and Near 1992). Our actions or inactions may be comparatively innocent, such as those of the supervisors who failed to pass along adverse drug reports or safety inquiries from ship captains. They may be more serious, such as those of Vandiver and Lawson, who prepared a report falsifying information. These people were all implicated in wrongs being committed, not because they were directly responsible for producing defective or unsafe products but because they played a role in obstructing accurate and timely communication about these wrongs. In some measure, they all recognized that they ought to speak up. Depending on the case, initially they either failed to speak or spoke up timidly and were rebuffed. Subsequently they either whispered further concern or remained silent, rationalizing that the matter was not that important or that they had tried as best as they could to speak up. As matters in question became more serious, in all cases they began to recognize that they ought to have acted more forthrightly earlier. They also recognized that they were implicated in the wrongs by their failure to speak up more forcefully. In some cases, such as the managers at Thoresend shipping company, they rationalized that the issues at hand were really insignificant and not worth further worry. The ferries had worked quite well in the past in spite of the concerns raised by the shipmasters. In other cases, such as the one involving the Air Force brake, the report writers became more agitated, began to prepare portfolios to protect themselves against accusation of wrongdoing, and finally spoke out. In all cases their temporary silence was occasioned and reinforced by their own feelings of being implicated.

Feelings of being potentially implicated by voicing concern about the wrongs of others produces two contrary but complementary apprehensions. On the one hand, we may worry about getting others in trouble when we are not really free from complicity, occasioned if nothing else by our own silence. On the other hand, we may worry that speaking up will eventually cause accusatory fingers to be pointed at us for tacitly condoning the wrongs, for failing to speak up, or for related errors of our own. Typically, our anxiety is caused not just about being found out but about being accused under circumstances that are potentially embarrassing and that will not allow us to easily explain and defend our own behavior.

Second, people sometimes remain morally mute and inattentive because they feel that speaking out or conducting further investigation will entail using means that are themselves morally questionable. Hesitation is provoked by a number of typical anxieties. For example, many people feel that blowing the whistle on questionable activities of peers and supervisors is like tattling. We often refer to this activity pejoratively as snitching or ratting, and we refer to the people who do it as finks or stool pigeons. Speaking up seems to be the equivalent of trying to get someone else in trouble because we are angry at them. Speaking up feels equivalent to tattling at least in part because people usually feel angry at any others whose questionable conduct has put them in the uncomfortable position of having to decide whether to speak up or not. Tattling is frowned upon as an intentionally malicious act, so many people pause a long time before voicing because initially speaking up has the feel of an act that is itself questionable. Additionally, talking with colleagues and friends about the questionable behavior of third parties feels like gossiping, which may be innocent but often assumes a malicious tone and often passes along, while embellishing, misleading information. Because gossiping is often entertaining, albeit at the expense of absent but known third parties, we may find it both difficult to resist but also mildly discomforting. Gossiping often makes us feel two-faced because we are adopting a public face by which we respect and defer to others whom we discredit in private conversations behind their backs. Raising questions about the questionable conduct of others, however, places us in the equivalent position whereby we are adopting a public attitude that at the moment differs from the one we voice privately with friends and associates.

People sometimes hesitate and draw back rather than investigate further clues about possible wrongdoings because of morally questionable features often associated with these investigations. Thus, pursuing investigations often entails suspecting others who have heretofore been recipients of our trust. Doubting and suspecting feel like betrayal, especially if it turns out that the initial clues were not symptoms of greater wrongs but really quite explicable and defensible acts. Suspecting itself seems like a minor weakness compared to launching a private, surreptitious investigation of telltale signs. The latter often involves taking liberties, discreetly to be sure, to make inquiries (that may inadvertently shed unjustifiable doubts among others), to use informants, and to look through private papers. These acts may turn out to be not only excusable but justifiable whenever investigations provide telling evidence of suspected wrongdoings. In the meantime these acts seem questionable, and hence the reluctance to engage in them.

Some people are reluctant to speak up or become more responsive regarding particular incidents of wrongdoing because such voicing or inquiring necessarily involves them in breaking prior promises. Overtly or tacitly we make many promises as we participate in organizational life. Whatever other specific promises we agree to, we inherently promise to support the organizations we work for, to protect their technical and trade secrets, and to perform the tasks assigned to us. As we contemplate speaking up about observed wrongs, sometimes we begin to feel that such actions would compromise or slight the promises we have made: By speaking up, we might be exposing the organization to potentially hurtful publicity and in some ways exposing organizational secrets. When considering particular organizational wrongdoings, whether manufacturing risky products, violations of public regulations regarding marketing, or working conditions, outsiders characteristically ask how organizational members aware of these wrongs could remain silent. They often raise this question as if the alternatives faced by organizational members aware of these wrongdoings were simply posed between doing what was morally right, on the one hand, and acting in their own self-interest, on the other hand. Many times, however, organizational members may not experience this kind of dilemma in such clear-cut terms. They often experience a tension between opposing moral claims: either keeping promises they have made to the organization, which seems to call for them not to speak up loudly or publicly, or speaking up and investigating wrongs in ways that will involve them in not honoring these prior promises.

In the Yale University studies conducted by Stanley Milgram, subjects of the experiments often continued administering apparently increasingly powerful electric shocks to persons who made errors in the experiment and also acted as if they were suffering from increasing pain as a result of these shocks. The subjects had been instructed to administer the shocks as a learning device to help the other persons learn to make correct answers by being punished for wrong answers. The overall experiment was designed to discover what factors would lead people to ignore the apparent suffering of others, to violate their own inner sense of right and wrong, and instead to continue to follow the original orders set by the researchers. Although this was how Milgram formulated the matter, this understanding of what was taking place seems too restrictive. After all, the research experiment began with an interchange of promises between the researcher and the subjects. The researcher promised that no one would be harmed by the research and instructed subjects to continue when they raised questions about whether everything was okay. The veracity of the researcher's promises—that no one would be harmed—seemed to be validated by his status as a university professor, a scientist, and the administrator of an ongoing research project for which the subject was only one of many like subjects, as well as by his objective, calm manner. The subjects correspondingly promised to follow instructions and abide by the rules governing the experiment. Many subjects felt mildly if not extremely apprehensive about keeping this promise as they witnessed the apparent, but actually faked, pain of the other person, who was in fact a hired actor. Many hesitated to act even as the apparent pain of the others became more severe. The factors motivating these subjects to act or not act were complex. I will later argue that the most decisive factor that led some people to call a halt to the experiment sooner than others was not a personality trait but the opportunity to talk about their reactions and feelings with another person, whether that was another subject, the researchers, or the hired actor. At this point, however, I wish to focus on a different feature, namely how the reluctance to call a halt was in part occasioned or reinforced by the moral act of interchanging what seemed to be valid promises. To call a halt required the subjects to undertake an act that was in part immoral because it violated promises they had just made in good faith (Milgram 1974).

We have now reviewed a variety of ways in which people may feel implicated if they decide to speak out or respond more directly to the concerns of others. I have attempted to give an empathetic account without defending or justifying in any way the failures of these people to act more forthrightly. If we hope to foster more speaking up and attentive responsiveness, we need to be able to identify and address factors that seem to impede the development and expression of active consciences. Although we may discover cases in which the fears of being implicated are more or less realistic and cases in which the extent and seriousness of implication are greater or smaller, it can be argued that forthright moral action often involves the possibility of being implicated in some way or another. Although we often imagine moral actions that are wholly virtuous and innocent of any ambiguity, responsible moral action frequently lacks this purity and innocence (Niebuhr 1932). Often, responsible moral action entails acknowledging our prior complicity or undertaking actions that are morally ambiguous. In order to gain support for disenfranchised workers, for example, we may need to organize and exert power so that corporate representatives will be persuaded to listen to us. If a given corporation wants its suppliers and customers to comply with its own environmental and safety standards, such as those now being adopted in the chemical industry, they often have to use pressure to gain this cooperation. If we are going to alert others about perceived violations in accounting procedures, we may need to reveal confidences. Clearly the subjects in Milgram's studies could only halt applying supposed electric shocks to others by breaking promises to comply with instructions and abide by the rules of the experiment. If officials at A. H. Robbins who had initially remained silent when alerted of possible dangers associated with their products decided subsequently to speak up, they would necessarily have to acknowledge their own initial inactions.

The existentialist philosopher and theologian Paul Tillich described this predicament in the following terms. Often, in order to act with a strong conscience in ambiguous settings, we must foster the courage that allows us to accept authentic feelings of bad conscience that often accompany these acts. He had in mind examples such as the acts of courage that led some pacifist Germans to join in attempts to assassinate Hitler or the willingness of others to lie to officials in order to protect hidden Jews from being discovered (Tillich 1963). The more mundane cases we have already reviewed exemplify the same basic phenomena: Responsible moral actions often entail recognizing that we have already been, or are allowing ourselves to become, implicated in some morally questionable activities in order to address forthrightly more serious wrongs that would otherwise not be dealt with in a timely and effective manner. In their attempts to avoid the possibility of being implicated and in their corresponding aspirations to be or seem morally innocent and uncompromised, however, many otherwise conscientious people remain morally mute and deaf.

The Claims of Other Preoccupations

Many businesspeople fail to voice their moral concerns because they feel so extended by other commitments that they think they do not have the time and energy to take on additional involvements. They feel that their plates are full. Although they may recognize the injustice in the treatment of junior staff and mentally approve of the efforts by their businesses to help with a community clean-up campaign, they feel that they have no reservoir of extra time and energy to draw upon so that they can speak out and become more involved. They feel overwhelmed by the claims already made by their jobs and their families, as well as by their neighborhood, professional, friendship, and religious commitments. They experience what the sociologist Harold Wilensky (1961) referred to as "life-cycle squeeze." They feel that numerous demands are being put upon them at the same time and that often it required a good deal of juggling and cutting corners to get done what they hoped to do. They may well feel that they are not fully doing justice to their current commitments and feel hounded by their own sense that they could and ought to do more. Wilensky observed the way "life-cycle squeeze" was experienced by younger and middle-aged adults as they were starting and rearing families, seeking to advance their careers, and establishing themselves in new neighborhoods and communities.

People who feel preoccupied by other commitments not only become hesitant about speaking up and getting involved but also typically become less attentive and more blind about moral issues and concerns in the first place. As if they were wearing blinders and mufflers, they just do not see many moral problems and do not focus their attention enough to comprehend other issues about which they may be vaguely aware. Like most people they will respond with alacrity to urgent cries for help they directly witness, whether in the form of a worker injured by a machine or a friend desperate for a short-term loan. They regularly practice the art, however, of tuning out other less immediate and critical calls for assistance. Sensing that they are near their own limits of energy, identification, and time, they seem to pull in the moral antennae by which they might sense and keep track of issues and concerns affecting the organizations and communities of which they are a part. They are correspondingly prone to exhibiting many of the symptoms of moral deafness and blindness that we have already reviewed, such as the tendencies toward shortsightedness and blurred moral vision as well as the disinclination to investigate questionable circumstances.

Many businesspeople feel especially preoccupied by advancing their own careers. What counts is winning successive promotions and not being passed over. These concerns especially affect younger businesspeople when their reputations as good, effective managers are being formed or not formed. Accordingly, ambitious younger managers will often demonstrate a willingness to work long hours, to take on extra assignments, and to consider geographical displacements in order to further their career aspirations. Often in the process, they become preoccupied by seeking to please and win recognition from relevant superiors and senior executives. To a considerable degree they may decide what projects to work for and what positions to support publicly on the basis of what these significant others are likely to favor and find worthy of note. As a result being career-minded ordinarily involves something more than simply working hard. Ambitious managers often devote considerable energy and imagination attempting to establish those kinds of networks and track records that will gain advancements for them given the particular patterns of organizational opportunities and politics (Jackall 1988). These efforts in turn frequently become enormously preoccupying.

The fact that many businesspeople possess other preoccupations explains in part why they may become morally mute, deaf, and blind. People possess only limited amounts of time, energy, and imagination. There are limits to the amount of commitments we can take on. Nonetheless, possessing other commitments does not really justify moral deafness and blindness. Even if we cannot readily assume additional responsibilities and engagements, we can still remain aware and sensitive to moral concerns that surround us. The fact that we are already busy does limit our ability to pursue additional activities, but it does not necessarily affect our capacity to perceive, foresee, recognize, and acknowledge moral concerns that bear upon our lives. Although the existence of existing commitments explains our inability to make additional commitments, it does not prevent us from being attentive to concerns raised by others. Likewise, although our current involvements may render us emotionally unavailable for fully sympathizing with problems voiced by others, they do not necessarily obstruct or prevent us from empathizing with these concerns and indicating our interest in them. The existence of other commitments may be able to explain our reluctance to voice our views about moral issues to the extent that speaking up also entails the probability of further follow-up involvements. In these settings moral silence results from a tactical judgment by which we choose not to speak up on particular issues at this point in time, not because we do not recognize their importance but because we judge them to be less compelling of our attention and efforts than other issues to which we have already committed ourselves.

When businesspeople become morally mute as a result of other preoccupations, however, it is rarely on account of such tactical judgments. Often the opposite occurs. It is those who are already very involved responding to prior moral issues who are most willing to think about new concerns. The saying is:

"If you want something to get done, you will get a busy person to do it." People do not usually become morally mute, deaf, and blind simply because they are already overcommitted but because of the character of these prior involvements. Problems occur when these involvements become overly preoccupying and distracting. This occurs when these other involvements are especially anxiety provoking or require considerable energy to defend against criticism or too close scrutiny. Many people, for example, become preoccupied by career advancement not simply or primarily because they are ambitious but rather because they feel vulnerable to losing recognition, to receiving adverse evaluation, or to being passed over. Similarly, any questionable business or personal involvements that require considerable tending to protect from being too closely observed by others or too critically examined by ourselves are also likely to preoccupy us excessively. Examples of such involvement include everything from managing private companies on the side in addition to our regular employment, personal habits that might bring disfavor if more widely known, and the excessive use of discretionary time for personal purposes. As a personal defense to being exposed too openly because of these other preoccupations, people characteristically become morally silent and inattentive, nearsighted and tunnel-visioned. Although they possess ready-to-hand excuses because of the extent of their current involvements, these excuses at the same time obscure people from recognizing the extent to which they have tacitly allowed themselves to become morally deaf and blind. In the end it is not other commitments as such that occasion or reinforce moral silence. Rather this deficiency is brought on by involvements that become so preoccupying that they cause us to become morally inattentive, insensitive, and unseeing because they overly distract us and consume our energy, attention, and imagination.

Ethical Inarticulacy

Businesspeople often do not speak about or respond to moral concerns because they do not know quite how to frame issues about which they feel concerned. Sensing that particular staffing arrangements are unjust or that current advertising campaigns make dubious comparisons with competitors' products but not knowing quite how to state these issues, they silence their own misgivings. Intuitively they may recognize the existence of a number of moral concerns related to their businesses, but they do not feel comfortable in speaking up about them. Like a beginner just learning to speak a foreign language who worries about using words the wrong way with incorrect tenses or inappropriate word orders, they fear that when they speak up they will sound strange, perhaps incomprehensible, and certainly unaccomplished and awkward. Not wanting to sound like babbling fools and not wishing to put themselves in positions where they might be soundly put down by others capable of skillfully countering their statements, they remain silent and make no efforts to comprehend the complex moral concerns raised by others.

The sense of inarticulacy assumes several forms. It arises when we think that we don't have sufficient information or fear that we don't have a large enough view. How can we speak up, we think, until we can obtain a fuller, clearer picture? Often we fear that we will really be out-argued. We do not feel confident in being able to counter the arguments we expect to be marshalled against our own statements. We sense that others will clearly possess the last word because we do not feel capable of stating our own positions with sufficient vigor and rigor and demonstrating persuasively the reasons why alternative views are wrong. We are not used to articulating moral arguments. Consequently, we may possess strong intuitive feelings that particular practices are wrong or that specific objectives are good and worthy of being pursued, but our primitive knowledge of moral logic and arguments leave us incapable of expressing our thoughts except in what seem like simplistic and overly naive terms.

Whenever we experience this sense of inarticulacy, we often initially feel that it arises because we lack appropriate vocabularies and necessary knowledge. This may indeed be the problem at least to a degree. Before we speak out about any issue, whether dealing with risk levels, marketing practices, the uses of privileged information, or proper exercise of fiduciary responsibilities, we need to seek out and review relevant information. Nonetheless, we need not become experts. We can raise questions on the basis of available information. Typically, our inarticulacy is not fundamentally occasioned because we lack knowledge and vocabularies, even though we tend to think of the problem in these terms. For the most part we can, if we are disposed to do so, readily raise questions, attend to the concerns of others, and comprehend moral issues utilizing our current vocabularies and funds of knowledge that we can easily acquire.

Practically, articulacy, the capacity to communicate clearly and intelligibly and with a coherent grasp of the issues at hand, is related to four factors:

1. the ability to assert one's own position;
2. the capacity to take into account the views of others;
3. the skill at phrasing ideas to show the connection between things being discussed;
4. the talent for stating these things clearly.

These factors are important because we can communicate articulately only if at the same time we assert our own points of view in ways that our audiences are likely to find comprehensible and in ways that simply connect the issues under discussion both to our concerns and the concerns of our audience. Correspondingly, we are likely to feel inarticulate to the extent that we do not really assert our own positions, that we do not communicate coherently to our audiences, that we cannot find intelligible ways of showing the relationships between the matters we are discussing, and that we cannot communicate these matters clearly.

One, unless we firmly assert our own particular concerns, we are likely to feel inarticulate no matter how logical or how informed our statements become. If we are not really saying what we wish to say, if we are hiding our true positions behind what we think are more-palatable cover stories, we are likely to feel that we are not getting our messages across. Unless this is done for temporary tactical reasons, we thereby misrepresent our concerns. In order to state our views clearly, we must first work on making sure that we vocally and forthrightly represent our positions. In order to accomplish this objective, we need not develop arguments that leave others, who may oppose us, either speechless or without retort. To assert is not necessarily to convince others, to overcome their arguments, or to gain their agreements. Assertion represents a medium point between persuading others to give in to our positions and us giving in to their position. Assertion calls for an emotional directness by which people state their views and why they are important in settings that allow others to do likewise. Clearly, people can gain experience learning how to assert themselves (Waters 1982).

Two, unless we attempt to communicate in relation to the terms used and the concerns raised by our audiences, we are likely to feel that our messages are not being comprehended. If we make no attempts to translate our concerns into images they readily understand, then our communications are likely to go over their heads and pass by their sides. Our communications will not appear articulate to others unless they are intelligible to them. We can work at making our discussions intelligible by striving to make them syntactically coherent and logically consistent, by seeking to state our ideas simply, and by trimming them of distracting elements that do not substantially add to what we want to say. We can make these efforts quite independent of any consideration of our audiences. Our well-crafted messages, however, may still seem practically unintelligible to our audiences unless we attempt to phrase our concerns in relation to their beliefs, assumptions, and interests. Correspondingly, our communications can become unintelligible and thereby inarticulate to our audiences to the degree that we fail to restate our arguments in relation to images, objectives, and turns of phrase with which they are familiar. To be sure, it is not necessary to reduce our concerns to terms they already accept. We may wish to challenge their assumptions and call them to change or expand their objectives. But if we hope that our messages will be regarded as intelligible and articulate, we must at least show some connections between what we wish to emphasize and points of reference and contact in the worlds of our audiences.

Three, we are likely to feel inarticulate to the degree that we are unable to find and express connections among the several concerns we are trying to communicate. In making this statement, I am making a very broad claim that needs to be explained. The root from which the word "articulate" comes means to join together. Articulate people do just that. They are able to see configurations and patterns among things and make these interconnections and gestalts apparent to others. We can describe this connecting activity in a variety of ways. For example, in a comparative study of accountants, Gaa and Ponemon (1993) found that accountants who were most professionally sophisticated about moral concerns were more likely to use analogical and configural patterns of reasoning about moral issues. Because they were able to see patterns and use metaphors, they were able to discern problems with greater facility and state their observations more concisely. From another perspective, we could say that articulate people are more likely to use their imagination actively to sort and re-sort information in order to find patterns and relationships that make sense of otherwise bewildering data. By hitting upon fitting metaphors, which in turn refer to relationships between phenomena, articulate people can make heretofore opaque matters seem interesting and comprehensible. Correspondingly, people are likely to feel inarticulate to the extent that they cannot identify or state these kinds of connections, whether by seeing patterns, by using analogies and metaphors, or by making straightforward associations.

Four, unless they can state their observations comparatively clearly, people are likely to feel inarticulate. To be sure, we do not become articulate by oversimplifying complex matters. We must do justice to the intricacies and subtleties of matters under consideration. With respect to simple issues, ones that involve clear rights and wrongs, it is important to be direct and straightfor-ward. More elaborate statements are obfuscating. However, the same cannot be said with respect to more complex issues. In fact, moral talk in business often errs by adopting too simplistic and too moralistic modes of expression. Many moral issues facing businesspeople cannot be formulated in relation to simple right/wrong standards. To be morally articulate in these cases calls for attempts to state matters clearly while still indicating the complexities of the issues at hand. People feel inarticulate to the degree that they feel they cannot express their concerns without either delivering elaborate accounts and long stories or being simplistic and superficial.

People become ethically inarticulate for several different but interrelated reasons. What fundamentally matters is being able to communicate our own views directly in comprehensible terms to others in ways that allow them to see simply the interrelationship between matters being discussed. Articulacy is a skill that can be cultivated and developed. We can learn more forthrightly to assert and more attentively to phrase our concerns in terms recognizable and intelligible to our audiences. We can likewise learn to use analogies and metaphors and recognize patterns to make what we want to say more compre-hensible. Inarticulacy springs not primarily from lack of learning or from the inability to state our concerns more precisely in sophisticated terms. Rather it is severally occasioned and reinforced by not asserting ourselves, by not addressing our audiences in language they understand, by presenting material without indicating how it fits together, and by sounding either overly simple or confusing. Fundamentally it arises from lack of experience. Although some may be more gifted than others at these several skills, we can learn and improve our competencies, thereby becoming more morally articulate.

Conclusion: The Strengthening and Weakening of Individual Consciences

I have reviewed separately five factors that play a role in bringing about or reinforcing moral silence, deafness, and/or blindness. I conclude this discussion by examining the overall impact of these factors, inquiring at the same time about what might be done to reduce their influence. Taken as a whole, I am interested in analyzing those factors within individuals that cause them to muffle, constrict, stifle, starve, and silence the sensuous expression of their consciences.

We can learn something about weak consciences by reflecting on factors associated with unusually strong expressions of conscience. People who at great personal risk protest against abuses, people who commit time and personal resources to furthering particular moral causes, and people who steadfastly support their organizations through difficult times in spite of opportunities to go elsewhere demonstrate considerable strength of conscience. Their beliefs in specific moral commitments are so strong that they are willing to put up with criticism, adverse circumstances, and depleted personal resources. We can think of many people like this: people like Gerald Durrell, who established the Jersey Wildlife Preservation Trust to help endangered species; people like Rosa Parks, who refused to move from her seat on a Montgomery, Alabama, bus and thus initiated a bus boycott that led to the desegregation of the transportation systems in that town and the beginnings of the contemporary civil rights movement in the southern United States; and people like Rev. Leon Sullivan, who persuaded General Motors to defy apartheid laws in South Africa. These people were not afraid of further, uncertain engagements—they seemed to invite them. They did not allow themselves to become resigned—whether they were successful or not in their actions, they were determined to act. Like the major characters in Camus' *The Plague*, whether they succeeded or not in overcoming the evils they were fighting, or whether they realized or not the ideals they pursued, it was important for them to resist the forces that brought distress and injustice. They were not afraid of being implicated because they might adopt questionable means, which included evading laws and ignoring conventional wisdom. Although they might already possess other commitments, they did not worry about taking on additional ones: The former neither distracted them nor consumed their energy in defensive cover-ups. They were able to articulate their concerns forcefully because they asserted their positions directly in ways clearly comprehensible to their audiences. Consider Rosa Parks not budging from her seat, or Gerald Durrell collecting wildlife from endangered species and transporting them to the preserve he established on the Isle of Jersey. These people required no enlarged vocabularies or training in moral reasoning in order to speak articulately about the moral issues that concerned them. In a profound way the strength of their convictions overrode any of the distracting influences we have just been considering. Although their devotion to particular moral projects probably fostered a degree of tunnel vision and inattention to other moral issues, they exhibited few additional symptoms of moral silence, deafness, and blindness.

We can see from these kinds of examples that people with strong, vibrant consciences are not bothered by the factors we have been discussing largely because they are moved often single-mindedly by intense convictions. Powerful convictions overcome the fears, anxieties, feelings of resignation, distractions, and hesitancy we have examined. People with these kinds of strong convictions are exceptional in many ways. Few humans exhibit such extraordinary commitments. Few humans are moved by such saintlike devotion to particular moral concerns. Still, strong convictions do matter. They render negligible these other fears, distractions, and hesitancies.

We can take two steps to strengthen our consciences and correspondingly reduce the degree to which we allow ourselves to become morally mute, deaf, and blind. One, we can work at developing our own sense of priorities. Two, we can distinguish between the moral objectives of being responsible and being morally worthy and focus more of our energies on the former rather than the latter.

Establishing priorities. It is important that we establish our own moral priorities, clearly distinguishing concerns that really matter to us from ones we regard as being less vital and worthy of our response. This is not a simple matter. To do so at any moment in time, we must be able to evaluate and determine the relative weight of at least three distinct considerations:

1. The question of importance asks which issues or concerns we judge to be the most important because of how many people are affected, because of the dangers and risks or opportunities involved, or because they touch upon matters we regard as especially compelling.
2. The question of competence and calling asks which issues or concerns we are in a position to be able to affect most tellingly and to which we can contribute most appreciably. To which issues and concerns do we sense that we may have a calling to respond?
3. The question of timeliness asks which issues and concerns compel the most immediate attention; which are most urgent or timely (Bird and Gandz 1991).

These are three distinct sets of judgments. Our internal perspective on moral concerns reflects our judgments on these questions, whether we make these overtly on the basis of reflection and discussions or tacitly as we act. De facto we establish our moral priorities whether we are aware we are making these judgments or not. Implicitly we determine what is important to us, what we feel competent to respond to, and what we have time to consider.

To the extent that we do not establish our priorities reflectively and thoughtfully, to the degree that we fail to see that distinct questions of importance, competency and calling, and timeliness enter into our judgments, we become vulnerable to feeling overwhelmed and confused. We are likely to respond to a particular issue simply because it is urgent, even though we would reflectively judge it to be of little significance; or we are likely to respond to a different concern because it seems very weighty, even though we are not well placed to have any impact upon it. Many moral issues arise in the context of our personal, professional, and civic lives. We cannot respond effectively to all of them. In order to become effectively engaged with respect to some issues, it is necessary to be able to draw a line and to stay uninvolved with other issues. In order to say "Yes" to particular involvements, it is necessary to be able to say "No" to others. Saying "No" to issues with which we do not become involved is integral to the process of focusing and taking an interest, which are in turn constitutive dimensions of being attentive.

As discussed in Chapter 2, there are a number of reasons why we might choose at least momentarily not to speak up about specific moral concerns. For example, we may remain silent temporarily to await a more opportune moment to voice our concerns. Recognizing that others are already effectively acting to remedy a given problem, we may choose to act on issues less attended to. We may decide that we are not very well placed to make a difference on particular concerns and instead invest our energies where our contributions are more likely to matter. We may choose to work on some issues quietly out of public view rather than publicly and thereby announce a disinterest tactically in order to pursue a line of problem solving that might not work as well if it were open to public scrutiny. Consider the way the Norwegian government used its good offices quietly in order to arrive at the beginnings of a diplomatic accord between the Israelis and Palestinians. In these examples people remain attentive and comprehending of moral issues about which they at least temporarily choose to remain publicly silent. Because they possess a clear sense of their moral priorities, they do not need to become either unresponsive or partially blind about moral issues about which they have chosen tactically not to speak.

This capacity on a practical basis to set moral priorities works to reduce and overcome two of the factors that directly weaken the sensuous expressions of conscience: The fear of other, uncertain engagements and the claims of other, competing commitments. To the degree that we feel confident about saying "No" to some moral issues because we have voiced our "Yes" to others, to the degree that we have a clear workable sense of moral priorities, neither of these fears needs to distract us or make us needlessly defensive. Contrariwise, to the degree that we have not worked out a sense of moral priorities, we are likely to experience these fears and distractions, and we are likely as well to become correspondingly morally deaf and blind.

Distinguishing between being morally right and being morally worthy. When we judge the morality of specific actions, we often ask two quite different questions. We inquire first about whether the action itself is right. We often use diverse criteria to answer this question, focusing in varying degrees on the character of the action itself and on its outcomes. For example, we may debate the pros and cons of reducing polluted air emissions using incineration by considering beneficial and costly results and by evaluating the merits of this approach compared to others. Or, we may debate the merits and shortcomings of extra efforts at promoting visible minorities again by examining likely outcomes as well as the fairness of the procedures involved. In addition to this question about the rightness or fittingness of the actions themselves, we also often ask a second question about whether the people involved in these actions are acting in ways that are morally worthy. Should those involved be praised or blamed, applauded or criticized? In order to answer this question, we need to consider factors beyond the actions themselves: We need to inquire about the intentions with which people acted and we need to know how easy or difficult it was for them to do what they did. Generally we assign greater praise when people act in more altruistic ways, especially when their generosity arises in spite of the limitations of their means.

These are both important moral questions but they address different although related concerns. We may well defend a number of actions because we judge them to be right even if people initiated them with morally indifferent or morally questionable intentions. For example, we may applaud added customer services of banks because these actions have greatly helped low-income clients with their finances while still recognizing these services were largely introduced to gain competitive advantage and they cost the banks next to nothing. We may thus conclude that this action is morally good in its execution and consequence but not one meriting much moral praise for those who introduced it.

We often conflate these two questions. We may from one side assume that people are acting in morally worthy ways simply because the action itself, in this case offering additional customer services in low-income neighborhoods, seems correct. Or we may assume that people are acting in morally unworthy ways because we judge particular actions to be unfairly executed, such as, for example, the failure to provide sufficient warnings with respect to corporate lay-offs. From the other side, we may presume that a particular action is indeed right or wrong simply because it is undertaken with high-minded moral intentions or quite amoral business instincts. Clearly, the question of whether an action or policy is right or wrong is different and distinct from, although related to, the question of whether particular individuals are acting in morally worthy ways.

Our moral vision is diminished and distorted whenever we base our judgments about the rightness or wrongness of actions solely or primarily on our evaluations of the moral worthiness or unworthiness of those involved. Our moral vision becomes correspondingly reduced whenever judgments about particular actions are primarily if not exclusively shaped by our preoccupation with bolstering and enhancing our own sense of moral worth. Morally minded people in particular are prone to becoming overly concerned if not distracted by their efforts to protect and shore up their own feelings of moral worthiness. Correspondingly, decisions about how to act are influenced more by considerations of what will make them feel virtuous rather than considerations of which actions in these circumstances are most appropriate.

Whenever we are motivated to act morally in order to largely gain or maintain the approval of others, we are as much or more moved to maintain our own sense of moral worth, in this case shored up by the judgments of others, as we are to perform acts we judge to be responsible or right on their own terms. Frequently our attempts to be virtuous are undertaken to enhance and protect our own sense of goodness as they are acted out to extend justice or promote charity for others. Because we are so concerned to avoid acts that may leave us with bad consciences or may be judged improper by others who are morally concerned, we often go out of our way to retain feelings of innocence or virtue.

A number of Christian thinkers—including Augustine, Luther, and Calvin—argued that personal feelings of moral worth or goodness are indeed valuable but should not or cannot be directly sought without making the character of moral action too self-centered. They used language that at times obscures their observations for contemporary secular audiences. They used the word "justification," referring to the good or favorable judgment of God upon human actions and hence, to refer to the highest or most fundamental experience of moral worth. They argued that a personal apprehension of one's ultimate moral worth, referred to here as God's good judgment or justification, could not really be won by numerous well-meaning moral acts, especially acts of penance, undertaken primarily to obtain this apprehension. Rather, they argued that this sense ought to be viewed as a gift bestowed by God or as a gracious by-product of acting responsibly. Trusting—having faith—that God would grant this gift appropriately, it was the responsibility of Christians, these authors argued, to follow the commandments and fittingly honor God's creation through lives well lived (Augustine 1955; Luther 1961; Calvin 1960).

From our perspective, the tendency to think of moral action too closely or exclusively in terms of the direct pursuit of moral worth or moral goodness in turn directly reinforces two of the factors that weaken personal expression of conscience. Not only does this pursuit often render individuals excessively self-preoccupied, it also tends to occasion and reinforce feelings of resignation and to aggravate worries and anxieties about being morally implicated. If we too ardently seek to feel morally worthy, if we too single-mindedly seek to feel morally good, several morally questionable consequences follow. We are liable to assign moral priorities not in relation to need, importance, or urgency but in relation to calculations about what will make us feel good. We become like the religious prohibitionists who felt proud about their temperance while maintaining a color bar against blacks in their congregations and neighborhoods and being judgmental about immigrants. We are liable to deceive ourselves about our own moral slips. As managers we become prone to institute programs that gain us good repute—perhaps showy corporate sponsorship—rather than instituting more difficult and less easily recognizable personnel or marketing reforms. Additionally we are likely to become resigned because we see no way that we can become the kinds of morally pure saints who never have to compromise, never have to seek the lesser of alternative evils, or never have to tolerate morally questionable practices in order to pursue valued objectives. To the degree that we become preoccupied by the pursuit of moral worth, we are liable to think of moral action as necessarily virtuous and correspondingly become resigned and cynical because genuinely virtuous acts seem too self-sacrificing or too personally or organizationally costly.

ORGANIZATIONAL FACTORS

I have examined how both cultural and individual influences occasion and aggravate moral silence, deafness, and blindness. I now examine organizational influences. In this case my focus is double and mixed. I examine the degree to which organizational factors affect the likelihood that individual constituents will be morally mute, deaf, and blind as well as that organizations themselves will act morally mute, deaf, and blind. These are distinct but overlapping questions. Organizations vary in the degree to which they vocalize moral concerns, respond attentively to concerns raised by their members and stakeholders, and perceive and acknowledge these concerns with vision and perspective.

Organizational factors powerfully affect the kinds of issues their members tend to respond to, the terms in which they classify problems, and the vocabularies by which they discuss them. They influence the stories people recall as they address current concerns. The cultural anthropologist Mary Douglas (1986) argues that it is possible to examine the ways organizations think. In particular she notes the distinguishably different ways contrasting types of organizations perceive risks and assign blame (Douglas and Wildowsky 1982). Drawing upon models developed by Williamson (1985) and Ouchi (1981), she argues that perceptions of risk and blame worthiness are raised and handled much differently by organizations that are market driven, hierarchical, or more like voluntary associations. She argues that differences in organizational types affect which kinds of problems organizations become blind to. When crises occur, she contends, market-oriented organizations tend to blame their leaders, bureaucratic organizations point to the loss of group commitment, and voluntary associations assume individual treachery (Douglas 1992).

Other observers have also attempted to examine the relationship between types of organizations and typical responses to the moral issues they face (Jacobs 1992; Waters 1978). Jackall (1988) in particular analyzes at length the constellation of moral blinders that modern bureaucratic organizations create for their members. He maintains that these organizations engender a morality-in-practice that causes members to defer excessively to their superiors and to overlook important ethical concerns.

Even though analyses by Douglas, Jackall, and others are often instructive, they tend to overstate the actual influence of these very general organizational patterns. They overlook other, less general features of organizations, which may often decisively influence their moral orientations and practices. Additionally, by focusing attention on these general organizational types, they leave their readers with the fatalistic sense of the predetermined ways typical organizations behave and with little sense of the more immediate and manageable factors that are subject to modification in ways that these general structures are not. In contrast, in the following discussion I examine a set of attributes that in varying degrees may afflict a wide variety of organizations. I analyze the degree to which these attributes seem to be fostered by different organizational forms. I have chosen to discuss these organizational attributes because of the ways each occasions and reinforces the moral silence, deafness, or blindness of individuals and organizations. Each thereby contributes to the weakening of these sensuous expressions of organizational conscience. Additionally all these attributes can be altered to the benefit of the organizations undertaking these changes and the individuals who are constituents of them.

I analyze four organizational attributes that contribute to moral silence, deafness, and blindness (see Table 6.3).

Table 6.3
The Impact of Organizational Factors on Moral Silence, Deafness, and Blindness

Organizational Factors	Characteristic Features	Impact on Moral Silence, Deafness, and Blindness
Organizational blocks to dissent, questioning, and criticizing	Discourages or penalizes moral questioning and criticizing	Fosters and fortifies moral silence
Top-down organizational accountability	Occasions one-way communications that do not include overt moral discussions	Reinforces moral deafness in upper levels of organization and moral silence in lower levels
Barriers to horizontal communication	Horizontal communication blocked by division and unit rivalries and by the avoidance of open discussions of conflicts	Occasions and reinforces moral silence and deafness between colleagues and coworkers
Blocks to organizational learning	Success and stability can occasion complacency and overconfidence that impede organizational learning	Occasions and reinforces moral blindness and moral deafness

If conscience represents a kind of self-knowing, these factors weaken organizational consciences by markedly reducing either the scope of what is being examined or the patterns of communicating, which allows organizations and their constituents to know themselves.

Organizational Blocks to Dissent, Questioning, and Whistle-Blowing

Organizations often welcome positive comments from their constituents more readily than critical comments. Individuals often feel freer to compliment or voice ideals than they do to dissent, question, or make accusations. Even organizations that go out of the way to encourage open communication often find that few people use the stated opportunities to make complaints or call into question activities by the organization or its constituents. One fairly large business placed sealed metal boxes in its offices and plants so that managers and employees could confidentially report on or raise questions about any actions that seemed to be out of line. Even though a number of questionable activities occurred within this corporation, including a number of conflict-of-interest cases as well as instances of employees abusing corporate resources for their own ends, almost no one used this device to voice concerns. In what ways did this organization discourage speaking up? How did this business, and how do others, create blocks so that their members and constituents do not more readily raise questions and make useful criticism?

In what ways do organizations create blocks that prevent critical observations from rising from the lower-downs to the higher-ups within organizations? Critical observations may assume any of several forms, which include the following: articulated dissent from stated policies; raising questions about specific activities; overtly criticizing either individuals or organizational practices; making complaints about practices that seem unfair or dangerous or questionable; suspecting others of wrongdoing; and accusing others of improprieties. Whistle-blowing represents a range of these kinds of critical observations insofar as the reason for speaking up is to disclose activities that are suspected to be illegal, immoral, or illegitimate (Miceli and Near 1992). It is worth noting that the range in the types of these critical observations is quite broad. In many cases these critical observations could potentially be made by raising questions, initiating inquiries, or making comments rather than making overt accusations or open criticisms.

Organizations block the voicing of critical comments in at least four distinguishable ways.

Not providing effective vehicles for communicating concerns. Many organizations provide no effective vehicles for raising questions, dissenting, or criticizing questionable activities of organizations as a whole or of other individuals within them. They establish no channels for communicating critical comments or neutral fora where really candid questioning can take place. They have established no times for open-ended, freewheeling discussions as part of their executive council or management team meetings. They allow for no hot lines by which ordinary members might raise vital concerns with senior management. They provide no media so ordinary members can raise questions. Often, even if they do establish some means for employees to voice concerns, they do not clearly and fully inform employees of this. Many employees complain that they do not know where to go to raise concerns about moral issues

(Keenan 1990). If critical comments can be made only openly and directly with superiors who are likely to be offended by probing and disturbing questions or upset that things are amiss, ordinary members are likely to hold their tongues.

Most companies provide no other institutions for employees to voice concern other than formal grievance procedures. Of more than 350 Canadian companies surveyed, only 20 percent of the unionized and 6 percent of the nonunionized companies had established some regular procedures for employee voicing. More than half of the institutional means established assumed the form of grievance procedures (Saunders and Leck 1993). Few nonunionized companies have established formal due process procedures to allow employees to raise complaints or questions or resolve disputes (Ewing 1989).

Sometimes organizations that attempt to establish media for making critical comments fail in their efforts in spite of seemingly good intentions. For example, one transnational corporation annually sent out forms to 2,000 upper-level managers and executives and asked them to indicate confidentially if they knew or suspected that any of their actions or those of others in any way violated their corporate code of conduct. Twenty to thirty people each year mentioned questionable activities, more than half of which referred to well-known and acceptable instances in which particular managers had outside interests that might potentially conflict with their corporate responsibilities. Most of the dozen or so additional cases mentioned referred to activities that were already known about by the people in the internal audit department. This annual and moderately expensive exercise turned up almost no new information about questionable activities in an organization of 11,000 employees. Part of the reason this vehicle was not more effective in allowing for and welcoming critical comments was that it did not really allow for neutral question raising. It called for suspicions, confessions, and accusations. A few executives used this medium to shore up their defenses in case anyone might suspect their outside interests. Others, who might well have raised questions or made comments, chose not to use this vehicle, which seemed primarily dedicated to identifying wrongdoing. It was, after all, administered by the internal audit department rather than by human resources, public affairs, or quality assurance.

Nynex, a communication company with 7,000 employees, obtained much better results by establishing a series of confidential phone numbers and mailboxes. By means of these vehicles, overall called Guide-Lines, employees were invited to raise questions and talk about any ethical concerns they had. Initially, in 1990, only a few hundred employees used these media. By 1994, however, over 3,000 inquiries of one kind or another were made. The high volume of use reflected the fact that the range of topics about which organizational members were invited to comment was very broadly set. Forty percent of the calls and letters dealt with personnel matters. Over 55 percent concerned ethical issues broadly defined rather than the more limited focus of misconduct. Nynex was able to solicit extensive participation in its Guide-Lines program by leaving the scope of substantive issues open and wide (David 1994).

Inviting only the most accusatory forms of criticisms. Organizations block the voicing of many critical comments not because they do not invite criticisms but because they seem to invite almost exclusively the most accusatory forms. We have seen this phenomenon in the two examples already cited. The annual survey of 2,000 managers asked them to comment on behavior that seemed to violate the organization's code of conduct. The surveyed managers were in fact asked to sign a statement, which they sent in with their form, acknowledging that they had read the code, recognized its content, promised to abide by its stipulations, and knew of no instances of others violating these standards except for a few well-known cases. This survey had a policing function. It did not invite more general commenting or questioning. The sealed metal boxes were even less successful in eliciting critical or exploratory comments. They were viewed almost exclusively as a means of reporting on the misdeeds of others. Their confidential character did not seem to lead to or invite debates and discussions. If no serious dangers were involved, employees indicated that they felt reluctant to tattle on what often seemed to be minor indiscretions by fellow employees. Their reluctance was reinforced by an announced corporate policy that threatened suspensions for employees caught cheating on expense accounts or raiding company stocks. It did not seem fair to many other employees to expose a fellow employee to economic insecurity for real but moderate wrongs that were not greatly different from excesses tolerated in the previous decade. In both examples, if these corporations had invited their members and constituents to raise questions, to make dissenting comments, and to initiate inquiries, they would probably have received a wider and fuller range of critical comments than they did when the range of comments was much more narrowly focused on instances of behavior that violated or seemed to violate organization codes.

For reasons similar to these, the automobile workers union reacted strongly and negatively when General Motors of Canada established what the company named its Awareline, which company members could use to report on anything from emergencies to possible wrongdoings by the company and its members. Calls on the Awareline were to be anonymous. Callers were to be given a number in case there would be any need for further communications. The union felt the program was an insult to the employees. The union's reaction may be overblown and may reflect the fact that they were not actively involved in setting up this program. Nonetheless, the union was reacting as well to the way the program was largely directed at detecting errors, wrongs, and violations and that it was not inviting two-way consultations but something more like one-way surreptitious surveillance (Gibb-Clark 1995).

Penalizing people for raising valid concerns. Many organizations block the forthright voicing of critical comments because they either penalize those voicing these comments or allow others to penalize them. It is risky to be the bearer of bad news. Organizations do not like to hear that senior executives have been defrauding them or that expensive projects have been poorly planned so as to put others or the environment in danger. In the end this kind of information may help them deal with serious problems. In the meantime it functions largely to endanger their reputations and occasion costly remedial actions. Hence, rarely are the messengers bringing this kind of news honored. Many such informants have subsequently suffered from reprisals at the hands of those they rightly criticized or accused. Although laws have been enacted to protect the employee rights of whistle-blowers in a number of states, provinces, and countries, still many people who have exposed serious corporate wrongs have subsequently lost their jobs (Miceli and Near 1992). Many others have suffered less drastically. Many are temporarily shunned or disfavored.

Penalizing people for raising concerns later proved to be wrong. Organizations block the raising of critical comments whenever they penalize people whose suspicions, accounts, accusations, and conjectures prove to be wrong. In the preceding section, I discussed instances when question raisers were penalized even though the observations and suspicions they voiced seemed to be valid. That is not always the case. Sometimes, those making critical comments misperceive or mishear. Their misapprehension results from honest errors without any malicious intent. Let us assume further that they make their comments professionally and judiciously in ways that do not expose those accused to rumors, public censure, or aggravated and acrimonious litigation. Often organizations reprimand or otherwise penalize those whose criticisms prove unfounded. Most people would agree that whistle-blowers and critics ought to be appropriately sanctioned if they needlessly expose others to public criticism, if they maliciously spread rumors, and if they aggravate acrimonious discussions on the basis of unsubstantiated evidence. But it is not clear that they ought to be penalized for making what later turn out to be erroneous critical comments if they voice their concerns in reasonable and fitting manners. When organizations shun, censure, or otherwise penalize people who raise questions or make critical comments on what subsequently prove to be mistaken observations and conjectures, they will effectively stifle much potentially useful speaking up. Organizational members become reluctant to speak up when they perceive that they will be punished for making honest errors in their observations and reasonable but mistaken judgments about activities that seem to them to be wrong or dangerous or questionable. If members fear such censure, organizations will have silenced most critical comments except with regard to the rare cases for which members have gathered overwhelming evidence that the activities in question are illegal, immoral, or harmful. If organizations genuinely want their constituents to raise critical comments, they need to reward people for speaking up, even if their observations and suspicions prove to be mistaken, so long as they voice their concerns professionally with due respect for the reputations and presumed innocence of those at whom they are pointing their finger.

Organizations often confuse two quite different concerns with respect to the voicing of critical comments: namely, whether those making critical comments do so in ways that are wrong or do so appropriately but on the basis of observations and conjectures that are judged to be wrong. As they attempt to guard against the first set of concerns through various penalties and warnings, organizations often also too severely punish those who innocently or carelessly speak up on the basis of erroneous observations and conjectures.

The Asymmetrical, Top-Down Character of Organizational Accountability

Certain patterns of organizational direction and accountability, more so than others, foster moral silence, deafness, and blindness. Many organizations adopt patterns of direction and accountability that tend to be asymmetrical and one-way. The basic pattern is for directives and policies to begin at the top and to be disseminated down through the organization. Subordinates report on how well they are performing. Superiors hold them accountable but are not in turn held accountable by subordinates. Strictly speaking, the difficulties that this pattern of authority creates are not due to its hierarchical character. Most authority patterns are hierarchical. Rather, problems arise because the relationships between superiors and subordinates are not two-way and interactive. Superiors are thought of as establishing the conditions with which subordinates are expected to comply. Subordinates are expected to have little or no role in establishing priorities, in defining environments, and in setting expectations for superiors. They are expected to comply and to gain corresponding rewards in the forms of remuneration, status privileges, and career opportunities when they perform as expected or better.

A major problem with this administrative pattern, which is indeed wide-spread, is that subordinates are expected to remain comparatively mute with respect to many moral issues that concern them. When interacting with their superiors, subordinates are expected to defer to the latter and to let the latter set the agenda for these discussions and establish the tone and character for them. Accordingly, superiors indicate what topics will be covered, communicate directives, and determine how these matters will be considered. Subordinates in turn report on requested information, follow the lead in these discussions, and indicate how well the directives are being followed. Occasionally subordinates may draw attention to particular problem areas that need more careful scrutiny. They may offer suggestions when asked (Westley 1990). This administrative pattern allows for top-down direction and control. In practice, however, it functions to keep a number of possible topics off the agenda.

For example, subordinates are typically not invited in an exploratory fashion to raise questions and highlight concerns not related to the performance objectives set by superiors. In multidivisional firms this pattern of interaction typically works to keep social issues off the corporate agenda. Superiors at corporate headquarters usually audit the performance of subordinates at divisional centers by financial controls. Superiors set objectives and then determine how well the subordinates are doing using ordinary economic measures. Subordinates are thereby counseled to raise and highlight moral concerns only insofar as these are likely to affect the financial measures of corporate performance. Subordinate managers might well possess a range of moral concerns from promoting women and training young adults with histories of irregular employment to reducing pollutants in air emissions and liquid wastes in excess of legal requirements. Given the characteristic administrative patterns of accountability, divisional managers are likely to defend concerns like these in terms of their impact on short- or long-range financial performances. As a result many of these concerns are likely not to be raised at all, unless they can be construed as improving marginal returns. Because subordinates work within the parameters set by superiors, they are unlikely to raise moral issues that cannot be contained within these parameters (Ackerman 1975).

In broad terms this administrative pattern tends to view the communicative interactions between superiors and subordinates too much in strictly administrative terms and not enough in contractual terms. Interactions tend to focus on how well subordinates are complying with directives of superiors rather than how together, each fulfilling their own tasks, they can cooperate for their mutual benefit. This latter contractual pattern is a possible approach to organizational accountability with employees, subordinate managers, and stakeholders. The difference in relation to our concerns about moral silence, deafness, and blindness is that the contractual approach allows for mutual agenda setting, for debates about the priorities of competing objectives, and for some mutual criticisms and corrections (Culbert and McDonough 1980). The contractual approach by its very nature additionally mandates greater moral attentiveness. Good contracts result not only from forthrightly asserting one's own interests but also from attentiveness to those of others so that the eventual agreement will be attractive and compelling to them as well.

Excessive Barriers to Horizontal Communication

Organizations foster moral silence, deafness, and blindness when they impose excessive barriers to horizontal communication between members and constituents. When organizational members do not regularly communicate about a variety of topics, they are not likely to bring up or respond to the moral concerns voiced by others. They are less likely to speak to others about moral dilemmas, ideals, or problems or set aside time to thoughtfully consider topics raised by others if they are not already used to communicating with each other in ways that are more and other-than-purely formal. Businesspeople arrange deals more often with colleagues with whom they talk about nonbusiness concerns than those with whom they regularly converse about business. The same holds true for moral discussions. Such discussions occur more often and more readily with others with whom we have already been used to conversing about a range of business and nonbusiness topics.

Business organizations, however, often block or frustrate these kinds of horizontal communications. They do so in several ways. They do so structurally by isolating work units and divisions from each other. People in different functions or in different job classifications often have little or nothing to do with each other. Moreover, their relationships with each other can be further distanced by deliberate policies that encourage units and divisions to compete against each other. As a result people in different areas—like accounting, marketing, purchasing, production, and workplace diversity—may have little or no sense of the issues and constraints of other workers. Consequently they may not be well placed to comprehend moral issues arising in relation to the specialties of these other fields or to find among these others persons who could readily understand and respond to complex dilemmas they might voice (Ackerman 1975).

Many individual managers feel that they cannot talk openly with colleagues about moral issues. They confess to being personally concerned about a number of issues affecting their organizations but about which they have never forthrightly talked with other employees. Organizations foster this sense of moral isolation not by overt policies but by de facto practices that not only discourage people from raising conflicts but also discourage them from disclosing any kind of vulnerability. However, this is exactly what people expose when they talk about dilemmas they do not know how to address and problems they do not know how to resolve. Many moral issues arise as practical dilemmas for which several different responses may be adequate. One recent *Harvard Business Review* case illustrates the character of typical moral dilemmas. In this instance several consultants and human resource experts gave varied answers about whether a very competent woman executive should continue to be assigned responsibility for managing a promotional project due in several months and at the same time as the term for her only-recently-disclosed pregnancy. It is not always easy to know how to respond appropriately to these kinds of cases. It becomes even more difficult when managers are effectively told to handle these matters on their own without involving others, especially their superiors. Managers assigned the task of handling these kinds of dilemmas may feel perplexed and uncertain. They are not likely to disclose this state of mind in organizational environments where managers are expected to act with confidence, direction, and competence. To ask others to help sort out this kind of dilemma can make them feel vulnerable to the criticisms of others who seem to handle these kinds of problems without second thoughts. Still, organizations can make a difference to the extent that they encourage and mandate collegial conferring about these kinds of management issues.

It is possible to demonstrate the importance of collegial and peer discussion for this kind of problem solving by again considering the experiments by Professor Stanley Milgram (1974). In these experiments, subjects were asked to administer what seemed to be increasingly strong electric shocks for learning errors to an actor posing as another subject in a supposed learning experiment. Sixty-five percent of the baseline group of subjects continued administering what were supposed to be shocks up through those that they were told were lethal as the actor posing as a would-be learner continued to make learning errors. Only 20 percent of the baseline group had discontinued administering shocks at level 17 after the would-be learner cried out in pain and acted as if he experienced a severe shock. When subjects were given the freedom to discontinue when they chose to, 95 percent had stopped by level 17 and 97.5 percent before the end of the experiment. When subjects had a mandate to choose as they wished, they experienced little stress. They experienced much greater stress when they were instructed to continue with the experiment. In a number of variations on the experiment, however, subjects were allowed to discuss what they ought to do either with another subject, a second experimenter (who disagreed with the first), the experimenter, or the actor posing as a would-be learner. In these instances the rate of compliance with the experiment was markedly lower than for the baseline group. Depending upon variations introduced in the experiment, the rate of subjects continuing to administer shocks to the end dropped from 65 percent to 20 percent and lower and the rate of those who continued after level 17 dropped from 80 percent to 40 percent and lower. Clearly, being able to discuss perplexing dilemmas with others helps people to resist and to determine their own course of action with respect to what they judge to be the erroneous or misguided instructions from superiors. Correspondingly, when organizations neither directly mandate nor encourage these kinds of exploratory discussions among colleagues, individual managers are much less likely to seek help from colleagues with perplexing dilemmas they must address. They are also more likely to acquiesce with orders they privately consider to be morally question-able. Organizations directly occasion both moral silence and deafness by not encouraging both broader and more frequent horizontal communication among their members.

Too Much Success, Stability, and Other Blocks to Organizational Learning

Organizational learning is important not only for practical and economic reasons but also for fostering a vital sense of moral responsiveness. The social, political, and economic environments in which businesses operate continuously change. If businesses are to be responsive, they need to be alert to these changes and discover ways of taking advantage of them or at least adapting to them. Alert attentiveness is especially needed in relation to ethical concerns. Firm moral resolve is not enough. Businesses need to be ready to respond to unprecedented incidents; they need to be able to expand the scope of moral concerns as additional issues are raised; and they need to be able to recognize the moral ruts they have fallen into. Steady moral commitments are not sufficient. To be sure, they help considerably, especially when organizations with clear moral philosophies are contrasted with those without self-acknowl-edged ethical perspectives. Staying morally alert requires something more. It means being ready continuously to learn. It calls for ongoing reassessments.

Stable and successful organizations can sometimes become less morally attentive and observant without really noticing it. Their stability and success make them complacent. Having gained public repute for their various projects—such as their environmental policies; their employment equity programs; their fair marketing practices; and/or their assistance to small, struggling suppliers—they may then take increasing pride in their own guidelines, which become in turn a new orthodoxy. Stability and success can lead organizations to become overly confident. Occasional failures and turbulence, in the form of external challenges or internal mistakes, often make organizations more resilient insofar as they recognize the ever-present possibility for these kinds of destabilizing factors (Holling 1995).

In *The Icarus Paradox*, Danny Miller (1990) examines how a number of exceptional companies brought about their own downfalls. He analyzes how companies can concentrate too much on those factors that contribute most to their success, whether this be their excellence in research, marketing, investing, or production. The companies he analyzed moved from success to success. They were good learners in the sense that they made excellent use of new information in order to strengthen their positions. However, they lacked mirrors. They were not given to self-evaluation. They were too egocentric. They excelled at what Argyris and Schon (1978) refer to as single-loop rather than double-loop learning. What they failed to do was to build in periodic reassessments so that they could periodically take good, hard, critical looks at themselves, their accomplishments, and their limitations (Miller 1990). Failing these kinds of critical reviews, these companies eventually fell upon hard times.

Needless to say, these companies would probably also not welcome ethical evaluations of their moral performance. To the degree that they do not invite self-scrutiny of their business performances, firms are also not likely to favor evaluations of their activities judged by ethical criteria. Still, it is equivalently possible for organizations that develop good track records in relation to the moral standards to become overconfident and complacent. Many would argue that something like this happened at General Electric, which developed a corporate ethics program that seemed exemplary. It prepared an excellent code of ethics and developed an ombuds office that allowed organization members to voice their criticisms, complaints, and suspicions confidentially. G.E. developed these programs in response to public charges of contract violations in dealings with the government. G.E. did seem serious about these programs, but ethical abuses continued, including charges of wrongful dismissal, violating environmental regulations, and declaring fraudulent trading profits. It might be argued that these abuses continued because the new ethics programs had little time to be instituted or because the company became complacent because it assumed that its newly designed ethics program would take care of these kinds of problems. It is probably more accurate to surmise that although it instituted these programs, G.E. did not at the same time take a long and hard look at factors within its organization that helped to give rise to the various abuses with which it was charged. It did not use these external challenges as an occasion to learn more about the potential for abuse that it either allowed, encouraged, or did not know how to limit (Byrnes 1994).

The Body Shop, the international cosmetics firm, handled public criticisms of their performances quite differently. The Body Shop began as a small firm that expanded quickly not only by producing attractive, highly marketable products but also by trying successfully to realize a number of ethically defined objectives. The latter included using and helping Third World suppliers, honoring environmental guidelines in their resourcing and production, and abiding by fair employment practices. This proved to be a highly successful formula that reaped sizable profits for the firm. It had gained a reputation as a socially aware, environmentally concerned company, and it had successfully used this image to expand its sales. By 1994 it had more than 1,000 outlets. It is certainly possible that an organization that has grown as quickly and become as large as The Body Shop might find it difficult to monitor carefully all its activities. Then in the fall of 1994 The Body Shop was roundly criticized for a number of abuses in articles appearing in *Business Ethics* and the new left newspaper *In These Times*. This list was fairly long, including the following: lifting the name and idea for The Body Shop from a small, local business in Berkeley, California; using in its products chemical substances that were either toxic or poorly rated; sourcing extremely few of the substances used in its products from Third World areas; treating some franchisees in a high-handed manner; not being honest about not testing its products on animals; discharging pollutants from a manufacturing plant; and using lax quality control procedures, especially during one pre-Christmas season (Entine 1994; Moberg 1994). As we shall see, some of these criticisms were petty, some were beside the point, and some were more telling. Fundamentally these critics were accusing The Body Shop of hypocrisy. The Body Shop had attracted considerable renown as an exemplary, socially responsible business and had cleverly leveraged this reputation as part of its own marketing policies. In many ways, it was not much different from other businesses that from time to time violate their own standards in spite of the best of intentions.

At the moment, I am interested in examining not the validity of these criticisms nor The Body Shop's counter-claims but the way The Body Shop used the occasion of public criticism as an opportunity for learning. A major critique of The Body Shop had been launched but suppressed two years earlier. A television program had been produced for BBC. The Body Shop learned of it, sued to have it suppressed for presenting a malicious and distorting picture of its company, and won the suit so that the defendants had to pay damages. However the matter did not stop there. In the meantime The Body Shop began to institute a number of steps to deal with the criticisms that had been voiced about it and would become public only later. It began the process to establish formal social, environmental, and animal protection audits of its business. It solicited the help from well-known scholars and from environmental groups to assist in these endeavors. Although these audits were not completed until later in 1995, the groundwork was being laid more than a year before. By means of these audits, conducted by neutral assessors, The Body Shop invited its members, constituents, and stakeholders to speak up and voice their criticisms and concerns (The Body Shop 1996). The Body Shop also recognized that it was vulnerable to criticism on Third World sourcing. It did know how very difficult it was to establish good working relations with suppliers from underdeveloped areas. To address this problem, The Body Shop persuaded the executive director of another organization, Bridgehead Canada, to come to work for The Body Shop with the aim of helping it develop better fair trade practices. Bridgehead had been very successful in identifying and developing contacts with groups of skilled craftsmen in underdeveloped areas who produce attractive items sold through catalogues and a few stores.

As the critical articles appeared in the fall of 1994, The Body Shop variously attempted to defend itself. For example, an open letter was sent to all the subscribers of *Business Ethics*. The letter explained that The Body Shop had already in 1987 formally acknowledged its debt to the firm in Berkeley and through a mutually satisfactory agreement had formally paid for its use. The letter went on to argue that many of the criticisms were exaggerated: that rare or isolated cases were treated as symptomatic of general problems, and that there were other sides to some of the examples cited. After all, the letter noted, it was not unusual to find a few aggrieved franchisees in an organization that dealt with more than 650 of them, almost all of whom were well pleased with their treatment (Roddick 1994). However, the most significant defense by The Body Shop was not found in the formal counterarguments it made in the fall of 1994 or in the months following as this story gained greater public attention. Rather its best defense consisted in what it was already doing to learn what it could do so that its actions more closely approximated its own exemplary standards. It had invited people to speak up in the arenas that mattered most: not in the public media but among its own employees, franchisees, suppliers, customers, and the community groups with which it regularly interacted.

Conclusion: The Weakening and Strengthening of Organizational Consciences

Although individuals can rise above their organizational environments, these environments do place constraints on people's ability and readiness to voice, hear, and see moral concerns. I have examined four typical organizational patterns that function to stifle, frustrate, and muffle the capacity and dispositions of individuals to recognize, attend to, and express moral concerns. These organizational syndromes each in different ways restrict or block potential avenues for communicating moral issues, standards, beliefs, and arguments. In different ways they limit opportunities for moral voicing, attending, and comprehending.

Many organizations block or stifle the voicing of critical comments, thus making it harder for individuals to voice questions, suspicions, or dissents. Additionally many organizations adopt top-down patterns of accountability that correspondingly discourage or exclude both the raising of moral concerns by subordinates as well as interactive moral discussions. Many organizations complicate these matters further by variously discouraging substantive and thereby potentially conflict-occasioning discussions about moral issues between co-workers and colleagues. Finally, by avoiding periodic reassessments, many organizations block opportunities for organizational learning and hence clearer understandings of their own moral blocks.

These organizational blocks have a double effect. They not only set constraints on the expressions of conscience by individuals, they also limit and constrain the expression of conscience by organizations. They function to weaken the voice of organizational conscience as well. What does this mean?

As individuals, our consciences are weak when their concerns are voiced too quietly or cannot be heard or comprehended because of the din of other distractions. Approximately the same observation can be made about weak organizational consciences. They are weak when moral concerns are voiced too quietly or when they are not heard or understood because of noise and the bother of other distractions. In the case of individuals, we need to add that we sometimes fail to hear our consciences because we have developed defenses or blocks that muffle and distort the voice of conscience. Similarly for organizations, they fail to hear the voice of conscience because organizational barriers muffle and suppress the concerns that are felt.

I speak metaphorically of organizations as having consciences, because it is impossible to regard organizations as individual persons with a sense of individual consciousness. Metaphorically for moral and legal purposes, we can regard organizations as being accountable and responsible like individuals. They can sue and be sued, borrow, and initiate actions as distinct entities just as individuals can. When we say the organization is acting in a particular way, however, we are using shorthand to characterize a much more complex reality, which involves actions by various members of organizations to realize objectives often by mobilizing still other groups of members. Thus, when we say that an organization began production of a new model, we are using shorthand to talk about a wide range of activities by a number of organizational members that enabled production of the new model to begin.

The words "organizational conscience" are an abbreviated way of describing a much more complex reality. If by their consciences individuals gain a sense both of what they ought to do as well as of how well they are actually doing what they ought to do, then organizational consciences, metaphorically understood, ought to operate similarly to guide, remind, and correct. For individuals, although conscience-pricking awareness always occurs within the same person, it may be occasioned by any of a number of different relationships. In organizations, conscience-pricking awareness arises similarly, but here the multiple different relationships are represented by the far greater number of interrelationships among organizational members, constituents, stakeholders, and critics. The voice of conscience may initially be spoken by many different people who raise criticisms, state ideals, consider dilemmas, reconsider judgments, and reassess policies. To stifle or silence any of these voices is to muffle one source of organizational conscience. As with individuals, the goal we strive for is to achieve some sense of integration among the voices of con-science. Given the possibility of being involved in quite different and complex relationships, individuals may find it difficult to realize a sense of integrity. Competing loyalties may make it difficult for individuals to feel integrated. This remains the goal of anyone not wishing to become a divided self (Allport 1955; Laing 1959; Fingarette 1969; Jung 1953). The same is true for organizations. They must also work at achieving an overall integrated sense of themselves. They cannot do that well, any more than individuals can, by attempting to ignore, suppress, or silence some genuine aspect of themselves (Fingarette 1969). As individuals, we can gain a sense of integration and integrity only through self-reflecting considerings or meditations, which hopefully allows us to see the fit between our multiple involvements. The equivalent is true for organizations as well. A real sense of integrity can be achieved only by listening to the multiple voices of conscience, reflecting different constituencies, individuals, and involvements, and then through considerings and vision gain a clear sense of the way they may fit together.

As individuals' consciences are weakened by not hearing or attending to conscience-pricking events or sensations, the equivalent is true for organizations. The organizational voice of conscience is weakened by not hearing and attending to constituents, members, stakeholders, and critics as they variously voice their moral concerns. Many organizations doubly suppress the sources of their own conscience both by discouraging people from speaking up and then by not attending to their voiced concerns when they do.

In the end an organization can develop a strong and vibrant voice of conscience only by finding ways to harmonize its multiple voices of conscience corresponding to its multiple constituents. Such harmonizing calls for vision and leadership but also for attentive listening. I will discuss ways of realizing this kind of moral vision in the next chapter. At this point, I want to underline that the groundwork needed to realize any common moral vision for organizations must include allowing the genuine moral concerns of constituents to be voiced and heard. Organizational patterns that block or muffle this voicing and attend-ing—whether by impeding horizontal communications among constituents or stifling bottom-up criticisms or rendering accountability into one-way polic-ing—correspondingly still the sources of organizational conscience.

CHAPTER 7
Good Conversations

To the degree that we act morally mute, deaf, and blind, we not only occasion and reinforce weak individual and organizational consciences, but we also allow harms and dangers to go unattended. We aggravate organizational accountability. We add to extraneous organizational transactional costs. We frustrate efforts at organizational sense-making. Additionally, to the degree that we are morally mute, deaf, and blind, we reduce opportunities for organizational learning, we increase the occasions for moral stress, and we tolerate and ignore various forms of deceit. We become less humane in our personal interactions.

We have explored extensively the causes and consequences of moral silence, inattention, and blurred vision. It is time now to explore in practical terms what can be done to help people become morally more vocal, responsive, and seeing.

BLOCKED, FRUSTRATED MORAL COMMUNICATION

I have noted that the vices of moral silence, moral deafness, and moral blindness give rise to each other in self-perpetuating ways. Correspondingly, it is difficult to attack this problem by simply aiming at only one of these vices. Many do not hear or see moral issues because others fail to speak out. Others fail to voice their concerns above practically unrecognizable whispers because the audiences they address do not seem prepared to listen. Some people fail to speak up because they fail to observe or acknowledge moral concerns that impinge upon their lives. These difficulties, however, at the same time represent a challenge and an opportunity. For these vices become less intractable when they are considered as aspects of a fundamental problem of which they are both symptoms and causes. The basic problem here is one of blocked or frustrated moral communication. The problem is interactive. Although it is as individuals that we are morally mute, deaf, and blind, these vices arise and flourish as a result of interactive patterns to which we contribute as persons in relations (Macmurray 1961).

We may choose to consider this problem of blocked and frustrated moral communication from several perspectives. We may, for example, continue to view this problem from an individual point of reference. Clearly, it is valid to argue that moral communications become blocked, frustrated, or never really get initiated because particular individuals remain morally silent, inattentive, and sightless. These problems will be reduced only as individuals find ways to become more morally vocal, attentive, and seeing. To think of this problem exclusively in individualistic terms, however, is to misconstrue it. Moral communications fizzle, become derailed, and never really emerge as reciprocal exchanges not only because individuals fail to speak, hear, and see but also because of the ways in which these interactions begin and proceed. Moral speakers often turn off their otherwise attentive audiences by the ways in which they voice their concerns. Moral listeners frequently shut up those addressing them by the ways they respond. Many times otherwise morally concerned persons utilize existing patterns or fall into new patterns of communication that do not serve well as fitting media for speaking and hearing moral issues that concern them.

Many people assume that moral communications fail to arise and become blocked primarily because people utilize inappropriate or inadequate vocabularies and forms of argument. I have already observed that articulate spokespersons for particular ethical traditions characteristically argue that problems of moral blindness can be reduced and eliminated by utilizing the ethical spectacles that these traditions have developed. The basic assumption is that we fail to speak recognizably in ways that get the attention of others, we fail to hear the moral concerns of others, and we fail to recognize moral issues because too often we use moral languages and forms of discourse that obscure rather than reveal these concerns. Partisans of one or another moral logic can demonstrate how specific issues have been misrepresented or hidden by the use of particular languages and forms of argumentation. Clearly these critiques possess merit. Often the use of one type of ethical discourse rather than an alternative affects how problems are defined and solutions are considered. For example, businesses are likely to respond in markedly different ways when concerns about the failure to promote more women into positions of senior management are articulated as an issue related to minority rights and/or as an issue related to the underutilization of human resources and talents. Similarly, ethical issues related to privacy look quite different when they are posed in relation to universal principles or utilitarian calculations (Benn 1971; Fried 1970).

Although the choice for one or another moral logic or language does affect our communicative interactions, it is easy to exaggerate the impact of these kinds of choices as the primary causal bases for blocked and frustrated moral communication. Clearly, moral communication can be transmitted with greater facility when those involved use the same language and logic. Shared moral values do enhance the sense of community (Durkheim 1964). Still, possessing common moral spectacles does not necessarily lead people to voice their concerns or to attend to the concerns of others. Fears of being implicated and fears of venturing into evolving and larger commitments are not affected by the use of one moral philosophy rather than another. In any case, because we are in no position to insist on the primacy of any one moral vocabulary or any one form of moral argumentation, we cannot hope to overcome the blocks and frustrations of moral communication by promoting any one particular ethical philosophy. Such advocacy is best thought of as a way of clarifying moral debates to the extent that open, reciprocating communication is already taking place.

We often feel that clear moral sight is the way to guarantee effective moral communication because we have inherited a long ethical tradition that assumes that clear moral knowledge necessarily leads to active moral practice. Whether knowingly or not, most of us have been influenced by the assumption, first persuasively set forth by Socrates and Plato, that people who clearly see their moral duties will act accordingly. Correspondingly, those who act immorally are presumed to do so in large part because they are ignorant of or blind to relevant moral truths. The task of moral instructors, therefore, is to help them see these truths either through skillful questions and answers, à la Socrates, or by rationally demonstrating truths they could not arrive at by their own means, à la Aquinas. This ethical tradition assumes a decisively cognitive bias. It presumes that effective communication is determined primarily by possessing a clear vision of moral knowledge. It assumes that good moral communication is especially shaped by the kinds of reasoning we utilize (MacIntyre 1988). Utilizing this tradition as a point of reference, people attempt to foster good communications largely by addressing and hoping to overcome forms of moral blindness that cause people not to observe, recognize, and acknowledge moral truths.

Clear, lively, and observant moral sight is not as fundamental to interactive, moral communications as are the virtues of moral voicing and moral hearing. Various forms of moral blindness limit the range of topics about which we may communicate. They reduce the vocabularies in ways that can signal our concerns and interests. In these ways, moral blindness occasions and reinforces blocked and frustrated moral communications. Moral blindness by itself, however, does not prevent this kind of communicating from happening. Moral blindness is not in itself constitutive of blocked and frustrated moral communication in the ways that moral silence and deafness most certainly are. Moral silence and deafness directly create and sustain blocked moral communication. The combination of these vices is basic to this problem. The primary importance that we often assign to moral blindness tends to obscure this recognition. It is by speaking and responding that we communicate. Blocked and frustrated moral communication is immediately the product of speaking and hearing that has become in some measure mute and deaf.

When we view moral silence and deafness as aspects of blocked and frustrated moral communication, our understanding of these vices shifts in two decisive ways. First, we treat these vices as interactive as well as individual. By not speaking up, we help to occasion moral deafness in others. By not being morally attentive, we occasion moral silence in others. And the same is true of others in relation to us. Vicious cycles such as these, however, can also become virtuous ones. As we speak up and others speak up, they and we are likely to become more attentive. Furthermore, as we and they become more attentive, they and we are likewise more likely to find ways of voicing our concerns. An interactive perspective not only allows us to see ways in which particular moral vices give rise to and reinforce each other, it also suggests clues about how these interlocking problems might be addressed.

Second, this perspective allows us to view these vices in time. Communications take place over time. They have beginnings, middles, and ends. They unfold. They happen as historically contingent occurrences whose outcomes are not necessarily predictable. When we initially consider moral silence and deafness, we often think of these in relation to specific acts of not speaking and not hearing. When we view these as parts of communications taking place over time, however, the opportunities for voicing and hearing occur not once but several times. Correspondingly, the initial task of our voicing and hearing is not necessarily to persuasively state our whole message or to hear, understand, and accept the full messages addressed to us. Rather, the initial task is to initiate a communicative interaction in ways that encourage us and others both to speak and to be attentive over time to each other. Initially, we do not need either to seek, demand, or consent to final agreements. Minimally, we need only to work at voicing and hearing and responding to each other so that we can explore over time ways we and others can (or cannot) reach agreements made possible by these unfolding communications. Viewed from this perspective, moral silence and moral deafness refer to specific ways of not acting that result not only in not voicing and not hearing moral concerns but also in impeding or obstructing real possibilities for initiating or continuing interactive communications.

Our fundamental question now becomes: Are there practical ways in which we can foster and facilitate interactive communications that help individuals and organizations become less morally mute, deaf, and blind? We can best see what can be done by initially considering the diverse ways in which we ordinarily enter into interactive moral communications.

MORAL COMMUNICATION AS A SOCIAL PRACTICE

Communicating about how people ought to behave is a basic social practice. Work, play, and rearing children are also social practices. These activities are both typical and constitutive of human life. Humans disagree not on whether to enter into these practices but on how, when, and where they should be conducted. By means of communicative moral interactions, humans seek to establish and gain compliance with social agreements that set forth standards of how people are expected to behave. We engage in moral communication whenever we are trying to persuade others to consent to such conduct-shaping agreements by intelligible arguments. Whenever we are seeking their voluntary cooperation by making comprehensible cases for our positions, we are enacting this social practice. In varying degrees practically all humans enter into these communicative exchanges whether they regard themselves as being particularly virtuous or not. These standard-setting agreements and the communicative exchanges that give rise to them and function as means of maintaining them are simply convenient and useful means for arranging social interactions.

The social practice of moral communication assumes varied forms. We engage in this activity as we negotiate contracts or seek to enforce them, as we consider joining associations, and as we seek consent for agendas we are proposing. We engage in moral communication as we debate the terms for collaborating with others and as we endeavor to sustain continued collaborations when these terms are ignored or neglected. Moral communication, understood from this neutral, anthropological perspective, is integral to all socializing activities: both as we educate and train the young and instruct them in the ways they are expected to speak, dress, play, and work and as we restrain those who as adolescents or adults seem to have forgotten or chosen to evade these expected patterns of conduct. Moral communication takes place in both formal and informal settings. As a young couple tentatively explores the explicit and tacit understandings that govern their living together, they engage in moral communication to the extent that they seek to work out this arrangement through intelligible discursive exchanges. An organization more formally engages in moral communication as it bargains with its stakeholders on the conditions that will regulate their interactions. People engage in moral communication as they make promises to each other and as they develop shared plans for their ongoing cooperation. In all these cases, they communicate in order to arrive at agreed-upon understandings that will then guide their subsequent behaviors. People engage in moral communication as well when they protest against these arrangements, in the process explaining the bases for their positions. Although at the outset they are objecting to particular conduct-governing agreements, implicitly they are really calling for alternative arrangements. Whether in the end they consent to given standards or not, they are directly engaging in moral communication.

In these communicative exchanges, people seek to arrive at and seek compliance with agreed-upon understandings that they defer to as respected and compelling guides for their behavior. These understandings function to regulate interpersonal relations (Habermas 1984) not only in the form of regulations and codes but also more frequently as shared goals, action guides, compelling examples, challenging stories, and informal agreements. These agreed-upon understandings possess a compelling and constraining character such that people

(1) feel obliged to act in keeping with them or be able to offer good reasons why not and (2) respect and value them both because of the benefits compliance seems to offer and the identification and commitment they assume and occasion (Durkheim 1974). Social scientists use the word "normative" to describe the constraining and compelling character of these agreed-upon understandings that people treat as authorizing how they are expected to act. Through the social practice of moral communication, we seek to establish, modify, and gain compliance with these normative understandings.

There are alternative ways of communicating in order to establish and arrange interpersonal relations. The characteristic features of moral communicating can be seen by comparing it with these alternatives. The social practice of moral communication represents one of five distinguishable ways in which people communicate in order to establish and regulate their interpersonal relationships (see Table 7.1). People use several different nonmoral forms of communicating to initiate and structure their interactions. Nonmoral communicating may also assume imperative, subjective, strategic, and customary forms.

Table 7.1
Forms of Social Communication Used to Order and Regulate Human Interactions

Types of Social Communication	Characteristics
Imperative	Issuing orders and commands
Subjective	Stating personal feelings (typical in arenas of indifference)
Strategic	Achieving desired ends by offering rewards and punishments
Customary	Invoking traditional customs
Moral	Seeking voluntary cooperation by establishing, maintaining, and interpreting normative agreements

In imperative communication, people regulate their relationship with others through commands and orders. We tell others how they are expected to act. We may do so by issuing imperative orders, by presenting detailed instructions, by crying for help, or by making assertive demands. When we command others, we do not seek their understanding in order to elicit their voluntarily given cooperation. We simply inform them of how they are to conduct themselves. At the same time, typically, we let them know the penalties they will suffer if they fail to comply. As parents, as supervisors, as caretakers for the incapacitated, and as security officials, we voice commands when we judge strict compliance to be crucial and when efforts aimed at generating agreed-upon understandings seem futile, especially difficult, or overly risky. Sergeants, coaches, and parents often seek compliance through commands when quick and unwavering responses are deemed necessary. We issue commands when we become especially concerned that our interactions with others succeed along the lines we judge to be important if not critical. To the extent to which we seek not only to influence but to control our interactions with others, we are often inclined to seek compliance through some form of commands (Habermas 1984). This kind of imperative communication, however, shades into a moral form whenever those issuing commands also seek to gain from their respondents voluntarily chosen compliance based upon the latter's understandings. To the degree that those making commands discursively justify their orders in hopes of engendering consciously chosen compliance, their communications become moral as well.

People often defend their own choices and seek the tolerance if not acceptance of their choices from others by subjectively expressing their feelings They describe their choices as matters of personal taste and inclination. Questions of taste are notoriously subjective. Correspondingly, they defend their actions as reflections of their own histories and idiosyncratic feelings. Assuming that all people, or at least those capable in some measure of managing their own lives, have the right to form and hold their own opinions, they justify their choices as personally formed judgments reflecting their own views. Consequently, they adopt a "live and let live" attitude toward interpersonal relations. As long as others do not interfere with my possibility of living out my own choices, then I will not interfere in the ways they live out their choices. When we are expressing subjective feelings, we make no attempts to persuade others about the choices we think they ought to make. We do not attempt to arrive at agreed-upon understandings that can govern our interactions. We do not state in phrases that can be argued and discussed what kinds of standards ought to guide our interpersonal relations. Rather, we express our own personal points of view. We implicitly hope that others will at least tolerate us by not directly countering our views. Tacitly we appeal to others to appreciate our stance. Insofar as we object to the actions of others, we state our views as subjective feelings. We express our disfavor as personal opinions rather than as sustained critiques of the positions held by others. Our objection to their conduct in practice becomes much like our objection to music or food we don't like: These are reflections of our personal feelings and tastes.

People regularly employ subjective communication to manage interpersonal relations in zones of indifference within relationships whose basic parameters are structured by mutually acknowledged norm-setting agreements. This is true of most communication within friendships, families, and larger communal and business organizations. The basic pattern of interactions is established by highly valued and readily defended norm-setting agreements. In varying degrees, these agreed-upon understandings allow for areas and times of free play in which individuals can act as they choose. Within these domains people typically arrange their interactions by both pursuing their own interests while making room for the choices of others through loose give-and-take adjustments. By means of subjective communications we cue each other, letting others know where we are at the same time as we keep track of their intentions, activities, and feelings. Subjective communication functions well to facilitate comings and goings within these zones of indifference as long as those involved share mutual respect for, and hence deference toward, each other. We can playfully express and comment on the feelings of others, responding frequently with humor, aesthetic appreciations, or simple curiosity to what others say. We can thereby assert and save each others' dignity and repute in ways that allow for us casually and informally both to pursue our own choices and not interfere with the choices of others (Goffman 1967).

People engage in strategic communication whenever they seek to gain the cooperation of others to work to accomplish particular projects by directly appealing either to the benefits that they may gain or the costs that they may experience if they do or do not act in proposed ways. By means of strategic communication, we direct others on how to act in order to achieve desired objectives. Our discourse becomes instrumental. We indicate what kinds of actions need to be performed in order to realize the goals we have in mind. In order to motivate people to perform the necessary tasks, we indicate the benefits they will earn as these objectives are reached and the costs that will accrue if they do not. Strategic communication is task oriented. We spell out ends, the steps that need to be taken to work toward these goals, and the reward and penalties that will be distributed in relation to the degree people contribute to or obstruct these activities. Unlike both imperative and subjective communication, strategic communication incorporates reasons for acting. By means of strategic communication, we solicit the conscious, voluntary cooperation of others. We convey reasons why people ought to act in specified ways (Habermas 1984). We neither invoke nor attempt to establish agreed-upon understandings as normative guides. Rather, we connect the reasons for acting both with the effective realization of desired objectives and with the corresponding promises and threats to earned benefits and costs.

Much of our everyday behavior-guiding communication is strategic or instrumental in this sense. For example, we may ask a friend's help to clean up our yard and offer him drinks and camaraderie. We direct subordinates to complete their assignments quickly so that our unit will fulfill its tasks on time. We charge employees to perform their work with skill and diligence so that these tasks do not have to be repeated a second time when poor quality products are returned. We ask our supervisors to take it easy in order to gain more willing cooperation from team members.

People also regulate their interactions by customary communications. People use customary communications whenever they answer the question about how to conduct themselves with respect to a particular activity by describing the ways people have previously conducted themselves. Customary communication is largely descriptive. We spell out at length and in detail the ways people are expected to interact by referring to what people have already been doing. The boundary between nonmoral customary communication and what we might describe as moral, conventional communication, however, is fuzzy and not always clearly demarcated. As soon as we begin to give intelligible and persuasive reasons why people ought to adhere to traditional or accepted patterns of conduct, our discourse becomes moral. Customs are then treated as agreed-upon conventions (Weber 1978). Still, in practice people often regulate their interactions by naming and describing customary ways of eating, dressing, speaking, working, and playing as authoritative guides without directly attempting to justify them as legitimate and compelling standards. They often do so in two contrasting ways that roughly correspond to the forms of imperative and subjective communications as previously discussed. On the one hand, they do so in many settings where moral arguments are presumed and where strict compliance is expected. In the process, customary communication becomes similar to imperative communication. Although articulated in declarative statements, the latter are regarded implicitly as commands or orders that are to be accepted and that require compliance. For example, descriptive accounts of how children have been raised, what marketing practices have been used, or how managers have been promoted become in practice authoritative guides to be regularly consulted and respectfully followed. On the other hand, it is also possible for customary accounts to be treated with an indifference that is typical of the way we convey technical information. In these contexts customary communication serves as a means of conveying information, often regarded as extremely useful, that indicates the ways in which other people have sorted out their interactions. Like manuals for how-to-do projects, these customary communications provide information on what has been done by others addressing similar projects and problems. As such, customary communication is similar to subjective communication insofar as it is treated as useful and interesting rather than directly obligating and compelling.

Moral communication constitutes one of several forms of communicating by which people regulate their interactions. Several characteristics distinguish this form of communication from imperative, subjective, strategic, and customary communications. It differs from these others because, by means of moral communication, not only do people attempt to establish, modify, and sustain agreed-upon understandings that set forth normative standards about how they are expected to act but they also seek to gain the consent of others to these understandings by providing intelligible arguments. Imperative, subjective, and customary communications do not attempt to establish or sustain agreed-upon understandings; nor, with the exception of strategic communication, do they attempt to gain the willful consent of others by providing intelligible and persuasive supporting accounts. Still, each of these other forms of communication plays a role in how humans develop and arrange their interactions. They are all social practices.

All forms of communicating play a role in the way we regulate our interactions. Our interactions may become difficult when any one form of communicating becomes too dominant. Excessive reliance on subjective communication occasions feelings of confusion and anomie. Excessive use of customary discourse threatens to make our interactions seem mindless and overly routinized. Excessive strategic communication turns all decisions into cost/benefit analyses. Excessive imperative communication is likely to occasion feelings that all decisions are arbitrary. Correspondingly, excessive reliance on moral communication can have the effect of shrinking our zones of indifference, tainting otherwise morally indifferent strategic considerations with questions of moral (or political) correctness, and undermining many otherwise relaxed routines with demands that we act always with purpose and clear intent.

I have described moral communication in neutral terms as a social practice because by itself such communication merits neither our applause and approval nor disdain. It represents one of several ways by which we shape and sustain our interpersonal interactions. It plays an integral role in our interactions, especially in organizational settings. The critical question is not just whether we engage in moral communication but how we engage in this social practice.

THE MICRODYNAMICS OF MORAL COMMUNICATION

Moral communication is not fundamentally an expert or saintly activity. It is the ordinary social practice by which humans seek to establish and sustain agreed-upon understandings they regard as normative. Prophets, judges, philosophers, seers, and confessors articulate moral messages that are often both influential and memorable. But they are atypical at least with respect to the ordinary practice of moral communication. Their communications are typically one-way: They are addressing others, sometimes—as in the case of seers and confessors—in response to queries and sought-after counsel, but usually to comment upon and change the characteristic ways others engage in moral communication. The communications of these ethical experts and saints are supplementary rather than central. They speak out to criticize, correct, shape, support, and inspire the ways ordinary people engage in moral communication in their everyday activities. Moral saints and experts act as professional ethicists to help ordinary humans as lay ethicists engage in moral communication that is, from the perspective of the experts and saints, more morally fitting.

The ethical communications of moral saints and experts are often extraordinary in several ways. They are often more learned and more eloquent. They know better how to cite relevant traditions and to employ literary and historical references in support of their arguments. They often exhibit a poetic sensitivity in their choices of words and images. Compared to better known moral experts and saints, most of us feel somewhat clumsy and unsure in our efforts to communicate morally (Taylor 1989). By making this kind of contrasting comparison, however, we commit a disservice to the ordinary practice of moral communication. We fail to appreciate this social practice on its own terms. In the process, we may inappropriately attempt to model our ordinary moral communications on these more exalted, more philosophically articulate models in ways that can at times undermine rather than support effective ordinary moral communication. Unlike ordinary moral communications, the ethical statements of seers, prophets, judges, philosophers, and other professional ethicists are often not truly interactive in form in the way ordinary moral communications primarily are. Many of the expert and saintly communications are one-way announcements and declarations uttered to inspire, challenge, and reprimand others. They are treated as revelatory and final in ways that ordinary moral communications typically are not.

Typical moral communications are interactions that take place over time as those involved seek to reach, interpret, or renegotiate normative agreements between themselves or make judgments about the bearing of these agreements on particular actions. They are either attempting to arrive at or to apply these agreements. These normative agreements represent focal points for actions. Once established, they embody our commitments to act in expected manners. Together they constitute constellations of signposts in relation to which we identify the basic contours of our lives and steer our interactions. By means of negotiated agreements, we construct our families, our friendships, our organizations, and our societies. Although we often treat certain norm-setting agreements as more paramount and authoritative than others—such as those by which we form sovereign states, commit ourselves to religious communities, and enter into marriages—our ordinary working relations are produced typically not by single, determinative agreements but by the interaction between numerous smaller, more private norm-setting understandings (Strauss 1991). The sociologist Anselm Strauss, for example, demonstrates how the working order of a typical hospital is the product of a large number of negotiated understandings between doctors, nurses, patients, staff, technicians, and others about how they will interact with each other. Sometimes sets of rules are established to aid this process. More often those involved in several different ways negotiate with each other informally as well as overtly about how they will understand these rules. The subsequent working arrangement, therefore, represents what Strauss describes as negotiated social orders.

As they seek to establish norm-setting, agreed-upon understandings, people represent their own views and interests and attempt to respond to the views and interests of others. Characteristically, those involved may communicate back and forth several times as they attempt not only to explain their positions, but also to persuade others of the positions they would like them to take, to indicate their assessment of the views held by others, and to communicate the degree to which they think they can accommodate these views. Where parties seem ready to agree, these discussions may take place fairly simply, with few misunderstandings, little need for mutual criticizing, and little need for extended argumentation. Parties communicate back and forth to clarify their understandings, to work on the wording of their agreements, to affirm that they are in fact making agreements, and to explore the implications for their ongoing endeavors. These communications serve several vital functions. They enable parties to sort out exactly what they are agreeing to. They provide the means for all to publicly commit themselves to the agreement they are establishing. They constitute the mechanism for establishing normative agreements as social facts and for the parties to affirm their importance for them.

In many cases the discussions leading up to normative agreements are not so cordial, spontaneous, and easy. Rather, they are characterized by sharp critiques, by impassioned pleas, and by sustained arguments. As they seek to arrive at norm-setting agreements, parties often engage in strenuous negotiating and hard bargaining. Such preliminary negotiations can become very partisan and political as parties seek to defend and protect their own interests against the encroachments of others. Still, these bargaining sessions over time often eventually result in normative agreements, which then commit the parties to various common objectives and patterns of acting (Zartman 1976; Zartman and Berman 1982; Bazerman and Lewicki 1983; Putnam and Roloff 1992; Lewicki and Litterer 1985). Negotiations may not be easy. They may require much time. Arriving at agreements may call for parties to find face-saving formulas so that none of the bargaining groups is viewed as giving up too much or becoming too accommodating (Goffman 1967). Through much of the bargaining sessions, the parties may not be especially friendly to each other. Furthermore, achieving agreements may only be possible with the help of neutral third parties.

Once people have committed themselves to act on the basis of particular agreements, they are called upon to communicate them to any people who may be affected by them and to exercise judgments about how to interpret and enforce them. This is rarely a straightforward and individual matter. For example, the moral education by which we seek to teach people about the norm-setting agreements relevant to their lives is best viewed more like a dialogue than a one-way process of transferring information. Those being educated learn more effectively to the degree that they ask questions about the meaning of specific stipulations, talk over their understandings in relation to typical dilemmas, and rephrase normative standards in their own words and in terms of their own experiences. In the process, educators often learn about how these standards may be phrased to deal with situations not originally envisioned, about the perspectives from which others view these standards, and about the character of their own responsibilities as moral teachers.

Often, once we have arrived at normative understandings, we take them for granted, adjust our behaviors accordingly, and refer to them only in passing. Whether we have agreed to address each other now as friends and not just associates, we settle our disputes without calling names, or we have promised to be more forthcoming about our private lives, we often carry on our interactions without directly invoking these new agreed-upon norms until we suspect that someone has slipped up. As we become members of organizations, for example, we often initially learn of and then consent to abide by a number of formal and informal codes governing deference and demeanor and then only infrequently discuss or debate these standards and their interpretation so long as they function to facilitate harmonious and cooperative interactions. From time to time, however, people slip up in the ways they follow these agreements, and the standards themselves occasion something less than harmony and cooperation. Then the matter of applying these codes becomes more complicated.

Rarely is the application of norm-setting agreements to concrete situations a matter of passive compliance. We are called to make judgments in several often quite different settings. In practically all cases the making of judgments typically includes consultations with others. For example, we may need to determine what to do when others have directly violated our prior norm-setting agreement. In order to render a fair judgment, we need at least minimally to hear their side of the case and to let them cross-examine any witness we may solicit and respond to any arguments we may make. We would also want to cross-examine any witness they may bring and raise questions about arguments they may make in their defense. Additionally, we may wish to consult with others in order to determine what forms of making amends, restitutions, and/or penalties seem appropriate. Furthermore, any judgment that is made ought to include reasons for its conclusions. These norms of due process, often referred to as standards of natural justice, call for at least some form of formal dialogue both prior to and in conjunction with fair judgments (Ewing 1989).

Judgment-making is seldom a strictly rational, deductive process. When we are making judgments, we are typically engaged in several overlapping activities, most of which call for us to respond to or seek out the views of others. For example, as we try to identify relevant evidence, we ordinarily consult with others, for help in determining what evidence is relevant and in evaluating the evidence for its bearing, its credibility, and its importance. It is useful as well to consult others when we are attempting to explore viable alternatives. Often we are able to exercise greater imagination in this process as our own reflections are both shaped and occasioned by the suggestions of others. As we deliberate, we also need to identify and interpret the norms in relation to our judgments and to articulate the justifications that explain and defend our positions. Even though we often end up stating our decisions and rationale as individuals, the quality of our decisions is often improved by listening to the suggestions and reasons of others involved. To the degree that we indeed take others' views into account, our judgments are likely to be more persuasive and to be regarded as more reasonable and fair. Empirical studies demonstrate that people are more likely to regard judgments as just and authoritative to the degree that their voiced concerns have been listened to and thoughtfully considered (Lind and Tyler 1988). When we make judgments, we are normally not content simply to arrive at a verbalized decision about the matters at hand. We also want to elicit the commitment of those involved to the particular solution, resolution, or judgment we are putting forward. Simply put, we want them to treat our judgments as agreed-upon normative understandings. Hence, we are well-cautioned to articulate our judgments in terms likely to gain the assent of those whose cooperation we seek and expect.

Whether we are negotiating, educating, or judging, we are engaged in interactive, communicative activities that unfold over time. These activities are all conversational. The archaic or root meaning of "converse" is "to keep company with." The word "conversation" nicely evokes the sense that these kinds of moral communications typically take place in the company of others as people communicate back and forth over a period of time in unplanned as well as planned ways. Responding to this or that cue, ongoing communicative interactions often lurch from side to side, digress, and move on as statements are occasioned by what others say as well as our own agendas. We might use the word "dialogue" to characterize typical moral communications. It has a tradition associated with the philosopher Plato, which characterizes moral communications as interactive, thoughtful explorations. This word, however, has several limitations. It suggests that moral communications ordinarily take place between two parties rather than among more diverse groupings. In addition, the word "dialogue," because of its association with written scripts, suggests that these communications move forward in ways that are well crafted. The word "dialogue" does not capture as well as the word "conversation" the contingent, happenstance character of most moral communications. Whichever term we use, the point is that moral communications are interactive; that the agreements, learning, and judgments that result are products of these interactions; that the interactions themselves develop and unfold over time; and that what parties communicate at any moment is conditioned as much or more by what it is timely to say in keeping with the ongoing flow of interactions as by considerations of what seems to be right considered without respect to what has been said. Hence, moral communications possess a narrative quality insofar as these exchanges take place over time influenced by our memories of previous exchanges, our anticipations of what we hope will occur as a result of our communicating, and the contingencies of the present (Ricoeur 1992).

CONSTRUCTIVE AND PROBLEMATIC MORAL COMMUNICATIONS

Our concern is to limit, reduce, and overcome moral silence, deafness, and blindness. We can do so, I argue, by finding ways to develop good moral communications that, because they are interactive and take place over time, help individuals address and master their moral reluctance, inarticulateness, inattentiveness, and blurred visions. Not all instances of moral communication, however, are likely to have that effect. We have already briefly discussed moral communication that assumes the form of carping, rationalizing, moralizing, and ideological posturing. These instances of speaking up frequently bring interactive conversations to a halt. People often do not respond to these kinds of discourse or they respond in ways that lead parties to speak past each other, rallying their own supporters more than listening and speaking to each other. Because people so often voice moral concerns by carping, rationalizing, moralizing, and ideological posturing, it is not surprising that some observers argue that it is better to frequently view many moral concerns in neutral terms as issues of political policy, legal liability, deterrence, and punishment and restrict ethical discourse only for matters more narrowly related to personal conduct and virtue. James Q. Wilson (1989), for example, argues that discussions regarding all of the following matters ought to eschew ethical discourse: developing policies regarding investments in South Africa, identifying fitting strategies for closing plants and reducing work forces, considering the proper use of bankruptcy provisions, deliberating on responsible ways to handle environmental and safety risks, and establishing appropriate measures for managing toxic wastes illegally dumped in the past. I sympathize with Wilson's argument insofar as he is proposing that we discuss these kinds of issues reasonably and professionally without moralizing ranting. But none of these issues can be treated exclusively as legal and/or political concerns. They are inextricably bound up with moral considerations of justice, fair treatment, and responsibility. Rather than adopting a morally mute, blind, and deaf stance in relation to these kinds of concerns, we need to foster more interactive and reasonable forms of moral communications. Even though moral talk often assumes morally off-putting characteristics, the best way to address this problem is to find and foster alternative, constructive forms of moral communication. In the remainder of this chapter, I describe the character of these forms, how they can be developed, and what difference they can make.

In general terms, we can fairly readily identify instances of good and bad moral communications. Good moral communications are constructive. They help to clarify and do not obscure issues. They elicit and foster ongoing participation, helping people to overcome their shyness and reticence to speak and to attend to the concerns of others. They occasion and do not stifle interactions. They assume the form of good conversations.

Bad moral communications are not so constructive and interactive. We can see how they differ by examining several examples of dysfunctional moral communication. Clearly, not speaking up and not attending to the vocalized concerns of others prevent moral communications from occurring. We are now examining instances where moral communications do take place but where they occur in ways that are generally problematic. For example, insulting is often a form of moral communication. People make and trade insults partly in order to put down others for specific moral failings. They attend to the words of others primarily to find chinks in their armor and fresh material that they can seize upon for new assaults. They are not really interested in building on each others' comments in order to resolve differences. They often hope that their insults will serve to silence the others or at least discredit them sufficiently so that others will not listen to them.

Carping represents another example of problematic moral discourse. As I noted in Chapter 1, people carp when they use moral discourse to complain about circumstances they feel they have little power to change. They point to wrongs, not primarily to understand these and finds way to address them, but to air their own sense of being both morally offended and frustrated. How could their supervisors possibly expect them to begin a downsizing exercise by determining casually which subordinates would likely make less noise if they were let go? Why should subordinates be monitored strictly on their use of company time to engage in outside political activities when several senior executives have been playing a very visible and vocal role in the latest referendum? Why were they passed over for advancements when another, who was an alumni of the same university as their boss, moved ahead in spite of less seniority and a record that seemed not much different than theirs? Carping is a bit like gossip. In both cases, we share disparaging comments about another who is not present. We do so in part to bolster our own feelings of well-being in relation to events that make us feel weak, wronged, and ineffective. We do so, however, to vent these feelings, not to find ways of dealing with the issues that upset us. Moreover, we do so without attempting in some manner to address others who might be able to help us raise these concerns. Carping invites others to sympathize with our sense of distress. At times it may well reinforce feelings of commonality among others similarly upset. Bolstered by such feelings, groups of people may more directly raise moral concerns, focusing on discrete problems and how they may be solved. In the meantime, insofar as we are for the most part voicing our own feelings of moral offense and frustration, we are seeking primarily a sympathetic response for our positions rather than collaboration in thinking about and responding to issues that concern us.

Rationalizing represents another example of problematic moral communication. When we rationalize, we use moral discourse to make excuses for our conduct or the conduct of others. Rationalizing assumes several typical expressions. We may explain how things come to pass, citing plausible causal accounts and noting in the process how these turns of events made other, more desirable responses difficult if not impossible. We may make reference to other commitments that preoccupy us or others, rendering us and others at least temporarily unresponsive. For example, we may defend our company's inattention to its poor safety record by its greater preoccupation with workplace equity concerns and its current difficulties in a highly competitive market. We may rationalize that it is perfectly acceptable to charge different customers markedly different prices because that is simply the way the market works. We may rationalize promising to deliver greater quantities than we know we can deliver of a manufactured product by an agreed-upon date by arguing that we would not get a number of contracts unless we made such promises and that customers in any case have more leeway than they claim.

When we rationalize, we usually substitute causal explanations for moral justifications. We thereby confuse the two distinct activities of explaining how things have come to pass and justifying our actions as morally defensible. Justifications constitute moral arguments. Justifications connect claims and judgments to invoked moral beliefs and standards. Justifications cannot be verified by neutral empirical investigations. They represent judgments of value rather than judgments of fact (Durkheim 1974). In contrast, explanations are descriptive statements that delineate circumstances, causal relationships, and other factual matters. Explanations can be verified or falsified by neutral empirical investigations. Explanations do not directly make moral claims. Still, explanations can legitimately form parts of moral arguments insofar as we cite them in order to indicate how someone's capacity to respond as morally expected was limited by specific circumstances. Explanations may thereby function to describe mitigating conditions. Explanations can correspondingly and appropriately affect our judgments about the degree or extent rather than about existence of culpability. By themselves, without justifying arguments, they provide no basis for direct judgments of culpability (Hart 1968). We invoke mitigating conditions in order to argue that individuals ought to be punished less severely for actions for which they are indeed guilty because their capacities for response were reduced by the circumstances we have described and explained. Justifications assume a different form. When we make justifications, we invoke moral beliefs and standards to argue why particular actions are morally acceptable or unacceptable. We make justifying arguments when we are attempting to defend someone else's innocence or accuse someone of being guilty. When we are rationalizing, we characteristically cite explanations as if by themselves they constituted justificatory rationales. We skip over and tacitly assume moral beliefs and normative standards and the arguments that need to made for their relevance and bearing on the cases at hand. Typically, we provide explanations to elicit the sympathy or outrage we hope to invoke. Correspondingly when we rationalize, we avoid and do not really welcome moral debates about the bearing and relevance of specific moral beliefs and standards. We offer rationalizations in order to lend sympathetic perspectives on our positions while at the same time limiting the agenda to topics calling for the discussion and interpretation of facts rather than exploration of moral questions.

THE MARKS OF GOOD CONVERSATIONS

Good moral communications are like good conversations. Seven features characterize good conversations.

1. Good conversations are recognizable.
2. Speakers are attentive.
3. Conversations move forward reciprocally.
4. Communications are rational.
5. Communications are honest.
6. Speakers keep the promises they make.
7. The exchanges remain civil.

These seven features are not accidental. They represent minimal normative standards that are integral to, and hence inherent in, the actual activity of conversing insofar as this activity realizes its aim and is indeed constructive and interactive. Another way of expressing this idea is to say that insofar as conversations actually work such that the people involved feel that their conversing has not been blocked or frustrated and has enabled the parties involved to reach norm-setting agreements, to make good judgments, and to educate themselves and others, these communications will exhibit these seven features. Adhering to these standards makes good conversations possible. To the degree that these standards are ignored or evaded, moral communications become blocked, frustrated, less constructive, and less fulfilling.

In the remainder of this chapter, I use the term "good conversations" to identify interactive moral communications that exhibit these characteristics. Communications corresponding to this model can and do occur in diverse forms and settings, from friendly discussions among colleagues to negotiations between organizations and their stakeholders, from executive strategy meetings to hard bargaining sessions, from special visioning exercises to thoughtful deliberations, from private encounters to public debates. Good conversations can and do take place in varied settings and proceed along both formal and informal lines. I use the term "good conversations" to refer to teleologically-oriented communicative exchanges that seek to reach, interpret, or maintain normative agreements. Although from time to time parties involved in these exchanges may engage in chatter and banter, for the most part these conversations remain purposive and goal oriented. The term "good conversation" is used not to define a particular form of communicating but to characterize common features of diverse patterns of interactive communicating that unfold in keeping with the seven norms identified above.

Speakers Voice Their Concerns Recognizably

Good conversations are recognizable. They are vocal, but more than that. It is important to speak up and not just whisper our concerns. As I have already noted, we often whisper our moral concerns. We do so by giving only part of our message or by speaking too quickly or too briefly. We do so by speaking timidly without elaborating on what we really mean. We whisper when we only hint at our concerns and fail to follow up initial, exploratory presentations with fuller accounts. We whisper when we expect others to grasp our meaning immediately without needing supporting arguments, illustrations, and/or testimony. In addition if we are to be vocal, we should not mask our feelings. If an issue is important to us, we ought to express the outrage, compassion, or concern we feel. When we suppress the overt expression of these moral passions, our moral communications are more likely to lack energy and become as a result more like whispers: timid, understated, unassertive, and unassuming. It is not enough just to speak up. We must address our intended audience(s) so that what we say is recognized by them. Often we speak up without being especially clear about just whom we are addressing. As a result we may well be quite audible to our own supporters but not to those with whom we are bargaining. Frequently political and ideological discourse has this characteristic. Speakers invoke revered symbols, myths, and legends dear to their own followers, leaving the opponents whom they are ostensibly addressing feeling baffled if not put down. Because political and ideological discourses are characteristically voiced in order to mobilize existing supporters and to move would-be supporters, they are often not fully recognizable in readily understandable terms to less sympathetic opponents.

Our initial attempts to address our audience(s) recognizably may not be very successful. We may whisper our concerns. We may speak past our audience(s). We may initially address them in language more fitting for still different audience(s). It is well to remember that whether our conversations are recognizable or not is not determined by what we say at our first encounters. These encounters may be too brief to allow much discussion. We may initially be so suspicious of each other that our utterances are designed more to protect our own sense of self than really to address the other. It is helpful, therefore, to remember that whether our conversations are recognizable or not is best judged by gauging the overall conversation rather than any one exchange. Initially, we are challenged as much just to get these conversations under way as we are to raise particular concerns. Depending upon the setting, our initial statements may occasionally assume the form of attention-getting ploys rather than substantive arguments. We may, for example, begin by voicing strong protests, by complimenting our audience(s), and/or by introducing humor. If we are going to voice our concerns recognizably, we must find ways to initiate conversations that are likely to unfold over time.

Speakers Are Attentive

Good conversations require that participants be attentive to each other. To be attentive to others requires that we listen to them, focus on what they are saying, and take at least minimal interest in their messages. We cannot really hear what another is saying if we allow ourselves to be distracted by other messages and our own reveries. Frequently something like this happens. We listen with half an ear. We get a sense of what is being said but remain largely insensitive to innuendos, mixed messages, and leaps of logic. We are not fully present. When we become distracted, we characteristically respond to arbitrary features of what others are saying to us. We seize upon particular phrases or examples and lose track of the overall direction of what is being communicated. We do not listen attentively because we become preoccupied with preparing our own response. As the other person speaks, we busy our minds considering how to address them. We may, for example, be busying ourselves with thinking of ways to counter their arguments. Alternatively, we may be feeling anxious about our responsibilities. Feeling a need to respond positively, we may be framing answers to the questions we think they are raising. These acts of ruminating are not in themselves inappropriate except insofar as they have the effect of shifting our focus away from what others are attempting to say. As a result of this kind of preoccupation, our responses to others usually lack fit. We begin proposing solutions before they have finished explaining their problems. We allow the conversation to shift away from the concerns they have been raising to questions about our own former, existing, or future responsibilities. We become defensive. In all these instances, we have become more intent on preparing and presenting our own communications than we are on listening attentively to the other.

It is well to remember that listening attentively to others involves more than hearing their words. People often communicate at several different levels at the same time. They often have a difficult time in being direct about underlying concerns that matter most to them. Or they may be trying to raise a number of issues at the same time with the result that their several messages get interwoven in confusing cacophonies. With their rational intellects they may be saying one thing while gesturing and sighing in ways that communicate quite different things. Ordinarily, we are not expected to make greater sense of what others say than they make themselves. Correspondingly, we need to work at not allowing ourselves to become so distracted by parts of what they are communicating—such as their verbal arguments or their emotional outbursts—that we fail to pay attention to the other ways they are voicing their concerns.

We need not be either sympathetic with others or in agreement with them to be attentive to them (discussed in Chapter 3). All that is required is that we respect others as human beings enough that we are willing to pay attention to what they are trying to say to us. Without this degree of respect, we cannot converse (Rawls 1971). Still, greater respect may be ideal, but it is not necessary. We can converse with those whom we do not particularly like just as we can negotiate and reach viable norm-setting agreements with others whom we may oppose and compete with on a number of counts. Antagonistic parties, representing political opponents or labor and management, can bargain their way to normative understandings that function to regulate amicably their otherwise conflictual interactions. These negotiations can proceed successfully so long as the parties, at a minimum, respect each other sufficiently to listen attentively to what each says to the other.

It can be argued that attentively listening to others is the critical factor in making good conversations possible. As people learn to attend to each other, they begin talking to rather than past each other. To the degree that people feel they are respected enough to be attentively heard, they also feel more encouraged to speak up. To the extent that we attentively listen, we also learn how to respond. We discover from the responses of others how our communications are being heard and understood, and we learn how to craft our messages so that they are recognizable to the particular audiences we are addressing. Correspondingly, many people become morally mute after first whispering their concerns because others whom they are addressing fail initially to respond with much attention. Failures at attentiveness stifle conversations, just as attentively listening makes good interactive communications both possible and lively.

The importance of being attentive is signalled by the recent study of American social institutions by Robert Bellah and associates. They conclude their book, *The Good Society*, with a chapter entitled "Democracy Means Paying Attention" (Bellah et al. 1991). They argue that being attentive means not allowing ourselves to become too distracted. It calls for us to keep track of each other in our families, organizations, communities, and societies. They likewise maintain that paying attention to each other makes moral discourse possible. Borrowing from *The Responsible Self* by H. Richard Neibuhr (1963), they observe that paying attention makes it possible to be responsive and that at the core is what responsibility is: the ability and readiness to respond.

Conversations Move Forward Reciprocally

Good conversations are reciprocal. They unfold over time as parties respond to each other in a give-and-take fashion. No one party completely sets the agenda of what is discussed. No one party is allowed to establish the feeling tone of the interaction. All parties are given room for saying how they would like the communicative interaction to proceed (Westley 1990). In really good conversations, parties communicate these expectations naturally as their interactions begin and proceed and they adjust to the concerns and expectations of the other. At the outset, parties usually indicate where they think their communications will go and how they would like them to proceed. They engage in initial discussions aimed at what the sociologist Irving Goffman (1959) referred to as "defining the situation." Communicative interactions are reciprocal to the degree that all parties have a say in these matters so that conversations unfold in response to the interests of all parties involved. There are no passive observers. Nor are there any parties who act only either as inquisitors or the subjects of someone else's inquiries.

Good conversations are reciprocal because as each party speaks, each responds in part to what the other has just said. Parties may well use their alternating moments for speaking to voice their own concerns, to reinforce their own arguments, and to clarify their own positions. If communications are to proceed as interactive conversations, however, the parties must also connect what they wish to say with what has just been said. At times, they may then need to defer until later bringing up concerns that cannot be easily introduced into the middle of interacting communications currently focusing on other topics. The possibilities for making points and reaching agreements in conversations are much like the corresponding possibilities for making telling arguments and gaining consent in history: It is possible to achieve results at particular moments that are impossible at other moments. We often must initially prepare the ground for further communications by working now to initiate conversations and allow them to gain momentum. What we can say at any one moment is contingent upon how conversations have been developing and what has previously been said. To introduce comments not in some way connected to the flow of conversation is typically experienced as being intrusive and often abrasive. To continue to make statements, asserting one's own point of view in a manner unconnected to the comments of other, is to turn what might be conversations into bypassing monologues (Piaget 1951; Taylor and Cameron 1987).

Occasionally, we begin new conversations in the middle of existing ones. Because we judge some issues to be particularly important, we are, therefore, willing to interrupt other conversations in order to interject our concerns. If we did not allow for this possibility, we might become even more morally mute out of deference for existing patterns of communication. Raising concerns in this manner, however, commits us to staying with the ensuing conversations long enough to allow the parties involved to get a sense of the matters at hand and, if possible, commit themselves at least to preliminary sets of conversations about them.

Good, reciprocal conversations are open-ended. They have no necessary ends. They develop and move along, guided not only by logic or dialectics but by the contingent give-and-take of those involved. As a result, good conversations can open up new ideas and thoughts in unplanned ways occasioned by the interacting responses of those involved. Because by their nature good conversations are open, people cannot genuinely converse with others about nonnegotiable demands. These kinds of demands are like commands or orders. They are a means of insisting on recognition of and deference to specific positions. They represent demands for compliance, not invitations to conversation. As participants in reciprocating, open-ended interactions, conversants do not insist on having the last word. Many people, however, at least nominally enter into conversations with precisely this intent: to speak in such a way that others feel that they can make no reasonable response apart from ceding the positions they had been asserting. Parties can have the last word in a number of ways. Typically they do so by insulting or shaming others either directly by personally belittling them or indirectly by their own show of logic, verbal artistry, or one-upmanship. As a result of these demonstrations, others feel discredited with respect to current possibilities for ongoing conversations. Many supervisors act this way toward inquiring subordinates who are seeking fuller explanations and justifications for new and personally distressing policies with which they are called upon to comply. The supervisors cut off further questions and debates by implying that subordinates really do not know or understand the larger contexts in which these decisions were made. The problem with having the last word—as well as the rationale for this practice—is that it cuts off any further discussions. As a verbal ploy, it becomes a conversation stopper. In contrast, good conversations are in principle open-ended. They remain open until the parties involved reach norm-setting agreements. Even then, they remain open for give-and-take discussions, deliberations, and even bargaining regarding the meaning and interpretations of these agreed-upon understandings in relation to issues, problems, and contingencies that arise from time to time.

Those who fully and openly engage in conversations with others thereby relinquish a measure of control over the outcomes they seek to realize. How conversations unfold depends as much on the role that others play as on our own efforts. In many settings where we have regularly conversed with others, we are not really aware of this relinquishing: We have become accustomed to how these interactions typically proceed. Our expectations already take into account our anticipations of how others will raise issues and respond to our concerns. In other settings, especially where we are just initiating new conversations, we are more aware of uncertainties and our own inabilities to manage events just as we please.

The technical, legal phrase "bargaining in good faith" establishes reciprocity as a norm for labor and other difficult organizational negotiations. "Bargaining in good faith" means several things. It calls for parties to participate in negotiations genuinely and to do so seriously with the objective of reaching workable agreements. This norm is violated if parties make only a show of negotiating, using these discussions as a ploy while preparing for other, unilateral actions. This norm is also violated if parties deliberately and systematically misrepresent their positions. Naturally, bargaining in good faith is a form of bargaining. Correspondingly, bargainers seek to advance their own positions as cleverly and persuasively as they can. They seek to avoid any unnecessary compromises. They yield as little as possible. Nonetheless, as negotiators inherently work to support the interests they represent, they also necessarily as bargainers seek to reach viable, mutually satisfactory agreements. Bargaining in good faith, therefore, implies that negotiators in the process seek to match the concessions and disclosures of those with whom they are bargaining. They are expected to be neither altruistic nor transparent as they negotiate. They are expected in a reciprocating fashion, however, to follow up the conciliatory or concessionary moves of others with corresponding moves of their own. Especially in situations where they will continue to work or otherwise interact with the parties with whom they are negotiating, they then have vested interests in not duping them or letting them walk into traps. If the others feel abused by the bargaining process, they will then be more likely to renege on parts of the agreements or to find other ways to undermine their effects or render them unworkable. Bargaining in good faith transforms negotiating even in fairly adversarial relationships into a kind of collaborative process whereby bargainers not only pursue their own advantages but also in reciprocating ways attempt to respond when possible to the mediating moves of others.

Communications Are Rational

Good conversations are rational. I use the word "rational" on purpose—but not to argue that our individual discourses need to be either strictly logical or scientifically valid. Both standards represent particular but not exclusive criteria of rationality. When adhered to too closely with respect to moral judgments, both standards can place excessive weight on these gauges of rationality as opposed to others. Both have been invoked by philosophers from Plato to Kant and their disciples. A number of ethicists have attempted to identify those moral rules that were in keeping with reason. They have variously argued for something like a science of ethics. For Example, Gewirth (1978) attempts to identify a supreme moral principle based upon an analysis of reason and the basic character of human action. Gert (1970) in turn attempts to identify a list of ten basic, universal moral rules guided primarily by considerations of what constitutes rational behavior. The philosophical tradition associated with attempts to identify natural moral laws has argued that it is possible to discern by using reason alone a number of universally valid moral standards that rational humans everywhere would recognize as valid (Donagan 1977). In all these examples reason and rationality are primarily associated with attempts to state universal moral principles. When we become concerned instead to deliberate about contingent moral issues and we seek to arrive at good judgments with respect to difficult cases, however, it is appropriate to think of "rational" in relation to alternative criteria. Correspondingly, it is fitting to associate rational with intelligible, reasonable, and thought-provoking communications (Nussbaum 1986) or with what Jonsen and Toulmin (1988) refer to as "topical argumentation" rather than "formal demonstration."

Good conversations are rational insofar as they are intelligible, reasonable, and thought-provoking. When we speak, we voice our concerns in terms that are comprehensible to others. Our discourse becomes irrational to the extent that others find our language or our modes of expression to be so unclear, obfuscating, or jumbled that they cannot readily get a sense of what we are trying to say. Intelligibility is the basic mark of rational communication. Intelligibility, however, can become problematic for a number of reasons. For example, people are often accustomed to speaking in coded terms that are readily recognized within particular groups but quite incomprehensible to outsiders. These coded discourses often function as informal badges of membership or status. Members of youth gangs, religious sects, and close friendships frequently use privately understood coded languages that are largely unintelligible to outsiders (Bernstein 1971). Organizational elites at times develop their own privately understood allusions, analogies, and argot, which new organizational members can initially only vaguely comprehend. It has been argued that men and women frequently speak in ways that differ enough to occasion typical misunderstandings when they speak to each other that do not occur when they are speaking to others of the same gender (Tannen 1990). Often when people from different regions, social classes, occupational groups, or cultures communicate with each other, they need to take special steps to rephrase their thoughts in terms familiar to their audiences, or what they are trying to say will remain largely incomprehensible. This latter concern has been raised by those involved in cross-cultural management. Hence, before venturing into a new culture, managers often receive special training to help them communicate intelligibly with people of the culture where they will be going.

Our discourse also can become unintelligible and thereby irrational to the degree that it functions largely to mystify our audiences. We may, for example, use technical terms not readily understood by others. Patients often feel that doctors address them in this manner, both by being overly brief in their diagnoses and explanations and by peppering their accounts with Latin-sounding phrases. In the world of business, many people seek to augment their claims to moral authority by making pronouncements that portray themselves like diviners possessing considerable untapped wisdom. As they speak, they may use ambiguous terms with multiple meanings, make indeterminate references, and refer to privileged information they cannot presently disclose. Audiences to discourses like these are often left somewhat dumb-founded. They recognize the knowledge and expertise of these speakers, their skill in speaking, and their capacity to draw upon their backgrounds to make cogent analyses. But these audiences remain fundamentally audiences. They feel that they lack the art or the knowledge to engage in an interactive communication. Executives, consultants, priests, and gurus are all tempted at times to assume mystifying stances because of the way these poses enhance the authority of their visions by rendering them other than ordinary.

Good conversations are reasonable. To be sure, standards of reasonableness vary. People utilize different modes of arguing and invoke different standards to demonstrate the reliability and credibility of what they are saying. They employ different patterns of reasoning and often challenge the validity of reasoning used by opponents. As a result, what is considered reasonable in Japan may not be considered reasonable in New York. In spite of these variations, we can nonetheless identify several marks of reasonableness that remain both unchanging and universally valid. Thus, it is reasonable in all settings to provide comprehensible and falsifiable explanations for all assertions about empirical observations and to support all moral claims with understandable and debatable justifications. There are parallel reasons why it is reasonable for empirical explanations to be falsifiable and for moral justifications to be debatable. In both cases, if statements are to be demonstrated, they must be capable of being proven by marshalling supporting evidence. In principle, others can question my explanations and justifications to the degree that they can marshall evidence that raises questions about my statements and lends support to their alternatives. My explanations and justifications can be genuinely demonstrated only so long as these possibilities exist so that I can regard my statements as proven or demonstrated and not just asserted or claimed. Correspondingly, all explanations and justifications implicitly lay claim to being better or more fitting than alternative views, which may or may not be known and discussed. At the same time insofar as I demonstrate my explanations and justifications, my audiences genuinely can accept them only insofar as they consider them, that is, they think about them enough to find my demonstrations more convincing than any voiced or unvoiced alternatives. As such, explanations and justifications are evidence of reasonableness because I must demonstrate their credibility and because these demonstrations call for thoughtful, considered, and not automatic responses from my audiences.

Moral statements that cannot be debated are not really reasonable. It is unreasonable, for example, to issue moral demands or make moral requests without providing justifying arguments, which can in principle be debated. Demands and requests that assume the form of commands or pleas seek compliance out of deference to the power and authority of the speaker or out of fear or caprice of the hearer. In contrast, reasonable demands always appeal to the considered judgment of their audiences. In this sense precisely moral arguments are debatable, not because they are dubious but because it is possible to discuss their meaning, to consider their bearing, to review their assumptions, and to explore alternative interpretations. From this perspective personal testimonials, individual opinions, and authoritative declarations are unreasonable because their claims are not open to debate (Bird 1991). Organizational judgments rendered to resolve conflicts or to discipline employees are not only unreasonable but unjust if they do not set forth their justifying reasons so that those affected can both know the basis for the actions taken against them and prepare for any available appeals.

Reasonable moral arguments may utilize one or more of several moral logics and still be rational. Ethicists have long argued over the validity and preeminence of particular logics. Debates continue between those favoring principled, consequential, and purposive arguments. Others favor patterns of argumentation that rely primarily on identifying relevant precedents, real or hypothetical agreements among those concerned, or their own feelings of conscience (Bird and Gandz 1991; Bird 1981a). Each of these modes of arguing possesses strengths and weaknesses. Each is rational—although in different ways. Whereas principled arguments invoke notions of consistency and universality, consequential arguments more closely examine causal interconnections. Purposive arguments call for thoughtful reflection on the basic character of our activities and organizations. Arguments citing precedents invite us to reflect on the wisdom of our predecessors. Consensual arguments force us to think about what we can agree to. Particular ethical philosophies often differ as much with respect to their moral logics as they do with respect to their underlying moral beliefs or the substantive normative standards they favor (MacIntyre 1988). Nonetheless, no particular form of reasoning, whether it be deontological or teleological, deductive or inductive, can claim to be either more rational or more morally fitting in all settings. Each form of reasoning presumes some largely nonrational moral beliefs regarding human nature or the character of human communities, or regarding the relevance of precedents or the goodness of valued objectives. Depending upon the setting, particular moral logics may well function better at clarifying issues, weighing alternatives, facilitating agreements, or persuading opponents. No one form of moral reasoning can assume a privileged position. In practice, people are likely to make better judgments when they utilize several forms of reasoning to complement each other.

Good conversations are rational additionally insofar as they are thought-provoking. They occasion and presuppose engaged thinking. Well-argued, interactive conversations call for people to use their capacities to think in lively, imaginative, and thoughtful ways. Rather than taking for granted current practices or present presumptions, they incite us to consider possibilities and alternatives. Thinking is a present-tense rational activity. It is not like a habit of mind that moves us primarily to consider established rationales. Thinking leads us to examine assumptions, review evidence, explore possibilities, imagine hypotheses, weigh arguments, and consider other points of view. In her analysis of what led many people in Nazi Germany to comply with immoral directives of their government, the contemporary philosopher Hannah Arendt (1964, 1978) argued that too many people associate the exercise of reason narrowly with attempts to gain certain knowledge and not with the broader activities of thinking and reasoning. Knowing reasons, she argued, is not the same thing as reasoning well. People can become unimaginative lackeys to current systems of thought to the extent that they fail to use their reasoning powers to reflect, question, criticize, imagine, and entertain alternative possibilities. They are likely to defer excessively to established political, philosophical, and religious authorities and the reasons they set forth to the degree they associate reason with highly regarded reasons rather than with the personal and interactive activity of reasoning and thinking well.

Communications Are Honest

Good conversations are honest. Lying, making deliberately misleading statements, and forthright deceiving undermine all attempts at reciprocal communication. Lying occurs whenever people intentionally deceive in their overt communications. People lie whenever they purposefully misstate information, make promises they do not mean to keep, and testify to holding beliefs they do not embrace with the deliberate intention of deceiving others. Lying is a deliberate act, not an inadvertent act. Lying thereby differs from honest errors or careless misstatements, both of which are essentially accidental and for which people willingly allow themselves to be corrected without any loss in honor or regard. To the degree that we suspect others of lying, it becomes difficult to continue with ongoing, unfolding conversations and it becomes impossible to reach norm-setting agreements. If we think that others may be intentionally deceiving us, it is hard to know where we stand. Feeling that we may well be taken advantage of, we are likely to become very guarded in what we say and to discontinue any real give-and-take communication. Because overt deception gives rise to suspicions, hostility, and retreats from existing cooperative efforts, people are rarely openly dishonest. Lying can be effective only so long as others do not know that we are doing it. As Bok (1978) has observed, lying is essentially a parasitic activity. People are able to lie to their advantage only in settings where everyone is assumed to be speaking honestly. Liars abuse the trust tacitly extended to them by others who assume that they are speaking honestly. Those who have been deceived characteristically feel abused and wronged. Lying is an exercise of force: It forces others to accept as real particular premises that have been made up to make the case of the liar look better than it is.

A number of other forms of communicating are similar to lying but do not constitute instances of intentional deception. For example, personal and corporate boasting often involves exaggerated statements that are for the most part recognized, just as puffery in advertisements often exhibits an inflated but acknowledged sense of bravado. People often appropriately make evasive statements to avoid gratuitous embarrassment at their own cost and for someone else's amusement or feelings of moral self-righteousness (Bonhoeffer 1955). We are not required to divulge personal secrets to others who possess no vital need for this information. Moral philosophers since Augustine have defended evasion as an appropriate means for silencing intrusive inquiries about these kinds of matters (Augustine 1956; Aquinas 1960). These instances of mild deception are similar to the traditional category of jocular lies: namely, instances of momentary deception that are recognized as such by most everyone involved and forgiven if not forthrightly accepted because of the good that they help to occasion.

In some settings withholding secrets, confidences, and privately held information becomes manifestly deceptive just like deliberate lying. For example, we feel that individuals with highly contagious diseases like the HIV virus are wrong not to inform those whom they may infect (such as their sexual partners). Comparably, we say that employers ought to inform their employees fully about the real and potential risks they are likely to experience. Before eliciting their consent, researchers are required to let their subjects know what their research exercises involve and what dangers they may face. More generally, we ought to divulge secrets, confidences, and privately held information if others have a legitimate right to know and would regard this information as vital to their interests if they knew about it. Correspondingly, people have a right to information about circumstances that put them at greater risk than they are aware. Executives have the right to know about any events or conditions that may markedly affect the well-being of units over which they have assumed managerial jurisdiction and for which they will be held accountable. Although in most of these cases the moral presumption for divulging partly arises from potential dangers or risks to those involved, it is also grounded fundamentally in the way withholding information distorts and damages the unfolding interactive communication between people. It takes advantage of others to advance our interests at their costs.

Timing matters because as conversations unfold over time the relationship between conversing parties may evolve. As it would be inappropriate to share personal secrets with strangers, we are not expected initially to share confidential corporate or union game plans with negotiating opponents. Sharing confidences, both personal and organizational, becomes more fitting as conversations develop to the degree that bargaining parties in little ways arrive at working agreements on how they will proceed and they begin to share some privileged information.

Speakers Keep the Promises They Make

Good conversations can proceed, establish agreed-upon understandings, and facilitate good judgments only to the degree that the parties involved are willing and able to make and keep their promises. Promise-making and promise-keeping are at the heart of good conversations. Often we engage in these communicative interactions precisely because we seek to form norm-setting agreements with partners, associates, or strangers. We would not engage in these exercises unless we believed that there was a good chance that our conversation partners were willing and able to make and keep the promises that in turn will constitute these agreements. We shy away from engaging in these kinds of conversations with those whom we judge to be unwilling or unable to make and keep agreements with us. We may, for example, simply judge their relationship to us to be insignificant and transient. We may regard them as immature, inexperienced, and not as yet capable of bearing the consequences of genuinely mistaken choices. They may be passing acquaintances with whom we may engage in frivolous banter but persons with whom we do not wish to establish any further agreed-upon understandings. We may judge them to be incorrigible liars.

Promises serve not only as a primary aim or objective for good conversations, they also function to facilitate them. Conversations develop beyond initial greetings and pleasantries only to the extent that parties establish among themselves how they will proceed. They need to signal each other about possible agendas, about whether their interactions will be formal or informal, whether they will speak colloquially or properly, about who will take the lead or whether this will be shared either randomly or by some other criteria, about the range of taken-for-granted assumptions, and about subjects that are likely to be regarded as off-topic. Although conversations do unfold in ways that are unplanned and contingent, they rarely proceed haphazardly. If conversations are to become reciprocating exchanges, the parties must arrive at some sense of how they will converse. Often tacitly, they address questions about agendas, formality, conversational leadership, emotional tonality, assumptions, and subject matter. They make informal procedural promises about how they will converse. To be sure, they often modify these promises as their conversations unfold: They may become more formal or informal, the topics of concern may shift, taken-for-granted assumptions and goals may become clearer. Nonetheless, ongoing interactive conversations become possible only to the degree that parties can make and keep promises to each other about how they will converse. Without such tacit promises, communicative interactions become one-way, distant, and stilted.

Exchanges Remain Civil

Good conversations are civil. Minimally, this means that we are expected to be polite and courteous and to avoid directly insulting or slandering our conversation partners. We are expected as well to avoid name calling and directly casting aspersions on each other's character. At the same time, we are expected to avoid excessive displays of anger, self-pity, or other emotions that may derail ongoing communications. We are expected to act with decorum, to wait our turns to speak, and not to interrupt others. Still the norms of civility do not require that we act dourly and exhibit no feelings. Rather we are expected to speak with wit and good humor and to voice our feelings directly but politely, without rancor or exaggeration.

The norms of civility direct how we ought to act not just with acquaintances with whom we are familiar but also with strangers and more distant acquaintances. As the sociologist Norbert Elias (1977) observed, norms of civility—unlike the more traditional norms for courtly life—involve fewer rituals, less flourish, and less ostentation. These norms grew up among the merchant and middle classes in sixteenth-century European cities. They were meant to facilitate commerce, political discussions, and social intercourse among people, largely unacquainted with each other and from diverse backgrounds, who met and contracted to develop the social, economic, and political institutions of cities as self-governing polities.

Good conversations are constructive, interactive communicative exchanges. With good conversations people reach and interpret norm-setting agreements, deliberate, make judgments, and in other equivalent ways shape and regulate their interactions. We have discussed seven characteristics of these exchanges. These features are not accidental or arbitrary. They represent norms that are immanent and integral to the very activity of conversing insofar as we aim to establish or interpret agreed-upon understandings. Insofar as we adhere to these standards, it becomes possible to engage in good conversations. Insofar as we adhere to some but not all of these standards or to part but not all of each standard, our interactive communications are likely to falter, become strident, foster misunderstanding, become uninteresting and unengaging, and occasion acrimony. These norms are fundamental precisely because complying with them makes good conversations possible.

THESE STANDARDS ARE PRACTICAL AND NOT UTOPIAN

These standards are basic, practical, and not utopian. For the most part people are capable of recognizably voicing their concerns; of being attentive to others; of engaging in reciprocating exchanges; of discussing intelligibly, reasonably, and thoughtfully; of speaking honestly and civilly; and of honoring their promises. For the most part we comply with these standards or at least seriously endeavor to adhere to them as a matter of course. We can see the way these standards are practical and nonutopian by observing that they do not assume that we need to become saints or moral experts to observe them.

First, we do not have to be of equal status or power to participate in good conversations. None of the immanent standards discussed presupposes that parties involved in negotiating, socializing, interpreting, or deliberating need to possess the same or equivalent power, authority, or status. Often these exchanges are between people of different status: parents and children, judges and litigants, instructors and students, preachers and congregants. In spite of these differences, the ensuing conversations can be constructive so long as the parties adhere to the guidelines we have outlined. Communications can be vocal, attentive, and reciprocating even though the parties hold asymmetrical positions. Communications between people of different status, like purchasing agents from powerful corporations and sales representatives from small suppliers, or like executives and their subordinates, can be reasonable, honest, and promise-honoring even though speakers are of different status. They can take turns setting conversational agendas and feeling tones (Westley 1990).

Occasionally people are prone to capitalize on greater power or status to advance their own interests. Those with less power are therefore well counseled to seek ways to reduce or neutralize the power of their opposition and to mobilize support for their own positions if they hope to advance their moral concerns. They are likely to get better hearings, especially from powerful opponents, if they find ways to reduce the discrepancies in power between themselves and others. Sometimes, the first step to initiating hard bargaining negotiations with opponents who attempt to ignore us is to explore ways to neutralize their influence and augment our own (Niebuhr 1932). Associations of laborers initiated conversations with their employers first by forming trade unions and then by engaging in various work stoppage and work-to-rule tactics until their opposites consented to negotiate. The Inuit in northern Quebec greatly improved the character of their ongoing conversations with the powerful Quebec utilities monopoly Hydro Quebec by a series of tactics that appreciably augmented their power. These tactics included successful efforts to win the support of international environmental groups, who in turn pressured utilities in the United States to consider the rights of Inuit as they bargained to purchase hydroelectric power from Hydro Quebec. These kinds of political tactics may improve the attentiveness extended by others. It would be foolish to attempt to work at making our conversations more reciprocal solely by resorting to more thought-provoking, reasonable, and intelligible discussions with others who at present barely accord us even the minimal respect of listening to what we have to say. It would also be naive, however, to dismiss the significance of good conversations in these kinds of cases. Both associations of workers and Inuit enhanced their own power and were able to reduce the legitimacy of their opponents by initiating good conversations with other parties. As a result they were able to mobilize significant people power on their behalf, to invoke the countervailing veto power from groups who could threaten not to cooperate, and to reduce the room of their opponents to maneuver in the face of greater public attention generated by publicity campaigns they had launched (Galbraith 1954; Pfeffer and Salancik 1978; Fisse and Braithwaithe 1983). In aggravated settings where opposing parties are not really talking with each other, political tactics often become the initial steps of what may become ongoing conversations; that is, they represent ways of getting others to become attentive. Subsequently, political tactics are often useful means for persuading others to be more forthcoming and less secretive.

Ethics cannot be divorced from politics as ancient philosophers like Plato, Aristotle, and Cicero recognized. Neither can good conversations be wholly separated from political actions. Insofar as the agreements and judgments that are the by-products of good conversations affect our public interactions or modify organizational relationships, these conversations are not politically neutral. Moreover, insofar as we utilize influence to get the attention of others, to foster greater reciprocity, or to encourage fuller disclosing, we engage in politics in order to foster more lively and constructive moral conversations. Because good conversations take place in the midst of our ongoing interactions rather than in some ahistorical, apolitical, and imaginary settings, they necessarily bear the marks of this world. If they did not bear these marks, if they were carried on without passion or politics, they would not matter to us. I have already observed that conversations change over time as parties make or resist agreements, reveal or disclose secrets, and respond to or ignore historical developments. If they stand still, they atrophy. From this perspective, differences in power affect the character rather than the possibility for engaging in good conversations. As we gain or lose power, the character of these conversations can change. In many cases, our conversations will become more transparent, honest, and reciprocal as power relations become more equivalent. However, there are limits. Many relations are by their nature asymmetrical but not necessarily for that reason incapable of fostering engaged, open, honest, intelligible, give-and-take conversations.

Second, we do not need to hold the same moral beliefs, utilize the same moral reasons, or embrace the same cultural values in order to engage in good conversations. We live in a pluralistic world. We hold different religious beliefs, embrace contrasting political ideologies, follow varied etiquettes, consult the wisdom of diverse cultural traditions, and adhere to dissimilar social norms. We phrase our moral arguments in genres that can be primarily legalistic or narrative, principled or aphoristic. Moral diversity is an omnipresent fact that cannot be wished away or overcome. People do not and will not agree on the forms of moral reasoning that they will regard as most reliable, valid, and truthful. Whereas some insist on using utilitarian formulations, others remain devoted to principled natural law arguments. Whereas some find deontological arguments most consistent and compelling, others remain intuitionists as an expression of their own veracity or cultural relativists out of respect for the historicity and wisdom of given moral traditions. It is impossible to convince people to develop moral arguments of the same form or even to persuade competitive partners to common agreements to defend them using the same justifications. Even within the same cultures we are inclined to phrase our arguments in different terms. Across cultures the diversity becomes even more marked. We cannot arrive at any common moral Esperanto to reduce or overcome this moral diversity (Stout 1988). Most decisively, we differ in the conception and ranking of what we regard as fundamentally morally good (Walzer 1983). With great passion we defend our particular views of what we regard as relevant moral goods—for example, personal autonomy, national sovereignty, the reduction of poverty, industrial expansion, or sustainable development. Religions differ markedly between themselves over what they regard as the objectives or aims of human life. These differences are not trivial. Nonetheless, in spite of all these differences we can still engage in good conversations with people of diverse moral persuasions.

None of the basic features for good conversations—speaking recognizably, being attentive, reciprocating, speaking reasonably and honestly and civilly, and keeping promises—requires that we hold common moral beliefs or utilize similar forms of reason. Accepting common beliefs and trusting in similar forms of reasoning can indeed make it easier to begin and sustain good conversations. Yet, in principle we can carry on in spite of these differences so long as we are willing and able to translate what we are saying back and forth between ourselves as we converse. This kind of "translating" is basic to any conversation. It is both more obvious and more difficult when we hold different beliefs and speak different languages. Even with comparatively simple conversations, however, people often extend themselves to rephrase their observations and arguments in terms and expressions they have heard their audiences use. They engage in this restating and rephrasing in part to make what they say seem more credible, in part simply because they want to be understood, and in part out of minimal empathy for the world view of others. With close intimate associates, who have engaged in conversations over long periods, this process of rephrasing and restating can become almost automatic. When people from different ethnic, occupational, national, or religious cultures begin to converse, they are often acutely aware of the need to listen and translate as well as to speak and translate out of mutual respect for their differences. One norm established for interfaith dialogues is that participants ought to phrase their observations about each others' religions in their own words that at the same time seem comprehensible and valid to the people of the religion they are describing (W. Smith 1976). When people within the same general culture meet, the need for translating is often neither as openly acknowledged nor as civilly managed. We often dance around the problem by using vague terms capable of multiple meaning or by diverting conversations to familiar grounds when we do not comprehend what was being said. Sometimes we evade the problem by jumping to inferences of what we think others are saying. If we are really to speak recognizably and to listen attentively, however, we often need to work at translating our respective jargons so that they are intelligible to those with whom we are negotiating, bargaining, and deliberating. This need to rephrase and restate would remain even if we were all to use the same moral language, simply because of our differences in beliefs, objectives, status, and power. The activity of translating so that we understand what others say to us and so that we speak in terms they find intelligible cannot be executed once for all time. It must be undertaken again and again on a case-by-case basis out of simple respect for others with whom we are speaking. It is an integral dimension of conversing well.

Good conversations address these problems of moral diversity over time. As people from different cultures, moral traditions, and bargaining positions find ways to initiate and maintain their conversations, they gain competence in finding more apt ways of rephrasing and restating their positions to make them intelligible to each other. Although there are no foreseeable ways of overcoming moral diversity, having good conversations can at least initiate and establish communicative links among people with differing positions. Although we may not be able to achieve agreements regarding either our visions of moral good or the moral logic we use to justify our positions, through good conversations we can from time to time reach practical agreements about specific projects.

Third, we do not need to be moral virtuosos to engage in good conversations. It is assumed that the people who participate in these communicative interactions are fallible, self-interested human beings who are nonetheless at least minimally capable of speaking up, attending to others, and commencing intelligible, honest, reciprocating discussions. We do not need to excel at any of these traits at the outset of any communicative interaction. It is not necessary that we be particularly altruistic, courageous, just, temperate, or prudent. Most of us can be encouraged or inspired to cultivate and further develop our moral character. Most of us are capable of and interested in acting with loyalty to our family, friends, and associates. But we are also prone to serve our own interests, to forget uncomfortable truths, and to be temporarily overwhelmed by anxieties and desires. From time to time, we all become selfish and greedy. Additionally, we are likely to act inconsistently and to waver when moral goals seem to call for excessive self-sacrifice. None of these traits either disqualifies or incapacitates us from engaging in good conversations. To the degree that we enter into and sustain constructive conversations with others, our own consciences are likely to be strengthened. We can begin these communicative interactions even though our consciences are comparatively fragile and weak, as long as we attempt almost with experimental mind-sets to see how these conversations will unfold.

These guidelines are practical and nonutopian. We need not become prophets or moral experts. We do not need to master new, technical languages of ethics. The competencies we need to develop are all within our grasp. The basic human vocation for ethics requires that we seek to cultivate a handful of skills together as part of unfolding conversations that lead us to make and sustain norm-setting agreements. In nascent form we already possess these skills: Voicing moral concerns recognizably; being attentive to others; speaking reasonably, honestly, and reciprocally; and keeping promises. In a cyclical manner good conversations often help us to cultivate them further.

HOW GOOD CONVERSATIONS OVERCOME MORAL SILENCE, DEAFNESS, AND BLINDNESS

We have examined at length the problems of moral silence, deafness, and blindness and reviewed their consequences for organizational life. These problems are pervasive, deeply engrained, and cannot be wished away. Many people are likely to resist attempts to strengthen either their own consciences or those of their organizations. Currently they are able to get away with question- able activities. They would prefer not to examine too closely the appropriateness of their own activities. They benefit from liberally construing corporate policies to their own private advantage. Although as a result they may remain estranged from their own moral instincts, they willingly defend their weak consciences against the anxiety, disruptions, and conscious guilt that they associate with more lively expressions of conscience. Similarly, organizational members often defend their organizations against more lively organizational consciences because they sense that the latter involve more confrontations, questioning, and conflicts.

Still these problems are not intractable. There are a number of good reasons for attempting to address them: to reduce unnecessary harm and damages, to improve organizational accountability, to enliven organizational sense-making, and to reduce extraneous transactional costs. I have been arguing that moral silence, deafness, and blindness become less intransigent when they are viewed as being aspects of blocked or frustrated moral communication. Although we still recognize that it is particular individuals who are being morally mute, deaf, and blind, we additionally see that these problems emerge as features of disturbed communicative interactions. Correspondingly, if we can find ways to encourage individuals to enter into and engage in good conversations, they will as a result over time learn to become less morally mute, less morally deaf, and less morally blind. I realize that I am making a large claim for a relatively ordinary human activity. In order to redeem this claim, I must be able to succeed at several tasks. I must be able to show that good conversations can and do in fact address and reduce the vices of moral silence, deafness, and blindness; that good conversations can and do in fact also address the underlying causes that function to give rise to these vices; and that it is indeed possible and practical to cultivate good conversations as a social practice.

The first step is to notice that people vary in how well they engage in good conversations. Each of us probably finds it easier to comply and excel with some of these standards than with others. Some people find it easier to be intelligible than others. Others can be more thought-provoking. Some of us are more ready to make and keep promises. Others find it much easier to be attentive listeners. Some people quite readily can put together good arguments; others of us feel inarticulate: We know what we want to say but just can't seem to find the right words. Although we naturally possess these capacities in varying degrees, all of these competencies can be cultivated and enhanced. We are not destined to be inattentive, not vocal, inarticulate, or unresponsive. We can learn to accomplish each of these tasks with greater proficiency.

Table 7.2
How Do Good Conversations Help to Overcome
Moral Silence, Deafness, and Blindness?

Features of Good Conversations	Communicative Functions
Occur over time	Allow time for reconsidering and for negotiating
Cultivate the sense of partnership	Develop as part of the process
Educational	Allow for imagination, learning, mutually instructing
Foster trust	Encourage people to take more risks, to collaborate
Strengthen conscience	Help in the forming of conscience, in decentering and recentering
Occasion gracious initiatives	Occasion acts of forgiveness, humor, wit, face-saving, and "reckoning without sharing"

Whether we cultivate these competencies or they remain dormant in large part depends upon whether any of our current interactions helps us to develop, divert, or suppress these competencies. Our communicative interactions tend to become either virtuous or vicious cycles insofar as these competencies are concerned. With self-fulfilling momentum, what begins as fairly good conversations often becomes better, at least for a period of time; whereas forced, directionless, bantering, bypassing, or one-way conversations usually retain these features, which often become even more pronounced. Still, few conversations remain always constructive. From time to time, even good conversations become diverted or blocked, lose their momentum, or turn in upon themselves. Because the parties engaging in them have gained competence in voicing concern, attending to others, speaking intelligibly and reasonably, however, these people are better positioned to initiate other conversations or renew the ones that stall, drift off course, or reach impasses.

Several features of good conversations give them a self-realizing momentum. These features are listed in Table 7.2.

Good Conversations Unfold over Time

A conversation is not just an exchange of greetings. Ongoing conversations often develop through a number of encounters, periodically recessed to take care of other concerns and then recommenced. The fact that conversations take time matters. The fact that conversations have duration means that people have time to reflect, reconsider, and adjust their positions. Conversations would neither build trust nor be educative if they did not unfold over time. Correspondingly, good conversations are able to reduce the resistance of many people to raising and talking about moral concerns. Many people who will initially reject new ideas are often willing to reconsider if they are given time to search for alternatives that seem more acceptable. If negotiations had to succeed in one setting on the basis of initial proposals, political opponents, labor and management, and competitors would reach fewer formal agreements and working understandings. Good conversations provide the time for bargaining, for thoughtful deliberating, for rethinking in ways that allow and foster greater attentiveness to others and more lively sight of what is going on.

Good Conversations Cultivate the Sense of Partnership

As they proceed, these communicative interactions elicit tacit promises from participants first to explore the possibilities of the conversations themselves and then to proceed at least tentatively toward some kinds of agreed-upon understandings that seem from time to time to be worthwhile pursuing. The ensuing sense of partnership develops among participants to the degree that they actively listen, voice their views, and overtly commit themselves to continue to participate. These feelings of involvement, however, develop only to the degree that people participate in good faith without intentional dissimulation. None of these feelings of being involved or committed arises for those who join these discussions only as a ruse, ready later only to protest against them. Those who converse in good faith develop what amounts to something like vested interest in the work of their conversing: In the implied and overt agreed-upon understandings that these interactions occasion. For hypocrites who converse in bad faith, debates, discussions, and deliberations constitute only pro forma rituals from which they remain personally aloof and emotionally distant.

A sense of partnership—of being involved in particular matters together with specific others—is a by-product of conversing in good faith. These feelings even arise for people whose interactive discussions primarily consist in hard bargaining. Individuals who regularly represent their respective organizations in industrial bargaining sessions sometimes develop toward each other collegial feelings of mutual respect. Although their negotiations sometimes become protracted and difficult, they frequently develop a sense of mutual and shared pride in their respective capacities to represent the interest of their constituents while putting together agreements that they regard to be in everyone's best interests. They often act toward each other with esteem and regard as worthy opponents who, much like ongoing contestants in sporting competitions, experience a sense of accomplishment in the way they can work together to produce something worthy and highly valued: A well-played sporting event in one case and a new treaty or collective agreement in the other case. Although negotiators often use tricks and ploys to advance their positions, they frequently will warn their adversaries about them when they feel that the resulting agreements may become too advantageous for themselves. Imbalanced agreements are likely to occasion resentment, they reason, and thereby make the next round of negotiations even more difficult. Many negotiators feel that the best bargaining sessions are ones that allow all parties to feel that in some measure their interests have been well represented but in ways that are good for all involved (Zartman 1976; Zartman and Berman 1982).

These feelings of partnership are important because, to the degree that we experience them, we also feel more ready to voice our concerns, be attentive to the concerns of others, recognize issues being discussed, and acknowledge our own involvements. As we develop feelings of affiliation or collegiality, we also become implicated in the process in ways that both facilitate speaking up and listening attentively and make these activities more obligatory. As we and they make the small tacit agreements to initiate and maintain our conversations, whether these be for negotiations, meetings, or debates, we also find ourselves becoming less reticent both to voice and to pay attention. The emerging sense of affiliation or partnership acts both to push and to pull us into further speaking and hearing. Given the willingness of the others to voice and hear our accounts, we correspondingly feel that we ought to speak and listen to them. By showing a willingness to listen, to speak personally and forthrightly, and to wait for the reciprocating character of conversations gradually to emerge, we can often coax others to speak their view and listen to ours.

Good Conversations Are Educational

We can and do learn from our communicative interactions about how to converse well and correspondingly how to be morally more vocal, attentive, and observant. As previously discussed, many of us feel morally inarticulate. Conversations represent ideal schools for learning how to speak, how to listen, and how to observe. Through trial and error as conversations proceed, we learn more apt ways of phrasing our thoughts and more felicitous turns of phrase for expressing our ideas. We learn by reflecting on how well our various formulations communicate what we mean and by imitating the telling examples of our conversation partners. Good teachers know the power of conversation for learning. They know that students are less likely to learn from lectures, however brilliant they may be, for which they sit like audiences than from interactive discussions in which they play a much more active role. Raising the prepared participation levels of students is a key to better learning. The critical element is not just more student participation but more conversation-like participation.

Given the chance, students are quite capable of generating noisy sessions in which they mindlessly express feelings, cite random pieces of information, and state opinions that remain largely unconnected.

We learn through repeated conversations how to exercise our judgments better. As conversational partners consider related topics over a period of time, they learn of and from the perspectives each brings. They gain fuller and clearer senses of the issues themselves as these have been sorted in past conversations. They comprehend more empathetically the attitudes of their conversation partners toward typical alternatives. Two examples, both drawn from studies of hospital management, nicely illustrate this process. The first example involves a neurosurgeon and the parents of children suffering serious nervous system disorders. Initially it was often very difficult to decide which of several alternative courses of action was most appropriate. The doctor discussed the cases with the families almost like textbook cases in bioethics. They attempted to understand and weigh considerations regarding extraordinary means, pain and distress levels, risks, and viabilities of alternatives. Over time, however, as the doctor discussed the declining health and care for the children with the parents, they all found it easier to talk about the decisions that needed to be made. The surgeon as well as the parents felt that they learned in the process. They gained a better sense of what the alternatives meant. They found it easier both to express their feelings directly and to listen to what was being said to them. Even though from a textbook perspective the decisions were becoming more difficult, the doctor and the families found it easier, having been educated by their developing conversations, to make the judgments they felt needed to be made.

The second example involves doctors and nurses on an intensive care unit. They often had to make decisions very quickly about whether or not to operate, resuscitate, connect a patient to a heart or lung machine, or do nothing. Any medical intervention was likely to be very expensive. Because the ICU was located in a Canadian hospital, this expense was not paid directly by the patient and/or his family. Nonetheless, costly but needless interventions for some patients might function to drain the financial resources of the hospital enough so that similar interventions were not as available later for others with more pressing needs. The medical staff also recognized that it is more difficult to disconnect a patient from a heart or lung machine than it is to connect a patient in the first place. They knew how distressing and traumatic the interventions they ordered could become. They faced a number of very difficult cases, about which they had to decide very quickly. In retrospect, staff members felt more comfortable with some decisions they had made than with others. Regularly without making any criticisms, without blame or praise, they confidentially reviewed troubling cases among themselves. Over time, as a result of these conversations they achieved a better sense of what was at stake in the cases they saw. They found themselves being better able to arrive at decisions quickly, with which they also felt more at ease. Difficulties in making decisions only arose when new doctors, who had not been party to the previous conversations, joined the staff. As a result of these open, considerate, thoughtful conversations, participating doctors and nurses learned how to raise concerns more clearly, how to attend more sensitively to the concerns raised by others, and how to discern with greater sophistication central issues from peripheral matters.

These kinds of communicative interactions can additionally be educational because they provide ways for us to rethink, reconsider, and thereby change our minds. For this purpose the personal, contingent, narrative character of conversation is decisive. Because conversations—even those involving negotiation or formal deliberating—do not always unfold according to plan, they provide free space that participants often use to reposition themselves. We often use off-hand comments, pauses, and digressions as springboards to take new tacks. Our conversation partners act similarly. Pauses are especially important, as the sociolinguist Basil Bernstein (1971) observed. Pauses occur in discursive interpersonal communications, he noted, as speakers carefully think about what they want to say to particular audiences. They pause because they are searching for words and phrases they think will be intelligible and thought-provoking to their audiences and because they feel a need to attempt to incorporate into their own comments concerns expressed in the previous statements of their conversational partners. As a result conversations often wander, momentarily pause, and cycle through previous topics on slightly modified terms. In the process these maneuverings allow us to maintain "face" while both altering our stances and seeking to become more accommodating. As ordinary conversations unfold, in settings other than courtrooms and formal debates, we often allow each other to add to and revise what we are saying without exposing these modifications as inconsistencies. In fact, intentionally shaming conversation partners in this way is viewed as unmannered bad form (Goffman 1967). In good conversations, participants often mutually contribute to this face-saving out of ordinary respect for the other and partly out of a sense of civility. As a result conversational interactions often promote learning because they frequently provide narrative space for participants to rethink and reexpress their positions without losing face.

Through conversation we often receive information so that we gain a clearer view of our own concerns and at the same time become more articulate. There is a recurrent pattern in which interested individuals initiate a number of conversations with diverse people in order to obtain relevant information regarding problems they want to address. In the process of these inquiries, we meet other people who share similar concerns. If we were just seeking facts, then we might obtain little else. But insofar as we engage our respondents in conversation, then we often gain interested allies as well. These allies actively instruct. As our investigations proceed, we find ourselves beginning to pass along relevant concerns and information among our respondents, who begin to form loose networks of potential collaborators. Informed by these multiple, overlapping conversations, we can become very sophisticated about the issues at hand. Instructed by the people we have consulted, we gain an educated sense of the value and cost of various alternatives. As a result these investigative conversations position us much better to champion the causes that interest us.

The experience of Gail Mayville, an employee with Ben and Jerry's Homemade, Inc., illustrates this process. In 1986 she was hired as an office manager for the president. She had an interest in environmental issues and informally began to see how well Ben and Jerry's was performing. The reputation of the company was excellent, based largely on its efforts to help preserve the Brazilian rain forest by buying nuts from native producers and making donations through its corporate charity. It marketed a product, called Rainforest Crunch, which reinforced this image in the public's eye. Nonetheless, on the basis of her informal surveys of the company, Gail Mayville thought that they could and should do more right at home. The company was being cited for its milky wastes, which exceeded what the local sewage system could handle. After making a number of phone calls, Mayville helped solve this problem, which was not part of her job, by identifying a farmer who had just sold off a herd of cattle and was willing to buy pigs and to use Ben and Jerry's milky waste to feed them. As she reviewed the corporation's efforts, Mayville felt it could go further toward recycling corrugated cardboard, office paper, and plastic pails. Between 1986 and 1988 she collected detailed, up-to-date information both on the company's actual performance and on possibilities for doing something more. She collected this information in much the same way she had helped to address the milky waste problem, by contacting lots and lots of people, by getting leads and following them up, and in the process forging some very useful informal alliances. She developed a close relation with the Association of Vermont Recyclers. She discovered and forged informal links with like-minded contacts in government offices, the post office, and other businesses. She discovered a local businessman, for example, who mostly hired handicapped workers. He was hoping to expand his cardboard recycling business if larger supplies could be collected and transported to him. In a short time the conversations Mayville had initiated had become something more than ways for her to obtain information. They had become part of an informal, supportive networking alliance. Ben and Jerry's later utilized these contacts to develop sets of pickup points for recycling plastic pails and office paper (Weiss 1991).

Good Conversations Cultivate Trust

Good conversations help to overcome moral silence, deafness, and blindness because they often cultivate trust. To the degree that people experience trust in their relations with others, they feel that they can take risks. This general observation applies especially to the risks involved in voicing moral concerns, attending to the moral concerns of others, and seeing these concerns with a lively vision.

A number of observers have recently commented on the importance of trust for successful economic endeavors. In a book titled *Trust*, Fukuyama (1995) argues that the most prosperous economies are those in which trust flourishes. He points to the much higher productivity levels in high-trust societies like the United States, Japan, and Germany compared to other low-trust societies. Economies become especially productive to the degree that people learn how to work together for common purposes in groups and organizations. Their capacity for collaborative and cooperative work is in turn boosted by social arrangements that foster trust. Fukuyama argues that high-trust societies all foster the development of numerous community groups, professional organizations, and voluntary associations, which function as practical laboratories for generating various social virtues including trust. The historical development of these kinds of social arrangements is therefore decisive. Whether we agree or not with Fukuyama's broad historical speculation, we can see the merit in the parts of his argument in which he observes how trust as "social capital" fosters effective collaborations and how particular institutional arrangements in turn seem to cultivate trust.

For the present, we are concerned about trust at a more micro level. Trust is born of interactions that seem reliable in the face of uncertainties. If there were no uncertainties, there would be no need to trust because everything would be predictable (Moorman et al. 1993). The sense of reliability in turn is generated by experiencing continuity and reciprocity in given relationships. We initially learn to trust specific others when our actions engender familiar and complementary responses from them (Ring and Van deVen 1994). Trust is generated within families and friendships in these ways. Trust is also generated whenever people succeed in establishing ongoing, unfolding good conversations among themselves. The reasons for this overlap with the reasons why trust is born in families and friendships. Uncertainty exists with respect to any conversation. As we begin them, we do not know how they will turn out. We do not know for sure how others will respond to specific arguments or questions we introduce. As conversations develop, however, we do sense that specific others indeed attend to what we say, even if initially they disagree, and respond reciprocally if not always supportively in give-and-take fashion to our comments. As we proceed, we and they tacitly enter into agreements that we will continue to converse at least for the time being and about how we will do this. As our conversations develop, we begin to trust enough so that often we become less guarded and defensive. Correspondingly, we become more attentive to what our conversation partners are really saying and, depending on the nature of the conversation, we become more willing to openly disagree, to be more conciliatory, or both.

Trust is integral to good conversations. It arises to the degree that our communicative interactions are vocal and attentive, are reciprocating and civil, and give rise and faithfully adhere to mutual promises. When conversations become uncivil or one-way, we are less likely to extend our trust. Verbal exchanges filled with insults and challenges do not occasion trust. Neither does overly close surveillance or aloof responses. Attempts to foster greater cooperation within organizations by multiplying ordinances, strengthening enforcement, and other legalistic remedies generally do not succeed in this aim because they undermine trust. They are built upon strengthening both top-down and bottom-up one-way communications rather than upon building more reciprocating, interactive ones (Sitkin and Roth 1993). Trust is occasioned by good conversations. In a circular fashion, trust also makes good conversations possible. To the degree we feel that we can trust others not to abuse or scorn our statements, we are likelier to be bolder in saying what we really mean rather than voicing only neatly trimmed versions. Because good conversations are more likely to work well to the degree that people engage in them fully and forthrightly, increases or decreases in the feelings of trust are correspondingly likely to give rise to more energetic and constructive exchanges on the one hand or more timid, halting, desultory exchanges on the other hand.

Some institutional arrangements more than others foster both good conversations and trust, and for equivalent reasons. The extent to which they foster trust is in large part the by-product of the degree to which they allow and encourage reciprocating, interactive, and purposive exchanges through which people reach and sustain agreed-upon understandings. Trust at the group or community level is in part the cumulative effect of the sense of trust occasioned by multiple, overlapping, good conversations taking place within them. At the same time, institutional arrangements at the group or community level often facilitate and encourage these exchanges. Institutional arrangements that frustrate the formation of informal groupings, that discourage unofficial consultations, and that seek to ensure only orderly official deliberations, stifle the development of reciprocating interactive exchanges and trust.

Good Conversations Strengthen Feelings of Conscience

I have argued that moral silence, deafness, and blindness are sensuous embodiments of weak consciences. Good conversations work to overcome this deficit. With the exception of a few incorrigibles, all humans possess moral sensitivities. We feel indignation at personal insults and resentment at injuries for which we are not compensated. We feel grateful as the beneficiaries of good deeds and wronged if punished without explanation or a chance to defend ourselves (Strawson 1974). We feel that we ought to keep our promises and that we ought to attend to others when they directly appeal to us. We feel that unprovoked harm is wrong and that we should, if possible, rescue someone in imminent peril. Finally, we feel uncomfortable when we violate our own moral convictions (Nabert 1969). By themselves, however, these moral sensitivities do not amount to genuine feelings of conscience. As Catholic moral theologians have long argued, these are sentiments of unformed consciences (Curran 1977). We often need help in learning how to evaluate these sentiments properly and balance them with customary social rules and visionary ideals. We need help in establishing priorities and integrating these multiple moral feelings along with our specific social obligations into an overall sense of integrity. If conscience is, as the psychologist Gordon Allport (1955) described it, the self-conscious striving by individuals to achieve a sense of self-unity in relation to distinctive values, then forming and strengthening our consciences is a life-long enterprise. The studies of developmental psychologists in turn confirm this observation: They note that the sense of conscience that people bring to problems differs and that these various senses can be ranked from less to more developed (Kohlberg 1984a, 1984b).

Good conversations occasion the formation and strengthening of conscience in several ways. For instance, as we grapple to determine how to act in specific cases, we gain a clearer sense of our own priorities. Through the give-and-take of discussions, we can explore ways of balancing claims. To the extent that the external debates represent partial reflections and manifestations of our own inner struggles, ensuing conversations often not only reach their own resolutions but help us find personal resolutions to our own comparable inner tensions. Most importantly, good reciprocating conversations call for us to empathize at least in part with our conversational partners. In order for the conversation to unfold, in order even to be able to form persuasive counter-arguments to their positions, we need to gain a sense of how they see the world. At least to a degree, we need to be able to take on their role. Developmental psychologists argue that precisely this activity spurs the growth and development of conscience. Piaget (1948) found that the primary difference in the moral judgment of young boys and adolescents was the capacity of the latter to comprehend the positions of their playmates. The older boys were as a result less judgmental, less punitive, less literalistic in their interpretation of rules, and more concerned to take into account how the motives of others affected their conduct. Kohlberg (1984a, 1984b) has confirmed and expanded on these studies. As people learn to try on the views of others, they also gain in their ability to look at themselves. Their consciences develop as they form a sense of themselves, and their moral values, as oneself among others (Conn 1981; Ricoeur 1992).

Good Conversations Occasion Gracious Initiatives

From time to time good conversations occasion gracious initiatives, which make it possible for stalled or blocked exchanges to revive and begin again. The fundamental problem is that good conversations are often difficult to sustain. Conflicts arise. People get bored. Distractions intervene. Genuine difficulties seem insurmountable in spite of the best intentions. Someone gets offended. Another becomes momentarily inattentive. New problems arise that challenge agreed-upon understandings. The inevitable frictions of communicative exchanges engender imbalances in even the most reciprocating of relations. What was once a self-sustaining virtuous cycle threatens to become a mutually off-putting vicious cycle. These are all instances of what we might describe as the force of social entropy, or the devolution of our communicative exchanges to less open, less reciprocating, less reasonable, and less trusting forms. What gracious initiatives do is reverse these trends. They serve to address and overcome the forces of social entropy.

The sociologist Alvin Gouldner published an essay in 1960 arguing for reciprocity as a universal norm. He argued that all societies insisted on this norm, which in turn provided the absolutely necessary basis for viable and sustained social relations. Gouldner argued that this norm called for more tit-for-tat exchanges but also sometimes more than is required. Basically people are expected to contribute to others in equivalent measures what they received from others. Sometimes, however, these exchanges become asymmetrical. What is important, if the norm of reciprocity is to be honored, is for the overall system of exchanges to balance. Parents, for example, extend themselves for their children, who in part return this investment by later caring for parents but in part respond by extending themselves for their children. Gouldner recognized that there is a tendency for systems of reciprocity to run down unless from time to time some people are willing and able to do more than is expected of them. He expressed these concerns in a subsequent essay entitled "The Importance of Something for Nothing" (Gouldner 1973). He argued that societies attempt from time to time to inspire or occasion extraordinary acts of generosity, courage, and forbearance, as well as the willingness to suffer unmerited deprivation by extending social honors to those who respond to the challenge. Thus societies have honored saints, crusaders, heroic warriors, and philanthropists. Without these extraordinary acts, which in various ways compensate for failings in existing patterns of reciprocity and inspire corresponding acts by others, systems of reciprocity falter. Forgetting their reciprocal obligations, people become only narrow-minded, self-seeking egoists.

Blocked, frustrated, and stalled moral communications often are revived and renewed because one or both parties are correspondingly inspired to extend themselves in ways that are not required. They extend themselves to do something for nothing. Like traditional notions of works of supererogation and imperfect duties, these are acts of "sharing without reckoning" (Schumaker 1992). They may do this in a wide variety of ways. They may help revive lagging negotiations, renew desultory deliberations, overcome bargaining stalemates, or revivify disinterested disputants by a number of different kinds of acta. They may introduce humor, relate distracting but engaging stories, call for a pause in discussions, willingly concede points, apologize, ignore insults, not take offense at offending comments, or make no attempt to have the last word. These gracious initiatives are indeed varied. None is required or called for. All of these actions, from the recourse to humor to apologies, make breaks with what has just been transpiring in the stalled or blocked communication. They serve intentionally not to follow up essentially negative discourse with additional negative discourse. They are like gifts in that they are not required, they are expressions of generosity even if this is muted, and they give or add something so that conversations have a possibility of moving again. They are like acts of grace (Deutsch 1963).

Forgiving epitomizes what takes place in these gracious initiatives. Forgiving is not the same thing as forgetting even though we sometimes use these words interchangeably. To forget is to lose any memory of a past event. If we still recall what has happened, forgetting is either impossible or it is pretense. Forgiving is different. It calls for us to treat past upsetting acts as if they were really past. When we forgive, we are saying that in spite of these acts that were upsetting, we seek to continue and to revive our relationship with the persons responsible for them. We will treat these events not as part of the present but as part of the past. We must, therefore, relinquish efforts to call up these events just to serve our own purposes or to make others feel ashamed. Because it is not always easy to let bygones be bygones, ordinarily we attempt to elicit from others some gesture(s) to aid us in keeping these past acts in the past. We may look for signs of regret, comparable commitment to keep these events in the past, complementary acts of generosity, genuine efforts to compensate for past injuries, or a clear signal of willingness to drop certain demands or insinuations. Depending upon the circumstances, a wide range of responses may suffice. What is critical is that others extend themselves by these gestures either in response to or in conjunction with us so that particular upsetting events, comments, or conditions can be treated as past and we can now focus on reviving our interactions in the present.

Gracious initiatives function in a parallel fashion. They signal that we have taken certain upsetting topics off the negotiating, bargaining, or deliberating tables. Sometimes we make these kinds of concessions formally, often as part of bargained exchanges. Mostly, gracious initiatives are like gifts. Although gifts typically elicit corresponding responses, gifts by their nature are still expressions of generosity (Titmuss 1973; Mauss 1966). The result of these gracious initiatives is that people find that they can pick up their conversations again, although on terms that usually are slightly altered. In some cases, these changes are forthrightly announced. In many cases, they are only tacitly acknowledged. Gracious initiatives give beleaguered, derailed, and frustrated conversations a second chance.

Gracious initiatives are important because they allow stalled or blocked conversations to begin anew. Even as they thus help to occasion good conversations, they are also themselves the by-products of these same kinds of reciprocating interactions. Many of these iniatives are already part of the repertoire of good conversations. We have already noted, for example, how acts like not having the last word correspond to the implicit standards for reciprocating interactions. At the same time, civility calls for people to ignore insults, introduce humor, and not take offense at offending remarks. Additionally, the implicating character of good conversations and the trust they occasion over time elicits from conversation parties increasing commitment to the unfolding communicative intentions themselves. This commitment is decisive. We know from comparative studies of charity that giving gifts is not purely an altruistic act even though it is an expression of generosity. Rather, gift giving is usually part of a tacit, sometimes asymmetrical, but reciprocating system of exchanges. These are undertaken not like market exchanges based upon individual calculations of self-interest and equivalent trade-offs at one point in time but as part of social systems in which gifts are often exchanged for deference over longer periods of time. What is especially characteristic of gift exchanges is the extent to which these are given and deference is extended in order to maintain the sense of community between those involved (Mauss 1966; Titmuss 1973). Charity, for example, is especially directed toward people whose marginality might lead them to oppose the larger community and yet whose loyalty can be counted on (Bird 1981b). With these comparative studies of charity in mind, we can see that gracious initiatives, like other acts of charity, are part of tacit systems of exchange that especially aim at sustaining the sense of community or relatedness between conversation participants. Having been bolstered by the experiences of conversation thus far, some individuals occasionally extend themselves through special gracious initiatives in hopes of reviving relationships among themselves that seem threatened.

Over time, good conversations directly work to reduce moral silence, deafness, and blindness by engendering feelings of partnership, fostering learning, cultivating trust, strengthening our sense of conscience, and occasioning periodic acts of for-gifting. These by-products of good conversations make participants feel that they can and that they ought to speak out, listen attentively, and become more observant and cognizant. At the same time, good conversations function to address a number of the underlying organizational and individual factors that encourage these vices. For example, to the degree that people feel free to talk about their moral concerns and to sort out possible responses, they will feel less moral stress. As they voice and listen, over time they can become at least moderately more articulate. Good conversations address and serve to reduce the influence of most of the individual factors that cause or reinforce moral silence, deafness, and blindness. Through these interactions we can reduce our fears of uncertain engagements. Conversations are in principle open-ended. As we learn through our conversing to manage this particular form of unpredictability, we also gain greater ability to manage our relationships to other uncertainties. Ongoing interactions can become points of reference. Good conversations also address the fears of being implicated by bringing into being manageable interactions that do indeed implicate us. Because these conversations foster feelings of partnership and collegiality, we often gain through them potential allies to help us in the larger issues we face. Although good conversations cannot help us reduce or manage other claims on us, they directly help us become less inarticulate in voicing our concerns.

WHAT CAN BE DONE: WAYS FOR CULTIVATING GOOD CONVERSATIONS

We have discussed the character and contributions of good conversations at length. We recognize that these communicative interactions may take place in diverse settings from bargaining sessions to thoughtful deliberations, from regular encounters to special workshops. We now need to consider how to bring these conversations into being or how to transform our current communicative interactions so that they more nearly approximate this model. In the following paragraphs I make a number of suggestions that I discuss at the general and at the institutional levels (see Table 7.3). The first set of suggestions is addressed to anyone concerned about moral silence, deafness, and blindness and how to reduce and overcome these vices by cultivating good conversations. The second set is addressed to those who manage businesses, corporations, and other complex organizations.

At the General Level

The first suggestion is simple and direct. Any persons who are at all concerned about these problems ought to take the initiative to limit and reduce the current ways in which they have allowed themselves to become either morally mute or morally deaf. These two traits directly produce blocked and frustrated communications. To what extent and in what ways have we failed to voice our concerns about problems, failed to speak up for ideals, failed to provide honest feedback, or camouflaged our moral commitments? To what degree and in what ways have we failed to notice problems, failed to hear attentively concerns voiced by others, failed to investigate potential problems, or failed to regard with empathy problems from the perspective of others? How many times and in what ways have we allowed conversations about moral concerns to stall or become derailed? How many times have we allowed ourselves to become uncivil or unreasonable? Because none of us probably is a saint, few of us could answer these questions entirely positively. We may well excel in some areas, just as we have decided difficulties in others. There is room for improvement. Few of us, however, are incorrigible sinners as well. Therefore, these questions matter to us. To the extent that we care, we need in our own ways to address and reduce these traits in ourselves.

We can review a number of reasons to do so, already discussed in Chapters 2, 3, 4, and 5. To the degree that we and others take the initiative to speak up, be attentive, and otherwise cultivate good conversations, we are likely to let fewer wrongs go unattended, provide more opportunities for organizational learning, make our organizations more just and caring, reduce the extent to which we and others feel morally compromised, foster cooperative collaborations, occasion organizational sense-making, and make of ethics a more central and less marginalized concern. In the process, we are likely to strengthen our own consciences and to live with a greater sense of integrity. I mention these objectives not to sound high-minded and idealistic but out of a realistic recognition that unless we regard these objectives as of paramount importance, we are not likely to do much about these problems, and the further suggestions I make will not have much impact.

Table 7.3
Ways of Cultivating Good Conversations

Generally
- Encourage people to speak up because it matters and makes a difference
- De-professionalize moral discussions and decision making
- Allow and encourage organizational dissent
- Help people to develop their abilities to hear and be attentive
- Allow conversations to develop: avoid premature closure

Organizationally
- Define speaking up as part of every manager's job description, not just as trouble shooters but as quality managers
- Transform auditing function from one-way policing to two-way interactive activities
- Institute regular discussions of ethics in each organizational unit
- Establish multiple media for employee voicing
- Establish training programs in conflict resolution

Second, we can and ought to act to deprofessionalize moral discourse and decision making. All of us are morally responsible for our own decisions. Still, we often treat ethics as the vocation of specialists who have received training and education in specific disciplines. When we face moral dilemmas, we seek out one or another of these professionals. We select among them depending on the character of the particular dilemma. We go to lawyers if issues may have been covered by statutes or if previous litigation might shed light on our alternatives. We consult accountants to explore both possible infractions of others and our own leeway. Government regulators inform us what we need to do to satisfy their inspections. We seek out rabbis and other religious scholars to explore for precedents in religious moral codes and teachings. We go to counselors, therapists, and pastorally-oriented clergy when we want help in integrating our own sense of conscience. We call upon professional ethicists to help us develop organizational codes or train us in the use of moral logic for problem solving. All these consultations can be helpful, and many are essential. But they are not substitutes for the consulting and deliberating we need to do with those immediately involved in whatever dilemmas we are facing.

Ethics does not primarily take place in consultations with these professionals. Ethics as reflective deliberations about moral concerns primarily takes place as ordinary people reflect on the issues they face, deliberate, decide, and formulate the reasons for their decisions. Ethics, as Aristotle described it, is practical wisdom (Aristotle 1953). The primary consultations ought to be those that occur with others directly involved. We need to talk over these matters even if this involves confrontations, disputes, and heated discussions. We need to converse about these issues even if initially we feel inarticulate. Ethics is not only and primarily a calling for professional specialists—lawyers, accountants, counselors, clergy, consultants, ethicists. It is a calling for all adults who accept responsibility for their own lives: It is the calling to make sound, discursively defensible judgments about our lives and to be accountable for the decisions we make. If we are to steer the course of our own lives, we cannot hand over to others the task of reflectively deliberating on the good(s) for our lives and the fitting ways to act. The role of professional experts is secondary and supportive. We consult with them in order to perform our own tasks as ethicists better. Fundamentally, their responsibility is to advise and counsel us so that we are better informed and more competent to deliberate and decide responsibly.

Several important correlates follow from this view of ethics. One concerns the language of ethics. If we are all ethicists, then the language of ethics need not differ from our ordinary discourse. To be sure, lawyers, accountants, theologians, rabbis, therapists, regulators, consultants, and professional ethicists frequently do use special, often technical languages. They do so largely because they perform additional tasks that may bear upon our day-to-day moral decision making but take place beyond the ordinary domain of ethics in languages appropriate for courts, financial audits, scholarly debates, learned treatises, and psychological analyses. These specialized languages allow for clear, precise, and analytically instructive communications in these professional arenas. However, when these professionals consult with ordinary adults about the ethical dilemmas the latter face, the ensuing exchanges ought to be as reciprocating as any other good conversations, whether these take place between business colleagues or members of differing cultures. Correspondingly, on a case-by-case basis parties need to attempt to translate and restate their messages so that they are intelligible to each other. Occasionally as a result of this process, technical terms from professional languages find their way into ordinary discourse. Problems arise when ordinary adults feel that they cannot deliberate about moral issues, which happen to overlap with specialized domains of law, accounting, theology, or professional ethics, because they do not know enough about these specialties or don't feel comfortable using their terms and phrases. The optimum situation occurs when we deliberate about our moral dilemmas in the forms of discourse with which we are familiar. In the process we may consult when relevant with corresponding professionals, but we do so as part of good conversations in which—as part of give-and-take discussions—genuine efforts are made to translate and restate our concerns and theirs into each other's usual forms of discourse.

Correspondingly, the best way to introduce ethics into organizations is to get everyone involved. This is nicely demonstrated by recent efforts to redesign the curriculum at Harvard Business School. The objective was to expand the role of ethics in programs offered by the business school. In part this aim was accomplished by revising and improving the number of courses devoted to ethics and corporate social responsibility. These efforts were matched with community outreach programs through which students used their business school skills to help community groups and local businesses in the Boston area. Efforts were additionally made to introduce class sessions on ethics, leadership, and social responsibility into courses otherwise devoted to finance, accounting, marketing, international relations, and organizational behavior. Changes of this order, although they gave increased attention to ethics, would have still left ethics as a special, prominent, but marginal topic area. What made the efforts at Harvard Business School different was the degree of involvement by the faculty. Efforts were made to engage the faculty so that they reexamined their own values, commitments, and ways of teaching and so that they explored ways of connecting ethics more closely to their programs of research. Decision making and managing the business school itself were reviewed in light of these concerns. As a result everyone got involved in the "ethics conversation," which had once primarily only involved specialists in this area (Piper, Gentile, and Parks 1993).

Third, we can and ought to encourage organizational members to dissent, raise questions, voice concerns, and declare their convictions. Without people speaking up, a number of potentially beneficial conversations will never take place. Instead, there will be one-way communications, silence, and resentment. It is important to encourage people to voice their moral concerns and convictions so that they can feel more a part of their organizations, so that they won't feel silenced and often wronged, and so that the organizations have a better sense of what is taking place within them. If we do not genuinely welcome dissent, we are not likely to get many people speaking up and voicing their concerns. Because so many people fear that they will be punished or isolated or attacked if they openly criticize or dissent, they are likely to remain silent no matter how extensively people are encouraged to ask questions, voice concerns, and declare convictions. Unless dissent and criticism are explicitly welcomed, and the people involved are supported and rewarded for speaking up, then speaking up policies are likely to be viewed as public relations ploys. If as a result of these efforts we are successful in getting people to speak up, life within our organizations and communities is likely to become more turbulent. Communications are likely to become louder, more vocal, and often more critical. Previously submerged conflicts are likely to surface. Still, these changes need not be a problem so long as we insist that people who dissent, criticize, and challenge abide by the standards of good conversations: That they speak civilly and reasonably, that they listen attentively to others and respond reciprocally to their concerns, and that they keep the promises they have made. While encouraging dissent and challenges, we can also quite sharply draw the line to discourage if not prohibit slandering, carping, insulting, and pontificating as uncivil, unreasonable, or one-way discourse.

Fourth, we can and ought to encourage people to develop their abilities to listen well and be attentive to others. As I have already observed, listening well is the key to fostering good conversations. Many would-be conversations never begin because we fail to hear and respond when others address us. Many existing conversations falter on account of failures to remain attentive. Because we are so anxious to defend ourselves against the criticisms that are either just hinted at or only intimated or because we are overly eager to give answers, we do not hear fully and clearly what is being said. People often listen to the words but do not really hear what others are saying because they have not taken time to consider what is being said. They feel that an immediate demand is being requested of them. Although they may appear to dither, they have in fact not really thoughtfully and imaginatively considered the case at hand. They give answers, much like the supervisors in the Air Force brake case, because they feel they have to give answers at this very moment. And at this moment, they do not want to consider more issues. Their answers do not so much reflect and respond to the substance of our questions but to their need to keep issues off the table.

Fifth, we can and ought to allow conversations to develop and unfold. Often one or more participants bring potentially constructive conversations to premature completion. Because they want clear, decisive answers, they become impatient with ambiguous, wait-and-see responses. Not used to long-term bargaining or drawn out negotiations, they can either seek to force resolutions—often eliciting heightened resistance—or they can too easily give in—feeling thereby compromised. Many potentially promising conversations end before they really begin. Managers raise concerns and make requests, and after getting initial rebuffs, take these first statements as final answers and make no more moves. They may grouse to their friends and feel internally divided, but they feel that the matter has been closed. They do not wish to expose themselves to further rejections.

An instructive example of this type of response is the case of a recently graduated MBA who began working in the African and Asian offices of a Canadian company selling communication technologies in Third World countries. He had been raised in Latin America as the son of missionary parents, who had voiced their concern at the extensive corruption of local officials. Upon preliminary investigations, he learned that the agents his company used seemed to be charging huge fees, up to 25 percent in some cases. He confronted his boss with his concern that although the company itself was doing nothing illegal either by Canadian or local laws, the agents they retained might be. His boss dismissed his concern. His boss argued that the company had to use agents in most of these areas simply because the latter had contacts and knowledge that the company lacked. He argued that if the agents used some of their fee money to grease the palms of the local government officials, this could be justified by arguing that it was customary, that the officials were underpaid and counted on the extra support, and that the practice was very similar to the way lobbyists acted back in Canada. Given this response, the MBA graduate felt that he had either of two options: to leave the company because it condoned unethical practices or to swallow his conscience and continue his work feeling that he had at least raised the question. Looking at this situation from a distance, we could argue, I think, that the MBA graduate had several options that fell between these extremes. Most importantly, he could regard his meeting with his superior as the initial session in an unfolding set of conversations in which these concerns could be further discussed. Approached from this perspective, he would not necessarily seek a resolution from his first several discussions. Rather, he would explore ways to initiate a conversation that might touch upon several topics including this one. Correspondingly, in subsequent sessions he might raise questions about why some agents received much higher fees and about the possibility of seeking to recruit other agents and thereby occasion competition among them, which might in turn lead to reduced fees. He might note ways in which the current practice was costly. He might also observe the extent to which local community groups frowned on corruption, as they have in many countries in the Middle East, Asia, and Africa (Gillespie 1987; Klitgaard 1988). He might also learn from further conversations more of the constraints that influenced previous practices and gain some insight about prospects for modifying these. Viewed as one of a series of discussions, engaged in civilly, he might well perceive a number of alternatives that lay between the initial opposing alternatives, both of which seemed intolerable to him (Bird and Gandz 1991).

At the Organizational Level

The first suggestion at the organizational level parallels the first suggestion at the general level. Organizations can and ought to explore ways to incorporate voicing moral concerns as part of the ordinary job descriptions for managers and for employees. We have learned from several comparative studies that organizational members are far more likely to speak up about moral problems if such acts are viewed as being part of their jobs. Many people perform jobs that call for them to look for things that might be out of line. People in these positions are much more likely to act as whistle-blowers (Miceli and Near 1992; Victor, Trevino, and Shapiro 1993). All of the following are troubleshooters of sorts, and all report on possible moral problems at much higher rates: quality control officers, health and safety inspectors, internal auditors, regular supervisors, managers of employee assistance programs, human resource people who counsel other employees, union representatives, and central office purchasing agents who check on the relations with suppliers arranged by working units.

My suggestion builds upon these studies in two directions. First, it is appropriate to broaden the mandate held by people in these kinds of positions. They should be called to speak up not just as troubleshooters but as quality managers. That is, their job descriptions would require that they monitor the quality of work, performance, and cooperation within the areas where they hold responsibility. Correlatively, they would be expected to speak up to encourage good performance, to propose more promising alternatives, to help people address problems faced in their work, to caution people who are performing poorly, to raise questions as well as to call attention to possible infractions. Many of the people holding these troubleshooting positions already see their jobs in broader terms. In the previous chapter I examined why it is important to broaden the scope of concerns about which people speak up. To the extent that speaking up is primarily associated with raising complaints or making allegations, the incidence of voicing is likely to remain quite low, and many cases of possible wrongs are likely to go unreported.

Second, it is possible additionally to assign a modest form of this quality-management mandate to all organizational members. It is not really possible to turn all organization members into troubleshooters. They would appropriately resist the proposal. Efforts to make all employees into potential whistle-blowers through special anonymous reporting systems have not worked very well. Rates of speaking up are higher, however, when reporting on problems is regarded as only one of a much wider range of reasons for voicing and when as a result people are primarily expected to speak in person although often confidentially. Organizational members are in these cases invited to raise questions, to propose solutions, to talk over dilemmas, to express concerns, to discuss apparent cases of conflict of interest as well as potential and real ones, and to report on possible dangers and wrongs. They are additionally expected to speak up with the intent of maintaining or enhancing the quality of work and performance within their organizations and to speak up civilly as part of give-and-take discussions. Depending upon the topic these discussions may be confidential. The difference between anonymous and confidential communication is crucial. The latter is usually two-way and allows for give-and-take. It provides means for people to explore topics and to become mutually informed. In confidential discussions people can be quite open with the other so long as they keep confidential the information passed between them and release it to others only on terms mutually agreed between them. Anonymous communication is quite different. It takes place only if neither party can recognize the other. Although systems using numbers or third-party intermediaries can be devised, anonymous communications are usually not two-way and do not allow for reciprocating interactions. They are additionally open to a number of abuses both by malicious and poorly informed informants. Many organizations refuse in principle to act on anonymous complaints except where threats of grave danger warrant cautious response.

The overall aim is to define work responsibilities so that speaking up is viewed as an integral part of them. To a degree, something like this occurs in highly collegial settings. Where people work together as teams, they cultivate and count on ready communications to foster better collaborations, the early detections of possible problems, and adaptive responses to exigencies. Correspondingly, giving existing settings a collegial character or creating more collegial settings is likely to encourage equivalently higher rates of speaking up.

My second suggestion complements the first. I propose that insofar as possible auditing and appraising tasks be undertaken interactively and collegially. Rather than treating these activities primarily as means of control, I think they ought also be regarded as interactive venue in which people set and adjust goals on the basis of realistic appraisals of where they have been. I suggest that financial audits, social audits, and performance appraisals be conducted regularly not only to evaluate performances and to arrange what needs to be done when performances fall below minimal expectations but also to educate, to foster improved communications, and to set realistic objectives. For example, both auditors and those audited could benefit from these changes. Auditors would then be viewed not only as agents of control, who announce and maintain limits, but also as resource people, who help others make better, more proficient use of the persons and assets of their organizations. Correspondingly, performance appraisals would change. Supervisors as well as subordinates would see them not only as occasions for rating past performances but also as settings in which they can instruct and learn from each other about their respective concerns and needs. Each would hold the other accountable, although in different ways. Supervisors might well insist on certain objectives. Subordinates in turn could indicate the resources and conditions they need to realize these objectives. As a result of these changes, audits and appraisals would become more like good conversations and less like one-way evaluations or bypassing monologues (Culbert and McDonough 1980; Mohrman, Resnick-West, and Lawler 1989). Employees regard as fair and just pay decisions and performance appraisals that seem to take into account their communications with their superiors. Good interactive communications about these matters foster not only feelings of justice but also correspondingly greater organizational commitment (Folger and Konovsky 1989; Folger and Lewis 1993).

My third suggestion is that work units within organizations regularly set aside time for ethics discussions in the broadest sense—about the particular good or goods that they are seeking to realize and how well they are doing, and about the principles that guide their work. These would be like "meta" discussions in which they step back from their day-to-day operations in order to look at their work and performance from a larger perspective. Some units engage in these kinds of discussion by conducting exercises in which they review their mission and the progress they have been making to live up to it. Johnson and Johnson reports that work units within the company have over many years regularly held sessions to discuss the company's Credo and its meaning for their operations. Correlatively, the Credo itself gained in significance so that members frequently invoked it to clarify or explain their decisions (Nash 1988). Often these kinds of "meta" discussions work best not by invoking abstract principles but by considering concrete cases. Probably the case approach has the most utility because it keeps discussions grounded. Principles are reviewed in relation to specific issues. Occasionally these larger discussions just happen as members within units attempt to sort out their feelings, judgments, and expectations in relation to a particular decision that has to be made. In hospitals surgeons often lead what they refer to as "hair shirt" discussions in which they review difficult cases, usually involving themselves, in which they analyze how they might have acted differently. These are all judgment-call discussions, not unlike many business school cases used for seminars or classrooms. Surgeons lead their associates and staff through these retrospective discussions in order to explore how they can make better judgments in the future. The discussions are nonjudgmental, often forthright, but also usually fairly well monitored by surgeons themselves (Bosk 1979). It is often useful to discuss cases where a serious problem almost occurred but was averted. People feel freer to talk more expansively, more critically, and less judgmentally about such cases than when serious wrongs are involved or serious accidents occur. Thus, for example, it is often easier for these kinds of educational purposes to analyze apparent or potential conflict-of-interest cases than real ones.

The fourth suggestion is that organizations can and ought to establish a variety of institutional means for employees to voice concerns. Employees speak up for quite varied reasons: from formally grieving decisions by their supervisors to complaining about the behavior of colleagues, from alerting superiors about dangerous and unsafe conditions to making allegations about wrongdoings by peers, from seeking help in resolving dilemmas to questioning existing policies. Given this variety, it makes sense to establish several means for employees to voice concerns (Saunders and Leck 1993). Organizations can address this need by establishing a number of arenas or forums for employees to speak up. They can stage regular, town-meeting-like hearings. Senior executives can set aside regular times to receive informal calls. They can invite confidential correspondence. They can establish formal due process systems by which employees can make complaints. They can work with unions to provide for formal grievance procedures. They can institute ombuds offices. They can train supervisors so that the latter are able to become more supportive, objective listeners. They can encourage employees to speak directly with their supervisors when they have problems. Finally, they can establish formal procedures for hearing allegations or blowing the whistle. All the above function as institutionalized conduits for employees to raise issues and speak about their concerns. All possess some merit. None is sufficient by itself.

The fifth suggestion is that from time to time organizations can and ought to hold workshops to help members develop their skills at resolving conflicts. Conflicts of diverse sorts do arise. Conflicts occur because people are different, because competing units become aggressive or feel threatened, because decisions seem to favor some at the expense of others, and for many other reasons. When conflicts emerge, people respond in ways that can make matters worse. Often they become angry or defensive, or they seek to suppress conflicts or evade them. All of these typical responses can aggravate conflicts. They all cut off constructive, interactive communication. When they are in the midst of conflicts, people shout at each other figuratively if not literally; they do not listen well; and they defend their turfs. It is impossible for a number of reasons to create organizations in which conflicts never happen. We cannot reengineer or restructure conflicts out of organizational existence. They arise if for no other reason than because people care about what they do, go about doing it in different ways, and because resources are limited. Therefore, we need to explore ways of managing and resolving conflicts as they come up.

Two quite different procedures are especially helpful: One is to help people develop skills for managing conflicts as they arise; the other is to elicit from among relevant members and stakeholders a revived consensus about the fundamental purposes that they value in common. Both procedures give people common terms that they can invoke to steer their way through conflicts. The first provides tools for handling small, everyday conflicts; the second both revives in more vivid images the common purposes of organizations and helps people recommit themselves to this vision. Workshops have been developed to help people with both of these procedures.

Many businesses have either developed their own conflict-resolution training programs or have hired outside consultants for this purpose. The training workshops help participants develop skills in listening, in assertiveness, and in viable alternative tactics for dealing with different conflict situations. They learn that they can respond to conflicts by seeking integrative solutions that allow parties to get pretty much what they want by understanding their situation in a new light and making adjustments. Alternatively they can seek out compromises in which parties yield in part in order to achieve possible solutions. Or they can seek to dominate, to be obliging, or to avoid conflict altogether. Participants gain skills in conflict-resolution strategies that work best for the situations they are in (Rahim, Garrett, and Buntzman 1992).

In the late 1970s a medium-size manufacturing company started up a new plant site. They decided that all 500 employees would be required to enroll in interpersonal skills/conflicts-resolution workshops that originally lasted 5 days. All new employees hired in subsequent years were required to take the course. The company decided upon these workshops because almost all work at the plant was done through teams. They felt that it was important that team members be able to cooperate and resolve conflicts that might arise among themselves quickly and amicably without interfering with production schedules. This policy bore considerable fruit over the years. The workshops helped to facilitate effective working relations among employees at the plant. Plant members took pride in their skills in politely confronting each other and working through problems when they arose. As they became used to speaking up, plant members also became used to making suggestions for better ways to operate the plant both technically and managerially. Over time they came up with hundreds of suggestions, many minor, that when implemented markedly enhanced productivity. They were working with the same basic technology that was found at other similar manufacturing plants but at much higher levels of productivity. People liked working at the plant. Partly as a result of having graduated from the same standard interpersonal skills/conflict-resolution workshops, managers and workers developed characteristic ways of talking about issues. This style was so noticeable that when individuals who had worked at the plant moved to other sites of the manufacturing company, their new colleagues immediately recognized where they came from by how they addressed problems. In disproportionate numbers former managers from that plant were appointed to more senior executive positions at other sites. The skills they had gained first from these workshops and then from the experiences of putting these ideas into practice had helped them develop very useful competencies in managing conflict situations.

A second basic approach to conflict resolution works by creating common, integrative visions to which organization members commit themselves. Conflictual situations are overcome not by developing skills to manage conflicts but by altering the focus and perspectives in which they are viewed. Often conflicts seem intractable as long as we come at them, even with new conflict-resolution skills, in the same ways on the basis of our old interests and loyalties. These often connect us in practice to our own units and careers. Future Search Conference workshops in contrast attempt to overcome these problems by involving all major players within organizations in putting together new common visions to which they, as co-creators, are all committed. Future Search Conferences work in the following manner. All the major players within the organization or unit sponsoring the workshop, including all the significant stakeholders, are expected to participate. In spite of differing positions and status, all participate as equals. Participants proceed through a series of exercises, all of which encourage full, active participation, until they come up with a vision of where they would like their organizations to be several years in the future. This vision is based on realistic assessments of historical trends as well as on sets of beliefs and principles to which participants commit themselves. If not overtly moral, these beliefs and principles usually include a number of statements about what participants regard as the good(s) that their organizations ought to seek to realize and right ways of pursuing this end. These exercises enable participants to experience the fact that they hold in common many important assessments and commitments. The workshops provide settings for them to voice strongly these underlying sentiments rather than their ordinary, surface work-a-day concerns, which are often divergent.

After having gone through the experience of articulating these shared visions, participants are then called to draw upon these in order to restate what they judge to be the mission of their organizations, their distinctive competencies and shared internal values (Selznick 1957). As a result of these workshops, which ordinarily require several consecutive days, participants come away not only with common vocabularies for talking about their organizations but also with common commitments to the aims and principles they have identified (Weisbrod et al. 1992). They have also learned through this intensive experience the importance of speaking up and listening to each other. Future Search Conferences are workshops in good conversations. They work especially well because of the intense efforts participants invest to overcome the latent dissonance between the common visions they co-produce and the divergent views reflecting their ordinary work experiences with which they began (Weick 1993).

HISTORICAL CIRCUMSTANCES AND POSSIBILITIES

In a famous line, Marx observed: "Men make their own history, but they do not make it just as they please; they do not make it under circumstances chosen by themselves, but under circumstances directly encountered, given and transmitted from their past" (Marx 1963, 15). Marx's statement can be interpreted as an expression both of optimism and pessimism. On the one hand, humans make history. They create their own futures. Within measure, to the extent that historical circumstances allow, they can humanize their working conditions, make more effective use of natural and human resources, and hope for a future in which "the free development of each will be the occasion for the free development of all" (Marx and Engels 1955). But the dead hand of the past often constrains what humans can actually accomplish. They can only move forward on the basis of their actual historical circumstances.

In this book I have attempted to balance realistic appraisals of current circumstances with reasonable assessments of the prospects for change. I have examined at length varied expressions of moral silence, deafness, and blindness. These vices do not just crop up exceptionally. Most of us from time to time exhibit these vices in one form or another. Most of us occasionally suffer from weak consciences. Sometimes failures to speak up about moral concerns, to respond when others do, or to recognize moral issues clearly result in significant harm, in missed opportunities, and in self-corrupting self-deception. Moral deafness, blindness, and silence aggravate a number of problems of organizational life. In addition, these problems are both occasioned and made worse by a number of individual anxieties, including ethical inarticulacy, as well as by a variety of organizational factors that discourage open, interactive communication. Still, while depicting these vices and their consequences at length, I have assumed throughout that it is possible to limit and reduce these problems. We can address these vices by promoting good conversations in a number of settings. I have just reviewed a number of suggestions for promoting good, interactive moral communications. I have described these not as high ideals but as practical possibilities.

What we can accomplish, however, depends on the circumstances of our organizations and communities. Robert Putnam recently finished a twenty-year study of the development of regional democratic governments, established in Italy for the first time in 1970. At the end of the twenty-year period, these governments were both more fully developed and more democratic in northern regions than in southern ones. In principle all areas had equivalent opportunities for developing workable institutions of representative government. After twenty years there were marked differences. Putnam (1993) argues that differences in performance were shaped by differing social contexts, which in turn were shaped by quite different histories. Correspondingly, what advances we can institute to overcome moral silence, deafness, and blindness and what progress we can make to cultivate good conversations will be influenced in part by the social contexts in which we find ourselves. Some situations are more promising than others. None of us lives and works in settings without possibilities, however, if for no other reason than that the forms of moral silence, deafness, and blindness are so variegated. All of us live and work in settings where we can initiate or revive some good conversations about issues that matter. Initially, we are not expected in a mechanically efficient way to resolve all conflicts that arise, to institute reforms, or to overcome all past injustices. We are, nonetheless, expected to help nudge conversations along.

It is in our real interest to take these initiatives not only because we may eventually have some impact on the organizations for whom we work or the communities in which we live. We ought to take these steps, to begin or revive these conversations, for the sake of our own integrity. If we do not, we threaten further to weaken our own consciences.

In spite of our best efforts, we may not succeed in measurably reducing moral silence, deafness, and blindness in our organizations and communities. We may meet fierce resistance. We may find it difficult to secure allies and collaborators in these projects. We may feel overwhelmed and exhausted and overly vulnerable. Nonetheless, there are good reasons for not resigning prematurely. Sometimes resignation is occasioned by overly naive expectations. There is a happenstance, contingent character to the way history unfolds not unlike the way good conversations proceed. Goodness is fragile (Nussbaum 1986). Our most promising prospects sometimes fizzle. In the cases we are discussing, however, they also always remain worth pursuing. As we work on addressing the vices of moral silence, deafness, and blindness in ourselves and others, as we correspondingly work on cultivating good conversations, and as we additionally often help our organizations and communities avoid problems and respond to opportunities, we are also doing something else. Because we seek to foster fuller, more honest, reciprocating conversations with those with whom we live and work, we will also more fully realize our own humanity.

Works Cited

Ackerman, Robert. 1975. *The Social Challenge to Business*. Cambridge: Harvard University Press.

Allport, Gordon. 1955. *Becoming*. New Haven: Yale University Press.

Altheide, David L., Patricia A. Adler, and Duane A. Altheide. 1978. The Social Meaning of Employee Theft. In *Crime at the Top: Deviance in Business and the Professions*. John M. Johnson and Jack D. Douglas, eds. Philadelphia: Lippincott.

American Institute of Certified Public Accountants (AICPA): Committee on Social Measurement. 1977. *The Measurement of Corporate Social Performance*. New York: AICPA.

Anthony, Dick, Thomas Robbins, and Thomas E. Curtis. 1974. Reply to Bellah. *Journal for the Scientific Study of Religion* 13(4):491-495.

Aquinas, St. Thomas. 1960. *The Pocket Aquinas*. Vernon J. Bourke, ed. New York: Washington Square Press.

Arendt, Hannah. 1964. *Eichmann in Jerusalem*. New York: Schocken Books.

———. 1978. *Life of the Mind: Vol I: Thinking*. New York: Harcourt, Brace, Jovanovich.

Argyris, C., and D. A. Schon, 1978. *Organizational Learning: A Theory of Action Perspective*. Reading, Mass., Don Mills, Ontario: Addison Wesley.

Aristotle. 1953. *The Nichomachean Ethics*. J. A. K. Thomson, trans. Baltimore, Md.: Penguin Books.

———. 1981. *The Politics*. F. A. Sinclair, trans. Harmondsworth, England: Penguin.

Asch, Solomon E. 1951. Effects of Group Pressure Upon the Modification and Distortion of Judgement. In *Groups, Leadership and Men: Research in Judgment*, pp. 177-190. Harold Guetzkow, ed. Pittsburgh: The Carnegie Press.

Augustine. 1955. The Spirit and the Letter. In *Augustine: Later Works*, pp. 182-250. John Burnaby, trans. Philadelphia: Westminster Press.

———. 1956. "On Lying" and "To Consentius: Against Lying." In *On the Trinity, Doctrinal Treatises, Moral Treatises*. H. Browne, trans. Grand Rapids: Eerdmans.

Axelrod, Robert M. 1984. *The Evolution of Cooperation*. New York: Basic Books.

Bazerman, Max H., and Roy J. Lewicki, eds. 1983. *Negotiating in Organizations*. Beverly Hills: Sage Publications.

Bear, Larry Alan, and Rita Maldonado-Bear. 1994. *Free Markets, Finance, Ethics, and Law*. Englewood Cliffs, N.J.: Prentice-Hall.

Bell, Daniel. 1976. *The Cultural Contradictions of Capitalism*. New York: Basic Books.

Bellah, Robert. 1970. *Beyond Belief: Essays on Religion in a Post-Traditional World*. New York: Harper and Row.

———. 1974. Comment on "The Limits of Symbolic Realism." *Journal for the Scientific Study of Religion* 13(4):487-489.

Bellah, Robert N., Richard Madsen, William M. Sullivan, Ann Swidler, and Steven M. Tipton. 1984. *Habits of the Heart: Individualism and Commitment in American Life*. Berkeley: University of California Press.

———. 1991. *The Good Society*. New York: Knopf.

Bendix, Reinhart. 1956. *Work and Authority in Industry: Ideologies of Management in the Course of Industrialization*. New York: Wiley.

Benn, Stanley I. 1971. Privacy, Freedom, and Respect for Persons. In *Nomos* 13:1-26. J. Roland Pennock and John W. Chapman, eds. New York: Atherton Press.

Bernstein, Basil. 1971. *Class, Codes, and Control. Vol I: Theoretical Studies towards a Sociology of Language*. London: Routledge and Kegan Paul.

Bird, Federick B. 1973. *The Poor Be Damned: American Perceptions of and Responses to Poverty, 1885-1970*. Ph.D. Dissertation. Berkeley: Graduate Theological Union.

———. 1981a. Paradigms and Parameters for the Comparative Study of Religious and Ideological Ethics. *Journal of Religious Ethics* 9(2):157-185.

———. 1981b. The Works of Charity in Christianity and Judaism. *Journal of Religious Ethics* 10(1):144-169.

———. 1991. Good Conversations: A Practical Role for Ethics in Business. In *The Role of "Good Conversations" in Business Ethics: The James A. Waters Colloquium on Ethics in Practice*, pp. 13-93. George Aragon, ed. Boston College.

———. 1992. Religious Leadership. *Journal of Religion and Culture*, pp. 1-26. Vol. 6.

———. 1996. Moral Universals as Cultural Realities. In *Ethical Universals in International Business*. F. Neil Brady and Peter Koslowski, eds. Berlin: Springer-Verlag.

Bird, Frederick B., and Jeffrey Gandz. 1991. *Good Management: Ethics in Action*. Scarborough, Ontario: Prentice-Hall.

Bird, Frederick B., and James A. Waters. 1986. The Nature of Managerial Moral Standards. *Journal of Business Ethics* 5:373-384.

Bird, Frederick, Frances Westley, and James A. Waters. 1990. The Uses of Moral Talk: Why Do Managers Talk Ethics? *Journal of Business Ethics* 8:75-89.

Bloom, Allan. 1987. *The Closing of the American Mind: How Higher Education Has Failed Democracy and Impoverished the Souls of Today's Students*. New York: Simon and Schuster.

The Body Shop. 1996. Measuring Up: A Summary of the Body Shop Values Report. Watersmead, Littlehampton, West Sussex: The Body Shop International.

Bok, Sissela. 1978. *Lying: Moral Choice in Public and Private Life*. New York: Vintage Books.

———. 1983. *Secrets: On the Ethics of Concealment and Revelation*. New York: Vintage Books.

Bonhoeffer, Dietrich. 1955. *Ethics*. Eberhard Bethge, ed. Neville Horton Smith, trans.

New York: Macmillan.

Bosk, Charles. 1979. *Forgive and Remember: Managing Medical Failures*. Chicago: University of Chicago Press.

Boyd, Colin. 1988. Zeebrugge Car Ferry Disaster. In *Good Management*, pp. 360-383, by Frederick Bird and Jeffrey Gandz. Scarborough, Ontario: Prentice-Hall.

Buber, Martin. 1958. *I and Thou*, 2nd ed. Ronald Gregor Smith, trans. New York: Scribner's.

Byrnes, Nanette. 1994. The Smoke at General Electric: GE Continues to Struggle with an Ethics Program That Is Not Producing Results. *Financial World* (Fall).

Calvin, Jean. 1960. *The Institutes of the Christian Religion*. Vols. 1 and 2. Ford Lewis Battles, trans. Philadelphia: Westminster Press.

Camus, Albert. 1942. *The Stranger*. Stuart Gilbert, trans. New York: Vintage Books.

———. 1947. *The Plague*. Stuart Gilbert, trans. New York: Knopf.

———. 1951. *The Rebel: An Essay on Man in Revolt*. Anthony Bower, trans. New York: Vintage Books.

———. 1956. *The Fall*. Justin O'Brien, trans. New York: Knopf.

Cohen, Albert K. 1955. *Delinquent Boys: The Culture of the Gang*. New York: Free Press.

Conger, Jay A. 1989. *The Charismatic Leader: Behind the Mystique of Exceptional Leadership*. San Francisco: Jossey-Bass.

Conger, Jay A., R. N. Kanungo, and associates, eds. 1988. *Charismatic Leadership: The Elusive Factors in Organizational Effectiveness*. San Francisco: Jossey-Bass.

Conn, Walter S. 1981. *Conscience: Development and Self-Transcendence*. Birmingham, Ala.: Religious Education Press.

Cowan, John Scott. 1994. Lessons from the Fabrikant File: A Report to the Board of Governors of Concordia University.

Culbert, Samuel A., and John J. McDonough. 1980. *The Invisible War: Interests at Work*. New York: John Wiley's Sons.

Curran, Charles. 1977. *Themes in Fundamental Moral Theology*. Notre Dame: University of Notre Dame Press.

Damasio, Antonio R. 1994. *Descartes' Error: Emotion, Reason, and the Human Brain*. New York: G.P. Putnam's Sons.

David, Gregory. 1994. Bringing Up Baby: The Ethics Program at NYNEX May Be First Rate But It Is No Panacea. *Financial World* (Fall):38-39.

Deutsch, Karl. 1963. *The Nerves of Government*. New York: Free Press.

Donagan, Alan. 1977. *The Theory of Morality*. Chicago: University of Chicago Press.

Douglas, Mary. 1986. *How Institutions Think*. Syracuse, N.Y.: Syracuse University Press.

———. 1992. *Risk and Blame: Essays in Cultural Theory*. London: Routledge.

Douglas, Mary, and A. Wildowsky. 1982. *Risk and Culture: An Essay on the Selection of Technological and Environmental Dangers*. Berkeley: University of California Press.

Durkheim, Emile. 1961. *Moral Education: A Study in the Theory and Application of the Sociology of Education*. E. K. Wilson and H. Schnurer, trans. New York: Free Press of Glencoe.

———. 1964. *The Division of Labor in Society*. George Simpson, trans. New York: Free Press of Glencoe.

———. 1974. *Sociology and Philosophy*. D. F. Pocock, trans. New York: Free Press.

Dutton, Jane, and Janet M. Dukerich. 1991. Keeping an Eye in the Mirror: The Role of Images and Identity in Organizational Adaptation. Unpublished paper.

Edwards, Jonathan. 1969. *The Nature of True Virtue*. Ann Arbor: University of Michigan.

Elias, Norbert. 1977. The Civilizing Process. In *The History of Manners*. Boston: Beacon Press.

Entine, Jon. 1994. Shattered Image. *Business Ethics* (Sept/Oct):23-28.

Etzioni, Amitai. 1961. *A Comparative Analysis of Complex Organizations: On Power, Involvement, and Their Correlates*. New York: Free Press of Glencoe.

————. 1988. *The Moral Dimension: Towards a New Economics*. New York: Free Press.

Ewing, David W. 1989. *Justice on the Job: Resolving Grievances in the Non-Union Workplace*. Boston: Harvard Business School Press.

Fingarette, Herbert. 1969. *Self-Deception*. London: Routledge and Kegan Paul. New York: Humanities Press.

Fisse, Brent, and John Braithwaithe. 1983. *The Impact of Publicity on Corporate Offenders*. Albany: State University of New York Press.

Folger, Robert, and P. Konovsky. 1989. Effects of Procedural and Distributive Justice on Reactions to Pay Raise Decisions. *Academy of Management Journal*, pp. 115-130.

Folger, Robert, and Debra Lewis. 1993. Self-Appraisal and Fairness in Evaluations. In *Justice in the Workplace: Approaching Fairness in Human Resource Management*, ch. 5. Russell Cropanzano, ed. Hillsdale, N.J.: Lawrence Erlbaum Associates.

Foucault, Michel. 1973. *The Birth of the Clinic: An Archaeology of Medical Perception*. A.M. Sheridan Smith, trans. New York: Vintage Books.

Frank, Robert H. 1988. *Passions within Reasons: The Strategic Role of the Emotions*. New York: Norton.

Freud, Sigmund. 1957. *The Future of an Illusion*. W. D. Robson-Scott, trans. New York: Doubleday.

————. 1958. *Civilization and Its Discontents*. Joan Riviere, trans. New York: Doubleday.

Fried, Charles. 1970. Privacy: A Rational Context. In *An Anatomy of Values: Problems of Personal and Social Choice*, ch. ix. Cambridge: Harvard University Press.

Friedman, Milton 1971. The Social Responsibility of Business Is to Increase Its Profits. *New York Times Magazine* (Sept. 13):32-33.

Fuller, Lon L. 1964. *The Morality of Law*. New Haven: Yale University Press.

Fukuyama, Francis. 1995. *Trust: The Social Virtues and the Creation of Prosperity*. New York: Free Press.

Gaa, James C., and Lawrence A. Ponemon. 1993. Toward a Theory of Moral Expertise: A Verbal Protocol Study of Public Accounting Professionals. Unpublished paper.

Galbraith, John Kenneth. 1954. *American Capitalism: The Concept of Countervailing Power*. Boston: Houghton Mifflin.

————. 1958. *The Affluent Society*. Boston: Houghton Mifflin.

————. 1967. *The New Industrial State*. Boston: Houghton Mifflin.

————. 1973. *Economics and the Public Purpose*. Scarborough, Ontario: Meridian Books.

————. 1990. *A Short History of Financial Euphoria*. New York: Penguin Books.

————. 1992. *The Culture of Contentment*. Boston: Houghton Mifflin.

Gandz, Jeffrey, and Frederick B. Bird. 1996. The Ethics of Empowerment. *Journal of*

Business Ethics. (April) Vol. 15(4):383-392.

Gardner, Howard. 1983. *Frames of Mind: The Theory of Multiple Intelligences*. New York: Basic Books.

Geertz, Clifford. 1973. *The Interpretation of Cultures*. New York: Basic Books.

———. 1983. *Local Knowledge*. New York: Basic Books.

Gert, Bernard. 1970. *The Moral Rules: A New Rational Foundation for Morality*. New York: Harper and Row.

Gewirth, Alan. 1978. *Reason and Morality*. Chicago: University of Chicago Press.

Gibb-Clark, Margot. 1995. "Snitch Line" Called Insult. *Globe and Mail* (Sept. 21):B5.

Gillespie, Kate. 1987. The Middle East Response to the Foreign Corrupt Practices Act. *California Management Review* 29(4):9-30.

Goffman, Irving. 1959. *The Presentation of Self in Everyday Life*. Garden City: Doubleday Anchor Books.

———. 1967. *Interaction Ritual*. Garden City: Doubleday Anchor Books.

Gouldner, Alvin W. 1960. The Norm of Reciprocity. *American Sociological Review* 25(2):161-178.

———. 1973. The Importance of Something for Nothing. In *For Sociology: Renewal and Critique in Sociology Today*. Harmondsworth, England: Penguin Books.

———. 1976. *The Dialectic of Ideology and Technology: The Origins, Grammar, and Future of Ideology*. London: Macmillan Press.

Habermas, Jürgen. 1971. *Knowledge and Human Interests*. Jeremy J. Shapiro, trans. Boston: Beacon Press.

———. 1984. *The Theory of Communicative Action. Vol. One: Reason and the Rationalization of Society*. Thomas McCarthy, trans. Boston: Beacon Press.

———. 1987. *The Theory of Communicative Action. Vol. Two: Lifeworld and System: A Critique of Functionalist Reason*. Thomas McCarthy, trans. Boston: Beacon Press.

———. 1990. *Moral Consciousness and Communicative Action*. Christian Lenhardt and Shierry Weber Nicholsen, trans. Cambridge: MIT Press.

Hammer, Michael, and James Champy. 1993. *Reengineering the Corporation: A Manifesto for Business Revolution*. New York: Harper Business.

Hampden-Turner, Charles, and Alfons Trompenaars. 1993. *The Seven Cultures of Capitalism*. New York: Currency Doubleday.

Hare, R. M. 1952. *The Language of Morals*. Oxford: Clarendon Press.

———. 1963. *Freedom and Reason*. London: Oxford University Press.

Hart, H. L. A. 1968. *Punishment and Responsibility: Essays in the Philosophy of Law*. New York: Oxford University Press.

Hegel, Georg Wilhelm Friedrich. 1952. *Philosophy of Right*. T. M. Knox, trans. London: Oxford University Press.

———. 1956. *The Philosophy of History*. J. Sibree, trans. New York: Dover Publications.

Hirschman, A. O. 1970. *Exit, Voice, and Loyalty: Responses to Decline in Firms, Organizations and States*. Cambridge, Mass.: Harvard University Press.

Holling, C. S. 1995. What Barriers? What Bridges? In *Barriers and Bridges to the Renewal of Ecosystems and Institutions*. Lance H. Gunderson, C. S. Holling, and Stephen S. Light, eds. New York: Columbia University Press.

Hume, David. 1972. *A Treatise of Human Nature*. Books II and III. Pall S. Ardal, ed. London: Collins.

Jackall, Robert. 1988. *Moral Mazes: The World of Corporate Managers*. New York:

Oxford University Press.

Jacobs, Jane. 1992. *Systems of Survival: A Dialogue on the Moral Foundations of Commerce and Politics*. New York: Random House.

Jonsen, Albert R., and Stephen Toulmin. 1988. *The Abuse of Casuistry: A History of Moral Reasoning*. Berkeley: University of California Press.

Jung, Carl Gustave. 1953. *Two Essays on Analytic Psychology*. R. F. C. Hull, trans. Princeton: Princeton University Press.

Kagan, Jerome. 1989. The Idea of Temperamental Types. In *Unstable Ideas: Temperament, Cognition, and Self*, ch. 3. Cambridge: Harvard University Press.

Kant, Immanuel. 1949. *Fundamental Principles of the Metaphysic of Morals*. Thomas K. Abbott, trans. New York: Liberal Arts Press.

———. 1956. *Critique of Practical Reason*. Lewis White Beck, trans. Indianapolis: Bobbs-Merrill.

Keenan, John P. 1990. Upper-Level Managers and Whistle-Blowing. *Journal of Business and Psychology* 5(2):223-235.

Kierkegaard, Soren. 1941. *Concluding Unscientific Postscript*. David F. Swensen and Walter Lowrie, trans. Princeton: Princeton University Press.

Klitgaard, Robert. 1988. *Controlling Corruption*. Berkeley: University of California Press.

Kohlberg, Lawrence. 1984a. *The Philosophy of Moral Development: Moral Stages and the Idea of Justice*. San Francisco: Harper and Row.

———. 1984b. *The Psychology of Moral Development: The Nature and Validity of Moral Stages*. San Francisco: Harper and Row.

Kotter, John P. 1988. *The Leadership Factor*. New York: Free Press.

Laing, R. D. 1959. *The Divided Self*. Harmondsworth, England: Penguin Books.

Lenin, V. I. 1963. *What Is to Be Done?* Alexander Trachtenber, ed. New York: International Publisher.

Levinas, Emmanuel. 1969. *Totality and Infinity: An Essay on Exteriority*. Alphonso Lingis, trans. Pittsburgh: Duquesnes University Press.

Lewicki, Roy J., and Joseph A. Litterer, eds. 1985. *Negotiations: Readings, Exercises, and Cases*. Homewood, Ill.: Richard D. Irwin.

Lewis, Michael. 1989. *Liar's Poker: Rising Through the Wreckage on Wall Street*. New York: Penguin Books.

Light, Stephen S., Lance H. Gunderson, and C. S. Holling. 1995. The Everglades: Evolution of a Management System in a Turbulent Ecosystem. In *Barriers and Bridges to the Renewal of Ecosystems and Institutions*, pp. 103-168. Lance H. Gunderson, C. S. Holling, and Stephen S. Light, eds. New York: Columbia University Press.

Lind, E. Allan, and Tom R. Tyler. 1988. *The Social Psychology of Procedural Justice*. New York: Plenum Press.

Lukacs, Georg. 1968. *History and Class Consciousness: Studies in Marxist Dialectics*. Cambridge: MIT Press.

Lukes, Steven. 1971. Moral Weakness. In *Weakness of Will*, ch. ix. G. W. Mortimore, ed. London: Macmillan.

Luther, Martin. 1961. "Two Kinds of Righteousness" and "The Freedom of a Christian." In *Martin Luther: Selections from his Writings*. John Dillenberger, ed. New York: Doubleday.

MacIntyre, Alisdair. 1981. *After Virtue: A Study in Moral Theory*. Notre Dame, Ind.:

University of Notre Dame Press.

———. 1988. *Whose Justice? Which Rationality?* Notre Dame, Ind.: University of Notre Dame Press.

Macmurray, John. 1961. *Persons in Relation.* New York: Harper and Brothers.

Malcolm X. 1973. *The Autobiography of Malcolm X.* With the assistance of Alex Haley. New York: Ballantine Books.

Mannheim, Karl. 1936. *Ideology and Utopia.* Louis Wirth and Edward Shils, trans. New York: Harcourt, Brace.

Marx, Karl. 1906. *Capital: A Critique of Political Economy.* Vol I. Samuel Moore and Edward Aveling, trans. Friedrich Engels, ed. New York: Random House.

———. 1963. *The Eighteenth Brumaire of Louis Bonaparte.* New York: International Publisher.

———. 1977. *Selected Writings.* David McLellan, ed. Oxford: Oxford University Press.

Marx, Karl, and Frederick Engels. 1947. *The German Ideology.* Parts I and III. New York: International Publishers.

Marx, Karl, and Friedrich Engels. 1955. *The Communist Manifesto.* New York: Appleton-Century-Crofts.

Matthews, Gwynneth. 1971. Weakness of Will. In *Weakness of Will.* G. W. Mortimore, ed. London: Macmillan.

Matza, David. 1964. *Delinquency and Drift.* New York: Wiley.

Mauss, Marcel. 1966. *The Gift: Forms and Functions of Exchange in Archaic Societies.* London: Routledge and Kegan Paul.

Mayer, Martin. 1990. *The Greatest Bank Robbery Ever: The Collapse of the Savings and Loan Industry.* New York: Charles Scribner's Sons.

McLuhan, Marshall. 1962. *The Gutenberg Galaxy: The Making of Typographic Man.* New York: New American Library.

———. 1964. *Understanding Media: The Extensions of Man.* New York: McGraw Hill.

Miceli, Marcia P., and Janet P. Near. 1992. *Blowing the Whistle: The Organizational and Legal Implications for Companies and Employees.* New York: Lexington Books.

Milgram, Stanley. 1974. *Obedience to Authority: An Experimental View.* New York: Harper and Row.

Miller, Danny. 1990. *The Icarus Paradox: How Exceptional Companies Bring About Their Own Downfall.* New York: Harper Business.

Mintz, Morton. 1985. *At Any Cost: Corporate Greed, Women, and the Dalkon Shield.* New York: Pantheon.

Moberg, David. 1994. Skin Deep. *In These Times* (Sept. 19), pp. 12-16.

Mohrman, A. M., S. M. Resnick-West, and E. E. Lawler. 1989. *Designing Performance Appraisal Systems: Aligning Appraisals and Organizational Realities.* San Francisco: Jossey-Bass.

Moore, Barrington, Jr. 1978. *Injustice: The Social Bases of Obedience and Revolt.* White Plains, N.Y.: M. E. Sharpe.

Moorman, Christine, et al. 1993. Factors Affecting Trust in Market Relationships. *Journal of Marketing* 57:81-101.

Nabert, Jean. 1969. *Elements for an Ethic.* William J. Petriçk, trans. Evanston Ill.: Northwestern University Press.

Nash, Laura. 1988. Johnson and Johnson's Credo. In *Corporate Ethics: A Prime Asset.* James Keogh, ed. The Business Roundtable (Feb.), New York, ch. 8, pp. 77-104.

———. 1990. *Good Intentions Aside: A Manager's Guide to Resolving Ethical*

Problems. Boston: Harvard Business School Press.

Niebuhr, H. Richard. 1963. *The Responsible Self: An Essay in Christian Moral Philosophy*. New York: Harper and Row.

Niebuhr, Reinhold. 1932. *Moral Man and Immoral Society: A Study in Ethics and Politics*. New York: Scribner.

———. 1944. *The Children of Light and the Children of Darkness: A Vindication of Democracy and a Critique of Its Traditional Defence*. New York: Charles Scribner's Sons.

Nielsen, Richard. 1987. What Can Managers Do About Unethical Management? *Journal of Business Ethics* 6:309-320.

———. 1989. Changing Unethical Organizational Behavior. *Academy of Management Executive* 3(2):123-130.

Nietzsche, Friedrich. 1927. *The Genealogy of Morals*. Horace B. Samuel, trans. In *The Philosophy of Nietzsche*. New York: Random House.

Nonet, Philippe. 1969. *Administrative Justice: Advocacy and Change in a Government Agency*. New York: Russell Sage Foundation.

Nozick, Robert. 1981. *Philosophical Explanations*. Cambridge: Harvard University Press.

Nussbaum, Martha C. 1986. *The Fragility of Goodness: Luck and Ethics in Greek Tragedy and Philosophy*. Cambridge: Cambridge University Press.

Ouchi, William G. 1981. *Theory Z: How American Business Can Meet the Japanese Challenge*. New York: Avon Books.

Parry, Susan, and Jim Dawson. 1981. *Nightmares: Women and the Dalkon Shield*. New York: Macmillan.

Perrow, Charles. 1984. *Normal Accidents: Living with High-Risk Technologies*. New York: Basic Books.

Perry, William G. 1968. *Forms of Intellectual and Ethical Development in the College Years: A Scheme*. New York: Holt Rinehart and Winston.

Peters, Thomas J., and Robert H. Waterman, Jr. 1982. *In Search of Excellence: Lessons from America's Best-Run Companies*. New York: Harper and Row.

Pfeffer, J., and G. R. Salancik. 1978. *The External Control of Organizations: A Resource Dependence Perspective*. New York: Harper and Row.

Piaget, Jean. 1948. *The Moral Judgement of the Child*. Glencoe, Ill.: Free Press of Glencoe.

———. 1951. *The Language and Thought of the Child*. Marjorie Gabain, trans. New York: Humanities Press.

Piper, Thomas R., Mary C. Gentile, and Sharon Daloz Parks. 1993. *Can Ethics Be Taught? Perspectives, Challenges and Approaches at Harvard Business School*. Boston: Harvard Business School Press.

Plato. 1960a. *Gorgias*. Walter Hamilton, trans. New York: Penguin Books.

———. 1960b. *The Republic*. In *The Republic and Other Works*. B. Jowett, trans. Garden City: Doubleday.

Plotnick, Robert, and Felicity Skidmore. 1975. *Progress Against Poverty: A Review of the 1964-1975 Decade*. New York: Academic Press.

Putnam, Linda L., and Michael E. Roloff, eds. 1992. *Communications and Negotiation*. London: Sage Publications.

Putnam, Robert. 1993. *Making Democracy Work: Civic Traditions in Modern Italy*. With Robert Leonardi and Rafaella Y. Nanetti. Princeton: Princeton University Press.

Rahim, M. Afzalur, Jan Edward Garrett, and Gabriel Buntzman. 1992. Ethics of Managing Interpersonal Conflict in Organizations. *Journal of Business Ethics* 11:423-432.

Rawls, John. 1971. *A Theory of Justice*. Cambridge: Harvard University Press.

Ricoeur, Paul. 1992. *Oneself As Another*. Kathleen Blamey, trans. Chicago: University of Chicago Press.

Rinehart, James W. 1978. Work Humanization and the Labor Process. Unpublished essay. University of Western Ontario.

Ring, Peter Smith, and Andrew H. Van deVen. 1994. Developmental Processes of Cooperative Interorganizational Relationships. *Academy of Management Review* 42(1):95-113.

Robbins, Thomas, Dick Anthony, and Thomas E. Curtis. 1973. The Limits of Symbolic Realism: Problems of Empathetic Field Observation in a Sectarian Context. *Journal for the Scientific Study of Religion* 12(3):259-271.

Roddick, Gordon. 1994. Letter to *Business Ethics* Subscribers (Sept.22), pp. 1-10.

Rokeach, Milton. 1968. *Beliefs, Attitudes and Values: A Theory of Organization Change*. San Francisco: Jossey-Bass.

———. 1979. *Understanding Human Values: Individual and Societal*. New York: Free Press.

Saunders, David, and Joanne D. Leck. 1993. Formal Upward Communication Procedures: Organizational and Employee Perspectives. *Canadian Journal of Administrative Studies* 10(3):255-268.

Scheler, Max. 1954. *The Nature of Sympathy*. Peter Heath, trans. London: Routledge and Kegan Paul.

Schumaker, Millard. 1992. *Sharing without Reckoning: Imperfect Right and the Norms of Reciprocity*. Waterloo, Ontario: Wilfred Laurier University Press.

Schutz, Alfred. 1967. *The Phenomonology of the Social World*. George Walsh and Frederick Lehnert, trans. Evanston Ill.: Northwestern University Press.

Scott, John. 1971. *The Internalization of Norms: A Sociological Theory of Moral Commmitment*. Englewood Cliffs, N.J.: Prentice-Hall.

Selznick, Philip. 1949. *TVA and the Grass Roots*. Berkeley: University of California Press.

———. 1957. *Leadership in Administration*. Berkeley, University of California Press.

———. 1969. *Law, Society, and Industrial Justice*. New York: Russell Sage.

———. 1992. *The Moral Commonwealth: Social Theory and the Promise of Community*. Berkeley: University of California Press.

Sennett, Richard. 1974. *The Fall of Public Man*. New York: Knopf.

Sitkin, Sim B., and Nancy L. Roth. 1993. Explaining the Limited Effectiveness of "Legalistic Remedies" for Trust and Distrust. *Organizational Science* 4(3):367-392.

Smith, Adam. 1970. *The Wealth of Nations*. Books I-III. Baltimore: Penguin Books.

———. 1976. *The Theory of Moral Sentiments*. Indianapolis: Liberty Classics.

Smith, Wilfred Cantwell. 1976. *Religious Diversity*. Willard Oxtoby, ed. New York: Harper and Row.

Srivastva, Suresh, et al. 1988. *Executive Integrity: The Search for High Human Values in Organizational Life*. San Francisco: Jossey-Bass.

Stevenson, Charles L. 1944. *Ethics and Language*. New Haven: Yale University Press.

Stone, Christopher. 1975. *Where the Law Ends: The Societal Control of Corporate Behavior*. New York: Harper and Row.

Stout, Jeffrey. 1988. *Ethics after Babel: The Languages of Morals and Their Discontents*. Boston: Beacon Press.

Strauss, Anselm. 1991. *Creating Sociological Awareness: Collective Images and Symbolic Representations*. New Brunswick, N.J.: Transaction Publishers.

Strawson, P. F. 1974. *Freedom and Resentment*. London: Methuen.

Sutton, F. X., S. E. Harris, C. Kaysen, and J. Tobin. 1956. *The American Business Creed*. Cambridge: Oxford University Press.

Tannen, Deborah. 1990. *You Just Don't Understand: Women and Men in Conversation*. New York: Ballantine Books.

Taylor, Charles. 1989. *Sources of the Self: The Making of Modern Identity*. Cambridge: Harvard University Press.

Taylor, Talbot, and Deborah Cameron. 1987. *Analyzing Conversation: Rules and Units in the Structure of Talk*. Oxford: Pergamon Press.

Tillich, Paul. 1963. *Morality and Beyond*. New York: Harper and Row.

Titmuss, Richard M. 1973. *The Gift Relationship: From Human Blood to Social Policy*. Harmondsworth, England: Penguin Books.

Tocqueville, Alexis de. 1955. *The Old Regime and the French Revolution*. Stuart Gilbert, trans. Garden City, N.Y.: Doubleday.

Toffler, Barbara. 1986. *Tough Choices: Managers Talk Ethics*. New York: Wiley.

Tönnies, Ferdinand. 1957. *Community and Society*. Charles P. Loomis, trans. New York: Harper and Row.

Toulmin, Stephen. 1950. *An Examination of the Place of Reason in Ethics*. Cambridge: Cambridge University Press.

Troeltsch, Ernst. 1960. *The Social Teaching of the Christian Churches*, Volumes I and II. Olive Wyon, trans. New York: Harper and Brothers.

Turner, Ralph. 1975. The Real Self: From Institution to Impulse. *American Journal of Sociology* 81:989-1016.

Tussing, A. Dale. 1975. *Poverty in a Dual Economy*. New York: St. Martin's Press.

Vandiver, Kermit, 1972. Why Should My Conscience Bother Me? In *In the Name of Profit*. Robert L. Heibroner et al. Garden City, N.Y.: Doubleday.

Vatican Council II. 1965. *The Church in the World Today: Schema of the Pastoral Constitution*. Vatican City: Vatican Polyglot Press.

Victor, Bart, Linda Klebe Trevino, and Debra L. Shapiro. 1993. Peer Reporting of Unethical Behavior: The Influence of Justice Evaluations and Social Context Factors. *Journal of Business Ethics* 12:253-263.

Walzer, Michael. 1983. *Spheres of Justice*. New York: Basic Books.

Waters, James A. 1976. Organizational Sanctions: A Process of Inquiry into Deviations. Ph.D. dissertation. Cleveland: Case Western Reserve University.

———. 1978. Catch 20.5: Corporate Morality as an Organizational Phenomenon. *Organizational Dynamics* (Spring), pp. 3-19.

———. 1980. Of Saints, Sinners, and Socially Responsible Executives. *Business and Society* (Winter), pp. 67-73.

———. 1982. Managerial Assertiveness. *Business Horizons* (September/October), pp. 24-29.

Waters, James A., and Frederick B. Bird. 1987. The Moral Dimension of Organizational Cultures. *Journal of Business Ethics* 6:15-22.

Waters, James A., Frederick B. Bird, and Peter D. Chant. 1986. Everyday Moral Issues Experienced by Managers. *Journal of Business Ethics* 5:373-384.

Waters, James A., and Peter D. Chant. 1982. Internal Control of Managerial Integrity: Beyond Accounting Systems. *California Management Review* 24(3):61-66.

Weber, Max. 1978. *Economy and Society: An Outline of Interpretive Sociology.* Guenther Roth and Claus Wittich, eds. Volumes I and II. Berkeley: University of California Press.

Weick, Karl. 1993. Sensemaking in Organizations: Small Structures with Large Consequences. In *Social Psychology in Organizations: Advances in Theory and Research.* J. Keith Murnighan, ed. Englewood Cliffs, N.J.: Prentice Hall.

Weisbrod, Marvin R., et al. 1992. *Discovering Common Ground.* San Francisco: Berrett-Koehler.

Weiss, Stephanie, and Kirk Hanson. 1991. *Gail Mayville A, B, C, D, E.* Stanford: Business Enterprise Trust.

Werhane, Patricia H. 1991. Engineers and Management: The Challenge of the Challenger Incident. *Journal of Business Ethics* 10:605-616.

Westley, Frances. 1990. Microdynamics of Inclusion: Middle Managers and Strategy. *Strategic Management Journal* 11:337-352.

————. 1992. Vision Worlds: Strategic Vision As Social Interaction. In *Advances in Strategic Management*, No. 8. P. Shrivasta, A. Hoff, and J. Dutton, eds.

Wilensky, Harold. 1961. The Uneven Distribution of Leisure: The Impact of Economic Growth on "Free Time." *Social Problems* 9:32-56.

Williams, Bernard. 1985. *Ethics and the Limits of Philosophy.* Cambridge: Harvard University Press.

Williamson, Oliver. 1985. *The Economic Institutions of Capitalism: Firms, Markets, and Relational Contracting.* New York: Free Press.

Wilson, James Q. 1989. Adam Smith on Business Ethics. *California Management Review* 32(1):59-72.

Winch, Peter. 1972. *Ethics and Action.* London: Routledge and Kegan Paul.

Wolff, Robert Paul, Barrington Moore, Jr., and Herbert Marcuse. 1965. *A Critique of Pure Tolerance.* Boston: Beacon Press.

Yankelovich, Daniel. 1981. *New Rules: Searching for Self-Fulfillment in a World Turned Upside Down.* Toronto: Bantam Books.

Zartman, I. William, ed. 1976. *The Fifty Percent Solution: How to Bargain Successfully with Hijackers, Strikers, Bosses, Old Management, Arabs, Russians and Other Worldly Opponents in This Modern World.* Garden City, N.Y.: Doubleday.

Zartman, I. William, and Maureen R. Berman. 1982. *The Practical Negotiator.* New Haven: Yale University Press.

Index

About the Author

FREDERICK BRUCE BIRD is Professor of Comparative Ethics at Concordia University, Montreal, where he teaches in the management and religion departments and directs the doctoral program in religion. He holds advanced degrees from Harvard Divinity School and the Graduate Theological Union and has authored or coauthored several previous books on management, business, and ethics.